INTERPERSONAL

COMMUNICATION

A GOALS-BASED

APPROACH

INTERPERSONAL

COMMUNICATION

A GOALS-BASED APPROACH

DANIEL J. CANARY
Ohio University

MICHAEL J. CODY
University of
Southern California

ST. MARTIN'S PRESS
NEW YORK

Editor: Suzanne Phelps Weir
Development editor: Cheryl Friedman
Managing editor: Patricia Mansfield-Phelan
Project editor: Amy Horowitz
Production supervisor: Alan Fischer
Art director: Sheree L. Goodman
Text design: Patrice Fodero
Photo research: Barbara Salz
Cover design: Carolyn Joseph
Cover art: Paul Klee, *Polyphonically Enclosed White*, 1930. Kunstmuseum Bern, Paul Klee Stiftung,
© 1993 ARS/N.Y.

Library of Congress Catalog Card Number: 92-50050

8 7 6 5 4
f e d c b a

For information, write:
St. Martin's Press, Inc.
175 Fifth Avenue
New York, NY 10010

ISBN: 0-312-03696-5

PREFACE

Three premises concerning the nature of people guided our thinking in this book: People are goal directed; they rely on other people to achieve their goals; and they use communication to accomplish their interpersonal goals. These premises also reflect important developments in the research on interpersonal communication. That is, much current research offers insight into three primary goals that people seek on a routine basis:

1. *Self-presentation goals:* how people present an image of themselves
2. *Relational goals:* how communication is tied to the escalation, maintenance, de-escalation, and possible termination of relationships
3. *Instrumental goals:* how people use communication to obtain personal favors or resources.

Interpersonal Communication: A Goals-Based Approach organizes the most current theory and research on interpersonal communication according to these goals. In doing so, it encourages students to identify how communication is used to achieve goals. Accordingly, this emphasis on goals will be personally relevant to the student. We want to challenge students to move beyond a focus on skills; instead we underscore how communication behaviors are variously associated with communicator effectiveness. In other words, this book is distinctive because it emphasizes the importance of goals and their relationship to how people communicate.

Organization of the Text

The fundamentals of interpersonal communication are presented in Part I, which discusses the nature of goals and how people pursue them interpersonally. We also define *communication* and give our assumptions about the nature of communication. This part concludes with an overview of verbal and nonverbal messages.

An extended overview of how people use communication to present an image of themselves is provided in Part II. Major topics include the process and strategies of self-presentation, threats to one's public image, the recovery from face-threatening situations, and self-disclosure as both a self-presentation and a relational development activity.

Part III focuses on how communication is linked to relational development. Here we discuss how relationships escalate from nonintimate to intimate, and we show how communication evolves over time. We then examine various communication behaviors people use to maintain relationships and conclude with a chapter on the process of relationship de-escalation and termination.

Instrumental goals are examined in Part IV, where we discuss such questions as: "How do people get others to do things for personal gain ('compliance-gaining')?" and "What happens when goals are incompatible?" When people experience conflict, they must rely on communication to manage that conflict. We therefore talk about various styles, strategies, and tactics people use to manage conflict interpersonally.

Part V presents an examination of personal communication competence. Each individual must develop personal communication competence, and this depends in part on the personality of the individual. Accordingly, we review some personality factors related to interpersonal communication. The final chapter offers a discussion of the implications of this text with respect to the concept of communication competence.

Pedagogical Features of the Text

Interpersonal Communication: A Goals-Based Approach offers many integrated pedagogical aids that help the student achieve the objectives of the course:

- Each chapter opens with a *scenario* either taken from a movie or developed specifically for the text. The scenarios illustrate interpersonal situations relevant to the chapter topics and to the lives of students.
- *Boxed inserts* throughout draw from current movies, newspapers, and magazines to provide concrete illustrations of important issues.
- End-of-chapter apparatus consists of a *chapter summary*, a list of *key terms, exercises for further discussion*, an annotated list of *suggested readings*, and a list of *references*.
- An extensive program of *photographs and cartoons* illustrates the concepts presented in the text.

Ancillaries to Accompany the Text

Interpersonal Communication offers a complete Instructor's Manual designed to facilitate class discussion as well as testing. Each chapter of the manual consists of additional discussion questions, in-class exercises, and test items (short-essay, true-or-false, and multiple-choice).

A computerized test bank in IBM (on 3-1/2- and 5-1/4-inch disks) and Macintosh versions is also available to adopters of the text.

Acknowledgments

Many fine people deserve to be mentioned for their advice and encouragement during the preparation of this book. First, thanks to Julia for being so patient. Next, to our students at Ohio University and the University of Southern California: Thank you. Your comments about the strengths and weaknesses of earlier drafts of the text have made this book more useful to everyone.

We also owe a debt of gratitude to the graduate students at Ohio University who read drafts and offered editorial advice. Three doctoral students at the university—Bonnie Farley-Lucas, Susan Messman, and Lisa Wallace—wrote the Instructor's Manual and commented on early drafts of the text. Jim Sahlman deserves thanks for his insights on Chapter 14. The advice and assistance of these students have improved this book significantly.

A number of graduate and undergraduate students at the University of Southern California provided help, suggestions, and feedback while the book was under way. Most important, Larry Kersten (now at the University of Nevada, Las Vegas) helped write the chapter on presenting the self. We also want to thank Diane and Jerry Burns, Dr. Lynn Miller, David Braaten (now at the American Graduate School of International Management in Arizona), Bill Brown (now at Regent University in Virginia), Jeff Robinson, Risa Dickson (now at California State University, San Bernardino), Valerie Manusov (now at the University of Washington), and Steven R. Phillips (now at the University of Montana). Thanks also go to a number of USC undergraduates for their help: David Tunnel, George Lyons, Jennifer Lively, Joel Miller, Jodi Wolf, Jason Faries, Jeny Esagian, Carrie Mukhar, and Bruce and Simone Friedman.

Several colleagues and experts in interpersonal communication also gave excellent suggestions. They include Kathryn Dindia (University of Wisconsin—Milwaukee), Steve Duck (University of Iowa), Mary Anne Fitzpatrick (University of Wisconsin—Madison), and Alan Sillars (University of Montana). In addition, Laura Stafford (Ohio State University) was very helpful reviewing our first drafts and offering excellent analytical advice. Finally, we want to acknowledge the help and support of Elva Veliz and Danny O'Hair. Like any publication, ours is significantly better because of the critical advice of these people.

Several fine editors at St. Martin's Press helped make this book a reality. Catherine Pusateri should receive an award for faithfulness, as she helped initiate the project and encouraged us to continue writing when setbacks occurred. We owe a debt of gratitude to Nancy Lyman, who helped us through the final stages of the book and reminded us that the top of the mountain was just over the next ridge. Both Cheryl Friedman and Amy Horowitz deserve mention for the fine job they did as development and project editors. There are many others at St. Martin's who have contributed, including Jane Lambert and Joyce Hinnefeld, and we sincerely appreciate their efforts. We are glad to have worked with these fine editors; they have represented St. Martin's Press very well indeed in their intelligent, calm, and confident manner.

Daniel J. Canary
Michael J. Cody

CONTENTS

INTERPERSONAL

COMMUNICATION

A GOALS-BASED
APPROACH

Interpersonal Communication
A GOALS-BASED APPROACH
by DANIEL J. CANARY and MICHAEL J. CODY

When ordering, please use this ISBN: 0-312-03696-5.

This examination copy is sent to you with the compliments of your St. Martin's Press representative. May we have your comments on it, please? They will help us estimate printing requirements, assist us in preparing revisions, and guide us in shaping future books to your needs.

- ☐ you may quote me in your advertising
- ☐ I have adopted this book for _____ semester, 19____.
- ☐ I am seriously considering this book for use with my classes.

Comments: Date_____

Name _____ Department _____

School _____ Phone Number ( ) _____

City _____ State _____ Zip _____

Course Title _____ Enrollment _____

Present Text _____

Do you plan to change texts this year? Yes ☐ No ☐ When is your decision due? _____

Is your decision individual ☐ committee ☐ department ☐ If committee or department, please list others involved _____

BUSINESS REPLY MAIL

FIRST CLASS   PERMIT NO. 1147   NEW YORK, NY

POSTAGE WILL BE PAID BY

College Department
ST. MARTIN'S PRESS, INC.
175 FIFTH AVENUE
NEW YORK, N.Y. 10010

P A R T   I

FUNDAMENTALS
OF
INTERPERSONAL
COMMUNICATION

Part I of this book defines our approach to interpersonal communication and introduces you to the basic concepts of the field. In Chapter 1, we discuss why we have chosen to use a goals-based model of communication and introduce three types of goals: self-presentation, relational, and instrumental. Chapter 2 provides an overview of the field of communication, including a review of four models of communication. We then present our own working definition of interpersonal communication. Chapter 3 examines language in interpersonal communication, including how language functions in general and, more specifically, the levels at which verbal messages function when people communicate. Chapter 4 examines the importance of nonverbal behavior in interpersonal communication. We present two theories of nonverbal interaction and discuss how nonverbal behavior is used in the communication of liking, intimacy, and deceit.

C H A P T E R   1

THE IMPORTANCE OF INTERPERSONAL COMMUNICATION IN ACHIEVING PERSONAL GOALS

After nine months of dating Kathy, Don wanted to get engaged. He realized that relationships took a lot of work and that it would not always be so romantic, but he loved Kathy more than he could imagine loving anyone. He believed that he had found the right person, and he felt ready to make the commitment.

Kathy was a photographer, going to school part time. She met Don in a class but didn't really think much about him until she saw him play baseball. He was a good athlete but didn't take himself too seriously, which she liked. So they began dating, and she found herself enjoying their time together more and more.

They both liked the beach in the late afternoon, when the sun wasn't too hot. One day Don packed a picnic basket with strawberries, soda, and a small box. After a great afternoon of swimming and sunning, Don pulled a ring out of the box and, without saying a word, presented it to Kathy.

Kathy could barely catch her breath; she didn't know how to respond. She was in love with Don, but she wasn't sure if she wanted to marry him yet. She knew that life was more complicated than baseball and beach picnics, and she wanted a career. So she told Don this. When he got up and went for a walk, she felt guilty.

Years from now you will recall your college experience. You will have engaged in many conversations, attended thousands of classes, taken hundreds of tests, and purchased a great many books. Naturally, you will recall best the ideas that are relevant and important to you. The ideas in this course on interpersonal communication should leave a lasting impression on you. Why? Because few things are as important to you as achieving your personal goals through interpersonal communication.

This book is about using **interpersonal communication** to achieve your **personal goals.** A basic assumption in this book is that people attempt to achieve a significant number of their personal goals in concert with other people. Pursuing goals interpersonally is perhaps so common that we don't stop to reflect on how often we do it. For example, you may need help when you move into a new apartment; you may want to initiate a relationship with someone you are attracted to; you may want to be seen as honest, sincere, and capable. All of these situations represent interpersonal goals that people pursue on a routine basis.

A second assumption of this text is that we use communication to achieve our goals. The way we communicate with others directly affects whether or not we will achieve our desires. The vast research on interpersonal communication indicates one simple principle: communication is the primary tool we use to achieve our goals with others.

Why Emphasize Goals?

We explore interpersonal goals for several reasons. First, as many scholars indicate (e.g., Davey 1976), we can understand social action in general because people's behaviors are goal-driven. Consider the story at the introduction of this chapter. Don's goal was to escalate his relationship with Kathy. Don's attempt to present a romantic proposal is clearly understood in terms of his goal. Kathy did not share in that goal, and hence we can understand her ambivalence. Second, an understanding of communication in particular should be placed in the context of communicators' goals. As Sanders (1991) observes,

> A concern with goals is unavoidable in studies of human communication. The proposition that what actors say and do in any instance is contingent on their goals is true by definition, insofar as we regard human communication as a form of social action. (p. 186)

Third, we emphasize goals so that you can understand how interpersonal communication affects your life in very real terms. Accordingly, the emphasis on goals is important to the extent that your communication functions to achieve goals important to you.

Types of Interpersonal Goals

Researchers have uncovered three general types of goals that people seek through interpersonal communication (Clark and Delia 1979; *see also* following Clark and Delia 1979: Dillard 1990; Dillard, Sergin, and Harden 1989; Hecht 1984; O'Keffe and Mc-Cornack 1987; Pervin 1989; Rule and Bisanz 1987; Tracy 1991; Tracy et al. 1984; Wilson 1990). The first type is the **self-presentation goal.** Self-presentation involves communicating an image of who we are and how we want to be perceived. The second type is the **relational goal.** This concerns how people develop relationships and then maintain or neglect those relationships. The third type is the **instrumental goal,** whereby we try to get others to do us a favor or offer some kind of resource.

SELF-PRESENTATION GOALS

We use interpersonal communication to present an image of who we are (Tedeschi and Norman 1985). Goffman (1971) has also argued that we are strategic in the pre-

We often plan how to make a favorable impression on others. Sometimes, however, our plans do not work out as expected.

(Gary Larson, *The Far Side*, copyright 1991 Farworks Inc./Dist. by Universal Press Syndicate. Reprinted with permission. All rights reserved.)

sentation of who we are. That is, we perform "facework" to make others see us in the way that we want them to see us. Our public image is something we work on every day.

By and large, we want to appear competent. That is, we want to seem intelligent, capable, expert, and effective. However, people may differ a great deal in their preferred public image. Whereas some want to be perceived as competent, others prefer a public image as being friendly and likable. These two self-presentation styles, competence and friendliness, involve using different communication tactics. Competent people often try to show others that they know what is best and that they are better trained and more capable. They talk more about themselves and their

People's self-presentation goals may differ a great deal. For example, some people may wish to be perceived as competent, while others may prefer to be seen as more friendly and likable.

(Joel Gordon)

achievements, and they engage in behaviors that draw attention to themselves. Friendly communicators do not want to show others up, and they try to get along without "rocking the boat." These communicators smile and nod more often, frequently express agreement with others, and find more sources of similarity with others (see Chapter 5).

Other communicators may want to appear weak and indecisive. Why? Some people appear weak so that they can exploit their dependence on others. By appearing helpless, such people get their friends to help them with their homework, car repairs, errands, and other tasks. Still other communicators may want to appear assertive and strong (to be "intimidating") or to appear to be more dedicated and worthy than others (e.g., Jones and Pittman 1982). As we shall see in Chapters 5 and 6, people use communication differently, depending on their desire to project a certain public image.

Table 1-1 provides examples of some self-presentation goals.

RELATIONAL GOALS
Nothing brings us more joy than our personal relationships. We spend significant amounts of time, energy, and emotion in the pursuit of quality relationships. The

Table 1-1
SELF-PRESENTATION GOAL EXAMPLES

Goal	Example
To present oneself to a peer	You want to appear friendly and intelligent to someone in class.
To present oneself to a superior	You want your supervisor to believe that you are reliable and honest.
To prolong an obligation	You want to postpone a debt of $50 that you owe a friend.
To defend oneself	You want to defend yourself against someone who likes to talk about you behind your back.
To protect a right	You want to make sure your roommate gives you your telephone messages.

Source: Adapted from Canary, Cody, and Marston 1987; Canary, Cunningham, and Cody 1988; Cody, Canary, and Smith 1993.

feelings of love and sharing we experience as a daughter or a son, a friend, and a romantic partner are unobtainable anywhere but in these relationships. Yet we also experience pain due to our interpersonal involvements. Every relationship eventually ends. Some seem to end naturally; others seem to end prematurely. Certain relationships stagnate and continue at a very basic level of social survival. Whether for joy or for sorrow, our interpersonal relationships are important to us. As several scholars have shown (e.g., Duck 1988), communication plays a vital role in our personal relationships.

Miller (1976) and Montgomery (1988) note that relationships are the products of our interpersonal communication and that the way we communicate depends in turn on the nature and quality of our relationships. For example, it is possible that you and your partner discuss how you will spend time with each other in the future (whose in-laws to visit at Christmas, where to vacation next summer, where to apply to school or seek a job, and the like). Such statements about the future may increase the level of commitment between the two of you; they assure you that the relationship will continue for a length of time. In turn, increases in levels of commitment allow you to dream and discuss plans with your partner for the future. In other words, interpersonal communication both reflects and affects the nature and quality of our relationships.

People have different goals in their various relationships. These goals involve escalating, maintaining, or de-escalating relationships.

(Stern/Peter Thomann/Black Star)

One useful way to look at relational goals is to break them into three types: *escalating*, *maintaining*, and *de-escalating*. Escalating a relationship involves learning more about one another and growing more intimate or more interdependent. Maintaining a relationship focuses attention on activities and communication behaviors used to sustain various personal relationships. De-escalating a relationship deals with how friends and lovers drift away from each other (or how relationships suddenly "explode") and how communication with these former friends and intimates decreases or ceases entirely.

Table 1-2 presents some examples of common relational goals.

INSTRUMENTAL GOALS

We also rely on interpersonal communication to achieve our instrumental goals. These goals refer to desires for self-advancement. For example, instrumental goals include everyday events, such as getting a ride to school, obtaining particular vacation time, or getting someone to help you photocopy some papers. Research indicates that our instrumental goals may be the most salient to us when we communicate with others, followed by our self-presentation and relational goals (e.g., Cody et al. 1986; Dillard et al. 1989). The point is that each of us has instrumental goals, and we rely on our interpersonal communication to achieve these goals.

Table 1-2
RELATIONAL GOAL EXAMPLES

Goal	Example
To share an activity	You want your friend to go with you to a party.
To initiate a relationship	You decide to ask a person in your class for a date.
To escalate a relationship	You want a more permanent commitment from your partner.
To maintain a relationship	You want to keep in touch with your friends from high school or from a previous job.
To de-escalate a relationship	You discover a friend of yours is not dependable, so you want to stop making plans to see that person.
To give advice to a peer	You want your sister to seek the advice of a counselor, because she has been depressed lately.
To give advice to a parent	You want your parents to take a vacation and relax a little more.

Source: Adapted from Canary, Cody, and Marston 1987; Canary, Cody, Cunningham 1988; Cody, Canary, and Smith 1993.

Table 1-3 (p. 11) lists some examples of instrumental goals.

Communicators sometimes pursue one type of goal at the expense of other goals. For example, it may be more important for you to go accept a job out of state than to keep dating a particular person. Alternatively, you might decide against taking the job in order to maintain your relationship at its current level of intimacy. In a majority of situations, however, we try to present ourselves favorably and seek satisfying relationships while we pursue our instrumental goals (you might accept the job *and* attempt to maintain a long-distance relationship).

In sum, interpersonal communication is used for three types of goals: self-presentation, relational, and instrumental. We present an image of who we are through our interpersonal communication. Most of the time we want to be seen as capable individuals, but people do differ in preferences for how they are viewed publicly. Our interpersonal communication also affects and reflects the very nature of our relationships. We use communication to develop, maintain, and de-escalate our relationships with others. Finally, we use interpersonal communication to achieve our

Instrumental goals can vary widely, from long-term goals, such as obtaining a college education, to more everyday goals, such as getting a ride to school, obtaining specific vacation time, or getting someone to help you with a paper.

(Harry Wilks/Stock, Boston)

instrumental goals. While pursuing instrumental goals, we typically also attempt to keep our self-presentation and relational goals intact.

The Nature of Goals

A **goal** is a state you want to achieve. As Cody and colleagues (1993) note, goals have both cognitive and emotional elements; they combine thoughts and feelings. An **interpersonal goal** is a goal you want that is linked to another person's thoughts, feelings, or actions. People who share interpersonal goals are interdependent (Kelley 1979). Scholars have identified several important properties of goals (e.g., Pervin 1989; Tracy 1991). We will examine seven general properties of goals that are relevant to interpersonal communication.

First, goals vary in their degree of abstractness. Relying on the research of Cantor and Mischel (1979; and also Cantor, Mischel, and Schwartz, 1982), we classify goals into three levels of abstraction: *supraordinate, basic,* and *subordinate.* **Supraordinate goals** are general and inclusive. "Be friendly," "be politically correct," and "be a winner" reflect supraordinate goal orientations. Likewise, the division of goals into self-presentation, relational, and instrumental types is a supraordinate distinction.

Table 1-3
INSTRUMENTAL GOAL EXAMPLES

Goal	Example
To seek assistance from a peer	You want a friend to help you with a task.
To seek assistance from a parent	You want to borrow $50 from your parents so that you can pay some bills.
To gain permission from a parent	You want permission to borrow the family car for a special night out.
To elicit support from a peer	You want your brother's friend to advise your brother to seek counseling.
To change a habit	You want your roommate to stop smoking.
To change an opinion	You want your friend to vote for a particular candidate in an upcoming election.

Source: Adapted from Canary, Cody, and Marston 1987; Canary, Cunningham, and Cody 1988; Cody, Canary, and Smith 1993.

Within each goal category, you will recall, we can make more specific, *basic* level distinctions (as shown in Tables 1-1 to 1-3). **Basic goals** provide more specificity in terms of actors' motives and relationships. For example, the goal "to share an activity" (see Table 1-2) identifies the motive for interacting (to go out and do something) as well as the role relationship with the other (friend or peer). Finally, **subordinate goals** are very specific and are quite distinct from other goals. For example, the goal "to get Kathy to go shopping on Friday night" is different from "to ask John to shoot baskets on Saturday afternoon," though both are specific instances of the basic goal of "to share an activity."

Second, goals differ in clarity. It appears obvious that the more specific the goal, the clearer it tends to become. Beyond this observation, we should note that goals sometimes have overlapping properties (Cody et al. 1993) and that goals sometimes lead to the same kinds of behavior (for example, wanting to appear competent and likable will help you obtain the job promotion you want). Finally, it appears that people are more motivated to achieve clear goals than ambiguous ones. Clear goals indicate standards that help us realize when our goals have been reached (Bandura 1989). For example, the goal "to do well in this class" is not as clear as "to get an A in

GOALS IN FILMS: THE CASE OF L.A. STORY

Self-presentation goals are pursued when communicators use tactics to offer a desired public image, usually to appear competent or friendly. But sometimes people want to appear weak or intimidating. One extreme type is the person who constantly adapts to others, projecting a different image to different audiences. An example of this is seen in the film *L.A. Story*. Throughout the film, Steve Martin conforms to what others are doing. He has a twist of lemon when everyone else has a twist of lemon, and he gets an enema when his date gets an enema. Further, he consistently agrees with what others are saying.

One scene illustrates how abruptly some communicators alter their public image. Martin's girlfriend (played by Marilu Henner) admits to having an affair:

Martin:	How long has this been going on?
Henner:	Three years.
Martin:	Three years!
Henner:	I'm sorry.
Martin:	This has been going on since the Eighties?

Martin appears to be in a state of shock and disbelief. Looking weak and vulnerable and about to cry, he says, "I'm sorry—I just can't be here right now."

We see Martin walk sadly down the stairs to the street, at first with heavy footfalls. But as he leaves the woman behind, his posture changes, and he starts to dance. He ceases to appear sad; he dances in the street. He screams with happiness, "Yes, yes, L.A. I love you. I'm out of my relationship, I'm out of the agency, and I only had to look like a jerk for three years. Now if I can just get out of doing the weather."

These last lines also reveal the three different types of goals people pursue: self-presentation ("I only had to look like a jerk for three years"); relational de-escalation ("I'm out of my relationship"), and instrumental ("Now if I can just get out of doing the weather"). Martin, the "L.A. yuppie," had learned to adapt strategically to his various audiences, presenting a self that was appropriate or desirable for particular audiences and situations (for a fuller discussion of self-presentation, see Chapter 5).

Whereas Martin's character in *L.A. Story* achieves what he wants by constantly adapting to others, Robin Williams's in *The Dead Poets Society* tells his students not to conform to others. This character, Mr. Keating, advises his students: "Now we all have a great need for acceptance. But you must trust that your beliefs are unique, your own, although others may think of them as unpopular, even though the herd may go, "That's baaaaad.""

We can contrast the many ways in which self-presentation, relational, and instrumental goals are pursued by looking at ourselves or others or by taking examples from the media (newspapers and films). Think about films like *The Firm, The Unforgiven, When Harry Met Sally . . . , Ordinary People, The Breakfast Club, Annie Hall,* and hundreds of other films and stories that show how people want and set out to obtain their important personal goals.

Excerpts from L.A. Story *by Steve Martin. Reprinted by permission of Steve Martin.*

this class." Knowing exactly what you want helps you achieve exactly what you want. As the saying goes, "You can't get what you want until you know what you want."

Third, goals vary in their degree of challenge. Some goals are more difficult to achieve than others. Some require a strong sense of determination and effort. According to Bandura (1986, 1989), people attempt to pursue challenging goals because they believe that they can succeed at reaching their goals—a property that Bandura calls **self-efficacy.** According to Bandura, a person with high self-efficacy persists in achieving challenging goals, even in the face of failures, and is more likely to achieve those goals. People who have little self-efficacy do not pursue challenging goals, nor do they achieve challenging goals. In other words, self-efficacy is crucial in determining the success you experience in achieving challenging goals.

Fourth, people often engage in multiple goals that vary in their level of importance. Dillard and colleagues (1989) separate goals into *primary* and *secondary* types. **Primary goals** are the most important to the communicator; **secondary goals** are less important to the communicator, but they function to constrain the primary goals. For example, imagine that you are caught speeding in a school zone. Your primary goal may be to avoid getting a traffic ticket. So you quickly decide what you'll say when the police officer knocks on your car window. But because you also want to be seen as honest and responsible, you decide not to lie or argue. These secondary goals thus moderate your communication behavior motivated only by your primary goal. So instead of lying or arguing, you explain why you were speeding ("I was not paying attention to the changes in zones"), and you apologize for speeding (see also Chapter 6, "Defending the Self").

Fifth, goals vary in terms of immediacy. Those that occur in the immediate future are called **proximal goals;** those that must be realized in the distant future are called **distal goals.** In many instances, the more proximal the goal, the more salient it is. That is, you are more likely to focus on proximal than distal goals, although the distal goals may be more important to you. For example, you may have the goal "to marry next year." But despite this goal's importance to you, you also want to have a good time now. So instead of pursuing a particular relationship, you prefer to date two or three people. In short, proximal goals may seem more urgent and may motivate us more than distal goals.

Sixth, people's goals are affected by the communication event itself. According to Hocker and Wilmot (1991), goals can be modified or changed during interaction. Hocker and Wilmot call these **transactive goals** (pp. 55–58; see also Berger 1986). The following example shows how Sandy's goal "to seek assistance from a peer" is transformed into the goal "to defend oneself."

Sandy:	Hey, Chris, what are you doing Tuesday afternoon?
Chris:	Why? What do you need?
Sandy:	Well, I really need a babysitter. I know it's short notice and all.
Chris:	Why is it that you only come around here when you need a favor or something?
Sandy:	What?
Chris:	Well, it seems that all I'm good for is babysitting.
Sandy:	(*defensively*) I can't believe this! Forget it. I thought you were a friend.

Finally, goals prompt plans for action. Planning consists of producing one or more mental models, detailing how you might achieve your goal through interaction (Berger 1986; Dillard 1990). Plans differ in complexity and completeness.

Plans that incorporate a number of elements, contingencies, and sequences are more complex than plans involving only a single message tactic ("I'll just go over there and tell Frankie not to do that anymore"). You may generate a complex plan by considering the many ways in which you can change an undesirable behavior, how the other person may resist changing, and how the resistance can be overcome. Complex plans, however, are not always the best ones. As Berger, Mann, and Jordon (1988) found, overly complex plans may actually lead to problems communicating (such as speech dysfluencies).

In addition, plans vary in the degree to which they are complete. Communicators may have a general idea about talking with their friends and "working things out" or "compromising" or "resolving our differences." But such plans are incomplete until communicators flesh out in more detail what they might work on, what exactly they would be willing to compromise, and how to search for common interests to resolve differences.

Overview of the Book

The purpose of this text is to present the research on interpersonal communication so that you can see the relevance of communication to important personal goals. This does not mean that we adopt a "skills" approach or that we want you to manipulate others. It simply means that we believe that human behavior, especially interpersonal communication behavior, is best understood when we frame those actions within a "goals" perspective.

The organization of the book is based on the literature associated with self-presentation, relational, and instrumental goals. We hope that by organizing the book in this way, you will learn how interpersonal communication is used to achieve important personal goals.

Part I, which includes this chapter, discusses the fundamentals of interpersonal communication. We offer a definition of interpersonal communication and review the basic tools used to exchange messages—verbal and nonverbal communication. In this chapter we discussed the importance, types, and nature of interpersonal goals. In Chapter 2 we present various approaches for examining interpersonal communication. We then provide our own definition of interpersonal communication and the assumptions underlying our definition. The different ways in which people exchange verbal messages and different properties of verbal messages are presented in Chapter 3. Chapter 4 concludes Part I by examining how people exchange messages nonverbally. Chapter 4 includes material regarding facial beauty, body image, and gender differences in communicating nonverbally.

Part II concerns self-presentation goals. Chapter 5 reviews what is meant by self-presentation and focuses on direct and indirect ways in which people present themselves, including intimidation, supplication, and ingratiation, among other strategies. But what happens when our desired self-presentation is threatened? Chapter 6 deals with the issue of how we defend our public image. It discusses how we restore our definitions of self in offering "accounts." Self-disclosure is the topic of Chapter 7, which examines the benefits and risks of self-disclosure, social penetration theory, and dimensions of self-disclosure and reviews the causes and consequences of self-disclosure.

Part III focuses on relational goals. Chapter 8 examines escalating relationships: why we are attracted to certain people, how we make ourselves more attractive through interaction, and how communication is linked to relationship development. Chapter 9 discusses relational maintenance, the important issues of why and how we maintain our personal relationships and the specific strategies we use. Chapter 10 concerns relational decay and termination. It explores the reasons for breakups, the ways in which people separate, and the emotional consequences of relational termination.

Part IV covers instrumental goals. Chapter 11 reports the findings on compliance gaining—how to get others to comply with your personal wishes. Processes underlying effective compliance gaining and basic rules of compliance are discussed. What happens when the goals of two people are incompatible? Chapter 12 concerns conflict: how conflict emerges, strategies for managing conflict interactions, and the effects of conflict. You will learn that conflict is a common communication event and that how people manage conflict affects their perceptions of the conflict episode as well the relationship.

Part V discusses factors related to achieving personal competence. We acknowledge that people vary in their orientations and predispositions to achieve goals. Hence Chapter 13 reviews research relevant to individual difference factors that affect our interactions with others. It points out that interpersonal communication is related to gender and the personality factors of self-monitoring, locus of control, loneliness, communication apprehension, argumentativeness, and cognitive complexity. In Chapter 14 we present criteria used to assess interpersonal communication competence and underscore findings presented in earlier chapters that are directly relevant to interpersonal competence.

This book focuses on the communication behaviors that people use to achieve their interpersonal goals. Many of these interaction behaviors will sound familiar, probably due to the fact that you or others you know have used them. Yet many of the ideas presented in this book will be new to you. As you will see, interpersonal communication behaviors vary according to the types of goals people routinely seek. Our primary objective is that you read this material so that you can achieve your own personal goals and become a more competent communicator.

KEY TERMS

interpersonal communication
personal goals
self-presentation goal
relational goal
instrumental goal
interpersonal goal
supraordinate goals
basic goals

subordinate goals
self-efficacy
primary goals
secondary goals
proximal goals
distal goals
transactive goals

EXERCISES FOR FURTHER DISCUSSION

1. In the past 24 hours, you have probably tried to achieve a number of self-presentation, relational, and instrumental goals—even if you were not aware of doing so.
   a. Try to think of as many of each type of goal as you can, providing an example for each.

    b.   Which of the goals that you listed is the most important to you?

    c.   How many different relationships were involved in your goals (parent, friend, etc.)? What were the relationships?

2.   Look again at Tables 1-1, 1-2, and 1-3.

    a.   Try to think of several self-presentation goals that you could add to Table 1-1.

    b.   Try to think of several relational goals that you could add to Table 1-2.

    c.   Try to think of several instrumental goals that you could add to Table 1-3.

    d.   Discuss the goals you have written down with other class members, and create a list of goals for your reference that includes as many different examples of each type of goal as possible.

3.   Consider the types of thinking and behavior that a goals-based approach to interpersonal communication encourages.

    a.   Does a goals-based approach stress self-conscious, rational aspects of behavior more than unconscious, irrational aspects of behavior?

    b.   When you think about your own behavior, do your goals involve feelings as well as rational thoughts?

    c.   What do you think the benefits of a goals-based approach to interpersonal communication would be? What would be the drawbacks?

4.   Think of people you know well and consider whether or not they seem to be aware of their goals.

    a.   Are most of the people you know aware of their goals? Or are most of the people you know unaware of their goals?

    b.   Do you think that people you know who are goal-directed are more effective communicators than those who do not have a clear sense of their own goals?

SUGGESTED READING

Cody, M. J.; Canary, D. J.; and Smith, S. W. 1993. Compliance-gaining goals: An inductive analysis of actor's goal types, strategies, and successes. In J. Wiemann, and J. Daly eds., *Communicating strategically*. Hillsdale, N.J.: Erlbaum. This chapter shows how we derive several of the goals presented in this book. Although this chapter focuses on interpersonal influence, virtually all of the principles can be extended to cover other types of interpersonal communication.

Dillard, J. P. 1990. Primary and secondary goals in interpersonal influence. In M. J. Cody and M. L. McLaughlin eds., *Psychology of tactical communication*. Clevedon, England: Multilingual Matters. Dillard presents a model of how goals lead to interpersonal communication. In addition, Dillard shows the relationship between primary and secondary goals.

Pervin, L. A., ed. 1989. *Goal concepts in personality and social psychology.* Hillsdale, N.J.: Erlbaum. This anthology offers some of the best thinking on the topic by social psychologists. Pervin's introductory chapter offers an excellent overview to the study of goals in social psychology.

Tracy, K., ed. 1991. *Understanding face-to-face interaction: Issues linking goals and discourse.* Hillsdale, N.J.: Erlbaum. Tracy provides a forum for scholars in communication to discuss how goals are related to communication behaviors. Several different approaches are offered. Virtually all, however, focus on microscopic levels of discourse.

REFERENCE LIST

Bandura, A. 1986. *Social foundations of thought and action: A social cognitive theory.* Englewood Cliffs, N.J.: Prentice Hall.

————. 1989. Self-regulation of motivation and action through internal standards and goal systems. *Goal concepts in personality and social psychology*, ed. L. A. Pervin, 19–85. Hillsdale, N.J.: Erlbaum.

Berger, C. R. 1986. Planning, affect, and social action generation. In *Communication, social cognition, and affect*, ed. H. Sypher and E. T. Higgins, 76–87. Hillsdale, N.J.: Erlbaum.

Berger, C. R.; Mann, S. K.; and Jordon, J. M. 1988, November. *When a lot of knowledge is a dangerous thing: The debilitating effects of plan complexity on verbal fluency.* Paper presented at the Speech Communication Association convention, New Orleans, La.

Canary, D. J.; Cody, M. J.; and Marston, P. J. 1987. Goal types, compliance-gaining, and locus of control. *Journal of Language and Social Psychology* 5:249–269.

Canary, D. J.; Cunningham, E. M.; and Cody, M. J. 1988. Goal types, gender, and locus of control in managing interpersonal conflict. *Communication Research* 15:426–446.

Cantor, N., and Mischel, W. 1979. Prototypes in person perception. In *Advances in experimental social psychology*, ed. L. Berkowitz, 12:4–52. Orlando, Fla.: Academic Press.

Cantor, N.; Mischel, W.; and Schwartz, J. 1982. A prototype analysis of psychological situations. *Cognitive Psychology* 14:45–77.

Clark, R. A., and Delia, J. 1979. Topoi and rhetorical competence. *Quarterly Journal of Speech* 65:187–206.

Cody, M. J.; Canary, D. J.; and Smith, S. W. 1993. Compliance-gaining goals: An inductive analysis of actor's goal types, strategies, and successes. In *Communicating strategically*, eds. J. Wiemann and J. Daly. Hillsdale, N.J.: Erlbaum.

Cody, M. J.; Greene, J. O.; Marston, P.; Baaske, E.; O'Hair, H. D.; and Schneider, M. J. 1986. Situation perception and the selection of message strategies. In *Communication yearbook 8*, ed. M. L. McLaughlin, 390–420. Newbury Park, Calif.: Sage.

Davey, A. 1976. Attitudes and the prediction of social conduct. *British Journal of Social and Clinical Psychology* 15:11–22.

Dillard, J. P. 1990. Primary and secondary goals in interpersonal influence. In *Psychology of tactical communication*, ed. M. J. Cody and M. L. McLaughlin, 70–90. Clevendon, England: Multilingual Matters.

Dillard, J. P.; Sergin, C.; and Harden, J. M. 1989. Primary and secondary goals in the production of interpersonal influence messages. *Communication Monographs* 56:19–38.

Duck, S. W. 1988. *Relating to others.* Homewood, Ill.: Dorsey Press.

Hecht, M. L. 1984. Persuasive efficacy: A study of the relationship among type and degree of change, message strategies, and satisfying communication. *Western Journal of Speech Communication* 48:373–389.

Hocker, J. L., and Wilmot, W. W. 1991. *Interpersonal conflict*, 3d ed. Dubuque, Iowa: Brown.

Jones, E. E., and Pittman, T. 1982. Toward a general theory of strategic self-presentation. In *Psychological perspectives on the self*, ed. J. Suls, 1:231–263. Hillsdale, N.J.: Erlbaum.

Kelley, H. 1979. *Personal relationships: A theory of interdependence.* New York: Wiley.

Miller, G. R. 1976. Introduction. In *Explorations in interpersonal communication*, ed. G. R. Miller. Newbury Park, Calif.: Sage.

Montgomery, B. 1988. Quality communication in personal relationships. In *Handbook of personal relationships*, ed. S. W. Duck, 343–359. New York: Wiley.

O'Keffe, B. J., and McCornack, S. A. 1987. Message logic design and message goal structure: Effects on perceptions of message quality in regulative communication situations. *Human Communication Research* 14:68–92.

Pervin, L. A. 1989. Goal concepts in personality and social psychology: A historical analysis. In *Goal concepts in personality and social psychology*, ed. L. A. Pervin, 1–17. Hillsdale, N.J.: Erlbaum.

Rule, B. G., and Bisanz, G. L. 1987. Goals and strategies of persuasion: A cognitive schema for understanding social events. In *Social influence: The fifth Ontario symposium in personality and social psychology*, ed. M. Zanna, P. Herman, and J. Olson, 185–206. Hillsdale, N.J.: Erlbaum.

Sanders, R. E. 1991. The two-way relationship between talk in social interactions and actors' goals and plans. In *Understanding face-to-face interaction: Issues linking goals and discourse*, ed. K. Tracy, 167–188. Hillsdale, N.J.: Erlbaum.

Tedeschi, J. T., and Norman, N. 1985. Social power, self-presentation, and the self. In *The self and social life*, ed. B. R. Schlenker, 293–322. New York: McGraw-Hill.

Tracy, K., ed. 1991. *Understanding face-to-face interaction: Issues linking goals and discourse.* Hillsdale, N.J.: Erlbaum.

Tracy, K.; Craig, R. T.; Smith, M.; and Spisak, F. 1984. The discourse of requests: An assessment of compliance-gaining requests. *Human Communication Research* 10:513–538.

Wilson, S. R. 1990. Development and test of a cognitive rules model of interaction goals. *Communication Monographs* 57:81–103.

C H A P T E R 2

DEFINING

INTERPERSONAL

COMMUNICATION

HUSBAND:	I don't think we have a lack of communication.
WIFE:	What? You have difficulty expressing your feelings on things. Other times you go and say whatever is on your mind, whatever you think. Or sometimes if my hair is a mess, or if it looks good, you always say, "It's fine." I would value your opinion if you'd just say, "It looks this way" or "It looks that way."
HUSBAND:	I guess my thoughts are, how you want to wear your hair is your business.
WIFE:	But I would like you to say whether you like it or not or why you like it or not.
HUSBAND:	Well, I think of hair and how it looks as trivial. Do you like my suits?
WIFE:	True, but you've been wearing your hair the same way for twenty years.
HUSBAND:	Do you like my suits?
WIFE:	No, if you want my honest opinion.

In this conversation, the wife wants more "communication" from her husband. In a word, she wants more direct expression regarding his opinion at times, while at other times she wants him not to offer his opinion. She does want his opinion regarding her hair. The husband doesn't feel that there is a lack of communication. Nor does he want to discuss how her hair looks because he thinks that it is a "trivial" issue. Whether or not they discuss her hair may not be the issue at stake.

Note how the wife criticizes the husband's hair ("you've been wearing your hair the same way for twenty years") and his clothes (in the last turn). Such communication by the wife may be the precise reason why the husband thinks there is plenty of communication between them. It is clear from this example that the amount of communication is not the issue; the quality of communication is the issue.

What is communication? How do you identify communication behavior when you see or hear it? As you will see, the answers to these questions depend on your perspective.

Perspectives on Communication

Dance (1970) reviewed ninety-five definitions of communication and was unable to come up with a comprehensive definition. According to Dance, "No one of the 95 definitions reviewed adequately covers the entire range of behaviors studied" by

People have different views on what constitutes effective communication. What is communication to one person can be noise to another.

(Spencer Grant/Stock, Boston)

communication scholars. And many other definitions of communication have emerged since Dance's study. Perhaps the primary reason why there is such diversity in definitions of communication is that scholars take different perspectives, or theoretic approaches that have different assumptions.

Fisher (1978) argued that the process of human communication is seen differently due to various theoretic perspectives, each focusing our attention on particular elements of communication. It should further be stressed that each perspective offers insights, although none offers a completely accurate account of communication.

We present these perspectives so that you can see the various ways in which scholars have approached the topic of interpersonal communication and place this book in the context of these perspectives. Then we will offer our own definition of interpersonal communication.

MECHANISTIC PERSPECTIVE

The **mechanistic perspective** on communication stresses that interpersonal communication operates like a machine, something like a conveyer belt. The conveyer belt is the channel through which a message links the communicators. Each communicator is a *source* and a *receiver*. The job of the source is **encoding,** or creating a message; the job of the receiver is **decoding,** or interpreting the message. The source sends the message, and the receiver offers **feedback** about his or her understanding of the message. For example, imagine the following interaction from a mechanistic perspective. The first person, Sandy, creates a message: "Hey, Chris, what are you doing Tuesday afternoon?" Chris decodes that message ("I'll bet Sandy needs something again"). Then Chris offers feedback: "Why? What do you need?"

From the mechanistic perspective, communication is effective when the decoded message matches the encoded message. When the message as interpreted matches exactly the message as created, the communication has **fidelity.** If the interpreted message does not match the encoded message, there is a problem (or a **breakdown**) in the communication process. One likely source may be **noise,** which is defined as an internal or external distraction from the message. Figure 2-1 illustrates a mechanistic model.

The mechanistic perspective is useful for identifying components of the communication process. We all readily recognize that each component (source, message, channel, receiver, feedback) must be functioning properly to ensure that high-fidelity communication takes place. Accordingly, we can trace where breakdowns occur in the communication process.

There are limitations to the mechanistic perspective, however. One limitation is the de-emphasis of humans as choice makers. In other words, in presenting communication as a machine, people are portrayed as elements of a machine, as reactors to messages said to them. Of course, people are not only reactors but are also **actors;** people are goal-directed and decide on their own actions. The mechanistic perspective also presents a **linear model** of communication, with communication moving in one direction (from source to receiver), and the receiver is limited to sending feed-

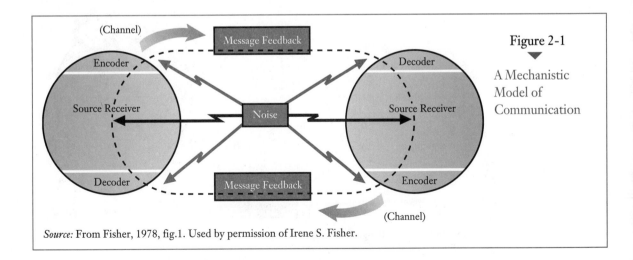

Figure 2-1

A Mechanistic Model of Communication

Source: From Fisher, 1978, fig.1. Used by permission of Irene S. Fisher.

back. In real-world interpersonal interaction, two people often send and receive messages simultaneously, blurring the distinction between source and receiver.

PSYCHOLOGICAL PERSPECTIVE

The **psychological perspective** on communication stresses the role of perception. According to this view, meaning is in the mind. Interpersonal communication occurs when the individual perceives stimuli (events or behaviors) as symbolic. For example, a wink from a co-worker may be perceived as a friendly gesture, as support when the boss is short-tempered, or even as sexual harassment.

Understanding occurs when people share perceptions; that is, each person perceives what the other person, or partner, is perceiving. In these instances, people share **co-orientation;** their perceptions of the event are similar and in agreement. True understanding occurs when people have actual, not just perceived, agreement on their perceptions. Regardless of whether or not people share perceptions, they respond to symbolic stimuli in some fashion. Also, note that the concepts of sender, message, channel, and receiver are not even discussed in the psychological perspective. Figure 2-2 presents a model of the psychological perspective.

The psychological view of communication has spawned much research on interpersonal processes. In fact, many of the theories regarding interpersonal communi-

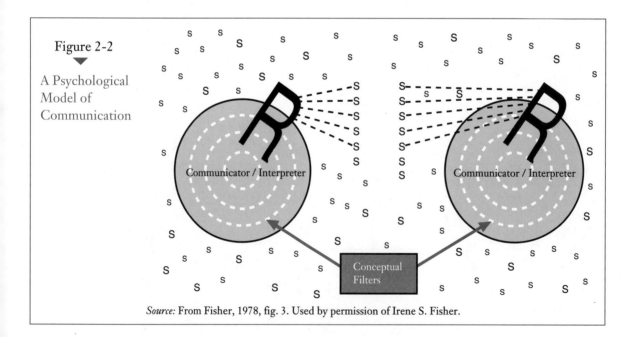

Figure 2-2

A Psychological Model of Communication

Source: From Fisher, 1978, fig. 3. Used by permission of Irene S. Fisher.

cation were born in the field of psychology, sociology, or social psychology, or they have at least a psychological orientation. In addition, the psychological view helps us focus on individual factors, such as cognitive processes and personality variables (see Chapter 13), and how such factors affect our interpersonal communication.

The primary drawback of the psychological perspective is the tendency to focus on cognitive factors to the exclusion of communication behaviors (Fisher 1978). Many researchers find psychological theories and constructs interesting but lose sight of how these psychological factors are related to interpersonal communication. A second and related problem is the overuse of questionnaires to study communication. Because questionnaires are helpful in measuring attitudes and other psychological constructs, they are also used to measure communication behavior when other methods are better suited for observing communication.

INTERACTIONIST PERSPECTIVE

The **interactionist perspective** on communication holds that the individual and society are bound together so completely that there is no distinction between the person and the society. Instead the person is defined by his or her interactions with society, and society is composed of a number of interacting people. The **self** is composed of our immediate actions as well as our belief about what others think of us, or what Mead (1934) refers to, respectively, as the *I* and the *me*. The I and the me are also said to interact in much the same way as a person interacts with others (Fisher 1978, 166–168).

According to symbolic interactionism, (Littlejohn 1989, 95–101), (1) society refers to the cooperative behaviors of individuals; (2) cooperation involves understanding the intentions of others, which involves **role taking,** or placing oneself in the partner's position; (3) people use symbols to convey meaning or assign significance to the gestures of others; and (4) meaning is also a product of social interaction. "Whatever meaning a person possesses for a thing is a result of interaction with others about the object being defined" (Littlejohn 1989, 98).

An important feature of interactionism is its concept of meaning as a process of interpretation. Actors interpret objects in terms of the relevance the objects have for them. Actors interpret their own behaviors in light of what they think others think of their behaviors. Finally, actors interpret others' behaviors in terms of what they think typical members of society would do in a similar situation. Figure 2-3 presents a model of the interactionist perspective.

Interactionism has taught us that people are creators of their social context and that they use what others think to define their own self-concepts. In addition, we recognize that people interpret our actions in terms of what is expected of our interaction roles. According to this perspective, understanding is achieved through role taking. For example, in the teacher-student relationship, it is appropriate for the teacher to offer verbal and written evaluation of the student's work; it is seldom ap-

Figure 2-3

An Interactionist
Model of
Communication

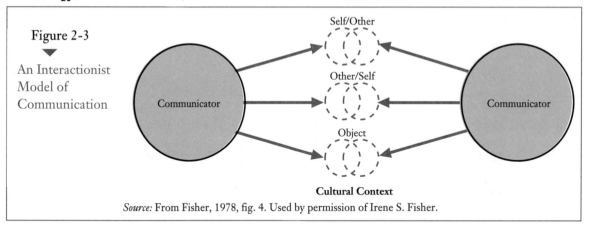

Source: From Fisher, 1978, fig. 4. Used by permission of Irene S. Fisher.

propriate for the student to evaluate the teacher's performance ("That was a good lecture, but it needs polish and better examples"). Appropriate social action is understood in terms of the teacher's and the student's roles.

Unfortunately, the interactionist perspective has spawned little recent research in the field of communication. One reason is that many of its theoretic statements are not readily observable. For example, the notions of *I* and *me* cannot be seen. In addition, by emphasizing the interactive nature of self and society, the issue of what we should research is made complex. That is, it is difficult to identify how particular variables are casually related from an interactionist perspective (Littlejohn 1989).

SYSTEMS PERSPECTIVE

The **systems perspective** on communication is a general approach to the study of human communication (Littlejohn 1989). Fisher (1978; see also Bahg 1990; Monge 1977) has outlined the critical components of the systems approach. (1) The principle of **nonsummativity** holds that the system as a whole is greater than the sum of its parts. Through interacting, for example, two people form a relationship, an entity that is something more than just the two personalities added together. (2) Persons in social systems have spatial and functional relationships to one another that evolve over time (e.g., how we interact as friends changes over time). (3) Interpersonal social systems are influenced by people outside the system; this property is called **openness.** (4) Systems have hierarchy, or organization. (5) Humans have choice and attempt to reduce uncertainty. (6) Finally, systems deal with events rather than material objects; hence social systems should be studied for redundant patterns that emerge over time. Figure 2-4 depicts social interaction portrayed from the systems perspective.

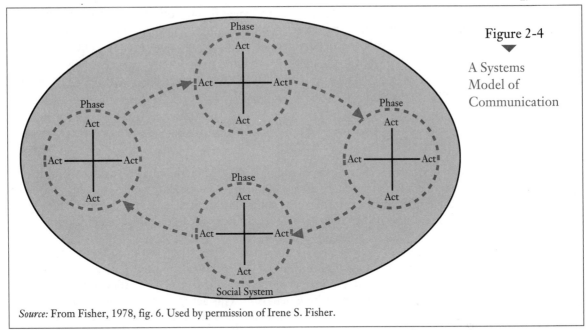

Figure 2-4

A Systems
Model of
Communication

Source: From Fisher, 1978, fig. 6. Used by permission of Irene S. Fisher.

The systems perspective is useful in drawing our attention to the relationship as a whole and not simply as the product of two individuals. For example, as Frank Millar once observed, if you want to know how to dance, you should look at how two people dance together—you can't learn how to dance by looking at each person separately. Similarly, if we want to understand interpersonal communication, according to the systems view, we need to focus on how both parties communicate with each other over time. Accordingly, the systems perspective has examined patterns of interaction over time to assess if there are any changes in the system.

The systems perspective also has limitations. First, like the interactionist approach, there is little recent research from the systems perspective on interpersonal communication. The reason for this may be that the complexities of interpersonal systems make them harder to research than isolated phenomena. Second, the systems perspective discounts the individual factors stressed by the psychological perspective (Watzlawick, Beavin, and Jackson 1967). Important personal factors, such as personality and individual goals, are not researched in the systems perspective.

In summary, interpersonal communication can be defined according to several different perspectives. Because each perspective focuses on different aspects of communication, each informs us about various facets of the communication process, and each has its drawbacks. The mechanistic perspective clearly identifies components of communication. The psychological view focuses on individual perceptions and individual differences that affect communication behaviors. The interactionist approach argues that the person cannot be separated from society. The systems approach has shown that relationships are more than the sum of the two individuals by focusing on both persons' communication over time. Table 2-1 presents definitions of these four perspectives on interpersonal communication.

Interpersonal Communication Defined

Our perspective is primarily psychological, although we also pay attention to features of communication discussed in the mechanistic, interactionist, and systems approaches. We define interpersonal communication as "the exchange of symbols used to achieve interpersonal goals." This definition is based on five assumptions.

ASSUMPTION 1: INTERPERSONAL COMMUNICATION REQUIRES AN EXCHANGE BETWEEN PEOPLE. One way to think of interpersonal communication is to think of it as action. At a minimum, one person sends a message to a second person. In very basic terms, that is an **act,** or one behavior. This act is then followed by a second act, and so on. In short, we can examine the communication process as a series of acts one person performs in the context of another person.

Table 2-1
DEFINITIONS OF COMMUNICATION
ACCORDING TO FOUR PERSPECTIVES

Perspective	Definition
Mechanistic	Interpersonal communication occurs when a source sends a message through a channel to a receiver.
Psychological	Interpersonal communication is the degree of co-orientation that two people achieve in their perceptions of symbolic stimuli.
Interactionist	Interpersonal communication involves taking the role of the other to interpret the symbolic significance of an event.
Systems	Interpersonal communication involves the patterns of interaction that depict the structural relationships between partners.

Like any phenomenon, communication can be analyzed from a variety of perspectives. Your perspective on communication reflects the aspects of communication that are important to you. Your perspective may differ from another person's perspective.

(Thomas Craig/The Picture Cube)

An alternative approach is to rely on the **interact** as the unit of analysis. An interact involves two behaviors: one person's act coupled with the second person's act. For example, the acts "What do you want to do?" and "I don't care, whatever you want to do" combine to form what is called a **submissive symmetrical interact** (Millar and Rogers 1976, 1987). That is, both persons want the other to take control of the situation, so they mirror the other's submissive acts.

A third way to examine communication is to think of it as the simultaneous sending and receiving of messages. This unit of message analysis is referred to as a **transact.** At a minimum, transactional analysis requires a focus on both actors, regardless of whose turn it is. From a psychological perspective, a transact also refers to both actors' simultaneous experience of the communication event.

Many, if not most, studies on interpersonal communication assess communication as an action. For example, much research on compliance gaining (how people attempt to influence their partners) does this (see Chapter 11). Examining communication as a series of acts is helpful when examining antecedents, or causes of an action. For example, if you wanted to borrow money from your parents for a couple of weeks, what would you say? If they refused your initial request, what would you say next? Would your approach be the same if you borrowed the money from a bank? Using acts as the unit of analysis helps us answer such questions.

Most systems theorists use the interact as the unit of analysis for studying interpersonal communication. Doing so, Courtright, Millar, and Rogers-Millar (1979), for example, could identify which married couples used *dominant* versus *domineering* interacts. A **dominant interact** is one in which one person's attempt at controlling the conversation is complemented by a submissive behavior, or vice versa ("Give me the keys to the car." "OK, honey, here you are"). A **domineering interact** is one in which one person's attempts to control the conversation are met with another control attempt or a neutral response ("Give me the car keys." "Not unless you fill the gas tank").

Studies on the transactional nature of communication are hard to find, possibly because they are the most difficult to conduct. One example is a study by Gottman (1982) in which the emotional responses of husbands and wives were simultaneously measured as they discussed how their days went. There are also several other studies that have had couples report on their perceptions of their communication. These studies examine the transaction in hindsight (and they depend on the accuracy of self-reports). For example, each person's self-report of the communication experience is correlated with the partner's to assess the couple's degree of understanding.

ASSUMPTION 2: INTERPERSONAL COMMUNICATION OCCURS BETWEEN PEOPLE WHO ARE IN THE "PROCESS OF BEING." One of the assumptions of communication scholars is that communication occurs between individuals who both act and react to one another and who are in the process of being (Brockriede 1978). This process of being means three important things. First, it means that people change over the life cycle, and their interpersonal communication reflects those changes (Nussbaum 1989). Second, it suggests that people are searching for meaning and develop strategies for adapting to their social world. Third, it implies that the communication exchanges we have now, as fleeting as they are, can never be exactly replicated. And when we try to repeat certain memorable communication episodes (such as a heart-to-heart talk or a particular discussion at a party), they are just not the same and may be quite disappointing.

ASSUMPTION 3: INTERPERSONAL COMMUNICATION INVOLVES THE USE OF SOCIAL SYMBOLS. Interpersonal communication occurs because people have created socially understood symbols for communicating their ideas. **Symbols** are both verbal and nonverbal representation of ideas, emotions, objects, or events. Burgoon (1985) identified social symbols as "behaviors that are typically sent with intent, used with regularity among members of a social community, are typically interpreted as intentional, and have consensually recognizable interpretations" (p. 348).

One often cited idea is that "one cannot not communicate" (Watzlawick et al. 1967). This catchy phrase is popular among students of communication. But recently this assumption has come under attack because, for one thing, it confuses the concepts of *signals* and *symbols* (see, for example, Cronkhite 1986). For example, if you have a fever, it is not symbolic behavior as much as it is a **signal** that you are ill. Likewise, if your eyes dilate when you are positively aroused (which they do), that is a signal. The fever or pupil dilation does not represent something else. We can obtain information from signals, but the process of communication involves symbols that are socially shared.

ASSUMPTION 4: INTERPERSONAL COMMUNICATION IS STRATEGIC.   We presented in Chapter 1 three supraordinate goals sought through interpersonal communication: self-presentation, relational, and instrumental goals. We are thus focusing on communication that is strategic. We use the term *strategic* in a broad sense to refer to all goal-relevant communication behavior. As Kellermann (1992) observed, "Communication is selected, structured, and patterned; it is not random, unrestrained, and lawless; it is voluntary, controllable, directioned, chosen, and purposeful" (p. 292).

At times our strategic interaction doesn't appear to us to be very strategic. For example, we may decide in advance that we won't bargain to lower the price of a stereo, only that we'll simply ask the salesperson once to reduce the price. In communication terms, such behavior is strategic, in that a message was constructed to achieve a goal. Kellermann (1992) has further argued that strategic behavior is often used implicitly; that is, our strategies are not always processed consciously.

We also recognize that there are instances wherein people behave without any clear goal in mind, such as in mindless behaviors (Langer 1989). And **mindlessness** can occur in routine interactions (Berger 1986). Our view is that mindless behavior probably occurs when the person's goals are distal or unclear in that particular interaction (see Chapter 1). For example, Langer, Blank, and Chanowitz (1978) found that you may not pay attention to someone giving you a poor reason for causing you a small inconvenience, but you would probably be very mindful if the inconvenience was large, and you would probably require a good reason for the inconvenience.

In this book, however, we emphasize behaviors that are strategic. Many people have plans for getting into a fraternity or sorority, getting into law school, finding a job, being introduced to a particular potential mate, arranging a particular schedule of courses, getting to the church on time, and so forth. In addition, most conversations are goal-directed. That is, people seek assistance from friends, attempt to clarify ideas, want others to like them and share activities with them, and the like. In other words, we all have goals that we pursue and communication strategies we use to help us achieve those goals.

ASSUMPTION 5: COMPETENT COMMUNICATION ACHIEVES SELF-PRESENTATION, RELATIONAL, AND INSTRUMENTAL GOALS.   Much research has concerned what it means to be a competent communicator (e.g., Parks 1985; Spitzberg and Hecht

1984; Wiemann and Backlund 1980). Many scholars have researched the behavioral properties of communication competence, including such factors as empathy, inter-action management, and involvement (Spitzberg and Cupach 1989; see Chapter 14). Most scholars do agree that competent, high-quality communication involves two fundamental properties: *effectiveness* and *appropriateness* (Spitzberg and Cupach 1984). **Effectiveness** refers to achieving our goals in the conversation, and **appropriateness** refers to maintaining the situational rules or expectations. You can be competent at achieving instrumental goals while also achieving self-presentation and relational goals. In other words, in most social situations, appropriateness and effectiveness are positively associated.

Atypical interactions occur, however, when you care only about your own personal goal regardless of what the other person thinks of you. In these situations you may be willing to sacrifice all concerns for self-presentation and relational issues in order to obtain your instrumental goal. We have studied how people gain compliance from others. In one project, students wrote essays on how they would get a friend to repay a loan. Some wrote that they would "hint" (for example, "Oh, I'd love to go out tonight, but my phone bill just arrived and I don't know how I am going to pay it"). Many of these hinters also wrote that if their friend didn't pay them back, they would not ask directly for the money. Why? Because these hinters did not want to embarrass their friends if the friends didn't have the money. These people sought to maintain the relationship over achieving an instrumental goal. One student, however, placed more emphasis on the instrumental goal of getting his money:

> Listen, we keep doing this. I mean, I loan you money and you take forever to repay me. I can't let you take advantage of me any longer. I want you to repay me by noon tomorrow or I'll never loan you money again. I don't care how you get it; just put the money on my dresser.

In sum, in most situations, competent communicators meet the dual requirements of appropriateness and effectiveness when pursuing their self-presentation, relational, and instrumental goals. However, there are rare situations in which people are primarily concerned about one goal at the expense of other important goals.

Functions of Interpersonal Communication

Our definition of interpersonal communication ("the exchange of symbols used to achieve interpersonal goals") is functional. In other words, we define interpersonal communication in terms of what it does. However, we should note that several scholars have identified other functions of interpersonal communication (e.g., Wilmot 1987). Here we present five functions of interpersonal communication: goal achievement, self-definition, structuring, linking, and need fulfillment.

OVERVIEW OF FUNCTIONS

First, in our view, the primary function of interpersonal communication is to achieve important self-presentation, relational, and instrumental goals. As mentioned, this function is a focus of our definition of interpersonal communication. The precise manner in which communication functions to achieve these goals is indicated in Parts II, III, and IV of this book.

Second, interpersonal communication helps us define who we are to ourselves in addition to others. As you will read in Chapter 5, our self-concepts are social concepts, and they are theories of what we are really like. We test these theories of self in interaction with others. In addition, by disclosing information about ourselves to others, we obtain feedback about what we have disclosed. In a word, our definitions of self are linked to the very process of communication, in the implicit as well as explicit presentation of self.

Third, interpersonal communication provides structure to our social world. Through interpersonal interaction people create and re-create norms for behavior, interpersonal rule systems, and standards for evaluating other people's behavior (e.g., Shimanoff 1980). For example, every time someone says "Gesundheit" or "God bless you" to someone who has just sneezed, that person reinforces the rule "Whenever someone sneezes, you should respond with a wish for that person to get well." Other more routine rules are created and reinforced through interaction over time (who changes topics most often, who has the final say, who decides where the couple goes to dinner, and so on).

Fourth, interpersonal communication provides links to other social systems. Information is diffused through various media. One important medium for the diffusion of information is interpersonal. Friends, family, and acquaintances discuss recent news events, technologies ("How do you block and move text in Word-Perfect?"), and opinion ("Do you agree with President Clinton's position on medical care?"). Links to social systems outside the relationship vary in their extensiveness (the degree to which you know people who are in contact with knowledgeable others), and links also vary in their intensiveness (the extent to which you engage in talk with one another).

Finally, interpersonal communication functions to meet interpersonal needs. Needs represent our primary requirements for living. Interpersonal needs refer to our social desires and requirements (needs involving other people). One theory on interpersonal needs has received widespread attention over the past few decades: Schutz's Fundamentals of Interpersonal Relationship Orientation (FIRO).

SCHUTZ'S INTERPERSONAL ORIENTATIONS

Schutz (1966) identifies three interpersonal needs: **inclusion, control,** and **affection.** According to Schutz, people need to include others as part of their world or to be included. People also need to direct others or to be directed. And people need to express or receive affection. People vary greatly in the extent to which they experience these needs. Schutz combines these individual differences to predict how compatible people might be in various relationships.

According to Schutz's "postulate of compatibility," these interpersonal needs are met when there is an equivalent amount of interchange involving them and when the individuals complement each other's ability to give and receive in fulfilling these particular needs. In other words, your needs for inclusion, control, and affection will be met by someone whose own needs balance out yours (Schutz 1966, 105–114).

Figure 2-5 illustrates the postulate of compatibility. The top half portrays a relationship (between Kay and George) that meets both people's needs. Each person's needs are complemented (balanced) by the needs of the partner. For example, Kay includes George by inviting him over to watch videos, to listen to her tapes, to play Monopoly, and so on. Kay also provides the direction in the relationship by deciding where to go for dinner, what time they should meet, and how often they get

Figure 2-5

The Balance of Needs: Schutz's Postulate of Compatibility

Relationship with High Compatibility: Kay and George

Offer affection — G   G → Accept inclusion
Offer control ← K   G → Accept control
Offer inclusion K   K → Accept affection

Relationship with Low Compatibility: Cindy and Sherry

Offer affection   Accept inclusion
Offer control ← CS   Accept control
Offer inclusion CS   SC Accept affection

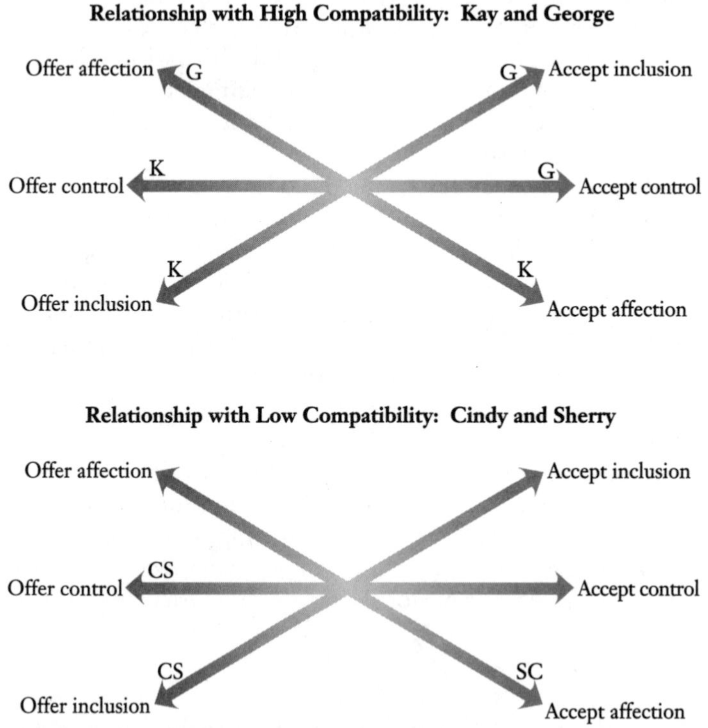

NOTE: Each person's needs are plotted on the lines, which represent continuums. The farther from center, the more intense the need. Needs are more likely to be compatible when the two persons' needs are equidistant from the center.

STRATEGIES TO GET A (SEXY) STRANGER TALKING

In this chapter we talked about five basic assumptions of interpersonal communication. Two dealt with the fundamental idea that communication is strategic and that communication is used to achieve one's goals effectively.

Much of the popular literature is devoted to providing readers with easy and simple ways to achieve goals. Here we have an example of strategic behavior as it is provided to readers of such popular magazines as *Cosmopolitan*. As you read the strategies designed to get a (sexy) stranger to talk to you, ask yourself these four questions:

1. Would using this strategy really be successful in gaining a man's attention?
2. If such a strategy is effective in gaining a man's attention, how do you know that the man who starts a conversation or responds to the strategy will in fact be a "sexy" one or one who is interested in starting a relationship?
3. Would you feel comfortable using such a strategy? Is it an appropriate tactic?
4. What effect would using this strategy have on your public image or the impression the man gets of you? If you used this strategy, would you be perceived as likable? Smart? Competent? Silly? Immature? Manipulative?

When reading the following article, always keep in mind that communication strategies often both affect success or failure in achieving a goal and have implications concerning creating and maintaining a public image:

Do you recoil at the thought of starting conversations with intriguing men you spot at the deli, on the beach, at the Laundromat? You probably still agonize over what to say—and worse, worry that you might seem too aggressive, maybe even predatory! Instead of sputtering and blushing, try a conversation piece. What's that? Any item that demands attention. It can be silly or seductive, quirky or heartwarming, even *startling*. And a conversation piece makes a definite statement about *you*. It says, "I'm friendly and *approachable*."

Pets.   Don't own one? Borrow a friend's, and take the creature for a walk. Tie a little red bandana around your dog's neck and stroll through the neighborhood. If you can't walk a dog, walk a cat. If you can't walk a cat, walk a snake.

Magazines.   You can actually target the kind of man you'd like to meet, by carrying a magazine that would appeal to his interests. Want an outdoorsy man? Try *Field and Stream*. Someone with a mechanical bent? How about *Motor Trend*? A doctor? Pick up the *New England Journal of Medicine*, and carry it (title showing) on your daily travels.

(continued)

(continued from previous page)

A camera. Invite a female friend to the beach. When you spot an attractive man, ask him to snap a picture of the two of you. Then offer to take his picture and mail it to him. Voilà! You now have his address, and when you mail the photo, you can drop him a note.

Children. If you believe having children hinders your chances for meeting men, think again! Women with children appear nonthreatening and nurturing—traits appealing to males. Take your tots to the park on Sunday afternoon; that's where you'll find the divorced men entertaining their own offspring. (No kids? No problem. Invite a niece or nephew along.)

Suspenders. With these racy little accessories in bright colors and quirky designs, you can bet you'll catch his attention. And when you do, tell him why you always wear these particular suspenders . . . —for luck!

A long loaf of French bread. Don't underestimate the power of a baguette carried European-style in a string bag. Men can't resist smiling at this homey sight and are bound to comment. What to do with the bread? Invite a few friends over for your special homemade pasta. And remember, there's always room for one more.

Sheet music. Do your knees go weak at the thought of meeting a musician? Carry sheet music geared to the type of music maker you have in mind. How about a Bach cantata for that cool, classical type?

Paints and easel. Loved to sketch in high school? Enroll in an art class and rediscover your talents. Set up an easel in the park and re-create the pastoral scene. You could be interrupted by a handsome passerby who'll want to model for you.

A telescope. If you go gaga over stargazing, why not take your telescope to the streets one summer night? When that curious man pauses to find out what you're doing, offer him a view of the moons surrounding Jupiter.

Stereo or VCR brochure. Is it time to upgrade your stereo system or replace your VCR? Pick up a few brochures and start reading them in public places. Ask a man if he knows where you can find a good pair of speakers for under one hundred dollars. When he stops laughing, ask about good speakers for under one thousand dollars.

Windup toys. Indulge your childish streak. Take a pal to a friendly saloon, set a small windup toy on the bar, and send it walking back and forth. Now what? Just wait!

Excerpted from "Twenty Conversation Pieces to Get a Stranger Talking," Sharon Wolf, C.S.W., for *Cosmopolitan*, March 1991.

together, which is fine with George. George shows affection (for example, giving praise), which Kay desires and complements by receiving.

The bottom half of the figure depicts a relationship in which the friends (Cindy and Sherry) do not complement each other's needs. Here both people want to include the other in their own social world. So they compete about whose tapes they are going to play, whose problems they will discuss, and the like. In addition, they both have a high need to control the other. So they interrupt one another and seek to wrest power from each other. Finally, both have similar needs regarding affection (in this instance, they both want to receive affection). So, for example, each is interested in opening her own Christmas present, getting (but not giving) compliments from the other, and receiving (but not sending) thank-you cards and phone calls.

In sum, interpersonal communication functions to achieve goals, to define who we are in our social world, to structure society, to provide links to other social systems, and to fulfill our interpersonal needs.

Chapter Summary

In this chapter we identified various properties of communication that have been emphasized in different theoretic approaches. Four theoretic perspectives were reviewed.

We view communication as a strategic activity. This implies communication that is purposeful and socially shared between partners. The remainder of this book further underscores the strategic nature of communication.

One of our secondary objectives in this chapter was to highlight various perspectives to provide you with a conceptual frame of reference for this book. In addition, in reviewing the various perspectives, you might be able to articulate, perhaps for the first time, your own theoretic perspective on interpersonal communication. Of course, your perspective might differ from ours. In fact, we would be surprised (and disappointed) if you accepted our position without reflection.

KEY TERMS

mechanistic perspective
encoding
decoding
feedback
fidelity

openness
act
interact
submissive symmetrical interact
transact

breakdown
noise
actors
linear model
psychological perspective
co-orientation
interactionist perspective
self
role taking
systems perspective
nonsummativity

dominant interact
domineering interact
symbols
signals
mindlessness
effectiveness
appropriateness
inclusion
control
affection

EXERCISES FOR FURTHER DISCUSSION

1. Try to come up with your own definition of interpersonal communication, using just one or two sentences. Now look at the definition you have written down.
   a. What are the key terms in your definition?
   b. What are some of the assumptions behind your definition?
   c. How is your definition different from the one that is outlined in this chapter?
2. Look at the four models of communication provided in this chapter.
   a. Which of the four perspectives on communication is most consistent with your definition?
   b. If none of the perspectives is consistent with your definition, try to articulate your own perspective.
3. Write down a definition of what it means to communicate strategically.
   a. Do you feel that most communication is strategic?
   b. Can you think of any instances when communication is not strategic?
   c. What implications does seeing communication as strategic have for your view of people in general? Does it imply that people are more calculating than you think they are?
4. Make a list of ten people that you know who provide your main links to the outside world.
   a. How much do you rely on these people for information about what is going on in the world?
   b. How reliable do you consider these people to be as sources of information about the outside world?

5. Think for a moment about whether Schutz's postulate of compatibility holds
   true in your own life.
   a. Do you seek relationships with others who complement your needs of inclu-
      sion, control, and affection?
   b. Which of your relationships do you consider most compatible?
   c. Are some of your relationships not compatible?

SUGGESTED READING

COMMUNICATION THEORY

Fisher, B. A. 1978. *Perspectives on human communication*. New York: Macmillan. This
   classic text shows how various perspectives on communication emphasize different aspects of interaction. Four perspectives are covered: mechanistic, psychological, interactional, and systems.

Littlejohn, S. W. 1989. *Theories of human communication*, 3rd edition. Belmont,
   Calif.: Wadsworth. This is perhaps the most comprehensive treatment of communication theories. Theories from both inside and outside the field of communication are presented and discussed.

INTERPERSONAL COMMUNICATION DEFINITION AND APPROACHES

Duck, S. W. 1988. *Relating to others*. Homewood, Ill.: Dorsey Press. This book focuses on how people form and develop relationships. In addition, Duck presents a
   chapter on repairing relationships.

Knapp, M. L., and Vangelisti, A. 1991. *Human communication and personal relationships*, 2nd edition. Boston: Allyn & Bacon. Based on a social exchange model, this
   book emphasizes stages of coming together and growing apart. Knapp and Vangelisti also discuss various communication behaviors associated with intimacy. The
   book concludes with a discussion of communication competence.

Roloff, M. E., and Miller, G. R., eds., 1987. *Interpersonal processes: New directions in communication research*. Newbury Park, Calif.: Sage. This reader is for the advanced
   student (upper level or graduate). The chapters emphasize diverse approaches to
   the study of interpersonal communication. In addition, particular domains of interpersonal communication are featured (e.g., emotion, conflict, self-disclosure).

Wilmot, W. W. 1987. *Dyadic communication*, 3rd edition. New York: Random
   House. Wilmot discusses how perceptions of the self, the other, and the relationship affect interpersonal communication. Perhaps the most innovative chapter is
   one that discusses various relational intricacies, such as paradoxes, double-binds,
   spirals, and dialectics (see also Chapter 9, this volume).

REFERENCE LIST

▼

Bahg, C. G. 1990. Major systems theories throughout the world. *Behavioral Science* 35:79–107.

Berger, C. R. 1986. Planning, affect, and social action generation. In *Communication, social cognition, and affect*, ed. H. Sypher and E. T. Higgins, 76–87. Hillsdale, N.J.: Erlbaum.

Brockriede, W. 1978. The research process. *Western Journal of Speech Communication* 42:3–11.

Burgoon, J. K. 1985. Nonverbal signals. In *Handbook of interpersonal communication*, ed. M. L. Knapp and G. R. Miller, 344–390. Newbury Park, Calif.: Sage.

Courtright, J. A.; Millar, F. E.; and Rogers-Millar, L. E. 1979. Domineeringness and dominance: Replication and extension. *Communication Monographs* 46:179–192.

Cronkhite, G. 1986. On the focus, scope, and coherence of the study of human symbolic activity. *Quarterly Journal of Speech* 72:231–246.

Dance, F. E. X. 1970. The "concept" of communication. *Journal of Communication* 20: 201–210.

Fisher, B. A. 1978. *Perspectives on human communication*. New York: Macmillan.

Gottman, J. M. 1982. Emotional responsiveness in marital conversations. *Journal of Communication* 32:108–120.

Kellermann, K. 1992. Communication: Inherently strategic and primarily automatic. *Communication Monographs* 59:288–300.

Langer, E. J. 1989. *Mindfulness*. Boston: Addison-Wesley.

Langer, E. J.; Blank, A.; and Chanowitz, B. 1978. The mindlessness of ostensibly thoughtful action: The role of the "placebic" information in interpersonal interaction. *Journal of Personal and Social Psychology* 36:635–642.

Littlejohn, S. W. 1989. *Theories of human communication*, 3d ed. Belmont, Calif.: Wadsworth.

Mead, G. H. 1934. *Mind, self, and society*. Chicago: University of Chicago Press.

Millar, F. E., and Rogers, L. E. 1976. A relational approach to interpersonal communication. In *Explorations in interpersonal communication*, ed. G. R. Miller, 87–103. Newbury Park, Calif.: Sage.

———. 1987. Relational dimensions of interpersonal dynamics. In *Interpersonal processes: New directions in communication research*, ed. M. E. Roloff and G. R. Miller, 117–139. Newbury Park, Calif.: Sage.

Monge, P. R. 1977. The systems perspective as a theoretical basis for the study of human communication. *Communication Quarterly* 25 (1) 19–29.

Nussbaum, J. F., ed. 1989. *Life-span communication: Normative processes*. Hillsdale, N.J.: Erlbaum.

Parks, M. R. 1985. Interpersonal communication and the quest for personal competence. In *Handbook of interpersonal communication*, ed. M. L. Knapp and G. R. Miller, 171–201. Newbury Park, Calif.: Sage.

Schutz, W. B. 1966. *The interpersonal underworld*. Palo Alto, Calif.: Science and Behavior Books.

Shimanoff, S. B. 1980. *Communication rules: Theory and research*. Newbury Park, Calif.: Sage.

Spitzberg, B. H., and Cupach, W. R. 1984. *Interpersonal communication competence*. Newbury Park, Calif.: Sage.

————. *Handbook of interpersonal competence research*. New York: Springer-Verlag.

Spitzberg, B. H., and Hecht, M. L. 1984. Component model of relational competence. *Human Communication Research* 10:575–599.

Watzlawick, P.; Beavin, J. H.; and Jackson, D. D. 1967. *Pragmatics of human communication: A study of interactional patterns, pathologies, and paradoxes*. New York: Norton.

Wiemann, J. M., and Backlund, P. 1980. Current theory and research in communication competence. *Review of Educational Research* 50:185–199.

Wilmot, W. W. 1987. *Dyadic communication*, 3d ed. Dubuque, Iowa: Brown.

C H A P T E R   3

FUNDAMENTALS

OF VERBAL

COMMUNICATION

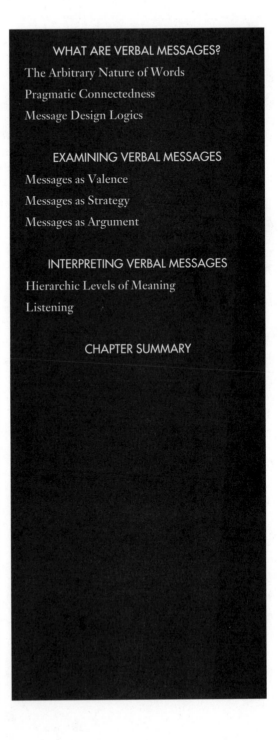

Alexander stood in the kitchen with Harold and brandished a plate of Danish over his head. "Tell me when I can find my own Prime Matter, or you will never see this Danish again."

"Tell me what the Prime Matter is," Harold said to him.

Alexander stared at Harold, walked out of the kitchen, and slammed the door behind him.

For days now, they had been having this nonconversation.

"When can I find my own Prime Matter?"

"Tell me what the Prime Matter is."

Harold said it now as if the answer was perfectly obvious, as if it was Alexander, not he, who had decided to hold something back.

It was not just a riddle when he said it now. It had become a plea.

From Lisa Grunwald, *The Theory of Everything* (pp. 295–296)

In *The Theory of Everything*, Alexander is a famous scientist who turns his mental powers to the study of alchemy (also known as the Work). Every Adept, or person who seriously undertakes the study of the Work, must obtain his or her own Prime Matter. The problem is that no one who knows is allowed to say what the Prime Matter is. So after months and months of reading and thinking, Alexander becomes very frustrated with Harold for not relating what the Prime Matter is. All that Alexander knows is that each Adept has his or her own Prime Matter and that Prime Matter forms the basis for all of alchemy.

People use words to create ideas, inspire action, and win hearts. People also use words to confuse issues, postpone obligations, and end relationships. In other words, verbal messages are used to achieve goals, whatever they may be. This chapter indicates that the process of exchanging words is linked to the nature of language, message choices by the actor, and ways of interpreting messages. Knowing these factors is fundamental to understanding how interpersonal communication functions to achieve personal goals.

What Are Verbal Messages?

Verbal messages consist of words, or everyday language. (Throughout this chapter we use the terms *verbal messages, words,* and *language* interchangeably.) Language helps us achieve goals, and social actors realize that. But people vary in their personal beliefs about language use.

THE ARBITRARY NATURE OF WORDS

Words are arbitrary metaphors. They are *arbitrary* in that they are created by people for any number of reasons. There is no deterministic reason why a person, event, or object is named what it is. *Metaphors* are symbols; they serve as substitutes for the person, event, or object. Accordingly, words are not reality; they merely *represent* reality.

Ogden and Richards (1927) proposed the *semantic triangle*, a model showing the relationship between words and the reality that words represent (for a brief review, see Foss, Foss, and Trapp 1991). In each corner of a triangle is a necessary element of meaning. In one corner is the thing being perceived (a person, an event, or an object), which is called the **referent.** In the second corner is the word, or **symbol.** In the third corner is your collective image of the class of the perceived person, event, or object, the **reference.** The reference is composed of your previous experience.

Meanings of messages depend on the communicators' use of shared symbols for the same referents using similar references. Of course, people often confuse meanings because their symbols, referents, or references are dissimilar. As Foss and colleagues (1991) illustrate, two people can have very different references for the apparently simple symbol "dog." One person recalls "dog" as a dangerous animal, while the other person recalls "dog" as a friendly creature. Of course, the picture becomes more confused with more abstract symbols or separately experienced references. Figure 3-1 illustrates how the semantic triangle shows the relations among words, referents, and references.

As Figure 3-1 shows, two people can have different mental images of the words *fur coat.* Of course, people have different associations for other words as well. For example, consider the different associations for "getting together" with someone. "Getting together" can mean having a romantic date to one person but just talking to another person. In short, words represent reality, and people have different realities represented by the same words.

Likewise, people may use different words to represent the same reality. For example, recall from the scenario at the beginning of the chapter that Harold wanted to know what the Prime Matter was. He knew the symbol but lacked a reference or referent. Once Harold discovers that Prime Matter is earth and that he can take any

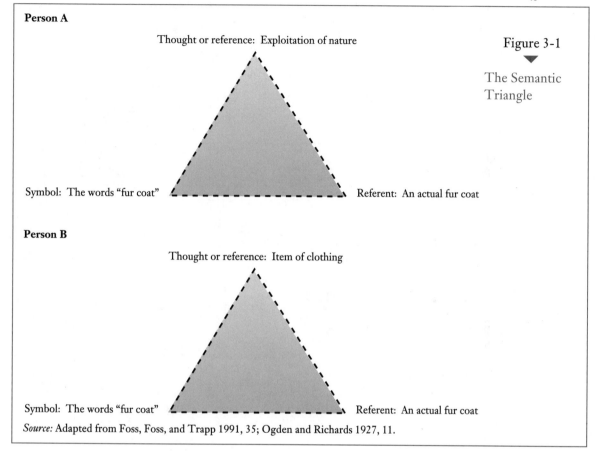

Person A

Thought or reference: Exploitation of nature

Symbol: The words "fur coat"   Referent: An actual fur coat

Person B

Thought or reference: Item of clothing

Symbol: The words "fur coat"   Referent: An actual fur coat

Figure 3-1

The Semantic
Triangle

Source: Adapted from Foss, Foss, and Trapp 1991, 35; Ogden and Richards 1927, 11.

portion of earth for his own Prime Matter, he immediately understands Alexander.
They now are using the same verbal symbol to represent the same reality.

PRAGMATIC CONNECTEDNESS

One of the most fundamental issues regarding language is the issue of coherence
(see Ellis 1992 for a discussion). In other words, how do people make sense of words
and relate them to one another? According to Jackson and Jacobs (1980; Jacobs and
Jackson 1983; Jacobs 1985), we see the relationships among words because they
serve a pragmatic purpose for the communicator. Both speakers and hearers link

People often have different realities for the same words.

(*Bloom County* by Berkeley Breathed. © 1985 Washington Post Writers Group. Reprinted with permission.)

messages to the communicator's goals and understand messages according to their **pragmatic connectedness,** or degree to which the words are relevant to a goal. Pragmatic connectedness lends coherence to words.

An excellent example of pragmatic coherence occurs during **presequences,** or message exchanges that precede the primary message (Jackson and Jacobs 1983). Consider the following presequence. In this example, Susan qualifies her part of the presequence so that she can learn more about Harry's goal.

Turn	Speaker	Message
1.0	Harry:	Hi, Susan, are you busy Saturday night?
2.0	Susan:	That depends. I've been promising my mom I'd come over for a visit soon. What's up?

3.0   Harry: I was wondering if you'd like to go bowling.
4.0   Susan: Well, I really can't, you know, change plans like that
                     with my mother.

The point worth emphasizing is that communicators understand the connection among words because of their inferred links to communicator goals. As Jacobs (1985) notes:

> The process is viewed . . . as a kind of problem-solving activity, involving the assessment of mutual knowledge in the generation of speaker plans and hearer inferences as to the most plausible solution for what the speaker plan might be. Language choice is based not on the force of normative regulation, but on speaker goals and general principles of rationality. (p. 336, original emphasis deleted.)

MESSAGE DESIGN LOGICS

Although people relate language to the communicator's goals, people may hold different conceptions of how language should be used. O'Keefe and associates (O'Keefe 1988; O'Keefe and McCornack 1987; O'Keefe and Sheppard 1987) present a theory of communication that explains why people use various messages based on underlying beliefs about communication. These beliefs are called **message design logics.** There are three types of message design logics: *expressive, conventional,* and *rhetorical.*

An **expressive message design logic** refers to the belief that communication functions primarily to express ideas and feelings. People who adopt the expressive logic present their ideas and feelings as they are experienced, without much editing, not really discriminating between thoughts and feelings (O'Keefe 1988). A **conventional message design logic** refers to the view that communication is a kind of a game, with commonly understood rules (conventions). People who use this logic are concerned with both expression and achieving their goals within the boundaries of social appropriateness; communication functions primarily to uphold social conventions. A **rhetorical message design logic** refers to the belief that communication functions primarily to create a person's social world. People who adopt the rhetorical logic believe that self-expression and social conventions can be used or changed to meet their interpersonal objectives.

According to O'Keefe (1988), when goals are easily achieved by simply expressing our needs, all three message design logics lead to similar kinds of communication. But when situations become more complex due to competing goals, differences in logics will lead to differences in message use.

O'Keefe (1988) demonstrates how verbal messages reflect these three logics. An expressive message typically is not edited, nor does it necessarily conform to social norms or apply to the partners' current activities. For example, imagine that you are

TAGGERS' CODES

In Los Angeles, teenagers who make it a business to paint graffiti on street signs, walls, and other visible backdrops are called *taggers*. Regardless of how we might feel about graffiti, taggers have their own subculture, complete with a set of common codes. These codes illustrate how words can serve as arbitrary metaphors. Here is a sample of terms taggers use.

- Tag: Your graffiti signature.
- Crew: Your tagging group—also known as a posse, mob or tribe.
- Homies: Fellow members of your crew.
- Kicking it: To relax with your homies.
- Toy: A novice, amateurish tagger.
- Ranker: A person who chickens out, doesn't defend his tag.
- Slipping: Being caught by rival taggers without homies to back you up.
- Mob: To hit a target with graffiti.
- Kill: To completely cover with graffiti.
- Seek and destroy: To tag everything in sight.
- Map the heavens: To tag hard-to-reach freeway overhead signs.
- To be down: To be a dedicated tagger, accepted by your crew.
- Buster: Someone who claims he's down but isn't.
- To get up: To spread your tag in as many places as possible.
- To battle: To go up against another crew to see who gets up the most.
- To be rank: To have the privileges of deciding who is in and out of your crew.
- Hero: An adult who would turn in a tagger.
- Landmark: A prime spot where a tag won't be erased.
- To be buffed: To have a tag cleaned off by authorities.
- To be crossed out: To have a tag erased by rival tagger.

"Leaving Their Mark: Youths Risk Everything to Tag Walls, Buses and Traffic Signs With Graffiti," by John Gilonna. Copyright © 1993, *Los Angeles Times.* Reprinted by permission.

You can think of your own relationships as subcultures, complete with special uses of language. Friends and partners in romantic relationships often develop their own codes, as do members of particular groups. What words have special, perhaps unique meanings in your relationships?

in a work group and one of the members has not performed his assignment. You might offer this expressive message:

> "Ron, you lazy idiot! Did you think we wouldn't notice you were this far behind? All you have is a rough draft! I can't believe it. I am so mad! I'm getting you out of our group because I don't want a bad grade" (adapted from O'Keefe, 1988).

Note that the message primarily expresses the frustration of the communicator but does little to change the situation. A conventional message implies appropriateness norms and links a person's goal to the fulfillment of these norms; for example:

> "Ron, you owe it to us to get your job done because each of us has spent a lot of time and energy to make an excellent presentation. You must know that the teacher will see who has spent the most effort during the presentation, so I doubt that your grade will be very good" (adapted from O'Keefe, 1988).

A rhetorical message would use the conditions and information in the situation to persuade others; for example:

> "Ron, I'm sorry you're not prepared for tomorrow. Can you think of some reason why you are so unprepared? Both the group and the teacher will want to know. You also need to see how your personal problems affect others. I sympathize with you, but you must help us out right now with all you've got. So get as ready as you can by tomorrow" (adapted from O'Keefe, 1988).

Knowledge of these message design logics makes it possible for you to "choose" which logic to adopt in a given situation. O'Keefe's theory implies that the rhetorical logic is superior. Our view is that the most sophisticated communicators can use all three logics and corresponding messages to achieve their most important goals.

Examining Verbal Messages

Imagine the following situation. Steve reaches for Linda's hand while they watch TV.

Turn	Speaker	Message
1.0	Linda:	Steve, listen, I don't want to get affectionate anymore. I don't want you try to hold hands or kiss me or do anything affectionate.

Turn	Speaker	Message
2.0	Steve:	Why? You know I like you.
3.0	Linda:	I know. But I hate it when you show affection and then say we're only friends. I want more than just being friends. I want more than physical affection every now and then too.
4.0	Steve:	But there's nothing wrong with showing someone you care about her.
5.0	Linda:	Yes, there is. It's frustrating. It's also confusing, and it hurts to realize that you don't really mean it. You complain that I don't act happy anymore. Do you want me to go on being miserable?
6.0	Steve:	No, no. It's so natural between us, and you seem to like it.
7.0	Linda:	It's not natural! How many other friends do you know who make out and then act like nothing has happened? No couples I know do this! They're either friends or they're in a relationship.
8.0	Steve:	But we *have* a relationship. So?
9.0	Linda:	Not like that, not anymore! Look, either you stop leading me on, or you can find someone else to be your "friend."

Poole, McPhee, and Seibold (1982) observed that people can examine messages at three levels: as **valence,** as **strategy,** and as **argument.** We can study the words exchanged between Steve and Linda at each of these levels. First, as valence, we can identify each sentence as being either for or against Linda's goal "to de-escalate the relationship." We simply do this by counting the number of messages that favor (positive valence) or disfavor (negative valence) Linda's proposal to stop being affectionate. Second, we can observe the strategies that unfold during the course of the discussion. For example, Linda begins by using the strategy of simple statement (turn 1). She then uses reason giving (turn 3), altruism (turn 5), an appeal to social norms (turn 7), and finally a threat (turn 9). Third, we can analyze the words as they function as argument. For example, in turn 7 Linda challenges the idea that showing affection between friends is natural and supports this challenge by referring to other friends' behaviors. Linda concludes turn 7 by making the inference that either people are friends or they have a relationship. We now examine each of these levels of verbal messages more carefully.

Verbal messages between individuals can be understood on several levels. Any message can be understood in terms of its valence, its strategy, and its argument.

(Joel Gordon)

MESSAGES AS VALENCE

Valence refers to the positive or negative value of a message. There are several important ways in which messages impart valence. First, messages indicate positive or negative reactions to another person's ideas or proposals (positive reactions such as "Great!" and "That sounds good," negative reactions such as "I don't think so" and "No way"). Second, messages convey an evaluation of your partner and the relationship. Recall from Chapter 1 that communication functions to achieve three types of goals: self-presentation, relational, and instrumental. Your messages confirm or disconfirm the other's self-presentation and definition of the relationship, in addition to indicating your attitude toward the other's ideas and proposals.

Sieburg (1976) specifies how messages confirm or disconfirm others. According to Sieburg, a **confirming message** contains the following elements:

1. Recognition of your partner's existence
2. Recognition of your partner as a unique individual
3. Expression of your partner's significance
4. Acceptance of your partner's way of experiencing life
5. Expressions of concern and willingness to become involved with your partner

These elements are indicated by showing yourself as involved in what the other is saying. Indeed, showing that you are conversationally involved is a primary criterion of communication competence (see Chapter 14). Note, however, that you do not necessarily have to agree with your partner's opinions to be confirming and positive. Simple messages, such as "I see" and "I understand" indicate your positive regard for your partner without expressing agreement with the ideas expressed.

Disconfirming messages, by contrast, convey a negative evaluation of your partner and the relationship. According to Sieburg (1976), disconfirming messages fall into three categories: *indifference, imperviousness*, and *disqualification*. Indifference means disconfirming the other through silence (not giving a sound or an utterance), through absent (mindless) responses, or by interrupting or disrupting what the partner is saying. Imperviousness involves being inattentive to the other's thoughts and feelings. Impervious responses reflect this lack of attention ("What, huh, I don't know," "Yeah—what?"). Disqualification means being unaware of the other. Disqualification is exhibited as monologues, wherein one person talks endlessly about his or her own concerns; either as irrelevant responses to messages ("So, do you think I should get married?" "Let's get an ice cream"), or as tangential responses, whereby the communicator responds incidentally to the issue and then proceeds with a different thought ("So, do you think I should get married?" "Who knows? Let's get an ice cream").

MESSAGES AS STRATEGY

Much research has been devoted to messages as strategy (for a review, see Seibold, Cantrill, and Meyers 1985; see also Chapter 11). A *strategy* refers to a general approach that people take to achieve their goals. **Tactics** are the specific behaviors taken to implement the strategy. Tactics usually occur in sequences. For example, imagine that you want to take your midterm examination a week late. You decide on the strategy of rationality (offering reasons to achieve your goal). You enter your professor's office and first compliment her on the nice print on the wall (ingratiation; see also Chapter 5). Next you relate how busy you've been on the debate team and that there is a debate tournament the weekend before the midterm, so you have no time for studying (reason giving). Finally, you present a desired image of yourself by indicating that you've never asked for this kind of favor before and that you are a good student (a self-enhancing message; see Chapter 5). Your overall strategy was one of being rational, but three tactics were used to implement the strategy behaviorally.

Several typologies of message strategies have been offered (e.g., Cody, McLaughlin and Jordon 1980; Cody, McLaughlin, and Schneider 1981; Clark 1979; Marwell and Schmitt 1967; Wiseman and Schenck-Hamlin 1981). Wheeless, Barraclough, and Stewart (1983) organized these various typologies according to how various strategies reflect three different power bases of *consequences, relationship identification,* and *values.* **Consequences** relate to your power to reward or punish the individual. **Relationship identification** concerns your power over the other based on how the other regards you or identifies with you as a role model. **Values** are the attitudes and beliefs that motivate individuals to act. Table 3-1 presents a sample of message strategies that reflect these three power bases.

Use of these strategies depends on a variety of factors. Research indicates that people select various strategies to achieve their self-presentation and relational goals, in addition to seeking their purely instrumental goals (e.g., Cody et al. 1986; Sillars 1980). In addition, use of these various strategies depends on the relationship with the other as well as a person's perceived rights to persuade that person (Cody et al. 1981). Finally, the way these strategies unfold during the interaction depends very much on the other person's response.

MESSAGES AS ARGUMENT

The third level of messages is argument. Argument is defined as convergence-seeking discourse (Canary, Brossmann, and Seibold 1987), that is, seeking agreement or understanding about our ideas. Accordingly, when a message is analyzed at the level of argument, we focus on how ideas are developed and shared.

The examination of interpersonal argument is a relatively new endeavor, compared to the centuries devoted to the study of public argument. The theories and prescriptions for public argument do not really portray how people argue in interpersonal contexts. Hence a category scheme for tracing argument in interpersonal situations was developed and has been used in several studies (e.g., Canary et al. 1987; Canary, Weger and Stafford 1991; Meyers, Seibold, and Brashers 1991).

There are six major categories of interpersonal argument. *Starting points* are positions you want the other to accept. These are supported with *developing points.* Showing agreement to another's idea or understanding (without agreement) indicates growing closer in terms of ideas, so these messages are called *convergence markers.* Their opposite are messages indicating nonacceptance of the other's views.

Table 3-1

MESSAGE STRATEGIES AND EXAMPLES ACCORDING TO POWER BASES

Power Base: Consequences

Strategy	Example
Promise	"If you loan me your car, I'll wash your windows."
Threat	"If you don't loan me your car, I'll never call you again."
Aversive stimuli	"I am going to keep criticizing you in public until you apologize to me."
Suggest negative alternatives	"If your dog doesn't stop barking at night, I'm going to buy it a muzzle."
Positive expertise	"If you stick by me, people will find out how talented you are."

Power Base: Relationship Identification

Strategy	Example
Cooperation	"Listen, I thought you should know that some of your neighbors are getting pretty mad about your dog barking at night."
Positive esteem	"You know we would like you a lot more if you were less selfish with your car."
Negative esteem	"People are really going to think you're a jerk if you don't keep your dog quiet."
Altruism	"Please think about how badly I need to get some sleep—quiet your dog for my sake."
Simple request	"Would you loan me your car on Saturday night?"

Power Base: Values

Strategy	Example
Moral appeal	"It isn't right that you delay the rest of the group because your job isn't done."

Positive altercasting	"You are a fair teacher. Please let me take the midterm exam at a later date."
Negative altercasting	"Only irresponsible students fail to get their work done on time."
Debt	"Look at how many times I have covered for you. The least you can do is loan me your car."
Negative self-feeling	"You will feel guilty later if you don't get your assignment to me tomorrow."

Source: Adapted from Wheeless, Barraclough, and Stewart 1983, 129–130.

These are called *prompters* because further communication is needed if convergence is to be achieved. Some messages contextualize or limit the discussion topic—these are called *delimiters*. Finally, there are behaviors that have no immediate argument function and are labeled *nonarguments*. Table 3-2 presents this classification scheme.

Finding that *relationship identification* tactics don't work, Calvin resorts to a *consequences* tactic.

(*Calvin and Hobbes,* copyright Bill Watterson. Dist. by Universal Press Syndicate. Reprinted with permission. All rights reserved.)

Table 3-2

CONVERSATIONAL ARGUMENT CLASSIFICATION SCHEME

Starting Points

ASRT: *Assertion.* Statement of belief or opinion.
PROP: *Proposition.* Statement that calls for discussion or action.

Developing Points

ELAB: *Elaboration.* Statement that supports other statements by providing evidence or clarification.
AMPL: *Amplification.* An explicit inferential statement.
JUST: *Justification.* A statement that advances norms, values, or rules of logic to support the validity of other statements.

Convergence Markers

AGMT: *Agreement.* A statement that indicates agreement.
ACKN: *Acknowledgment.* A message indicating recognition or understanding of another's point.

Prompters

OBJC: *Objection.* A statement that denies the truth or validity of other statements.
CHAL: *Challenge.* A message presenting a problem, question, or reservation that must be addressed to reach agreement.
RESP: *Response.* A statement that defends other statements met with an objection or a challenge.

Delimiters

FRAM: *Frame.* A message that provides a context for or qualification of another message.
F/SE: *Forestall/Secure.* An attempt to forestall discussion by securing agreement.
F/RE: *Forestall/Remove.* An attempt to forestall discussion by not permitting something to be discussed.

Nonarguments

NARG: *Nonargument.* A statement with no argumentative function.

*N: *"Asterisk N."* An asterisk plus a turn number, indicating that the thought is completed elsewhere (read: "see turn *X*").

Source: Adapted from Canary, Weger, and Stafford 1991, 161.

Consider two exchanges at the level of argument, referring to the codes in Table 3-2. In the first example, the husband and wife jointly construct an argument, showing convergence in their ideas. The wife offers support in turn 2.2 for the husband's assertion in turn 1.2. The husband elaborates a point, without really needing to finish his sentence (in turn 3.0), to which the wife agrees (in turn 4.0).

Turn	Speaker	Message	Code
1.1	Husband:	Ah, OK.	AGMT
1.2		Actually, the only time that I think cleaning and household chores are a problem is when one of us is really overworked.	ASRT
1.3		And we see work that needs to be done.	ELAB(1.2)
1.4		And we feel, "I'm just too tired to do that; it's the other person's turn."	AMPL
1.5		And we both yell at that point.	ELAB(1.4)
2.1	Wife:	Yeah.	AGMT
2.2		We're either overtired or being pressured by some event that's coming up and we want the house to be especially clean for that situation.	ELAB(1.4)
3.0	Husband:	Or if I spent too much money and you're feeling perhaps . . .	ELAB(2.2)
4.0	Wife:	There you go, yes.	AGMT

The second example shows less convergence of ideas and more disagreement. This example concerns a romantic couple not getting along with each other's friends.

Turn	Speaker	Message	Code
1.0	Female:	You think I spend too much time with Joyce.	ASRT
2.1	Male:	I do not.	OBJC
2.2		I just think that you kiss her butt.	ASRT
3.0	Female:	No, I do not.	OBJC
4.1	Male:	Yes, you do.	RESP(3.0)
4.2		You always do, every time.	ELAB(4.1)
4.3		You say, "No, no, Joyce is going to get mad."	ELAB(4.2)
4.4		And you never seem to care if I get mad.	ASRT

Recall from Chapter 2 how turns can be coupled to form interacts. Research has shown that particular argument interacts are positively associated with relational quality and that others are dysfunctional (Canary et al. 1991). For example, developing points followed by either a convergence marker or another developing point (as we see in the first example just given) are positively associated with relational satisfaction and cooperation. But prompters followed by prompters and prompters followed by developing points (as in the second example) are negatively associated with cooperation and relational satisfaction. You can realize that a series of prompter-prompter interacts is an argumentative dead end. The following exchange clearly illustrates prompter-prompter interacts:

Turn	Speaker	Message	Code
1.0	Woman:	You don't trust me very much.	ASRT
2.0	Man:	I trust you—I just don't trust other guys.	CHAL
3.0	Woman:	That says to me that you don't trust me either.	RESP
4.0	Man:	No, it doesn't.	OBJC
5.0	Woman:	Yes, it does.	RESP

Interpreting Verbal Messages

You have probably learned from experience that people can interpret the same message in several ways. Here we highlight the various ways in which a message can be interpreted.

HIERARCHIC LEVELS OF MEANING

One of the most comprehensive models for showing the various ways in which people interpret messages is offered by Pearce and Conklin (1979; see also Pearce and Cronen 1980). In this model the various ways in which people interpret a message are arranged hierarchically. Each level of interpretation serves as the groundwork for the level above it. Figure 3-2 summarizes this model.

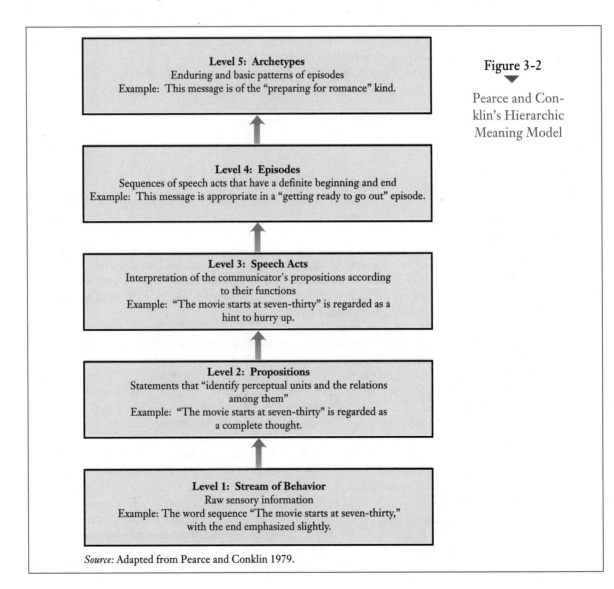

Level 5: Archetypes
Enduring and basic patterns of episodes
Example: This message is of the "preparing for romance" kind.

Level 4: Episodes
Sequences of speech acts that have a definite beginning and end
Example: This message is appropriate in a "getting ready to go out" episode.

Level 3: Speech Acts
Interpretation of the communicator's propositions according to their functions
Example: "The movie starts at seven-thirty" is regarded as a hint to hurry up.

Level 2: Propositions
Statements that "identify perceptual units and the relations among them"
Example: "The movie starts at seven-thirty" is regarded as a complete thought.

Level 1: Stream of Behavior
Raw sensory information
Example: The word sequence "The movie starts at seven-thirty," with the end emphasized slightly.

Source: Adapted from Pearce and Conklin 1979.

Figure 3-2

Pearce and Conklin's Hierarchic Meaning Model

Level 1 is the **stream of behavior** level. Raw sensory information, including all movements and sounds, potentially serve as message material. Certain of these movements and sounds (and smells, tastes, and sensations as well) are perceived and can be "punctuated" in a variety of ways. For example, using the raw sensory data in the sequence of words "The movie starts at seven-thirty," you might notice a slight emphasis on the end.

Level 2 consists of **propositions.** At this level, the literal meaning of the message is interpreted. "The movie starts at seven-thirty" is recognized as a complete sentence, with a subject and a verb, that has an identifiable reference in reality. However, no interpretation beyond the literal meaning is made.

Many times, responding only to the literal meaning of a message can be frustrating to the person who offers the message. Consider the following exchanges:

Alex: Could you please pass the milk?
Beth: Yes [but she doesn't pass the milk].

or

Beth: Excuse me, I'm wondering how to get to the Admissions Office
         from here.
Alex: That's nice.

Clearly, we often need to interpret a message beyond its literal content. We must also identify the goals of the communicator so as to realize that we are being asked a favor (to pass the milk or to give directions). Inferring the intentions of the communicator leads to the next level of interpretation.

Level 3 is **speech acts.** Pearce and Conklin (1979) identify speech acts as the smallest units of analysis having interpersonal significance. Speech acts interpret the message by answering the question, "What is the communicator's impact on the listener?" (Pearce and Conklin 1979). For example, the proposition, "The movie starts at seven-thirty" can be interpreted in various ways, depending what we think the intended goal of the communicator is. It can be seen as a hint to hurry up and get ready, it can be interpreted as an invitation to do something else before the movie, or it can be seen as information if we note that the other person was scanning the newspaper to find out when the show starts. In brief, the speech act level of interpretation indicates that propositions count as something beyond their literal meaning.

Level 4 is **episodes.** Episodes are coherent sequences of interaction that have an identifiable beginning and end. We use the information we have about various kinds of episodes to interpret messages. In other words, episodes also act as a frame of reference for interpreting messages. If you contextualize an interaction as a particular type of episode, you interpret behavior given your expectations for that given episode. For example, in the episode "getting ready to go out," the words "The movie starts at seven-thirty" could be taken as a hint to hurry up and get ready. But in the episode "meeting someone for the first time" the words "The movie starts at seven-thirty" are difficult to interpret. Imagine that you meet someone and introduce yourself ("Hello, my name is Charlie") and that is followed by the response, "The movie starts at seven-thirty." In this episode you might very well assign a negative attribution to that person ("What a rude person" or "That's one neurotic fool").

Wilmot and Baxter (1983) note that episodes can themselves be framed within the relational definition of the two communicators. That is, relationship definitions provide information about how to interpret what type of episode is occurring. Wilmot and Baxter found that the episodic interpretations of particular statements differ, depending on whether the relationship is growing stronger or declining. For example, a man turns politely to his wife and asks, "Where do you want to have dinner, dummy?" to which she replies, "Wherever you want, twit." In a loving couple, these statements might be interpreted as terms of endearment. If the couple were not getting along, they might use the very same words to convey displeasure, anger, or contempt.

Level 5 is **archetypes.** Archetypes are the basic patterns of episodes. At the archetype level, words are interpreted as part of a pattern. For example, Kellermann (1991) notes striking similarities in the structure of initial interactions. Specifically, she found that about 76 percent of informal interactions tend to progress through seven overlapping "scenes," although each interaction presents its unique version of the general pattern. Accordingly, the words offered during initial interaction could be interpreted as part of the repeated pattern of episodes known as the "initial interaction archetype." For example, consider the following two samples of conversations (both adapted from Kellermann 1991):

Hi there! (greeting)
How are you feeling? (health)
This weather is great. (weather)
Where do you live? (where live)
Do you know David Braaten? (persons known in common)
Do you play Frisbee golf? (sports)
Well, I have a class. (reason for terminating)
Bye. (good-byes)

and

Hello. (greeting)
My name is Charlie. (introduction)
This campus is great. (present situation)
Where are you from? (home town)

Do you know David Braaten? (persons known in common)
What is your major? (education)
Do you play Frisbee golf? (sports)
Maybe we could get a foursome together. (future activity)
It was nice to meet you. (positive evaluation)
See you later. (until later)
Bye. (good-byes)

Although these conversations are different, they progress in the same general manner. This observation suggests that during initial interactions, people likely interpret their exchange of messages in terms of a "greeting archetype."

LISTENING

Listening is one of the most frequent activities you perform. The average American employee spends approximately 60 percent of the workday listening (Wolvin and Coakley 1991). In social situations as well, you are more likely to listen than you are to talk.

Listening increases your likelihood of achieving your personal goals by raising your sensitivity to others' wants and needs, by giving you new insights into problems and solutions, and by garnering feedback regarding your behaviors. In addition, listening gives you access to other people's thoughts and feelings, allowing you to connect with them. And there is no denying that people like to be listened to, although what they say may tax our patience.

Listening is also fundamental to interpreting messages. Communicators often mistakenly assume that their messages are interpreted exactly as they are intended. In fact, the way you listen affects your message interpretations. Two kinds of listening approaches, or listening strategies, are represented in the literature.

The first listening approach is *empathic*. **Empathic listening** means associating with the speaker's cognitions and emotions, trying to interpret the message "as if" you were the speaker (Stiff et al. 1988). Empathic listening promotes maximal understanding of communication from the speaker's perspective. According to McComb and Jablin (1984), a number of behaviors are typically associated with empathic listening: using silence as a response and not interrupting, asking probing questions, providing verbal encouragement, restating the other's message, and seeking clarification.

The second listening approach is *deliberative*. **Deliberative listening** means evaluating the message's logic and support according to your own position. Deliberative listening increases interpretation of a message from your own perspective. Behaviors associated with deliberative listening include a predisposition to criticize, making internal summaries during the message, evaluating the message, and agreeing or disagreeing with the speaker during and following the message (Kelly 1972).

Empathic listening involves sharing the speaker's thoughts and emotions. The person engaging in empathic listening may show involvement with the speaker's experiences.

(Joel Gordon)

Empathic listening and deliberative listening are very different strategies. Some theorists hold that empathic listening is vital to communication effectiveness and interpersonal growth. Others contend that deliberative listening is critical in discussions requiring advocacy.

The selection of a listening strategy likely depends on the goal that is most salient to the listener during a conversation. Accordingly, you probably use empathic listening when taking the role of your partner into consideration is critical to meeting your goal (e.g., to present yourself as sincere during relational initiation or to understand your partner's emotions during a heated conflict). You select a deliberative listening mode when your goal is to make sure that your position is safeguarded (e.g., confronting your roommate about dirty dishes in the sink or presenting your side of a story to a judge).

It is possible to use a *combination* of empathic and deliberative listening approaches. You first listen for interpretation from the speaker's perspective so that you can interpret the message from that viewpoint; then you respond as you wish from your own viewpoint. Gross and O'Hair's (1988) prescription for listening skills suggests such an approach: (1) stop talking, (2) listen for ideas, (3) ask questions, (4) listen for unexpected situations, (5) avoid arguing until you comprehend the

Deliberative listening occurs when the listener evaluates the speaker's message in terms of its logic and whether or not it agrees with the listener's assumptions and attitudes. For example, a journalist listening to a politician often engages in deliberative listening.

(Reuters/Bettman)

other's points, and (6) avoid distractions. After these behaviors have been used, you could respond with your own view.

Chapter Summary

Words are arbitrary metaphors created by people to symbolize the real world. People sometimes refer to different realities when using the same word, and people often use different words to refer to the same reality. In addition, people have different beliefs about how communication functions, and these different beliefs are reflected in different types of messages. Given these differences, it is a wonder that we can communicate with each other at all!

The use and interpretation of verbal messages involve complex processes. Communicators select general strategies to influence others, and their partners simultaneously interpret these messages at various levels of meaning. To make sense of these exchanges, each party attempts to infer the other's conversational goal. The careful selection of words, phrases, or even entire speeches does not guarantee that the communicator will achieve the intended interaction goal. Much of that success also depends on the partner's goals.

KEY TERMS

▼

referent	disconfirming message
symbol	tactics
reference	consequences
pragmatic connectedness	relationship identification
presequences	values
message design logics	stream of behavior
expressive message design logic	propositions
conventional message design logic	speech acts
rhetorical message design logic	episodes
valence	archetypes
strategy	empathic listening
argument	deliberative listening
confirming message	

EXERCISES FOR FURTHER DISCUSSION

▼

1. First write down a definition for each of the following words: commitment, love, successful, open, family values. Then compare your definitions with those written by another class member.
   a. Are there any differences in the definitions that you came up with?
   b. Can you think of any situations in which the differences in definitions could lead to misunderstandings?
   c. Have you had experiences where an underlying difference in the definition of a word led to a misunderstanding?
   d. What do you do when such misunderstandings occur?
2. We generally understand how people use words because of the pragmatic connectedness of the words (that is, their relationship to an interaction goal).
   a. Have you ever misinterpreted someone by attributing a goal that the person did not in fact have?
   b. Has anyone recently misinterpreted your words by not accurately perceiving your goal?

    c. Have you ever had trouble interpreting someone's words because you were unsure of that person's goals? If so, what did you do?

3. Review the section on message design logics.

    a. Do you think that the people you know use different message design logics in different situations, or do they rely on the same message design logic regardless of the situation?

    b. What is your primary message design logic? Does it ever change? If so, in what circumstances and in what ways does it change?

4. Think of someone you know who is very confirming to be with and another person that you find disconfirming to be with.

    a. What communication behaviors does the confirming person use that make you feel that he or she is confirming?

    b. What communication behaviors does the disconfirming person use that make you feel that he or she is disconfirming?

5. Examine the strategies listed in Table 3-1.

    a. Does this list contain strategies that you have used?

    b. Can you think of strategies that could be added to the list? Try to provide a title and example for each.

    c. Which strategy do you find most effective?

    d. Discuss with other class members the specific way in which you have used strategies—your goal and the words you used to achieve your goal.

6. Review the section on listening styles.

    a. Which listening style do you use the most, empathic or deliberative?

    b. Can you think of some situations in which using one style would be more effective than using the other?

    c. Can you think of situations in which you might want to use a combination of the two styles?

SUGGESTED READING

LANGUAGE AND COMMUNICATION

Ellis, D. G. 1992. *From language to communication.* Hillsdale, N.J.: Erlbaum. Utilizing a chronological format, Ellis provides a fine overview of the various approaches for examining language. Ellis contends that the communicative functions of language should be emphasized.

Giles, H., and Coupland, N. 1991. *Language: Contexts and consequences.* Pacific Grove, Calif.: Brooks/Cole. Giles and Coupland show how people use language to "accommodate" one another. More specifically, this book presents research on how people from one culture accommodate those in higher status cultures and how language is used to defend one's group status.

Jacobs, S. 1985. Language. In M. L. Knapp and G. R. Miller eds., *Handbook of inter-personal communication* (pp. 313–343). Newbury Park, Calif.: Sage. Jacobs shows how language is best understood from a pragmatic view. That is, language is coherent because people recognize its utility in serving goals.

STRATEGIC COMMUNICATION

Cody, M. L., and McLaughlin, M. L., eds., 1990. *The psychology of tactical communication.* Clevedon, England: Multilingual Matters. This anthology presents different conceptions of interpersonal influence. An excellent representation of communication and psychology approaches is offered.

Seibold, D. R.; Cantrill, J. G.; and Meyers, R. A. 1985. Communication and interpersonal influence. In M. L. Knapp and G. R. Miller eds., *Handbook of interpersonal communication* (pp. 551–611). Newbury Park, Calif.: Sage. Seibold and colleagues offer a comprehensive review of interpersonal influence, drawing on several literature bases. The chapter also discusses particular strategies that have been emphasized in the research literature.

Wheeless, L. R.; Barraclough, R.; and Steward, R. 1983. Compliance-gaining and power in persuasion. In R. N. Boston, ed., *Communication Review and Commentaries* (pp. 105–145). Newbury Park, Calif.: Sage. This article focuses on compliance-gaining strategies. The authors specifically show how the various typologies of strategies can be organized according to three power bases.

INTERPRETING MESSAGES

Pearce, W. B., and Conklin, F. 1979. A model of hierarchical meanings in coherent conversation and a study of "indirect responses." *Communication Monographs, 46,* 75–87. Pearce and Conklin present their hierarchical model of meaning and show how the various levels of their model are linked. The authors then apply their model to the study of indirect responses (e.g., "Are you hungry?" Response: "Is the Pope Catholic?")

REFERENCE LIST

▼

Canary, D. J., Brossmann, B. G., and Seibold, D. R. 1987. Argument structures in decision-making groups. *Southern Speech Communication Journal* 53:18–37.

Canary, D. J.; Weger, H., Jr.; and Stafford, L. 1991. Couples' argument sequences and their associations in relational characteristics. *Western Journal of Speech Communication* 55: 159–179.

Clark, R. A. 1979. The impact of self-interest and desired liking on selection of persuasive strategies. *Communication Monographs* 46:257–273.

Cody, M. J.; Greene, J. O.; Marston, P. J.: Baaske, E.; O'Hair, H. D.; and Schneider, M. J. 1986. Situation perception and strategy selection. In *Communication yearbook 9*, ed. M. L. McLaughlin, 390–422. Newbury Park, Calif.: Sage.

Cody, M. J.; McLaughlin, M. L.; and Jordan, W. J. 1980. A multidimensional scaling of three sets of compliance-gaining strategies. *Communication Quarterly* 28(3):34–46.

Cody, M. J.; McLaughlin, M. L.; and Schneider, M. J. 1981. The impact of intimacy and relational consequences on the selection of interpersonal persuasion tactics: A reanalysis. *Communication Quarterly* 29(2):91–106.

Egan, G. 1973. *The small group experience and interpersonal growth*. Pacific Grove, Calif.: Brooks/Cole.

Ellis, D. G. 1992. *From language to communication*. Hillsdale, N.J.: Erlbaum.

Foss, S. K.; Foss, K. A.; and Trapp, R. 1991. *Contemporary perspectives in rhetoric*, 2d ed. Prospect Heights, Ill.: Waveland Press.

Goss, B., and O'Hair, H. D. 1988. *Communicating in interpersonal relationships*. New York: Macmillan.

Jackson, S., and Jacobs, S. 1980. Structure of conversational argument: Pragmatic bases for the enthymeme. *Quarterly Journal of Speech* 66:251–265.

Jacobs, S. 1985. Language. In *Handbook of interpersonal communication*, ed. M. L. Knapp and G. R. Miller, 313–343. Newbury Park, Calif.: Sage.

Jacobs, S., and Jackson, S. 1983. Strategy and structure in conversational influence attempts. *Communication Monographs* 50:285–304.

Kellermann, K. 1991. The conversation MOP II: Progression through scenes in discourse. *Human Communication Research* 17:385–414.

Kelly, C. M. 1972. Empathic listening. In *Bridges, not walls: A book of interpersonal communication*, ed. J. Stewart, 222–227. Reading, Mass.: Addison-Wesley.

Marwell, G., and Schmitt, D. R. 1967. Dimensions of compliance-gaining behaviors: An empirical analysis. *Sociometry* 30:350–364.

McComb, K. B., and Jablin, F. M. 1984. Verbal correlates of interviewer empathic listening and employment interview outcomes. *Communication Monographs* 51:353–371.

Meyers, R. A.; Seibold, D. R.; and Brashers, D. 1991. Argument in initial group decision-making discussions: Refinement of a coding scheme and a descriptive quantitative analysis. *Western Journal of Speech Communication* 55:47–68.

Ogden, C. K., and Richards, I. A. 1927. *The meaning of meaning: A study of the influence of language upon thought and of the science of symbolism*, 2d rev. ed. Orlando, Fla.: Harcourt Brace.

O'Keefe, B. J. 1988. The logic of message design: Individual differences in reasoning about communication. *Communication Monographs* 55:80–103.

O'Keefe, B. J., and McCornack, S. A. 1987. Message design logic and message goal structure: Effects on perceptions of message quality in regulative communication situations. *Human Communication Research* 14:68–92.

O'Keefe, B. J., and Sheppard, G. J. 1987. The pursuit of multiple objectives in face-to-face persuasive interaction: Effects of construct differentiation on message organization. *Communication Monographs* 54:396–419.

Pearce, W. B., and Conklin, F. 1979. A model of hierarchical meanings in coherent conversation and a study of "indirect responses." *Communication Monographs* 46:75–87.

Pearce, W. B., and Cronen, V. 1980. *Communication, action, and meaning.* New York: Praeger.

Poole, M. S.; McPhee, R. D.; and Seibold, D. R. 1982. A comparison of normative and interactional explanations of group decision making: Social decision schemes versus valence distributions. *Communication Monographs* 49:1–19.

Seibold, D. R.; Cantrill, J. G.; and Meyers, R. A. 1985. Communication and interpersonal influence. In *Handbook of interpersonal communication*, ed. M. L. Knapp and G. R. Miller, 551–611. Newbury Park, Calif.: Sage.

Sieburg, E. 1976. Confirming and disconfirming organizational communication. In *Communication in organizations*, ed. J. L. Owens, P. A. Page, and G. I. Zimmerman, 129–149. St. Paul, Minn.: West.

Sillars, A. L. 1980. Stranger and spouse as target persons for compliance-gaining tactics. *Human Communication Research* 6:265–279.

Stiff, J. B.; Dillard, J. P.; Somera, L.; Kim, H.; and Sleight, C. 1988. Empathy, communication, and prosocial behavior. *Communication Monographs* 55:198–213.

Wheeless, L. R.; Barraclough, R.; and Stewart, R. 1983. Compliance-gaining and power in persuasion. In *Communication reviews and commentaries*, ed. R. N. Boston, 105–145. Newbury Park, Calif.: Sage.

Wilmot, W. W., and Baxter, L. A. 1983. Reciprocal framing of relationship definitions and episodic interaction. *Western Journal of Speech Communication* 47:204–217.

Wiseman, R., and Schenck-Hamlin, W. J. 1981. A multidimensional scaling validation of an intuitively derived set of compliance-gaining strategies. *Communication Monographs* 48: 251–270.

Wolvin, A. D., and Coakley, C. G. 1991. A survey of the status of listening training in some Fortune 500 corporations. *Communication Education, 40:* 152–164.

C H A P T E R   4

FUNDAMENTALS

OF NONVERBAL

COMMUNICATION

Sarah Conner stood silently, smoking, watching a video recording she had made months earlier. In the recording, she talked about how the world was going to come to an end and everyone would die. After the television screen froze on Sarah's expression of anger, she spoke up. Without any vocal enthusiasm, she dryly, almost sadly, stated: "I feel better. . . . Things are clearer."

Later Sarah sat across from her psychiatrist and tried to convince him that she was making progress and that she should be able to see her son. When the therapist asked Sarah questions about the "terminator," she lied, denying that the "terminator" existed. As she did, her face was tense, and her tone of voice was forced, controlled, constrained, and lacking in emotion. Her body also became rigid as she leaned forward and held her hands together on her lap. The therapist heard her verbal message and considered her nonverbal performance. After a pause, he decided that Sarah really wasn't well, hadn't made progress, and was lying.

This story, culled from several scenes in the movie *Terminator 2*, highlights three features of nonverbal communication. First, the story deals with the communication of emotions. In the scene depicted on the video recorder, Linda Hamilton, the actress, did an excellent job communicating anger, one of the fundamental human emotions. Second, the scene with the psychiatrist accurately reflects some of the facts we know about deception. Her message lacked spontaneity and sounded rehearsed, her tone of voice was different than usual, and she sat rigidly while holding her hands and rubbing them together. Third, our story illustrates the concept of **channel discrepancy.** Liars often communicate messages that are discrepant—the words communicate one message, but the tone of voice, the face, or the body communicates another. For example, a person's words might express liking, positive feelings, and happiness ("I am better. Things are clearer"), but the tone of voice, body tension, and facial expression communicate that the person is not happy and is actually experiencing stress, anxiety, or dislike. Sarah, in our story, communicated verbally that she felt better; however, the message was contradicted by all other channels.

The Functional Approach to Nonverbal Communication

You may be familiar with some of the concepts of nonverbal communication from popular literature promising to teach how to "read a person like a book" or surefire ways to make a romantic connection. To sell such books, authors dramatize aspects of nonverbal behavior and often oversimplify. Sometimes these authors even make up their facts. For example, one author claimed that when a man jingles coins in his pockets, he is disagreeing with whoever is speaking. There is no evidence to support such a claim. One woman, dating a man who often jingled his coins, thought that he was evaluating her in some way. At a family reunion, however, she was startled to see that all of the men stood around the backyard engaging in this behavior.

Today serious scholars of nonverbal communication adopt what is called the **functional approach** (Burgoon, Buller, and Woodall 1989; Leathers 1992). **Functions** are the motives, purposes, intended goals, or outcomes of communication, including such things as communicating liking and intimacy, displaying power, and dominating others. The functional approach makes three assumptions. First, we assume that a cluster of behaviors are used together to communicate a function; we do not assume that a single behavior (such as gaze) can be completely effective in sending or receiving a specific message. Second, we assume that behaviors from different channels (face, body, tone of voice) are used jointly to communicate a function; liking for someone else is displayed by a number of behaviors in the face, body, and tone of voice. Third, we assume that any one behavior can be used to communicate several functions. Depending on the setting and other behaviors, for example, high levels of eye contact may communicate intimacy, dominance, attentiveness, or threat. Hence it is important to look for several behaviors from different areas of the body that combine to indicate that a person is friendly, domineering, threatening, and so on.

BEAUTIFUL PEOPLE

We like attractive people; we attribute positive qualities to them and find it rewarding when they appear to like us. Years of research have provided much information concerning beauty (Bull and Rumsey 1988):

1. *Stereotypes.* Even very young children are strongly biased in favor of good-looking children and adults. Good-looking people are expected to receive good grades, to be successful, to be paid higher wages, to marry other attractive people, and to be warm, sensitive, kind, interesting, and sociable.

2. *Self-fulfilling prophecies.* Stereotypes do not represent truth all the time; some attractive people are not really warm, sensitive, or kind. However, sometimes

we engage in **self-fulfilling prophecies** so that our stereotypes ("prophecies") will be confirmed.

For example, Snyder, Tanke, and Berscheid (1977) had males hold "get acquainted" phone conversations with female students. Each male was led to believe that the woman he was calling was either attractive or unattractive, when in reality attractiveness varied randomly. The conversations were rated on how sociable and outgoing the two speakers were toward each other. The results of the study indicated that when the men thought they were talking to a beautiful woman, they were sociable and outgoing, prompting the women to reciprocate friendliness over the phone and behave in a sociable manner. The men acted in ways to ensure that their prophecy (beautiful people are friendly) would be fulfilled.

3. *Attitude similarity.* We assume that physically attractive strangers will share our attitudes.

4. *Likely acceptance of dates and reaction to rejection.* When students are asked to rate their desire to date others, they indicate that they'd like to date attractive people, even people substantially more attractive than they are. However, when asked to rate the same potential dates on likelihood of accepting a date, most students indicated that people of substantially greater attractiveness would be less likely to accept the date. Most people think that real dates occur between people who are fairly similar in levels of physical attractiveness.

The research on this issue isn't always consistent—possibly because certain people believe that they can "win over" people far more beautiful than they are themselves. Less attractive people may also have beliefs and expectations about being rejected that are different from those who are more attractive. Weinberger and Cash (1982), for example, had females briefly interact with two males, separately, and indicate their interest in dating the men. When told that the first male had rejected them, the attractive women indicated (more than the less attractive ones) that it was important to win over and get a date offer from the second male. Presumably, rejection was more unsettling and bothersome to people who do not expect it.

5. *Bolstering self-esteem.* When we are associated with an attractive partner, others who observe us will rate us as more likable, friendly, and confident.

6. *Frequency of dating.* Good-looking people indicate that they have more dates and more dating partners than less attractive people. Also, members of a video-dating organization indicate that the more attractive members are selected more frequently for dates and are likely to have their selections reciprocated.

7. *Long-term dating.* Although beauty is preferred and certainly offers a number of advantages, a considerable amount of literature indicates that people date and become involved in long-term relationships when the two are matched in beauty.

People are more likely to remain in long-term relationships when both partners contribute equal amounts of inputs and benefits (we refer to this as **equity**). If one partner is vastly more attractive than the other, the attractive party may have more power in the relationship, and the other may have to work harder to make the relationship an equitable one. Indeed, people in stable, long-term relationships tend to be matched in level of attractiveness (see Figure 4-1).

In sum, we want to be associated with beautiful people, and our esteem is enhanced when we are linked to beautiful people. However, long-term relational stability is increased when people date and marry people of similar beauty.

THE FACE OF HUMAN EMOTIONS

No aspect of communication is as basic as the communication of human emotions. However, communicators vary substantially in how well or how clearly they communicate their feelings. Consider these common complaints:

"Bob thought I was angry, so he avoided me. But I was just preoccupied with my homework. I wasn't angry at all."

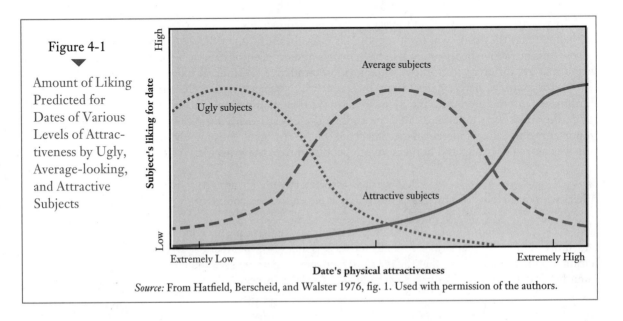

Figure 4-1

Amount of Liking Predicted for Dates of Various Levels of Attractiveness by Ugly, Average-looking, and Attractive Subjects

Source: From Hatfield, Berscheid, and Walster 1976, fig. 1. Used with permission of the authors.

"My boyfriend is so often hard to read. He'll be quiet and withdrawn, and then I'll later find out how mad he was."

"I have a hard time figuring out this one lady. I thought she liked me (because she smiles at me all the time). But we never get past superficial talk when we get together."

If communicating emotions is so basic, why do people appear to send the wrong message so frequently?

First, most of our emotional expressions are difficult to read quickly because they are **affect blends** of basic emotions. Ekman and Friesen (1984) claim that there are only six basic human emotions: surprise, anger, fear, sadness, disgust, and happiness. Many of our expressions are actually blends of two or more of these basic emotions, and the blends are often harder to read than "pure" expressions. For example, contempt combines disgust and anger. Figure 4-2 presents displays of the basic emotions that are pure and well defined. The faces are easy to read because the expressions were posed for the camera. In real life, reading emotions is often more difficult. Beside the fact that most of our daily expressions are blends, the culture in which people are raised has a very strong effect on publicly communicated facial expressions. In some cultures the expression of negative emotions in public settings is quite rare and is discouraged by parents and others. Cultures vary in **display rules,** the rules that govern the appropriateness of displaying various expressions in public.

Why do people in the same culture differ so much in communicating emotions? There are three important reasons: gender differences, internalization versus externalization, and differences in communication style.

GENDER DIFFERENCES. Women smile more than men; however, this does not mean that women are happier. Sometimes women smile when they are uncomfortable, even miserable. Men, by contrast, display a limited range of emotions and often wear neutral faces. To discuss why this happens, we must understand the concepts of masking and inhibition.

Masking is covering a feeling that you are experiencing with one that you are not. When you pretend to like something that you do not really like, you are engaging in the masking of negative affect, and when you pretend to dislike something that you actually like, you are engaging in the masking of positive affect. Masking substitutes one emotional expression for another. **Inhibition,** by contrast, means giving the appearance of having no feeling when you in fact do have feeling. Inhibition of negative affect involves putting on a neutral face when you are actually experiencing negative feelings (e.g., you are extremely angry and disappointed at losing a ball game, but your face is neutral). Inhibition of positive affect involves expressing a neutral face when you are experiencing positive feelings.

Figure 4-2

▼

Expressions of
the Six Basic
Human Emotions

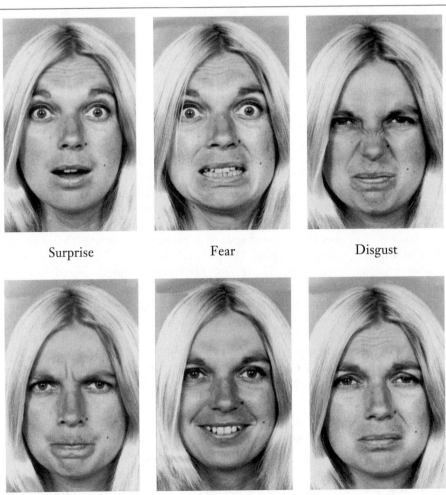

Surprise   Fear   Disgust

Anger   Happiness   Sadness

Source: From Ekman and Friesen 1984, copyright P. Ekman 1975.

Young children do not control their facial expressions. But limited control begins to develop between the ages of 6 and 12 (Shennum and Bugental 1982). Boys
demonstrate an ability to neutralize negative affect in the face as they mature; they
learn to look more neutral and to conceal emotions that they are experiencing. Girls,
however, do not learn precise control of the faces they are portraying; they don't
look neutral when experiencing a negative feeling. In fact, girls "overshoot" control

Children generally learn to control facial expressions by age twelve. Boys typically inhibit expressions to look neutral; girls mask expressions by displaying positive affect (smiling, looking happy).

(Joel Gordon)

and actually look more positive when attempting to be neutral. They tend toward smiling rather than appearing neutral.

There are a number of possible reasons for this control, one being that boys in our culture are encouraged and rewarded for exerting such control: "Don't pout or sulk," "Don't be a crybaby," "No one likes a poor loser," and so on. You may find it hard to read some men's negative expressions because they have been encouraged to inhibit them. Conversely, you may conclude that some females are happy when in fact they are not.

INTERNALIZING AND EXTERNALIZING. **Externalizers** tend to show emotions they are currently feeling. **Internalizers** tend to "bottle up" emotions and display neutral or muted faces. Generally, women tend to be externalizers; men, internalizers. But gender does not account completely for this difference. Externalizers are more extroverted and more socially oriented and have higher levels of self-esteem, and males who are externalizers tend to be more self-confident, less self-deprecating, more dominant, and more "heterosexually oriented" (Burgoon et al. 1989, 357).

STYLES OF COMMUNICATION. Communicators also differ in their style of sending expressions. Ekman and Friesen (1984) have identified eight styles; you probably know people who fit into each.

1. *Withholders* rarely show how they feel; they are expressionless. Withholders do not deliberately try to conceal their emotions; rather, they are naturally without expression. Marilyn, the doctor's receptionist on TV's "Northern Exposure," is an exemplary withholder.

2. *Revealers* constantly and consistently show their feelings—even when trying to conceal them. Such people are childlike in their inability to control their facial expressions. People often learn that they are revealers when they realize that others read their emotions so easily.

3. *Unwitting expressers* show an emotion without being aware of doing so, even when consciously trying to mask or inhibit facial expressions. They tend to restrict themselves to a few emotions; for example, Bob may show sadness or anger when thinking about the breakup with his girlfriend, even though he believes that he is controlling his expression.

4. *Blanked expressers* are convinced that they are expressing an emotion when in fact their faces look neutral or ambiguous. Many people do not know they are blanked expressers.

5. *Substitute expressers* substitute displays of one emotion for another without knowing why. For example, Annie may feel anger or disgust but actually exhibits signs of fear or sadness while nevertheless believing that she is signaling anger or disgust. It is difficult to convince substitute expressers that their displays do not reflect their true emotions.

6. *Frozen-affect expressers* show a trace of one emotion in some part of the face even when not actually feeling that emotion. For example, a trace of sadness or anger may be seen even when the person is trying to communicate neutral affect. This may be based entirely in anatomical structure, or the person may have experienced years of sadness or anger that left a lasting mark. It is hard to read other emotions on the face of frozen-affect expressers, who may be entirely unaware that this is their communication style.

7. *Ever-ready expressers* show a particular emotion as a first response to almost any event in any situation. For example, a person may have a tendency to show surprise as a first reaction whenever anything unexpected happens, whether the event is good or bad, happy or sad. After a flash of surprise, the face takes on the expression of the actual emotion the person is feeling. Many people, except for close friends and others familiar with the person's style, can find it difficult to decipher what an ever-ready expresser is actually feeling, and this difficulty may work against the person on a blind date or a job interview. Most ever-ready expressers are unaware that this is their style and require help from friends if they wish to change it.

8. *Flooded-affect expressers* usually show only one or two emotions, and the face is "flooded" all the time by those expressions. For example, a person in crisis might alternate between expressions of sadness and anger or fear, to the exclusion of any other emotion. This style is relatively uncommon.

In sum, it is sometimes difficult to read facial expressions because of cultural differences and differences in masking and inhibiting of facial affect. Further, people can also differ dramatically in their style of expressing emotions. It is obvious that communication problems stem from the fact that people communicate differently. For example, certain blanked expressers may believe that others should be able to read their expressions and know what they are feeling and are disappointed when people do not respond as expected. Similarly, a number of problems are likely to occur with substitute expressers; others respond to one emotional state when these people are in fact signaling a different one.

BODY IMAGE

Pliner, Chaiken, and Flett (1990) asked museum visitors about their concerns and beliefs on eating habits, body weight, physical appearance, and "appearance self-esteem." They found that females were more concerned than males about eating, body weight, and physical appearance and had lower appearance self-esteem. The different attitudes were not limited to young people—women at all ages expressed more concern and anxiety over eating and body image than men did.

We possess very strong stereotypes about body type. **Mesomorphs** are individuals who are muscular, **endomorphs** are plump, and **ectomorphs** are thin. Years of research indicate that we have positive attitudes toward mesomorphs and highly negative attitudes toward ectomorphs—very thin, frail individuals were stereotyped as nervous and high-strung (as played by Don Knotts on television). However, this has changed in recent years—today we have very positive attitudes toward both ectomorphs and mesomorphs. Ryckman and colleagues (1989) found that college students rated mesomorphs as most likely to have many friends; to be healthy, hardworking, and brave; and to be better-looking and less likely to be teased than either endomorphs or ectomorphs. However, mesomorphs were also deemed meaner and less intelligent. Ectomorphs were generally rated more positively than endomorphs and received the highest ratings on intelligence and neatness; both mesomorphs and ectomorphs were perceived as happier, cleaner, and faster than endomorphs. Also, there was a major sex-related bias: females were rated as popular and "good-looking" if they were either mesomorphs or ectomorphs, whereas the mesomorph male was rated as ideal (though lower in intelligence).

MOVEMENT

Many of the actions you engage in may contain information that others use to form an impression of you. Consider the way you walk, which communicates your emo-

WHEN A FAD DOES A BODY HARM

As the super-skinny "Twiggy look" re-emerges as the fashion ideal, many observers wonder if it might inspire women to starve themselves.

"Twiggy is the one who started the whole onslaught of anorexia," says Lynda Chassler, a Beverly Hills psychologist who specializes in eating disorders. "In our society, we measure beauty and admirability by weight—slim is beautiful—and it's perpetuated by magazines and designers. With a return to that ideal, it could make the problem even worse."

Says Barry Glassner, a sociologist and author of "Bodies: Overcoming the Tyranny of Perfection": "A change in fashion toward a really thin look is not just an innocent fad or trend; it's a serious health hazard for many women who are already inclined toward eating disorders."

The '80s, many observers say, ushered in a healthier ideal.

"The look of the late '80s, early '90s has been the strong, powerful woman," Glassner says.

But "there has been a lot of concern about women getting more power and position," he says. "As the power and strength of women in a lot of different spheres is coming under attack again, it's not surprising that that would be reflective in fashion. 'The [new] look' is weak, less powerful."

Says feminist Naomi Wolf, author of "The Beauty Myth": "It's uncanny how consistently the theory of the beauty myth—that any advance for women politically is met with punishment in terms of beauty ideals—is borne out. It's a law of politics meeting the collective unconscious that women are never allowed to imagine having Senate seats and adequate meals at the same time."

Twiggy Lawson, 43, insists she's never dieted—can eat just about anything—and says neither she nor fashion deserves blame for society's ills.

"In the fashion world, somebody decides to make someone a look, and people follow," says Lawson, now an actress. "I never condoned girls going on diets. I don't think anyone should stop eating. How they choose to live is up to the individual.

"The look that I had was a part of me then," she says. "It was not contrived, that's what I looked like. . . . I don't look anything like that anymore, nor would I want to."

—Andrea Heiman

Reprinted with permission from the *Los Angeles Times*, March 12, 1993, p. E2.

tional state and your confidence. Grayson and Stein (1981), in fact, filmed people walking the streets of New York and showed the films to prisoners, who indicated which walkers appeared vulnerable to attack. People who walked confidently with swinging foot movements were less likely to be selected as victims. Victims tended to lift their feet, used long strides (they were hurrying to leave the area), moved more rigidly, moved in only two dimensions rather than the normal three (forward, up and down walking, and swaying left and right), and moved unilaterally (one side at a time) rather than contralaterally, in counterpoint (right arm, left leg, left arm, right leg).

The most studied aspect of body movement involves hand movements. Ekman and Friesen (1969) proposed a set of four categories that have been universally adopted by nonverbal communication scholars. **Adapters** are hand movements that are used to satisfy physical or psychological needs. *Self-adapters* are used when a person scratches an arm, plays with hair, or wrings the hands together. *Alter-directed adapters* are used when a person is nervous talking to another—the nervous person may cross the arms to pull in from the other speaker. *Object adapters* are used when people manipulate objects in the environment—playing with rubber bands, pens, and the like.

Illustrators are movements that help emphasize a point that the speaker is making. Illustrators include pointing when speaking or any hand movements denoting space, time, or emphasis (for example, pounding the hands together when describing a violent, turbulent action). Illustrators show that we are highly involved in the conversation, that we are animated and interested.

Emblems are hand movements that have a particular meaning to a culture or subculture; they have a direct verbal translation that can be substituted without affecting meaning. The precise meaning of an emblem is known by most or all members of a social group. Emblems are often used with conscious intent and are perceived as being sent intentionally. Emblems include all hand gestures used by gang members, umpires, and other types of groups; common emblems include the gestures for "nice figure," "OK," "money," "hitchhiking," and "gossip."

Regulators are used to maintain or regulate turn taking between interactants. A speaker may raise a hand when nonverbally asking for a turn at speaking, and a speaker (who has the conversational floor) may hold a hand out with the palm toward the turn requester (as in "halt") to be able to finish speaking. Regulators are learned early in life and are used automatically with little thought. However, people do vary in their use of regulators—people from larger families, for example, use more marked regulators than people who are only children. You may have been in conversations with others in which your turn-requesting cues were ignored.

GENDER DIFFERENCES

Males and females differ fundamentally in nonverbal behaviors. Table 4-1 presents a summary of some of the major differences. Women generally display better skills and increased closeness in the facial and body channels—they send and receive most emotions accurately, smile more, engage in higher levels of eye contact, adopt a more direct position to other speakers, display increased levels of involvement, and are more expressive. They also display greater self-consciousness. Males seek, and are given, more interpersonal distance. They use greater amounts of space, even

Table 4-1
NONVERBAL GENDER DIFFERENCES AMONG ADULTS

Behavior	Increased Use by Females
Judging emotions	Females are more accurate at judging emotions (81–84 percent of studies)
Sending emotions	Females perform better in expressing emotions (71–59 percent of studies)*
Smiling	Females smile more (94 percent of studies)
Gaze	Females gaze more at others (83 percent of studies); females are gazed at more (90 percent of studies)
Body directness	Females sit more directly in front of other interactants (92 percent of studies)
Touch	Females touch more (67 percent of studies)
Involvement	Females are more involved (57 percent of studies)
Expressiveness	Females are more expressive (73 percent of studies)
Self-consciousness	Females are more self-conscious (67 percent of studies)

Behavior	Increased Use by Males
Distance	Males are given more space in natural settings (80 percent of studies); males are allowed more space by others (92 percent of studies)
Restlessness	Males are more restless (100 percent of studies)
Relaxation	Males are more relaxed (100 percent of studies)
Expansiveness	Males are more expansive (100 percent of studies)
Filled pauses	Males use more filled pauses (100 percent of studies)
Speech errors	Males make more errors (67 percent of studies)
Interruptions	Males interrupt more (56 percent of studies)
Volume	Males speak louder (67 percent of studies)

Source: Adapted from Hall 1984.
*Hall found that females sent emotions more accurately than did males in 71% of the early studies (those conducted before 1977). The studies conducted after 1977 demonstrate that females were more accurate at sending emotions in only 59% of the studies. The implication is that female superiority in sending emotions is dwindling over time.

when sitting, displaying increased expansiveness. Males also project greater body re-laxation. However, in the voice channel, men are louder, interrupt more, make more speech errors, and employ more "filled pauses" ("ah," "uh").

There are many reasons for these gender differences. One is a difference in mo-tivation. In general, men tend to be task-oriented and focus on the verbal channel to get their message across, speaking louder, interrupting more, and using filled pauses to keep the floor while thinking of their answers. We say that men are **status-assertive** (see Chapter 12). In contrast, women tend to focus greater effort on social harmony, cooperation, and friendliness; they are **status-neutralizing.**

Theories of Nonverbal Interaction

Scholars have proposed several theories concerning how our nonverbal behavior is affected by others during interaction. The first deals with arousal; the second, with accommodation.

AROUSAL MODELS OF INTERACTION

We have all experienced a situation like this: At a party we are talking with some-one. The person is somewhat boring, and we are not very interested in continuing the conversation. However, this person moves closer to us, looks more intently into our eyes, and touches us. We tense, stiffen, cross our arms, lean away, turn from the person, and start looking around the room. Why did we behave in this particular fashion?

Patterson (1976, 1983) has proposed an arousal model of intimacy that explains why people behave as they do in such situations. His model is presented in Figure 4-3. When Al is conversing with Beth at a party, they will adopt a distance and a commu-nicating style that they both believe to be normal and expected: they stand about 3 feet apart, smile a good deal, maintain a normal amount of eye contact, and face each other directly. Both look and feel comfortable.

Now suppose that Al moves closer to Beth, who notices this change in the level of intimacy (see the leftmost part of Figure 4-3). Because of this increase in inti-macy, Beth will experience arousal. How she reacts depends on whether she labels this experience a negative or a positive one. If Beth did not like Al's increase in the level of intimacy, she would experience anxiety, discomfort, and embarrassment. To cope with this situation, Beth might engage in **compensation**—behaviors that would maintain the level of intimacy and comfort that prevailed before Al attempted to increase intimacy. Beth may avoid eye contact, change her body orientation (to be less direct), lean away, cross her arms in front of her body, and engage in other be-haviors to distance herself from Al. However, if Beth liked Al or found Al attractive,

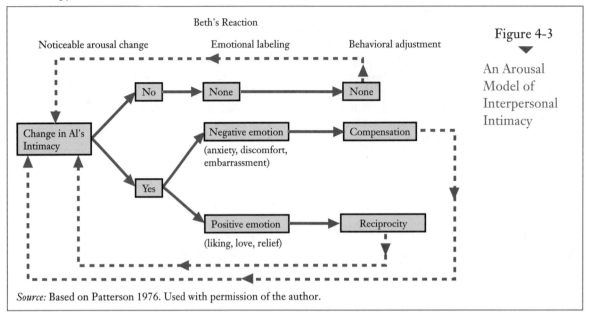

Beth's Reaction

Figure 4-3

An Arousal
Model of
Interpersonal
Intimacy

Source: Based on Patterson 1976. Used with permission of the author.

she would welcome Al's increase in intimacy as a positive experience. In this situation, Beth would react with **reciprocity,** matching Al's increase in intimacy by also moving closer, touching, and so on.

A somewhat different model of interaction is Burgoon's nonverbal expectancy violations theory (Burgoon et al. 1989; Burgoon and Walther 1990). Burgoon argues that any change from expected behavior is arousing, and we either reciprocate or compensate, depending on the direction of the violation of expectations and the reward value of the person doing the violating. If Beth found Al attractive (rewarding), she would probably reciprocate when Al moved closer; however, if Al reacted by moving away, Beth would find this behavior troubling and would compensate in order to "warm up" the interaction. If Beth found Al unrewarding, she would compensate if he increased intimacy and reciprocate when he moved away.

SPEECH ACCOMMODATION THEORY

Now suppose that Al was a likable person from Great Britain. As Beth talked to him, you might notice a change in her communication style. She speaks at his slightly faster rate, nods more frequently (like Al), and adopts his English accent. Beth has *accommodated* to Al's speech pattern. She altered her usual manner of speaking to *converge* toward Al's pattern. At another party, you see Beth conversing with someone who speaks with a very different accent, one you have never heard before. Here you notice that Beth *diverges* from the speech pattern of the stranger. Beth speaks more slowly and loudly, articulating and pronouncing her words carefully, employing a standard American accent.

The **speech accommodation** theory deals with the basic fact that we adjust our nonverbal and vocal behaviors in many situations to accommodate other speakers. Although we are not aware that we alter our behaviors, a number of speech, vocalic, and nonverbal behaviors may be involved in the accommodation, including dialect, utterance length, speech rate, speech volume, hesitations, silence between speaker's turns (known as **response latency**), gestures, head nodding, facial affect, posture, and eye contact.

Table 4-2 outlines why speakers converge or diverge in their communication behaviors. We often converge when we want approval (when we want to make a good first impression, have an enjoyable date, and so on), when we want to be efficient (for example, sales clerks often converge when they try to sell us items), and when we desire either a shared identity with others or a particular identity of our own. For example, members of social groups (from country clubs to street gangs) exhibit some convergence in speech patterns when they meet. The more valued the speech pattern, the more likely it is that people will converge; stigmatized speech patterns prompt speakers to diverge.

Communicators can exhibit **mutual accommodation** when they both switch their speech styles to move toward the partner's speech rate, volume, and so forth; accommodation can also be *nonmutual*, as in our example when Beth accommodated to the speech style of a person from Great Britain but Al did not accommodate to her style of speaking. There are many reasons for mutual and nonmutual accommodation. One important reason deals with our abilities to employ a particular repertoire of speech behaviors. Some people are not confident in their abilities to alter spoken dialects or to increase gestures, smiling, or eye contact, and such people are unlikely to show any convergence toward the style of their partners. Both speakers have to be motivated and skilled for mutual convergence to occur. (For more on the speech accommodation theory, see Giles, Coupland, and Coupland 1991 and Giles et al. 1987.)

Functions of Nonverbal Communication

We have organized our topic into four areas: general information about liking and intimacy, courtship and quasi-courtship behaviors, interest in dating, and mistakes in flirting. We will conclude with some comments concerning nonverbal communication and deception.

Table 4-2
OUTLINE OF THE SPEECH ACCOMMODATION THEORY

Causes of Speech Convergence

1. Communicators will attempt to converge toward the speech and nonverbal patterns *believed* to be characteristic of their fellow interactants when communicators seek
    (a) social approval
    (b) a high level of efficiency
    (c) a sense of oneness with other interactants
    (d) appropriate situational or identity definitions

Further, communicators will attempt to converge toward the speech and non-verbal patterns of others when
    (e) the target or targets of the convergence employ expected speech patterns
    (f) speech is positively valued (nonstigmatized)
    (g) the speech style is appropriate for all parties

2. The *magnitude* of speech convergence will be a function of
    (a) the extent to which a communicator has the ability to use a particular repertoire of speech behaviors
    (b) situational factors that may increase the need for social approval, efficiency, or social comparison

Causes of Speech Divergence

3. Speakers will attempt to maintain their communication patterns or even diverge away from their message recipients' speech and nonverbal behaviors when they
    (a) seek to communicate a contrastive self-image
    (b) seek to dissociate personally from the interactants or from the interactants' definition of the situation
    (c) define the encounter in intergroup or relational terms with communication style being a valued dimension of their situationally salient in-group or relational identities
    (d) wish to change interactants' speech behavior, for example, moving it to a more acceptable level

▼

Further, communicators will attempt to diverge away from other interactants' speech behavior when the interactants

    (e)   exhibit a stigmatized form of speech, one that deviates from a valued norm

    (f)   fail to meet the speakers' expectations regarding their performance

4. The *magnitude* of such divergence will be a function of factors similar to those cited in point 2.

▲

Source: Adapted from Giles et al. 1987. Used with permission of the authors.

BEHAVIORS THAT COMMUNICATE LIKING AND INTIMACY

According to Burgoon and colleagues (1989), the nonverbal expression of intimacy involves communicating several different, yet related themes that jointly characterize the total degree of intimacy in a relationship. We will highlight the three most important areas in intimacy and liking:

    1. *Involvement and immediacy.*   *Involvement* means signaling interest in a particular interaction; *immediacy* refers to psychological closeness. We communicate interest and closeness when we maintain a close conversational distance, maintain a direct body orientation, lean forward, increase direct eye gaze, nod, smile or display other pleasant facial expression, maintain an open sitting position, increase gesturing, and, sometimes, touch more frequently. In the vocal channel, people communicate increased levels of involvement by speaking louder and faster, lowering pitch, varying pitch, using fewer silences and briefer latencies, and using more coordinated speech and a warmer tone of voice.

    2. *Depth and similarity.*   Friends gaze more, smile more, show more positive facial affect, sit closer, and touch more while decreasing such signs of anxiety or discomfort as self-touching, crossed arms, and closed postures. Friends show depth and similarity by adopting similar dress, vocal patterns, hand movements, and posture while mimicking ways of walking, use of language, and facial expressions; there is a mutual convergence of speech styles.

    3. *Affection, attraction, liking, and love.*   People in love spend more time gazing into each other's eyes (mutual gaze) and at close range. Arousal is also indicated by pupil dilation, and dilated pupils are associated with attraction. Besides smiling and positive facial affect, good friends and potential intimates engage in **postural mirroring** (standing or sitting in exactly the same manner). Touching, holding, and ca-

Liking can be communicated nonverbally through a wide range of behaviors, including close distance, forward leaning, pleasant facial expression, touch, open posture, eye gaze, and postural mirroring.

(M. B. Duda/Photo Researchers)

ressing increase and are perceived as warm, friendly, loving, and intimate. Vocally, people express their love using "oversoft, slurred, drawling, resonant, high-pitched voices" (Burgoon et al. 1989, 321).

COURTSHIP AND QUASI-COURTSHIP BEHAVIORS

Very few studies have examined behaviors that parallel the process of actual courtship (see Burgoon et al. 1989). The term *quasi-courtship* has been used to refer to situations in which people (such as patients and doctors) engage in **courtship behaviors** but the flirting may or may not be serious and may never lead to any intimate act beyond merely showing liking. Scheflen (1965), credited for laying down the basic research in this area, identified five stages of courtship, quasi-courtship, and flirting:

1. *Attention.* Interested parties engage in signals and gain the attention of others. Catching a person's eye, a smile, handshakes, excited greetings, nervous laugh-

ter, or even childish expressions may be used to gain attention or elicit affectionate responses from a particular other.

2. Recognition. If the particular other ignores the attention-getting actions, the interaction is over (at least temporarily). However, the individual may signal recognition by raised eyebrows, improved posture, heightened alertness, a rosier complexion (due to blood flooding the capillaries of the face), or increased grooming or preening (smoothing hair, straightening clothing, tugging on socks, checking makeup). There is some anxiety in courtship behaviors. People may not be certain that they are the target of a person's attentions, and some people do not want to be obvious in sending signals; therefore, some ambiguity may be witnessed at this stage. Individuals may raise eyebrows and groom but then yawn or stretch. Also, communicators may exhibit submissive behaviors at this stage to show that they are not dominating or threatening and that they are likely to accept the approaches of the other. Givens (1978) describes the shoulder shrug composite, which combines a shrug, raised eyebrows, a head tilt, and an open mouth or a pout.

3. Positioning. People who are attracted to one another next engage in close face-to-face positions that make personal conversation possible while also possibly excluding others from interrupting.

4. Invitations and sexual arousal. Provocative gestures include the grooming of the partner, carrying or holding activities, and explicit sexual actions such as rolling or protruding the pelvis; protruding the chest ("chest thrust"); cocking the head; exposing the thigh when crossing the legs; stroking a wrist, arm, or thigh; to unbuttoning clothes.

5. Resolution. Either an approach is made, or the interactants decide to terminate the contact.

Unresolved is the issue of whether a person engaging in flirting is in fact serious about making an intimate commitment. Frequent mistakes in flirting occur (to be discussed shortly). Is a person being merely friendly, showing liking, or being seductive?

INTEREST IN DATING

Research by Muehlenhard has focused on relating specific behaviors of males and females to the intent to date (Muehlenhard and McFall 1981; Muehlenhard, Miller, and Burdick 1983; Muehlenhard et al. 1986). Both males and females watched videotapes of female-male interactions and rated the probability that the woman would accept if the man asked her for a date. In addition, men rated the attractiveness of her personality and her behavior; women rated how appropriate the woman's behavior was and how likely they would be to behave as the woman did. Table 4-3 presents a summary of the results.

Observers believed the woman would be likely to accept a date if she maintained high levels of eye contact, smiled, leaned forward, leaned sideways, maintained a direct body orientation, moved close to the man, touched him while laughing (when a person in the room made a joke), touched him while not laughing, caught the man's

---

Table 4-3
POTENTIAL NONVERBAL CUES SHOWING INTEREST IN DATING

Cues Indicating a High Probability of Accepting a Date

1. High levels of eye contact
2. High levels of smiling
3. More frequent forward leaning
4. More frequent sideways leaning
5. More frequent direct body orientation
6. Closer interpersonal distance
7. Touching while laughing
8. Touching when not laughing
9. Catching the man's eye while laughing at someone else's humor
10. Attentiveness—stopping what she's doing to give him undivided attention
11. No public grooming (as opposed to applying makeup in public)
12. Animated speech—speaking quickly, accentuating certain words with body movements and varied facial expressions

Cues Unrelated to Interest in Dating

1. Arm position—arms at side, hands on hips, arms akimbo or crossed
2. Crossing of legs—when the man sat down to join the woman, she crossed her legs with her foot pointed toward him, remained still, or crossed her legs with her foot pointed away from him
3. Type of leg cross—seated side by side wearing jeans, she sits with legs crossed at the knees, foot pointing toward him; with legs together; or with ankle on knee, foot pointed toward him.

Source: Based on Muehlenhard et al. 1986. Used with permission of the authors.

eye while laughing, showed undivided attention to the man (was not distracted by other people in the room), and used animated speech. Putting on makeup while talking to the man was interpreted as indicative of a lack of interest in dating him. Behaviors related to arms and legs were not related consistently to getting a date.

Male and female observers in the Muehlenhard studies generally agreed on which cues conveyed interest in dating. Females rated only three of the cues higher in probability than males did (forward leaning, touching while laughing, and touching while not laughing), apparently believing (more than males) that increasing closeness signals interest. Women also deemed certain behaviors inappropriate. In some cases, female observers rated too much smiling and too obvious a forward or sideways lean as inappropriate behaviors. Touching while not laughing was consistently rated negatively. However, touching while laughing was consistently rated as positive. The fact of humor and laughing being shared provides an excuse for engaging in the touching, whereas a touch without such an excuse would be inappropriate.

We conducted our own study on flirting in singles bars. Working in pairs and in small groups, our students would enter an establishment relatively early (before the dance music was turned up or the band played) and randomly select females to observe (males walk around these establishments so much that it is hard to follow them). The women's communication styles were observed in two phases: before the music was supplied (or turned loud) and while the dance music was being played. The question we sought to answer was: Which females would get dance offers in the first hour that dance music was played (or when the band played its first musical set)? Table 4-4 presents a summary of the results, based on observations of 287 women.

Women who appeared more outgoing and expressive before the dance music was supplied got more dance offers later in the evening. They engaged in more illustrating, more smiling, and more open sitting positions and were judged the "most talkative" in their group. They also engaged in a "jewelry flash," a "lip-moistening" action, and a "chest thrust" (types of courtship cues) more than women who did not get dance offers. Later, when music was supplied, women who displayed some of the courtship behaviors were quick to get dance offers. Dancing while seated, hair grooming, head or hair tosses, leg and foot movements, lip moistening, and chest thrusts helped attract dance offers.

Men do not want to be rejected or embarrassed when they ask someone to dance. So cues that indicate that a woman wants to dance, coupled with cues that indicate openness, an outgoing nature, and friendliness, help secure dance offers. We should note, however, that we did not assess eye behavior because it was impossible to do so reliably under the circumstances. Another study of this nature found that males approached females 60 percent of the time when the female repeated eye contact and also engaged in smiling (Walsh and Hewitt 1985). These authors concluded that males need a certain amount of encouragement before approaching a female and that this encouragement is most likely given when several behaviors are repeated in several channels.

Table 4-4

BEHAVIORS OF WOMEN WHO DID AND DID NOT RECEIVE DANCE OFFERS

Predance Observations

Variable	Females Receiving Dance Offers	Females Not Receiving Dance Offers	Was Difference Significant?
Group size (mean)	2.82	2.86	No
Illustrators (mean)	2.87	2.49	Yes
Smiling (mean)	3.34	2.84	Yes
Open sitting position (mean)	2.40	1.70	Yes
Time in talk	73%	49%	Yes
Eye contact	61%	51%	No
Hair grooming	56%	40%	No
Clothing adjustments	36%	35%	No
Glasses	10%	11%	No
Jewelry	39%	8%	Yes
Lip moistening	31%	16%	Yes
Body adapters	28%	30%	No
Chest thrust	22%	8%	Yes
Head toss	34%	35%	No
Thigh exposure	27%	22%	No
Leg or foot movement	61%	57%	No

Dance Music Observations

Variable	Females Receiving Dance Offers	Females Not Receiving Dance Offers	Was Difference Significant?
Postural shifts (mean)	3.17	2.73	No
Dancing in seat	67%	30%	Yes
Hair grooming	63%	40%	Yes
Clothing adjustments	41%	32%	No
Jewelry	35%	22%	No
Lip moistening	42%	16%	Yes
Body adapters	41%	46%	No

Dance Music Observations *(continued)*			
Variable	*Females Receiving Dance Offers*	*Females Not Receiving Dance Offers*	*Was Difference Significant?*
Chest thrusts	23%	8%	Yes
Head toss	48%	32%	Yes
Thigh exposure	22%	10%	No
Leg or foot movement	69%	49%	Yes

Source: Supplied by Michael J. Cody, University of Southern California.

MISTAKES IN FLIRTING

Abbey (1982) conducted a study in which male and female students engaged in a five-minute conversation. Neither partner was told to engage in any specific behavior. The pairs were observed from another room. After the conversation, both partners and the observers rated the extent to which the male and female were friendly, seductive, flirtatious, and promiscuous. Both male and female observers agreed in giving females high ratings in friendliness. However, male observers rated females as more seductive and promiscuous than did female observers. Also, the male interactants were rated as more sexually interested in the females. The conclusion was that males naturally perceive the world in more sexual terms than do females.

Abbey asked, "Do males misperceive females' friendliness as seductive?" This question raised a good deal of controversy because it implies that males believe that females are being promiscuous and solicitous when they are merely being friendly. Abbey and others indicate that males very often do perceive a higher level of sexual intent than females do, on the part of both male and female interactants (Abbey 1987; Abbey et al. 1987; Shotland and Craig 1988). Further, certain behaviors, such as excessive eye contact, leaning, touching, and the wearing of sexy apparel (Abbey et al. 1987), prompt high ratings of seductiveness by both males and females.

Shotland and Craig (1988) argue that males can distinguish between friendliness and seductive behaviors, or "showing sexual interest." Seductive encounters involve long eye contact, many short smiles, moving around, forward and backward) leans, softer speaking patterns, more frequent asking of questions, offers of help or assistance, comments that the other has been noticed before, and talkativeness. Encounters that were characterized as friendly rather than seductive included more frequent brief eye contact, being distracted by other activities (reading, eating, drinking), showing less undivided attention to the other by playing with inanimate objects, and taking longer speaking turns.

Research is still unraveling the problem of the individual's competence at distinguishing friendliness from flirtation from seductiveness. We all need to keep in mind that males have a greater sexual appetite and project this higher level of sexual interest onto others they encounter. Males who want to avoid making mistakes in flirting should continually remind themselves to look for multiple and repeated cues from more than one channel (face, body, tone of voice, words spoken) before taking action. Further, certain behaviors that females engage in that clearly denote more than friendliness should be used judiciously in order to reduce the chances of misinterpretation.

BEHAVIORS THAT COMMUNICATE DECEPTION

We began this chapter with a story about the character Sarah Conner. Communication scholars have devoted considerable time and energy to the attempt to detect when a person (a lover, an employee, etc.) is lying. We define **deception** as the deliberate attempt to foster a false belief in another person's mind. For example, deception occurs when you tell your sweetheart that you have been faithful when in fact you have not. Your intention is to mislead.

We behave differently when we lie than when we tell the truth. First, most of us have a fear of being caught, so we are nervous and aroused when we lie—our pupils are dilated, our eyes blink more frequently, our voice has a higher pitch, and we make more speech errors and hesitate more. Further, we have a negative attitude toward lying, so sometimes we are in a hurry to lie and change the topic. Also, when we lie we focus our efforts on one channel—the verbal channel—in preparing words that are not exactly true. As a result of these alterations (anxiety, arousal, negative feelings, and heightened attention given to the verbal channel), we behave differently when lying compared to when we speak the truth. Table 4-5 presents a summary of these differences.

Chapter Summary

Knowledge of nonverbal communication is fundamental to understanding interpersonal relationships. Nonverbal communication is used to communicate emotions, liking for others, and interest in dating, and understanding it can help you detect deception in others. Furthermore, ideas about what is "beautiful" may have a strong impact on dating and other aspects of interpersonal communication.

We also noted that communicators can vary tremendously in their ability to send or judge nonverbal behaviors, such as emotional expressions, interpersonal distance, frequency of gesturing, and so forth. In fact, we concluded that people should never infer too much from only *one* nonverbal behavior, communicated only once and by

Table 4-5

SUMMARY OF NONVERBAL BEHAVIORS
ASSOCIATED WITH DECEPTION

The following behaviors have been examined by communication scholars and have been found to be reliably and consistently related to deception:

Channel	Behavior
Face	
Pupil dilation	Liars' eye pupils dilate when lying.
Blinking	Liars engage in more frequent blinking when lying.
Body	
Adapters	Liars engage in some type of adapting, such as rubbing hands or arms together.
Paralinguistic	
Response length	Liars usually speak for a briefer time duration than truth tellers.
Speech errors	Liars usually communicate messages containing more speech errors, such as grammatical errors of mixing present and past tenses, and so forth.
Speech hesitations	Liars usually communicate messages containing more pauses and "filled pauses" (e.g., "ah," "err," "humm"). A liar's speech is not as fluent as a truth teller's.
Pitch	Liars usually communicate messages with a tone of voice higher in pitch (compared to when they are telling the truth).
Verbal	
Negative statements	Liars frequently include some negative statement, like "I was afraid you'd ask," "I hated it," or so forth, when lying.
Irrelevant statements	Liars frequently include some irrelevant statement in the lies they communicate; e.g., when asked "What is it like working in the governor's office?" a liar might talk about politics or about his or her own work habits, rather than answer the question.

(continued)

(continued from previous page)

Immediacy statements	Liars frequently include some expression of non-immediacy in the lies they communicate; e.g., they say things like "*that* girl over there," compared to a more immediate expression "this girl."
Leveling terms	Liars frequently include more vague terms such as "the usual stuff," "stuff like that," "the typical things," "you know" (as in "you know what I mean"); leveling terms may also include universal expressions: "all," "every," "none," etc.
Channel Discrepancy	At least one channel (face, body, paralinguistic, or verbal) fails or even contradicts the "message" communicated in other channels.

The following behaviors have been examined by communication scholars and have been found to be not reliably and consistently related to deception:

Eye gaze frequency
Smiling
Head movements
Illustrators or other gestures
Shrugs (as in the shrug emblem indicating uncertainty; "I don't know")
Foot/leg movements
Postural shifts
Response latency (the length of time it takes to answer a question; the hesitation that occurs between when a question is asked and an answer is provided)
Speech rate
Self-references (the number of times someone refers to the self, "I," "my," "me," "mine," etc.)

Source: Based on the analysis and review by Zuckerman and Driver 1985. Used with permission of the publisher, Lawrence Erlbaum Associates, Inc.

only one channel. We talked about specific nonverbal behaviors used to show interest in dating others, but also noted that there are many common mistakes in flirting; most obviously, women who show "friendliness" are often perceived as "seductive" and "promiscuous" by males. We also talked about specific nonverbal behaviors that are "leaked" when people lie. Again, it is worth emphasizing that no *one* nonverbal behavior should be used to judge a person as engaging in flirting or lying; one should rely on several cues, from several channels, repeated over time, in order to accurately judge or evaluate others.

KEY TERMS

▼

channel discrepancy	adapters
functional approach	illustrators
functions	emblems
self-fulfilling prophecies	regulators
equity	status-assertive
affect blends	status-neutralizing
display rules	compensation
masking	reciprocity
inhibition	speech accommodation
externalizer	response latency
internalizer	mutual accommodation
mesomorph	postural mirroring
endomorph	courtship behaviors
ectomorph	deception

EXERCISES FOR FURTHER DISCUSSION

▼

1. List the eight nonverbal communication styles: withholders, revealers, unwitting expressers, blanked expressers, substitute expressers, frozen-affect expressers, ever-ready expressers, and flooded-affect expressers. Then match people you know to each style.
    a   Is there a certain emotional style that you find yourself more attracted to than others?
    b. Do you have any friends who are revealers? If so, are you more likely to tell them personal information?
    c. Do you have any friends who are frozen-affect or blanked expressers? If so, do you have trouble knowing what they are thinking sometimes?
    d. Does any one communication style predominate in your family?
2. Write down the name of a male lead character from an action-adventure movie (e.g., Clint Eastwood's "Dirty Harry" or Arnold Schwarzenegger's character in *The Terminator*). Then write down as many different emotions that you can think of that the character expresses. Repeat this exercise for a female lead character from an action movie (e.g., Sigourney Weaver's character in *Aliens* or Geena Davis's or Susan Sarandon's characters in *Thelma and Louise*).

    a. Did you find that male and female lead characters express the same range of emotions? Or, as the research discussed in this chapter suggested, do female characters express a wider range of emotions?

    b. If you think that there is a difference in the range of emotions expressed, what do you think the effect of this difference is on the people who see these movies? Do people you know ever imitate or model themselves on characters that they have seen in the movies?

3. List five emotions, including pure emotions and blends. Working with other class members, try to express each of these emotions nonverbally, and see if others can guess which emotion or emotions you are trying to express.

    a. Who in your group was the most successful in expressing emotions?

    b. Were the men and women in your group equally successful in conveying negative emotions (fear, disgust, anger, sadness)?

    c. Were the men and women in your group equally successful in conveying positive emotions (happiness, surprise)?

4. Working with three other class members, have one person tell about an event that happened to only that person (e.g., an award or honor won, an incident that happened on a trip). Then have each group member prepare to tell the story to the rest of the class as if it happened to him or her. Next present the story to the rest of your class—one person will be telling the truth and three people will be attempting to deceive the class—and see if your classmates can determine who is telling the truth and who is not.

5. Review the section on mistakes made in flirting, and try to think of a situation that you were in where flirtatious behavior was misinterpreted.

    a. If you were the person misinterpreted, can you think of any nonverbal messages that could have caused the misinterpretation?

    b. If you were the person who did the misinterpreting, what nonverbal behaviors do you think led you to think that the person was interested?

6. List five recent television shows in which flirtatious behavior between characters is a common occurrence.

    a. Can you identify the nonverbal behaviors that were involved in the flirting?

    b. Which behaviors were effective in communicating flirting (that is, which got the other person's attention)?

    c. Which behaviors were not effective in getting the other person's attention?

SUGGESTED READING

GENERAL NONVERBAL COMMUNICATION

Burgoon, J. K.; Buller, D. B.; and Woodall, W. G. 1989. *Nonverbal communication: The unspoken dialogue.* New York: Harper Collins. This book provides a thorough treatment of nonverbal communication from historical roots to current applications. The book emphasizes the functions served by nonverbal communication, including intimacy, power, emotional expression, cultural differences, controlling interactions, and the communication of deception.

Knapp, M. L., and Hall, J. A. 1992. *Nonverbal communication and human interaction*, 3d ed. Austin, Texas: Holt, Rinehart and Winston. This book provides a detailed view of nonverbal communication and does so by focusing on different aspects or channels of communication; emphasis is placed on the role of gesture, eye contact and eye gaze, the face, vocal cues, and touch. Knapp and Hall also emphasize skills at sending and receiving nonverbal behaviors.

Leathers, D. G. 1992. *Successful nonverbal communication: Principles and applications*, 2d ed. New York: Macmillan. Leathers's treatment of nonverbal communication emphasizes the impression management function of creating and maintaining the communicator's public image. This book includes very good chapters on impression management, persuasion, and interviewing.

MISTAKES IN FLIRTING

Abbey, A. 1987. Misperceptions of friendly behavior as sexual interest: A survey of naturally occurring incidents. *Psychology of Women Quarterly* 11:173–194. In this article, Abbey used a survey in order to examine gender differences in perceptions of perceived sexual "availability" in naturally occurring events (as opposed to planned studies). Females reported experiencing more incidents of being misperceived (others see their friendliness as a "come-on") than males; the study also examined some of the issues that lead to misperceptions, including settings, how misperceptions were conveyed, and the consequences of misperception.

Koeppel, L. B.; Montagne-Miller, Y.; O'Hair, D. J.; and Cody, M. J. 1993. Friendly? Flirting? Wrong? In *Interpersonal communication: Evolving interpersonal relationships*. ed. P. Kalbfleisch, 19–45. Hillsdale, N. J.: Erlbaum. This chapter reviews research on mistakes in flirting, and reports the results of a study that manipulated the initiator of a conversation (a female initiator or a male initiator) and manipulated various "levels of intimacy" (casual, friendly, flirtatious and seductive). The authors suggest that people hold different beliefs about flirting. Flirting can be viewed as innocent common fun, as reflecting true sexual urges, or as an invitation to reciprocate a "come-on." Males who believed that flirting is an invitation were likely to view the woman as being seductive when she initiated the conversation.

INTIMACY AND NONVERBAL COMMUNICATION

Givens, D. B. 1978. The nonverbal basis of attraction: Flirtation, courtship, and seduction. *Psychiatry* 41:346–359. Givens focuses on how people show liking toward each other, possibly resulting in courtship and seduction.

Scheflen, A. E. 1965. Quasi-courtship behavior in psychotherapy. *Psychiatry* 28: 245–257. Scheflen published one of the first, and more comprehensive, set of observations concerning the display of liking and intimacy. Relying on observations of therapist-patient encounters, he employed the term "quasi-courtship" to denote flirtations behaviors (preening, unbuttoning and buttoning clothes, and so forth) that reflected an interest in intimacy that probably would not actually result in courtship (hence, the term "quasi-courtship").

DECEPTION AND NONVERBAL COMMUNICATION

Buller, D. B., and Burgoon, J. K. In press. Deception. In *Strategic communication*, ed. J. Wiemann and J. Daly. Hillsdale, N. J.: Erlbaum. Buller and Burgoon provide the most thorough review of current literature on deception. They provide their own theoretical framework for viewing nonverbal behaviors with possible links to deception.

Zuckerman, M., and Driver, R. E. 1985. Telling lies: Verbal and nonverbal correlates of deception. In *Multichannel integrations of nonverbal behavior*, ed. A. W. Siegman and S. Feldstein, 129–147. Hillsdale, N. J.: Erlbaum. Zuckerman and Driver conducted a "meta-analysis" of all studies on nonverbal communication and deception published from the 1950s to 1984. A "meta-analysis" is a way of telling whether a behavior (e.g., adaptors, eye blinks, and so forth) is consistently linked to deception across all of the published studies.

REFERENCE LIST

Abbey, A. 1982. Sex differences in attributions for friendly behavior: Do males misperceive females' friendliness? *Journal of Personality and Social Psychology* 42:830–838.

———. 1987. Misperceptions of friendly behavior as sexual interest: A survey of naturally occurring incidents. *Psychology of Women Quarterly* 11:173–194.

Abbey, A.; Cozzarelli, C.; McLaughlin, K.; and Harnish, R. J. 1987. The effects of clothing and dyad sex compositions on perceptions of sexual intent: Do women and men evaluate these cues differently? *Journal of Applied Social Psychology* 17:108–126.

Bull, R., and Rumsey, N. 1988. *The social psychology of facial appearance*. New York: Springer-Verlag.

Burgoon, J. K.; Buller, D. B.; and Woodall, W. G. 1989. *Nonverbal communication: The unspoken dialogue*. New York: Harper Collins.

Burgoon, J. K., and Walther, J. B. 1990. Nonverbal expectancies and the evaluative consequences of violations. *Human Communication Research* 17:232–265.

Ekman, P., and Friesen, W. V. 1969. The repertoire of nonverbal behavior: Categories, origins, usage, and coding. *Semiotica* 1:49–98.

————. 1984. *Unmasking the face.* Palo Alto, Calif.: Consulting Psychologists Press.

Giles, H.; Coupland, J.; and Coupland, N. 1991. *Contexts of accommodation.* Cambridge: Cambridge University Press.

Giles, H.; Mulac, A.; Bradac, J. J.; and Johnson, P. 1987. Speech accommodation theory: The first decade and beyond. In *Communication Yearbook 10,* ed. M. L. McLaughlin, 13–48. Newbury Park, Calif.: Sage.

Givens, D. B. 1978. The nonverbal basis of attraction: Flirtation, courtship, and seduction. *Psychiatry* 41:346–359.

Grayson, B., and Stein, M. I. 1981. Attracting assault: Victims' nonverbal cues. *Journal of Communication,* 31(1):68–75.

Hall, J. A. 1984. *Nonverbal sex differences: Communication accuracy and expressive style.* Baltimore: Johns Hopkins University Press.

Hatfield, E.; Berscheid, E.; and Walster, G. W. 1976. New directions in equity research. In *Equity theory: Toward a general theory of social interaction,* ed. L. Berkowitz and E. Hatfield, 1–42. Orlando, Fla.: Academic Press.

Leathers, D. G. 1992. *Successful nonverbal communication: Principles and applications,* 2d ed. New York: Macmillan.

Muehlenhard, C. L.; Koralewski, M. A.; Andrews, S. L.; and Burdick, C. A. 1986. Verbal and nonverbal cues that convey interest in dating: Two studies. *Behavior Therapy* 17:404–419.

Muehlenhard, C. L., and McFall, R. M. 1981. Dating initiation from a woman's perspective. *Behavior Therapy* 12:682–691.

Muehlenhard, C. L.; Miller, C. L.; and Burdick, C. A. 1983. Are high-frequency daters better cue readers? Men's interpretations of women's cues as a function of dating frequency and SHI scores. *Behavior Therapy* 14:626–636.

Patterson, M. L. 1976. An arousal model of interpersonal intimacy. *Psychological Review* 83:235–245.

————. 1983. *Nonverbal behavior: A functional perspective.* New York: Springer-Verlag.

Pliner, P.; Chaiken, S.; and Flett, G. L. 1990. Gender differences in concern with body weight and physical appearance over the life span. *Personality and Social Psychology Bulletin* 16:263–273.

Ryckman, R. M.; Robbins, M. A.; Kaczor, L. M.; and Gold, J. A. 1989. Male and female raters' stereotyping of male and female physiques. *Personality and Social Psychology Bulletin* 15:244–251.

Scheflen, A. E. 1965. Quasi-courtship behavior in psychotherapy. *Psychiatry* 28:245–257.

Shennum, W. A., and Bugental, D. B. 1982. The development of control over affective expression in nonverbal behavior. In *Development of nonverbal behavior in children,* ed. R. S. Feldman, 101–122. New York: Springer-Verlag.

Shotland, R. L., and Craig, J. M. 1988. Can men and women differentiate between friendly and sexually interested behavior? *Social Psychology Quarterly* 51:66–73.

Snyder, M.; Tanke, E.; and Berscheid, E. 1977. Social perception and interpersonal behavior: On the self-fulfilling nature of social stereotypes. *Journal of Personality and Social Psychology* 35:656–666.

Walsh, D. G., and Hewitt, J. 1985. Giving men the come-on: Effects of eye contact and smiling in a bar environment. *Perceptual and Motor Skills* 61:873–874.

Weinberger, H., and Cash, T. 1982. The relationship of attributional style to learned helplessness in an interpersonal context. *Basic and Applied Psychology* 3:141–154.

Zuckerman, M., and Driver, R. E. 1985. Telling lies: Verbal and nonverbal correlates of deception. In *Multichannel integrations of nonverbal behavior*, ed. A. W. Siegman and S. Feldstein, 129–147. Hillsdale, N. J.: Erlbaum.

ACHIEVING SELF-PRESENTATION GOALS

In Part II, we look more closely at the goal of self-presenta-tion, one of the three fundamental goals discussed in Chapter 1. Chapter 5 discusses the basic nature of self-presentation: what it is, when we engage in it, how it relates to interpersonal communication, and how we make self-presentations believable. We also discuss some of the tactics employed to create and maintain desired public images. Chapter 6 focuses on how we defend the self in situations that are threatening to our self-identity, particularly how we use "accounts" to justify our behaviors. Chapter 7 discusses how we disclose, or reveal, the self—to different degrees in different situations. We discuss what affects whether people will disclose, how they disclose, and how their disclosure is perceived.

C H A P T E R   5

PRESENTING THE SELF

When Dave was sixteen years old, he decided to spend the summer working at a Boy Scout camp in the mountains. Upon arriving at the camp, he was introduced to Bob, his supervisor. After moving into his quarters, Dave helped Bob stock food in the pantry. This was the first opportunity for Dave to get to know Bob, and Dave wanted to make a good impression not only because he was going to live and work with Bob all summer but also because he had often dreamt of living and camping in the mountains all summer, and he wanted to be liked, to do a good job, and to be rehired the following summer. As the two stored food, they began to talk and tell jokes and humorous stories. Dave took this to be a good sign. At one point Dave looked into the kitchen and noticed a large woman, whom he assumed was the camp cook. Keeping the humorous banter alive, Dave smirked and asked Bob: "Hey, who's the tank in the kitchen?" Bob stopped working, stood up straight, and gave Dave a questioning look: "That 'tank' happens to be my wife."

Although few of us have made errors as blatant as Dave's, we have all had similar experiences: We try our best to make a good impression, only to make some error in the process. Instead of creating a "correct" or "desired" impression, Dave became embarrassed, ashamed, and apologetic; what's more, he had to work hard to change a negative image to a positive one.

What Is Self-presentation?

Imagine being asked, "So what are you like?" by your instructor, an attractive lunch date, and a job interviewer. Your answers probably depend on how you want each person to see you. You would emphasize different aspects of yourself to each person. You may want your instructor to see you as intelligent and motivated, your lunch date to see you as attractive and interesting, and the interviewer to see you as reliable, competent, and honest. You are engaging in **strategic self-presentation,** or **impression management,** whenever you act in some way for the purpose of creating or maintaining a certain image in the minds of your audience.

Leathers (1992) defined impression management as an individual's conscious attempt to exercise control over selected communicative behaviors and cues "for purposes of making a desired impression" (p. 204). Any behavior can help achieve impression management goals, though some are obviously more effective than others. For example, something as simple as wearing sunglasses may be used to create the impression that you are "athletic," but a number of other actions (actually playing sports, exercising, and so forth) are more effective in creating and maintaining such a public image.

We are motivated by a desire to project a desirable social identity. Typically, desirable social identities include "positive" images that we are likable, competent, dedicated, skillful, strong, and so on. However, desirable identities may also sometimes include attempts to appear weak and helpless (so that others will help us) or to appear hostile and ruthless (so that others will respect us and leave us alone).

Table 5-1 lists five common self-presentational strategies. The **ingratiator** desires to be liked and to arouse the emotion of affection. To do so, the ingratiator will praise others, do favors, and engage in other "affinity-seeking" behaviors. However, each strategy also involves risks, and being perceived as a conformist or a "manipulator" are possible negative consequences the ingratiator risks. The **intimidator** seeks to be perceived as a dangerous, tough individual who should be feared; the **self-promoter** wants to be seen as competent; the **exemplifier** is dedicated, committed, and self-sacrificing; and the **supplicator** desires to be perceived as helpless and in need of nurturance. We outline how communicators go about creating these images later in this chapter.

MONITORING SELF-PRESENTATION

Sometimes we act to make an impression on others, while at other times we hardly give any thought to the impressions we are creating—we routinely greet people, carry on conversations, ask friends for favors, and so forth. An important question becomes, when are self-presentational goals relevant?

We answer the question by saying that self-presentational goals are relevant anytime our social identity is subject to evaluation by others. At one point in time, as when having lunch with a friend, we may pay little attention to our presentational goals. However, when we notice our lunch partner yawning or looking around the room, we acknowledge that we may be boring or not paying enough attention to the friend's interest. Because we prefer not to be evaluated as boring or insensitive, our presentational goals immediately become important, and we pay closer attention to what we are doing and the impression that might be communicated. We start consciously monitoring what we are doing and alter our actions so as to project a more desirable image. We joke to show that we are humorous or raise questions of interest to the partner to show that we are caring.

The point is that we do not always think about presentational goals, but the need to monitor such goals can be quickly activated by our surroundings. This is because we are able to monitor continually the success of our presentational goals at a *preattentive* or *nonconscious* level (Leary and Kowalski 1990). What this means is that our minds are often preoccupied with other goals involving work, relationships, and so

Table 5-1
A TAXONOMY OF SELF-PRESENTATION STRATEGIES

Strategy	Desirable Image Sought	Negative Image Risked	Desirable Emotion Sought	Typical Actions
1. Ingratiation	likable	sycophant conformist obsequious	affection	self-characterization opinion conformity other enhancement favors
2. Intimidation	dangerous ruthless volatile	bombastic wishy-washy ineffectual	fear	threats anger (incipient) breakdown (incipient)
3. Self-promotion	competent effective successful	fraudulent conceited defensive	respect awe deference	performance claims performance accounts performances
4. Exemplification	worthy suffering dedicated	hypocritical sanctimonious exploitative	guilt shame emulation	self-denial helping militancy
5. Supplication	helpless handicapped unfortunate	stigmatized lazy demanding	nurturance obligation	self-deprecation entreaties for help

Source: Adapted from Jones and Pittman 1982. Used with permission of the authors.

forth, and our concerns about how we are being perceived are relegated to the back of the mind. Relegating our concerns over impressions allows us to direct our attention to other matters (work, listening to others, and so forth). However, at the preattentive or nonconscious level of awareness, we still monitor how other people act or react toward us, and when we believe that we are being evaluated in some way, most communicators can quickly recall from memory what they can and should do to promote a desirable image.

Do we always monitor presentational goals? Yes, although we only give thought to the goals when prompted to do so by our surroundings. At one extreme, we think very little about our presentational goals unless the actions of others provide feedback that prompts us to put more effort into working on these goals. At the other extreme, there are communication situations involving blind dates, applying for membership in a country club, group job interviews, and the like, where we will be very preoccupied with presentational goals.

SELF-IDENTITY AND SELF-PRESENTATION

Socrates advised people, "Know thyself!" Though this may sound simple, it is really quite difficult. The difficulty arises from the fact that we often seem to have many different identities. Do members of your family see a different you than do your close friends? Do you present a different self at school than at work? There are many ways to view yourself. Schlenker (1986) says this is because a person's identity is a "theory of self that is formed and maintained through" interpersonal communication and agreement (p. 23). There are two important aspects of this definition: (1) Our identity is a theory and is dependent on available evidence, and (2) our identity is based on interpersonal agreement and is therefore dependent on communication.

Any good theory of the self must be believable. If we do not believe that a given identity is true, we will not internalize it and claim it as our own. For an identity to be believable, it must explain, predict, and guide behavior. First, an identity must explain our thoughts, feelings, and actions (Gergen 1989). For example, suppose that Jack notices the following about himself: he is very attracted to Jill, he enjoys spending time with Jill, and he thinks about Jill throughout the day almost constantly. Given these observations, Jack might conclude, "I'm in love with Jill."

But what if Jack also notices that he really misses his ex-girlfriend Mary and wishes that they could get back together and that he would also like to date Diane? In this case the identity "in love with Jill" is less believable. As an explanation of Jack's thoughts, feelings, and actions, being "in love with Jill" does not do a very good job. This is because the strength of Jack's explanation is influenced by how *inclusive* and *coherent* it is. The **inclusiveness** of an explanation refers to the number of different thoughts, feelings, and actions that it is able to account for. The greater the number of thoughts, feelings, and actions an identity is able to explain, the more inclusive it is. **Coherence** refers to how well the items we use to develop an identity fit together. The better they fit together, the more coherent the identity: Jack's first three observations fit together under the identity "in love with Jill"; the additional ones do not. If Jack believes in all of them, he can respond in at least three ways. First, he may attempt to explain all the relevant information and revise his identity. For example, after hearing popular talk shows, he may change his identity from "being in love with Jill" to "having a dependent personality." Second, he can maintain the identity of being "in love with Jill" but be less confident about it. Third, he may bias information in order to maintain the "I love Jill" belief—he can actually distort the available information or selectively attend to certain information, ignoring contradictory facts.

The second purpose our identities must serve is to help us predict future thoughts, feelings, and actions. If Jack believes that he is in love with Jill, he can predict that he will enjoy studying with her this weekend. Finally, in addition to explaining and predicting, our identities also help guide our actions. Because Jack is in love with Jill, he will not romantically date Diane.

The more believable an identity is, the more likely we are to internalize it as our own. But there is more to the adoption of identity than simply believing it. Imagine that you routinely receive the highest exam scores in class. Your possible explanations include (1) I understand the material better than my classmates, (2) I have really been lucky, or (3) I am benefiting from unfair grading practices. Which of these identities would you choose? Why?

Most communicators would choose the first alternative. This is because, in addition to the criterion of believability, we also strive for identities that are personally beneficial (Schlenker 1986). Identities that are beneficial include ones that suggest that we have the skills necessary to enter a specific profession, beauty enough to find and keep a mate, enough likability to have friends, sufficient competence to be promoted, and so on.

Our identities do not exist in isolation. We test them, develop them, and refine them using interpersonal communication. If you believe that you are friendly and likable, you will most likely enter conversations assuming that your partners will see you the same way. If you meet with resistance because your partners find you offensive (for example, they think your friendliness is insincere), you will probably attempt to "correct" their "misconception," especially if the others are important to you. If they persist in "misperceiving" you, you will have two choices: reject the others' opinion as insignificant, or rethink your identity. Cumulatively, our friends provide a "reality check" on our identities by indicating the degree to which they agree or disagree with our claims of being friendly, likable, caring, and so on.

But what happens if we begin with a negative identity? We are usually willing to exchange a negative identity (e.g., boring, unattractive) for a positive one. However, we often have a difficult time being convinced of its believability. We naturally enjoy hearing positive feedback about our good qualities; however, we usually prefer to hear accurate feedback about our negative qualities than be flattered with inaccurate positive feedback. Therefore, we often discount positive feedback and sometimes even provide self-deprecating information to "prove" that it is incorrect. This is a strong and reliable "test" of our identities. If someone says to me, "You're such a positive person. It's fun being around you," I might respond with, "Thanks, but I can be pretty moody. You haven't seen me on a bad day." This might be a way of saying,

"I would like to see myself as a fun person, but I don't. Before you jump to conclusions, consider this. . . ." But if I am convinced that they know the facts and still think I am fun to be with, I am more likely to adopt the identity of "fun to be with."

Two principles guide whether we will exchange a negative identity for a positive one: (1) If the positive identity requires us to fulfill new responsibilities, we may keep the negative identity. For example, adopting the identity "good student" may require an individual to spend more time studying and less time partying, or working at a night job. In this case, the "positive" identity is less beneficial than the "negative identity." (2) A person who believes it impossible to maintain the positive identity will choose to adopt the negative identity; a student who gets the highest score on an exam may claim that the grade was due to "luck" in order to avoid having others develop expectations that are too high.

In sum, our identity is best thought of as a theory that is developed according to the criteria of accuracy and personal benefit. To be accurate, our identity must help us explain, predict, and guide our thoughts and actions. To be personally beneficial, it must help us feel good about who we are and our potential for the future. Believability and personal benefit are often competing desires, and therefore we are very selective with the information we use to form our identity. Moreover, we test our identities as we pursue our presentational goals, and it is in the context of interpersonal communication that we become who we are.

INDICATORS OF ATTAINMENT

To make our identity claims legitimate, we need to engage in communicative activities that will make them believable. These activities are what Gollwitzer (1986, 145) refers to as **indicators of attainment.** These indicators operate as symbols of the desired identity that communicate to ourselves and others that we have attained an identity. Taking the identity of "student" as an example, indicators of attainment could include fulfilling the responsibilities associated with being a student (e.g., attending class), displaying material symbols (wearing a school sweatshirt), meeting institutional requirements (paying student fees), or making verbal claims ("I am a student"). Such a person could legitimately claim to be a student.

However, our identities lack a sense of completion until others acknowledge our possession of a desirable identity. Therefore, we develop ways of presenting ourselves to get the feedback desired to feel complete. Consider the following excerpt from a conversation with a student who desperately wanted to be seen as "graduate school material." It occurred two weeks before the semester was over and a paper was due. Notice how the student tries to indicate that he is a good student:

Professor: Hi, what's up?
Student: I need your help. Yesterday I spent seven hours in the library getting articles for my paper. [Spending long hours working symbolizes being a good student.]

Professor: You're not just getting started are you? [Good students do not put off papers to the last minute.]

Student: I couldn't think of anything to write on. But look how many articles I copied yesterday. This is a lot, huh? [I'm not a poor student because I have a good excuse for not starting earlier. Further, look at the sheer bulk of reading I plan to do. Only good students do this much work.]

Professor: What do you mean you couldn't think of anything? You've had over two months to work on this. Why did you put it off until now? [Your excuse is not legitimate.]

Student: I know I should have started earlier, but I really want to do a good job on this paper. This is really important to me. Will you show me which of these articles I should read and which ones I shouldn't? [Even though I may not seem like it, I really am a good student!]

Notice that the student continued to come up with new ways to assert his identity as a good student. This is because our desire to present ourselves as possessing a certain identity is often most acute when our identity has been challenged. We may resort to exaggerated verbal claims (see box on page 112) or increase performances related to proving the identity to ourselves and others. Gollwitzer (1986) demonstrated this nicely in an experiment with medical students, who were given a test that presumably measured whether or not each student had the personality necessary to be a competent physician. Although the test was bogus, half the students received feedback that they possessed the personality of a successful physician; the other half were told that they did not.

Later the students were given the task of solving a set of medical problems. The ability to complete this test symbolized their ability to be a successful doctor. The results indicated that those who had been given the negative feedback tended to show their completed tasks to the experimenter, whereas those who were given the positive feedback did not. Apparently, those who had been told by the experimenter that they were not suited for their desired profession were compelled to prove to the experimenter (and themselves) that they truly did have the skills necessary to be a good doctor.

The desire to create an acceptable identity can be so strong that it actually motivates us to engage in acts that are damaging to ourselves or others. For example, Norman and Tedeschi (1989) found that the desire to create a personally beneficial identity was a significant factor in motivating adolescents to start smoking. Six months after attending an antismoking seminar, adolescents who had rated smoking as being "cool" and who wanted to see themselves as "cool" started smoking and believed their friends would approve.

PART II ACHIEVING SELF-PRESENTATION GOALS

112

EXAGGERATED SELF-PRESENTATION MOTIVATED BY A LACK OF INDICATORS OF ATTAINMENT

One of the best ways to make a highly desired identity believable is to accumulate and display various indicators of attainment associated with that identity. Often, we are motivated to make exaggerated claims about our possession of a given identity when we don't have many indicators of attainment or when we receive negative feedback regarding our identity (Gollwitzer 1986; Jones 1989). The following commentary was written by a twenty-year-old male who had chosen to forgo going to college. Notice his exaggerated claims of competence to compensate for the lack of a college degree, which he disparagingly refers to as "the paper."

No Degree, No Job—Is It Fair?

I'm 20, and one thing that especially bugs me is that many older adults (don't tell me I'm not an adult) can't see through your age, no matter what kind of person you are. I've always wondered why no one talks about discrimination against the young, because it's certainly out there.

I also suffer from what I call the "lack of paper syndrome." I have many talents that could be put to use in a wide variety of fields, from accounting to writing, but I can't even be considered for jobs in these fields because I don't have a college degree—the "paper." It doesn't matter that I might have studied on my own and might have 10 times the knowledge of the person who went to college (I have one year of college). It doesn't matter that I can learn anything I want to very fast. After almost a year of working and paying my own bills, I know what the real world is like, yet most older adults would insist that I don't.

The people who are now in charge in the business world want us to go through the same irrational steps that they went through in order to get where they are now. That's the main reason the system remains the way it is. I think it's time for a change.

Reprinted with permission from *Parade*, June 16, 1991, p. 16.

The desire to create a beneficial identity can be so powerful that it motivates people to engage in violent acts. Studies indicate that when an insult threatened an aspect of a person's personality that he or she thought was important, the person was more likely to respond aggressively, particularly in the presence of a same-sex audience (Felson 1982; and Harris, Gergen, and Lannamann 1986). Insulted parties felt the need to protect their identity by attacking the other.

Direct Strategies of Self-presentation

The impressions you create in the minds of others have a profound impact on whether you are liked or rejected, popular or unpopular, hired or passed up in favor of someone else, and so on. Further, the development of presentational skills is one of the keys to reaching many other instrumental goals. As McCormack (1984) says in *What They Don't Teach You at the Harvard Business School:* "One of life's big frustrations is that people don't do what you want them to do. But if you can control their impressions of you, you can make them want to do what you want them to do" (p. 26).

There are two major methods that communicators use when managing impressions: direct and indirect methods. Direct methods include the tactics used to ingratiate, intimidate, self-promote, supplicate, and exemplify, discussed earlier. Indirect methods are used to bolster one's image and one's self-esteem.

INGRATIATION

A communicator can ingratiate others in order to appear likable by being humorous, warm, charming, trustworthy, and so on. There are many communicative choices available for the ingratiator. The choice to enact ingratiating behavior is influenced by three factors. The first is called the *incentive value* associated with being liked by a particular person (Jones and Pittman 1982). As the value of being liked by a person increases, so does the incentive or motivation to engage in ingratiating behaviors.

An ingratiator, however, can have either *illicit* or *authentic* motivations. Ingratiation is considered illicit or phony when a person acts solely to get something from the target. In other words, a person who wants to be liked for ulterior motives and employs **illicit ingratiation** runs the risk of being perceived as insincere. A typical example is when a student says, "Professor, I really like your class—it's my favorite this semester. Do you think it would be possible for me to take a makeup, since I have to be out of town during the next exam?" Though the student's primary goal is to persuade the professor to give a makeup exam, the student begins with a compliment. The success of the compliment depends on its being seen as honest feedback rather than apple polishing.

Authentic ingratiation, by contrast, occurs when a person's primary motivation is to meet the demands of the situation. In this case the reasons for engaging in the behavior are implicitly known by most people in the situation. The desire to be liked, though important, is secondary to other goals. For example, you may congratulate a classmate after a speech because she did a good job and deserves it. In this case, your congratulatory behavior may increase how much she likes you, but your primary motivation is to affirm her performance rather than meet your own personal needs.

Students often attempt to ingratiate themselves with their instructors. The important question is motive: Do students genuinely enjoy the class, or do they have a hidden agenda, such as an improved grade or a letter of recommendation?

(Frank Siteman/Stock, Boston)

The second factor that influences the decision to ingratiate is the **subjective probability of success.** Prior to deciding to ingratiate, we tend to size up the situation to determine the likelihood of our success. This requires that we assess our own skills and resources as well as the probability that our tactics might fail. For example, a friend receives the lowest score on a test on which you receive the highest. In your effort to be a friend, what do you do? One possible tactic is to offer to let your friend borrow your notes before the next exam. This may be appropriate if you believe that your resources (the notes) will help your friend and that he will be receptive to your offer. But if you think your friend will interpret your offer as an implication that he is stupid, that you are condescending, or that you are implying he cannot get good grades on his own merits, you will probably not use the tactic. However, we must be aware of the **ingratiator's dilemma:** as the need to be liked by a particular target person increases, the probability of successful ingratiation decreases. This is because the more obvious it becomes that an individual wants to be seen as attractive or likable, the more likely the target person is to attribute ulterior motives to the ingratiator.

The third factor affecting the decision to ingratiate is the **perceived legitimacy** of the ingratiating behavior. Each of us develops moral standards that govern whether we believe certain behaviors are appropriate or not, and any ingratiating behavior we choose must fit within those standards. Should you praise a friend's new haircut when she is desperate to hear words of approval, even though the haircut is awful? Perceived appropriateness strongly affects whether we ingratiate or not. People who are sufficiently motivated, believe that they are likely to be successful, and believe that certain ingratiation tactics are morally legitimate will usually choose to engage in one of three ingratiation tactics: Complimenting, opinion conformity, and rendering favors. We will also discuss affinity-seeking tactics.

COMPLIMENTING OTHERS.   One of the most commonly employed tactics, complimenting involves expressing a positive evaluation of the target by drawing attention to the target's strengths and virtues: "You did very well on this test. You are so smart!" "Wow, you look great this evening!"

There is a natural tendency for our attraction to increase toward those who compliment us. However, it is essential that the compliments be seen as genuine. Though this may seem simple, anyone who has tried it knows how difficult it can be. Consider the following situation: A friend tells you that she is worried about an exam because she desperately wants an A. Because you are confident of her abilities, you try to be reassuring: "I'm sure you will get one of the highest scores in the class. You always do." The complimentary nature of your response may seem obvious, but your response could be interpreted in five different ways (see Jones and Wortman 1974):

1. You want something from her.
2. That's just the kind of person you are.
3. Your comment was triggered by the situation.
4. You are just trying to be nice.
5. You are being honest and sincere.

First, your friend could believe that you are complimenting her because you want something from her. If your comment is interpreted in this way, it is likely to boomerang on you and produce a decrease in liking. To guard against this, a successful complimenter would play down any perceived dependence on the friend; praising her and asking for a favor (to borrow notes) at the same time makes the dependence too obvious.

Alternatively, she may think "That's just the kind of person you are. You always say nice things." A complimenter can avoid this interpretation by making it appear that he or she is a discerning complimenter who does, in fact, occasionally make negative statements about others—perhaps blending a negative comment on one minor point ("You may not be the most efficient person I know at studying") with a positive comment on a major point ("but you always remember what is important").

Third, your comment may be perceived as purely normal; friends are obligated to say reassuring things to each other. It is important to note that offering compliments in situations where they are considered normative may not increase liking, but failing to do so is likely to result in decreased liking. To derive the most benefit in such situations, the ingratiator should offer compliments that provide greater detail than usual. This could include not only expressing confidence in the friend's ability but also mentioning specific behaviors she engages in, such as "You study more than anyone I know. I've seen you get anxious about assignments in the past, yet you always seem to pull it off. I'm sure you will get one of the highest test scores."

Fourth, the friend might believe that you are "just trying to be nice." Your motives are good, but you are not being entirely honest in your estimation of her abilities. To avoid this, complimenters can provide "proof" concerning the positive evaluation. You could include reasons for your compliment, such as "I know some of the people in your class, and they're not putting nearly as much time into studying for this exam. Also, you had the same professor last semester and always did well on the exams. Considering that he grades on a curve, I'm sure you'll get one of the highest scores on the exam."

Finally, your friend might conclude you are being honest and sincere—that you really do believe that she is competent and will do well on the exam. In this case, the ingratiation tactic is likely to be successful.

AGREEING WITH OTHERS. **Opinion conformity** is based on the assumption that we tend to find people who are similar to us more attractive than those who are dissimilar. Similar others are often considered more attractive because they add support to the correctness of our world view, we expect them to be more cooperative, and we expect them to help us reach our goals. However, the value placed on independent thought and action makes opinion conformity a rather risky tactic. Communicators who are too quick to conform to others are often considered weak and indecisive or phony.

Opinion conformity is used in sales. Imagine a grandmother purchasing a graduation gift. A salesclerk first informs a gift-buying grandmother what is popular among high school students. Later the grandmother expresses an opinion, "I think I like the red sweater better." The salesclerk conforms to this opinion, "Yes, so do I," and the grandmother buys the red sweater. Note the difficulty for the salesclerk, however, if the grandmother changes her mind and says, "On second thought, I think I prefer the blue one." To agree again with the shopper would suggest that the salesclerk is insincere.

HELPING OTHERS. Rendering favors communicates to others that we respect them and are willing to help them pursue their goals. Like offering compliments, rendering favors is based on the principle that we reciprocate liking for people who like us. One of the ways to avoid the suspicion of ulterior motives is to do only favors that are considered appropriate for a given situation. A good example of doing favors beyond what was considered appropriate was reported in the *Los Angeles Times* ("Man spends $20,000 trying to win hand of girl who can say no"). After dating for two months, Keith, a thirty-five-year-old stockbroker, proposed to Karine, a twenty-year-old cocktail waitress, but Karine turned him down. Her refusal prompted a shower of gifts from Keith, including a Lear jet, a gold ring, a limousine waiting outside her door, $200 worth of champagne, 4,000 flowers, and musicians to serenade her. Karine was flattered but still said no. The inappropriateness of the behavior made Keith look foolish.

AFFINITY SEEKING AND LIKING. Bell and Daly (1984) explored the communication strategies specifically intended to increase liking for a communicator. They identified the twenty-five most commonly employed strategies people claim to use for **affinity seeking,** when they want to get others to like them. Table 5-2 lists these strategies. The most frequently used affinity-seeking strategies were conversational rule keeping, self-concept confirmation, eliciting disclosures, nonverbal immediacy, self-inclusion, listening, facilitating enjoyment, openness, and altruism. The least used were conceding control, influencing perceptions of closeness, and assuming control.

The use of these strategies has a strong impact on the perceptions of liking and loving for the communicator. As a general rule, the more frequently a communicator employed the strategies listed in Table 5-2, the more liked, loved, and effective the communicator was rated. Bell, Tremblay, and Buerkel-Rothfuss (1987) also found that individuals who score high on the use of affinity seeking are perceived to be less lonely, less apprehensive, and more socially assertive and to possess positive social abilities, as for making new friends or getting dates.

INTIMIDATION

The goal of an intimidator is to be seen as dangerous. Intimidators let it be known that they are both able and willing to inflict physical or psychological pain on anyone who gets in the way. In his research on criminal behavior, Toch (1969) found that intimidation was a common tactic among violent men. One out of four violence-prone men engaged in "self-image promoting," going out of his way to create the impression that he is formidable and fearless. Such men characterize their fights with others as necessary strategy to impress victims and the audience, and to promote their desired image. They challenge other men who invade their space and territory. Such men worry that if they don't act first to create the image of an intimidator, they will be mistaken as weak or cowardly. Such men challenge others at sporting events and in bars for the purpose of demonstrating that they are more masculine and more fearsome than others. A less extreme intimidator is the "self-

Table 5-2

AFFINITY-SEEKING STRATEGIES

1. *Altruism.* Strive to be of assistance to the other in whatever he or she is doing (e.g., doing a favor).
2. *Assuming control.* Present yourself as someone in control (e.g., taking charge of activities).
3. *Assuming equality.* Strike a posture of social equality with the other person (e.g., avoid acting snobbish).
4. *Comfortable self.* Act comfortable and relaxed when around the other person.
5. *Conceding control.* Allow the other to assume control over relational activities (e.g., where to go for coffee).
6. *Conversational rule keeping.* Adhere closely to cultural rules for polite, cooperative interaction (e.g., act interested in what the other is telling you, even if you are not).
7. *Dynamism.* Present yourself as an active, enthusiastic person (e.g., although you are very tired, you answer the phone using an upbeat, energetic voice).
8. *Eliciting disclosures.* Encourage the other to talk by reinforcing his or her conversational contributions (e.g., ask the partner for opinions).
9. *Facilitating enjoyment.* Maximize the positiveness of relational encounters (e.g., participate fully in an activity you know the other enjoys).
10. *Inclusion of other.* Include the other in your social groups (e.g., ask this person to a party your friends will be attending).
11. *Influencing perceptions of closeness.* Engage in behaviors that imply that the relationship is closer than it is (e.g., use nicknames for other; refer to "us" and "we").
12. *Listening.* Listen actively to the other (e.g., be attentive; ask for clarification).
13. *Nonverbal immediacy.* Show interest in the other through various nonverbal behaviors (e.g., smile at other).
14. *Openness.* Disclose personal information (e.g., "Don't be embarrassed, Sammy. I'm also afraid of Ferris wheels.").
15. *Optimism.* Present yourself as a positive person (e.g., offer positive comments about others).
16. *Personal autonomy.* Present yourself as independent and a free thinker (e.g., disagree with the other).
17. *Physical attractiveness.* Look and dress as attractively as possible (e.g., get rid of those sweats!).

18. *Presenting an interesting self.* Appear to be someone interesting to know (e.g., drop names of impressive people).
19. *Rewarding association.* Imply that you can reward the other (e.g., shower the other with gifts).
20. *Self-concept confirmation.* Show respect for the other and promote good feelings in the other (e.g., use compliments).
21. *Self-inclusion.* Arrange frequent contact with the other (e.g., show up where you know the other will be).
22. *Sensitivity.* Act warm and empathic (e.g., show your concern for the other).
23. *Similarity.* Convince the other about your similarity in interests (e.g., say that you really do like to go bowling).
24. *Supportiveness.* Support the other's social encounters (e.g., side with this person in an argument with a third party).
25. *Trustworthiness.* Present yourself as honest and reliable (e.g., fulfill commitments made to the other).

Source: Adapted from Bell and Daly 1984, 96–97. Copyright by the Speech Communication Association. Reprinted by permission of the publisher and the authors.

image defender" who doesn't go out of his way to challenge others but is extremely sensitive to invasions of his space and territory and quickly retaliates against any real or imagined slights against his public image.

Violence-prone men are the most extreme intimidators. Many public figures and executives work hard on impression management goals, including the perception of being intimidating. In some situations, intimidation is an important ingredient to success—as when you are playing sports or walking in a crime-ridden area and want to appear strong, dangerous, and fearsome. Also, certain jobs—police officer, probation officer, collection agent, candidate for certain political offices—require an intimidating style.

SELF-PROMOTION

The goal of the self-promoter is to be seen as competent. A successful self-promoter is usually competent in a particular context or in a particular activity (sports, singing, dancing, etc.). It would be arrogant to expect others to see us as competent at everything. Most of us realize that developing competence in one area requires a trade-off in another area. This leads to two implications for the potential self-promoter. First, self-promoting either too excessively or in the wrong context can lead to the attribution of incompetence. They are like Cliff, the self-promoting mail carrier on "Cheers." Although he presents himself as an expert on almost every topic, to everyone else he is obviously self-deceived. Second, in some situations self-promoters can enhance other's attributions of their competence by declaring their incompetence in other areas. This not only makes a competent person seem more human but also reinforces the perception of competence by generating the additional attribution of accurate self-awareness.

Consider the following story (Potter 1962, 287): About the time when Harvard University administers extremely difficult midwinter examinations, one of the students, Fitzjames, disappeared from the college. His classmates struggled with mounds of reading materials, anxious and worried about performing well on the important tests. When the tests were administered, all students were present in the lecture room except Fitzjames. When all others were furiously writing their answers, Fitzjames casually walked in five minutes late, well-tanned and wearing a light suit, strolling without an apparent care or worry in the world. He amusingly inspected the test questions and then began to write slowly. Later it become known that Fitzjames had received an A in the course. What is your perception of Fitzjames? How competent is he? Consider the full story:

Fitzjames did not go to Florida to vacation, nor did he take the exams any less seriously than the other students. The truth was that he checked into a cheap room in Boston, surrounded himself with the entire reading assignment, and spent virtually every day and night for three weeks reading and preparing for the exams, sitting between two sunlamps.

Now what do you think of Fitzjames? Though he cannot be commended for his honesty, Fitzjames was a shrewd self-promoter. He understood the "attributional arithmetic" used to determine the meaning of an accomplishment and staged the situation to increase his perceived competence. According to Jones (1989), accomplishments are produced by a combination of natural ability, motivation, and effort. Earning an A in a class, for example, requires a combination of intelligence (natural ability), a desire to get an A (motivation), and studying (effort).

The component most closely associated with competence is natural ability. This is because the greater one's natural ability (a stable factor), the less one has to compensate with motivation and effort (unstable factors). Therefore, the greater one's natural ability, the greater the potential for future success. Fitzjames disguised his degree of motivation and effort in the hope of appearing competent because of his natural ability; however, the truth (studying hard) reinforces an impression of being studious and dedicated but not quite as competent.

Self-promotion can be a risky proposition. Research indicates that people often fail to self-promote successfully. They either make strategic blunders in deciding how to self-promote (list too many accomplishments) or make mistakes in communicating their self-promotion strategies as the conversation unfolds, perhaps making a brash claim too early in the conversation or appearing arrogant, self-centered, and uninterested in their conversational partners (see Godfrey, Jones, and Lord 1986).

Common sense suggests that people who brag too early in a conversation would be perceived as competent but unlikable, relative to people who are humble early in the conversation and only later make self-promoting claims. McLaughlin and colleagues (1985) conducted a study on how people insert brags into conversations and found that females were more likely than males to plan or calculate how they would insert their brags. For example, a female may want to promote her world travels by revealing the fact that she studied in China the previous summer. Instead of blurting out this fact, she may introduce the topic of summer experiences and get the partner to talk about summer experiences first, knowing that a partner is likely to reciprocate the question, "So what did you do this summer?" Males, however, might merely blurt out, "I went to China last summer. What did you do?" It is probably the case that brags that are too obvious result in lower ratings of liking than brags that appear as part of a smooth-flowing conversation.

Miller and co-workers (1992) also found significant differences between males and females regarding reactions to bragging statements. The researchers first raised a fundamental issue: When do people perceive positive self-serving statements as "positive disclosures" or as "brags"? Consider the following statements:

"My softball team had its awards dinner last night. We had a good season and so everyone was in a great mood. I even got the most valuable player award. Boy, was I surprised. I played really hard this summer, but I did it for the fun and the exercise. So I was really pleased to get the award and the recognition. I was glad to help my team finish the season so well."

"My softball team had its awards dinner last night. I had my best season yet, and so I was in a great mood. They gave me the most valuable player award. But that was no surprise because I was the leading player all summer. Actually, I'm the best all-around player this league has ever seen. I could have my choice to play on any team I want next year, so I may be changing to a better team."

Most people will readily identify the first statement as a positive disclosure statement and the second as a boast or brag. Miller and colleagues identified three elements that make a statement a brag. First, a bragging statement is one in which the communicator emphasizes a personal and chronic quality of power, status, or wealth. Second, brags involve exaggeration, emphasis, or elaboration of how the speaker accomplished the achievement with no effort or of how much the achievement benefited others. Third, statements are perceived as brags if the communicators emphasize that they are better than others at a skill or a task.

Miller and associates found that communicators who employed bragging statements were perceived as competent but less likable. However, they also argued that bragging is perceived as a "masculine" behavior, characteristic of male competitiveness. Should you brag? If you are a male and you want other males to think of you as competent, you can significantly increase ratings of competence by bragging—although you will be perceived as less likable. However, if you are a female and you want males to think of you as competent, bragging does not increase ratings of competence as much as making mere positive disclosures does. Further, females who brag received low ratings of likability. Females, then, probably should employ positive disclosures because they will be perceived as just as competent as those who brag but significantly more likable.

There are a variety of tactics that self-promoters may use to help create credible claims concerning their competence. Three will be discussed here. First, self-promoters can have their accomplishments made known (perhaps by a third person, or when grades are posted, as in the case of Fitzjames) and then try to emphasize the role of natural ability while de-emphasizing the role of effort or motivation. This is what Fitzjames attempted.

Second, self-presentations can be made to appear credible and impressive by drawing attention to impediments that have been overcome. For example, Quattrone and Jones (1978) found that when actors learned they had auditioned successfully for the part of Scrooge in a production of *A Christmas Carol*, they went out of their way to point out that they had played other characters that were very different. The implication was that even though their experience was with an entirely different character, their natural acting ability made them quite versatile. You have probably heard fellow students make comments about how little sleep they got before an exam.

A third tactic is **self-handicapping,** described as an individual's attempt "to reduce a threat to esteem by actively seeking or creating inhibitory conditions that interfere with performance and thus provide a persuasive causal explanation for potential failure" (Shepperd and Arkin 1989, 101). In other words, self-handicappers sabotage their own performance. A typical example is the student who comes to class the day of an exam and says, "My friends and I went out last night and I haven't studied for this test at all."

On the surface, it may appear that self-handicapping would create an impression of incompetence, but actually it has the potential to create or maintain an impression of competence in two ways: (1) If self-handicappers fail, their competence is protected because people attribute the failure to the obstacle; and (2) if self-handicappers succeed, their natural ability is enhanced because they were able to overcome the obstacles.

SUPPLICATION

Communicators who attempt supplication base their self-presentation on the social norm that the strong are supposed to help the weak, and hence they attempt to create the impression of being weak or helpless. This style of self-presentation may not seem like it augments power, but the supplicant knows that many people who cannot be persuaded to act through reason alone can be moved to compassion through pity. Most people feel compelled to be supportive and encouraging when their friends are down. You may even have used this tactic yourself.

The potential danger associated with this tactic was illustrated in a *Los Angeles Times* article headlined "Playing for Sympathy." The article tells the story of a thirty-five-year-old corporate secretary named Anna. Shortly after her fiancé broke off their relationship, Anna told her friends she had terminal breast cancer. She shaved her head to resemble the side effects of chemotherapy, wore a wig, lost twenty pounds, and avoided any social activity that required physical energy— she did not want to appear too healthy. She eventually joined a support group for women with breast cancer and began counseling others on coping with the illness.

Her friends and co-workers embraced her with warmth and sympathy, she was unconditionally accepted in the support group, and she eventually developed a close group of friends at the hospital even though she had always had a difficult time making friends. When she sensed that her friends were growing complacent to her needs, Anna told them that her grandfather had been seriously injured in a fire (also a lie). Later people began to wonder why she never got any worse, and her physician was contacted. They discovered that none of the doctors she had mentioned had any record of her. The leaders of the support group confronted her, and she confessed that she had been lying.

The role had so overtaken her life that she had actually come to see herself as a cancer patient. She was eventually admitted to a psychiatric hospital to help with her recovery. Initially, her thoughts and actions were governed by the identity of being a cancer patient. However, she was released after four weeks and promised to stop lying. By then, however, she had lost her job, and many of her friends had abandoned her.

EXEMPLIFICATION

Exemplifiers attempt to project the image of integrity and moral worthiness. They appear to deserve our respect because they apparently do what we wish we could do or know we should do. The exemplifier's social power is based on the ability to instill respect, admiration, or even guilt in the minds of others. Prototypical exemplifiers include religious leaders who live a life of humility and self-sacrifice, political leaders who willingly endure hardship for the sake of their cause, and heroes who risk their lives for the good of others. However, co-workers or rivals in a sorority or fraternity may also try to be perceived as having high principles and to be of high moral worth. If you watch "The Simpsons," you will recognize Homer Simpson's neighbor, Mr. Flanders, as an exemplifier.

To maintain their standing, exemplifiers must be sincere and self-consistent. They must guard against being seen as self-righteous egotists or hypocrites. Consider the fate of televangelists Jim Bakker and Jimmy Swaggert: they lost much of their following when their extramarital indiscretions were revealed.

Gilbert and Jones (1986) attempted to determine the relative impact of moral failure on people's perceptions of an exemplifier compared with a moral pragmatist. Moral pragmatists do not maintain a stable, consistently applied set of moral principles; the decision regarding what is ethical varies from situation to situation. Exemplifiers, however, let it be known that they maintain high moral standards in all or most situations. The researchers gave participants self-presentation information about two hypothetical students (one exemplifier and one pragmatist) that the participants were led to believe participated in a similar study two years earlier.

The exemplifier made the following claims: he thought honesty was extremely important in both politics and in interpersonal relationships, he liked only jokes that had no potential to hurt anybody, he felt that rules should not be bent, and he thought about going into the Peace Corps because he liked helping people. The pragmatist made different claims: he liked practical jokes and had pulled some on friends, he thought that politics and interpersonal relationships should be managed with diplomacy because being truthful all the time was unrealistic, he thought rules were made to be bent, and he claimed he was going to become a lawyer or a public relations agent.

After hearing these two descriptions, students were led to believe that the hypothetical characters either cheated or resisted cheating on a test. The students were then asked to indicate their perceptions of the cheater and the resister. The results indicated that when they cheated, the pragmatist and the exemplifier were both disliked, but for different reasons. The pragmatist was disliked because he was seen as exploitive, manipulative, and devious, whereas the exemplifier was perceived as being a self-deceived hypocrite. In this study the negative consequences of the fallen exemplifier were less severe than those of the cheating pragmatist. This is because students saw the exemplifier's hypocrisy as pitiable but the pragmatist's deviousness as offensive.

Indirect Strategies of Self-presentation

So far we have talked about how communicators go about directly and actively trying to create public images. However, communicators may also rely, indirectly, on associations with others to bask in the glory or fame others have achieved, usually to bolster their self-image or public image. **Indirect self-presentation** management tactics are based on the idea that when seeking to enhance public image, a person can do so "not only by presenting information about his or her *own* traits, actions, and accomplishments" but also by presenting information "about the traits, actions, and accomplishments of his or her associates" (Cialdini, Finch, and De Nicholas 1990, 195).

Three indirect strategies investigated by Cialdini and associates have been labeled "basking in reflected glory," or BIRG (Cialdini et al. 1976), "blasting the opposition" (Cialdini et al. 1990; Richardson and Cialdini 1981), and "boosting" (Finch and Cialdini 1989). BIRG refers to the strategy of highlighting one's association with positively evaluated others (also see Cialdini and De Nicholas 1989), "blasting the opposition" is derogating one's enemies or rivals and "boosting" occurs when one elevates the assessment of an association, particularly a negative one.

An obvious attempt to impress others by indirect means.

Gary Larson, *The Far Side*. Copyright 1991 Farworks, Inc. Dist. by Universal Press Syndicate. Reprinted with permission. All rights reserved.

To test the concept of BIRG, Cialdini and associates (1976) studied the way students displayed their university affiliations by the clothing they wore after football games. They noticed that more students wore clothing with the university name or insignia on the Mondays after the football team won than when they lost or tied. In a follow-up study, Cialdini and colleagues tested how a threat to self-esteem influences one's tendency to use indirect tactics. Students were phoned and asked to participate in a survey designed to test their knowledge of the university. Half of the students were told that they did very poorly on the survey, and the other half were told that they did very well. They were then asked to describe the outcome of a university football game. Half of each of the success and failure groups were asked to describe a game the team had won, and the other half was asked to describe a game the team had lost.

The researchers found that when the team won, the students enhanced their association with the team by saying "we won." But when the team lost, the students denied their association with the team by saying "they lost." This shift in the use of pronouns occurred more in the failure group than in the success group. When esteem was reduced because of failure, students were motivated to bolster it by basking in the team's success.

Cialdini and co-workers (1990) also demonstrated that the basking effect is used to associate oneself with a university (or, by extension, a place of employment). The researchers hypothesized that students would enhance their self-esteem in two ways: by boosting their evaluations of the university they attended and by decreasing their evaluations of a rival university (blasting the opposition). Students were given a bogus test of their "latent creativity." Once again, half the students received a threat to their self-esteem by being told that they had failed, and the other half were told that they had done very well. Students were then asked to rate their university. The researchers found that not only did students who had been labeled low in latent creativity rate their own university significantly higher than those who had been told they rated high, but they also rated the rival university significantly lower than students who supposedly scored high on the creativity test.

This desire to boost one's associations also occurs when one's only target audience is oneself. Cialdini and colleagues (1990) gave students a story to read about Grigori Rasputin, the mad monk of Russia. Half of the students received a story that indicated that Rasputin's birthday was the same as their own; the other half received no information regarding Rasputin's birthday. Both versions of the story provided very negative descriptions of Rasputin. The students who received the matching-birthday stories thought they were the only ones who knew of the connection, yet they still rated him significantly less negatively than those who were given no birthday information. They boosted their evaluation of Rasputin based on the simple association of sharing a birthdate, even though nobody else supposedly knew the connection.

Self-promotion requires making one's accomplishments known to one's audience. The audience must also believe that the self-promoter possesses natural abilities and talents.

(Scianna/Magnum)

Nonverbal Communication and Self-presentation

Impressions are managed best if verbal statements and nonverbal behaviors are employed appropriately and jointly (see Chapter 4). Some nonverbal experts discuss impression management at length (see Burgoon, Buller, and Woodall 1989; Leathers 1992); Table 5-3 presents Leathers's summary of four general types of images: credibility/competence, likability, general interpersonal attractiveness, and dominance. The credibility/competence impression parallels the self-promotion

Table 5-3

NONVERBAL BEHAVIORS AND IMPRESSIONS

Credibility/Competence

1. Communicators who maintain a high level of eye contact with others (but not continuous eye contact) are perceived as more competent.
2. Vocal cues such as a relatively fast rate of speaking, substantial volume, and short, purposeful pauses are related to perceptions of increased competence.
3. Communicators who meet the personal appearance expectations of the persons with whom they interact will be judged to be more competent.
4. Communicators who speak general American dialect with a standard accent are viewed as more competent than those who do not.
5. Competence is negatively affected by looking down before responding to a question, characteristically downcast eyes, and a low level of eye contact.
6. Communicators whose verbal and nonverbal messages are inconsistent are viewed as less trustworthy than communicators whose multichannel messages are consistent.
7. Individuals who exhibit insincere smiles at inappropriate times will probably be viewed as less trustworthy than individuals who smile sincerely in context.
8. Communicators who exhibit behavioral "tension leakage" cues in the form of nonfluencies, shifty eyes, and lip-moistening will be judged to be less competent than those who do not.

Likability

1. Communicators who exhibit immediacy behaviors in the form of close interaction distances, a direct bodily orientation, forward leans, socially appropriate touching, in-context and sincere smiling, bodily relaxation, and open body positions are consistently perceived as more likable than communicators who do not exhibit such immediacy behaviors.
2. Communicators who signal interest and attentiveness via direct body and head orientations, direct eye contact, and smiling are typically viewed as more likable than communicators who do not similarly signal interest and attentiveness.
3. Communicators who dress in such a manner as to meet the dress expectations of those with whom they interact are better liked.
4. Impression managers should recognize that clothing that will make them appear likable (informal clothing) may also make them appear less credible or competent.

5. Sustained or direct eye contact and the maintenance of mutual eye gaze with the interaction partner are strongly correlated with positive judgments of likability.
6. Likability is positively associated with a speaking voice that is pleasant, relaxed, emotionally expressive, and friendly and sounds confident, dynamic, animated, and interested.
7. Nonverbal indicators of disliking, which reinforce the perception that the person exhibiting such behavioral indicators is unlikable, are unpleasant facial expressions, a relative absence of gestures, visual inattentiveness, closed body posture, and incongruent posture.

Interpersonal Attractiveness

1. Communicators whose nonverbal communicative behaviors seem to be spontaneous, disclosing, and uncensored are seen to be more interpersonally attractive.
2. Communicators who exhibit a high level of responsiveness via such nonverbal communicative behaviors as nodding, positive vocal reinforcement ("uh-huh"), forward lean, direct body orientation, and direct eye contact with their partner will be perceived as more interpersonally attractive than those who do not.
3. Nonverbally expressive communicators are viewed as more interpersonally attractive.
4. Communicators who exhibit emotional expressivity via facial animation, appropriate vocal volume, vocal warmth, smiling and laughing, and gestural and bodily animation are viewed as more interpersonally attractive.
5. Communicators who choose seating arrangements that provide for decreased interpersonal distance and increased capacity for visual contact with individuals with whom they interact are usually seen as more interpersonally attractive.
6. Communicators who exhibit a low frequency of nonverbal communicative behaviors and cues will be judged to be less interpersonally attractive.
7. Communicators who exhibit narrow voice pitch and volume range are often perceived to be uninterested.

Dominance

1. The eyes serve to define or reveal the distribution of power within social relationships.

(continued)

(continued from previous page)

2. Dominance is communicated strongly by staring and submissiveness by gaze avoidance; emotional states associated with gaze aversion include fear, guilt, shame, and social inferiority.
3. Communicators are perceived as increasingly dominant as their amount of eye contact increases.
4. Communicators become more dominant as their level of looking while speaking increases and their level of looking while listening decreases; that is, their visual dominance ratio increases.
5. Dominance is conveyed by controlling talk time, speaking in a loud voice, and frequently interrupting the interaction partner.
6. Communicators who use hesitations and hedges are perceived as less powerful than those who do not.
7. Nonverbal indicators of submissiveness include constricted and closed body postures, a limited range of movement, hunched body, downward-turned head, and bodily tension.
8. A soft voice with little volume communicates a lack of assertiveness.

Source: Adapted from Leathers 1992. Used with permission of the author.

image discussed in this chapter, and the likability impression and general interpersonal attractiveness image parallel the ingratiation image we have discussed. The behaviors that communicate dominance may be used by self-promoters (bragging and claiming to be better than others) or exemplifiers (when a person is more dedicated than we are); they can also be used during attempts to intimidate. By contrast, a person who employs supplication tactics would avoid the use of dominance gestures.

Chapter Summary

Self-presentation is one of the most important and pervasive goals we pursue through interpersonal communication. Self-presentation can be used to enhance our sense of self-esteem and to increase our confidence in other desired attributes. The way others see us determines how they respond to us and therefore governs the opportunities available to us. Certainly, people who are seen as hardworking and competent have different opportunities than those seen as lazy and incompetent. The impressions we create operate as deposits in a "power bank" that can be drawn on as needed. We examined five direct strategies: presenting oneself as likable, dangerous, competent, morally worthy, and helpless. Each of these images implies a different type of power relationship. The indirect tactics included basking in the reflected glory of another person, blasting one's opposition, and boosting one's current associations. Nonverbal cues are linked to the establishment of public images.

KEY TERMS

▼

strategic self-presentation (impression management)	illicit ingratiation
ingratiator	authentic ingratiation
intimidator	subjective probability of success
self-promoter	ingratiator's dilemma
exemplifier	perceived legitimacy
supplicator	opinion conformity
inclusiveness	affinity seeking
coherence	self-handicapping
indicators of attainment	indirect self-presentation

EXERCISES FOR FURTHER DISCUSSION

▼

1. Make a list of five main characters from movies or television shows that you have watched recently. Then write down the self-presentation style of the main character.
   a. Is the self-presentation style presented in a positive or negative way?
   b. Does the self-presentation style of the person allow him or her to gain love, money, or other types of rewards?
   c. Does the self-presentation style of the person result in conflict with others?
   d. What does the movie or television show tell us about this type of self-presentation?
2. Think of situations in which you or people you know have engaged in self-handicapping strategies. Were these strategies effective in protecting your sense of competence?
3. Identify your own style of self-presentation.
   a. Are you a self-promoter? ingratiator? intimidator? exemplifier? supplicator?
   b. Are you a blend of more than one style? If so, which ones?
   c. Why do you think you tend to use this style or these styles?
   d. Do you think that being male or female affects the style you use?
   e. Is your style similar to or different from that of your parents or siblings?

4. Think of a situation in which you would want to ingratiate yourself with someone (the parents of a person you are dating, an instructor, someone you would like to become friends with).
   a. What behaviors would you use to try to be ingratiating?
   b. Have you tried to be ingratiating in similar situations and failed? If so, what would you change if you could do it over again?
5. Think of each type of self-presentation behavior and consider whether, in your own experience, men and women can successfully use the same tactics.
   a. Are women perceived in the same way as men when they try to be self-promoting? ingratiating? intimidating? exemplifying? supplicating?
   b. If they are not perceived in the same way, why not?

SUGGESTED READING

IMPRESSION MANAGEMENT

Arkin, R. M., and Shepperd, J. A. 1990. Strategic self-presentation: An overview. In *The psychology of tactical communication*, M. J. Cody and M. L. McLaughlin, 175–193. Clevedon, England: Multilingual Matters. Arkin and Shepperd provide a detailed overview of the work on self-presentation, including historical notes and how work in this area has progressed over the decades.

Tedeschi, J. T., ed. 1981. *Impression management theory and social psychological research*. Orlando, Fla.: Academic Press. Although published over ten years ago, this volume continues to represent the single most important volume on the topic of impression management theory.

SELF-PRESENTATIONAL STRATEGIES

Jones, E. E., and Wortman, C. 1974. *Ingratiation: An attributional approach*. Morristown, N.J.: General Learning Press. Jones and Wortman look at four basic strategies designed to derive liking from others: praising or flattering others, conforming one's opinions to fit in with others, rendering favors for others, and self-bolstering (in which the communicator attempts to increase his or her status, competence, and so forth). The book details who uses the strategies on whom, and with what consequences.

Jones, E. E., and Pittman, T. S. 1982. Toward a general theory of strategic self-presentation. In J. M. Suls (Ed.), *Psychological perspectives on the self* (pp. 231–262). New Jersey: Lawrence Erlbaum. Jones and Pittman provide a thorough discussion of the five most fundamental strategies of self-presentation, including the competent communicator, the ingratiator (or likeable communicator), the intimidator, the exemplifier, and the supplicator.

INDIRECT METHODS OF PRESENTING THE SELF

Cialdini, R. B.; Finch, J. F.; and De Nicholas, M. E. 1990. Strategic self-presentation: The indirect route. In *The psychology of tactical communication*, ed. M. J. Cody and M. L. McLaughlin, 194–206. Clevedon, England: Multilingual Matters. Cialdini and his students review their work on indirect methods of presenting the self—including the work on "basking in reflected glory (BIRGing)," "blasting the opposition," and "boosting."

Finch, J. F. and Cialdini, R. B. 1989. Another indirect tactic of (self-)image management: Boosting. *Personality and Social Psychology Bulletin* 15:222–232. Finch and Cialdini report on two of their studies on "boosting," wherein an individual confronted with a personal connection to another, especially a negative other, elevates or "boosts" some aspect of the other.

NONVERBAL COMMUNICATION AND IMPRESSION MANAGEMENT

Burgoon, J. K; Buller, D. B.; and Woodall, W. G. 1989. *Nonverbal communication: The unspoken dialogue*. New York: Harper Collins. This book emphasizes the functions served by nonverbal communication, including the communication of intimacy, power, emotional expression, cultural differences, controlling interactions, and deception.

Leathers, D. G. 1992. *Successful nonverbal communication: Principles and applications*, 2d ed. New York: Macmillan. Leathers's treatment of nonverbal communication emphasizes the impression management function of creating and maintaining the communicator's public image. The book includes very good chapters on impression management, persuasion and interviewing, and other communicative goals.

REFERENCE LIST

Bell, R. A., and Daly, J. A. 1984. The affinity-seeking function of communication. *Communication Monographs* 51:91–115.

Bell, R. A.; Tremblay, S. W.; and Buerkel-Rothfuss, N. L. 1987. Interpersonal attraction as a communication accomplishment: Development of a measure of affinity-seeking competence. *Western Journal of Speech Communication* 51:1–18.

Burgoon, J. K.; Buller, D. B.; and Woodall, W. G. 1989. *Nonverbal communication: The unspoken dialogue*. New York: Harper Collins.

Cialdini, R. B.; Borden, R. J.; Thorne, A.; Walker, M. R.; Freeman, S.; and Sloan, L. R. 1976. Basking in reflected glory: Three (football) field studies. *Journal of Personality and Social Psychology* 34:366–375.

Cialdini, R. B., and De Nicholas, M. E. 1989. Self-presentation by association. *Journal of Personality and Social Psychology* 57:626–631.

134

Cialdini, R. B.; Finch, J. F.; and De Nicholas, M. E. 1990. Strategic self-presentation: The indirect route. In *The psychology of tactical communication*, ed. M. J. Cody and M. L. McLaughlin, 194–206. Clevedon, England: Multilingual Matters.

Felson, R. B. 1982. Impression management and the escalation of aggression and violence. *Social Psychology Quarterly* 45:245–254.

Finch, J. F., and Cialdini, R. B. 1989. Another indirect tactic of (self-)image management: Boosting. *Personality and Social Psychology Bulletin* 15:222–232.

Gergen, K. J. 1989. Warrenting voice. In *Texts of identity*, ed. J. Shotter and K. J. Gergen, 70–81. Newbury Park, Calif.: Sage.

Gilbert, D. T., and Jones, E. E. 1986. Exemplification: The self-presentation of moral character. *Journal of Personality* 54:591–615.

Godfrey, D. K.; Jones, E. E.; and Lord, C. G. 1986. Self-promotion is not ingratiating. *Journal of Personality and Social Psychology* 50:106–115.

Gollwitzer, P. M. 1986. Striving for specific identities: The social reality of self-symbolizing. In *Public and private self*, ed. R. F. Baumeister, 143–159. New York: Springer-Verlag.

Harris, L. M.; Gergen, K. J.; and Lannamann, J. W. 1986. Aggression rituals. *Communication Monographs* 53:252–265.

Jones, E. E. 1989. The framing of competence. *Personality and Social Psychology Bulletin* 15:477–492.

Jones, E. E., and Pittman, T. S. 1982. Toward a general theory of strategic self-presentation. In *Psychological perspectives on the self*, ed. J. M. Suls, 231–262. Hillsdale, N.J.: Erlbaum.

Jones, E. E., and Wortman, C. 1974. *Ingratiation: An attributional approach*. Morristown, N.J.: General Learning Press.

Leary, M. R., and Kowalski, R. M. 1990. Impression management: A literature review and two-component model. *Psychological Bulletin* 107:34–47.

Leathers, D. G. 1992. *Successful nonverbal communication: Principles and applications*, 2d ed. New York: Macmillan.

McCormack, M. H. 1984. *What they don't teach you at the Harvard Business School*. New York: Bantam Books.

McLaughlin, M. L.; Louden, A. D.; Cashion, J. L.; Altendorf, D. M.; Baaske, K. T.; and Smith, S. W. 1985. Conversational planning and self-serving utterances: The manipulation of topical and functional structures in dyadic interaction. *Journal of Language and Social Psychology* 4:233–251.

Miller, L. C.; Cooke, L. L.; Tsang, J.; and Morgan, F. 1992. Should I brag? Nature and impact of positive and boastful disclosures for women and men. *Human Communication Research* 18:364–399.

Norman, N. M., and Tedeschi, J. T. 1989. Self-presentation, reasoned action, and adolescents' decisions to smoke cigarettes. *Journal of Applied Social Psychology* 19:543–558.

Potter, S. 1962. *Threeupmanship*. Austin, Texas: Holt, Rinehart and Winston.

Quattrone, G., and Jones, E. E. 1978. Selective self-disclosure with and without correspondent performance. *Journal of Experimental Social Psychology* 14:511–526.

Richardson, K. D., and Cialdini, R. B. 1981. Basking and blasting: Tactics of indirect self-presentation. In *Impression management theory and social psychological research*, ed. J. T. Tedeschi, 41–53. Orlando, Fla.: Academic Press.

Schlenker, B. R. 1986. Self-identification: Toward an integration of the private and public self. In *Public and private self*, ed. R. F. Baumeister, 21–62. New York: Springer-Verlag.

Shepperd, J. A., and Arkin, R. M. 1989. Determinants of self-handicapping: Task importance and the importance of preexisting handicaps on self-generated handicaps. *Personality and Social Psychological Bulletin* 15:101–112.

Toch, H. 1969. *Violent men: An inquiry into the psychology of violence*. Hawthorne, N.Y.: Aldine.

CHAPTER 6

DEFENDING THE SELF

One sunny spring day a patrolman in Indiana saw a driver of a station wagon speeding and driving erratically. The officer turned on his siren and flashers and pulled the driver over. Later the officer said, as he examined the driver's license, "Sir, is there some problem?"

"Well, officer, I know you think I broke the law, and I did. But I didn't mean to! You see, I am allergic to bee stings, and there was a bee in the car (the driver at this time showed the officer a Medic Alert tag that indicated he was allergic to bee stings). At first I tried to roll down the windows and speed up to get it out of the car. Finally, I killed it with this newspaper." (The driver then displayed a folded-over newspaper on the passenger's seat and pointed to a dead bee on the dashboard.)

"I usually don't do things like this," he continued (referring to breaking the law), "but if I got stung way out here miles from a hospital or anything, I would get deathly ill. . . ."

The officer was just about to believe the man's story and let him go with only a verbal warning when he stopped to look at the dead bee. "This is odd, sir. But it seems that this bee isn't smashed at all. It looks dried out." The man then confessed that it was all a hoax. He kept a dead bee in a small vial in his glove compartment, and he'd pull out the bee and the newspaper props whenever he needed a good excuse to avoid a ticket. He had used this ruse many times in the past. However, it took an observant officer to see through the deception.

This chapter focuses on how we "defend" ourselves, or defend a particular public view of ourselves, when we have engaged in actions others find questionable. When we are accused of doing something wrong (like speeding, driving erratically), we frequently give an explanation for why the behavior occurred. When communicating these explanations we offer an *account* for our actions. Because the driver in our story didn't want to get any more tickets, he had devised a plan to convince police that he was not a person who routinely exceeded the speed limit (which was not the truth). He wanted the officer to believe that the bee (and the threat of being stung) caused his poor driving and that this single episode of violating the law was a one-time fluke. Police officers are more likely to forgive a victim of circumstances beyond human control. Accounts are commonly used to manage people's perceptions of our behavior and of whether we are responsible for our actions or are victims of external causes.

Police officers are familiar with the types of accounts people use when accused of questionable behavior, such as speeding.

(Gary S. Weber/Photo Researchers)

Chapter 5 focused on individuals' attempts to create and maintain a public image. We now focus on individuals' use of communication to escape responsibility for questionable behavior. Accounts are important because they are used to achieve several fundamental interpersonal goals. For example, we use apologies and excuses to repair relationships. We apologize to accept blame and ask for forgiveness. We use excuses to avoid being held personally responsible for an action.

What Are Accounts?

An **account** is "a linguistic device employed whenever an action is subjected to valuative inquiry" (Scott and Lyman 1968, 171). "Valuative inquiry" is a request for an explanation of either an inappropriate or unexpected behavior ("Why were you flirting with Pat?") or a failure to engage in an appropriate or expected behavior ("Why didn't you pay the phone bill on time?"). Such a request usually comes when one individual realizes that some failure event has occurred and wants to hear an explanation for it.

Scott and Lyman (1968) drafted a set of verbal statements that they considered to be a typology of accounts, and scholars relied on this typology for many years. However, Schonbach (1980) argued that the original list of accounts missed a number of important types of accounts that people use every day. We will present both typologies.

TYPES OF ACCOUNTS

The two most common forms of accounts are **excuses** and **justifications** (see Table 6-1). When using an excuse, the communicator admits that the act in question occurred, but claims not to be fully responsible for it. The *appeal to accident* is one of the most common forms of an excuse; it includes such claims as the dog ate the homework, the traffic was backed up, and the tire was flat.

An *appeal to biological drives* generally deals with an appeal to fate; men are men, women are women, boys will be boys, and so on. In the movie *Urban Cowboy*, an ex-convict is caught being unfaithful and claims, "You can't expect a cowboy to love just one woman," meaning that as a cowboy, he believed that he should not be blamed personally for his act. It is a cowboy's fate, he believed, to be unfaithful, and it cannot be controlled. When employing the *appeal to defeasibility*, the accounter claims that he or she did not have full knowledge about an action and its consequences and therefore should not be held responsible for what occurred. For instance, a teenage boy teases his sister about her boyfriend, and she begins to cry. When asked why he behaved so cruelly, the boy confesses that he didn't know the two had argued and separated (and hence that he should not be blamed or considered cruel). Cases of *scapegoating* are fairly common ("But my secretary told me this was the correct form"). In fact, the first excuse in recorded history may have been scapegoating: Adam blamed Eve for their eating from the forbidden tree.

When using a **justification,** the accounter accepts responsibility for the act in question but denies that it was harmful or tries to claim that there were actually positive consequences. When using a *denial of injury*, the accounter admits that an action occurred and that he or she was responsible for it, but because no harm came from it, no penalty should be assessed; for instance, "Yes, we took the car and stayed out last night, but nothing happened. Everybody's OK." In a *denial of victim*, the accounter argues that the person who was hurt isn't worthy of concern: "Who cares? She would have ripped me off if she could have."

When using an *appeal to loyalty*, the accounter asserts that loyalty to a group or a friend is more important than the rules that were violated. Some drivers do in fact claim that being late for a date is the reason why they are speeding, and police usually ticket such drivers. The claim that being on time for a date is a more important loyalty than obeying the speed laws is a poor communication strategy.

When using a *self-fulfillment* message, the accounter accepts responsibility for the act but claims that there was value to the act—growth, maturity, or self-fulfill-

Table 6-1

TYPES OF ACCOUNTS

Accounts	Examples
Excuses	
Appeal to accidents	The tire was flat when I went out to the driveway this morning.
	A truck carrying a load of fruit jackknifed on the freeway this morning, and two lanes were closed for hours.
Biological drives, fatalism	Boys will be boys.
	That's just the way people are.
Appeal to defeasibility	I didn't *intend* to burn rubber like that.
	I knew they were unhappy, but I had no idea that things had become so miserable.
Scapegoating	Satan made me do it.
	The dog ate my science project.
Justifications	
Denial of injury, minimization of harm	Oh, Mom! Nothing happened!
	Yeah, I did it. But it was no big deal.
Denial of victim	Who cares about a Gypsy palm reader?
	So what if he got hurt? Tourists usually cause their own trouble anyway.
Appeal to loyalties	I was speeding because I am late for work.
	I engaged in burglary in order to gain information helpful to my political candidate.
Self-fulfillment	Yes, I went bungee jumping. I wanted to prove to myself I could do it.
	Good LSD is great. You see everything so much clearer afterward.
Condemnation of the condemners	But officer, I was just flowing with traffic. Everyone else was doing seventy.
	Everybody cheats a little on their tax forms.
Sad tale	I am working two part-time jobs and taking two courses. My boyfriend and I just had a fight, and I just can't concentrate on a test right now.
	When you are from the streets like me, you learn to cut corners in order to get ahead.

Source: Adapted from Scott and Lyman 1968.

ment. Some drug users justify the use of LSD as expanding the mind. Some people may say that they wanted to prove something to themselves by bungee-jumping or skydiving. The *condemnation of the condemner* justification involves the claim that since others break the same rules, the accounter shouldn't be personally repri-manded; everyone cheats on tax forms, drives a little over the speed limit, and so on. In the use of a *sad tale*, the accounter claims that highlights of a dismal past can be used to explain current behaviors. Criminals employ the sad tale (unhappy child-hood, deprivation, etc.) to justify a life of crime.

AN EXPANDED TYPOLOGY OF ACCOUNTS

Schonbach (1980) added two categories to the taxonomy of accounts (see Table 6-2): *concessions* and *refusals*. In a **concession,** the accounter simply confesses or admits to the act in question. Some concessions are nothing more than admissions of one's guilt, but other forms of concessions contain any of several elements of **apologies.** Schonbach includes some elements of apologies in the higher levels of concessions (items 3.0 through 4.2 under "Concessions" in Table 6-2). Schlenker (1980) simi-larly noted five elements of a "full apology": (1) an expression of guilt, remorse, or embarrassment; (2) clarification that one recognizes what the appropriate conduct should have been and an expression of acknowledgment that negative sanctions ap-ply for having committed the failure event; (3) rejection of the inappropriate con-duct and disparagement of the "bad" self that misbehaved; (4) acknowledgment of the appropriate conduct and a promise to behave accordingly in the future; and (5) penance, restitution, or an offer to compensate the victim or victims.

The **refusal** category includes denying that the questionable act occurred or denying responsibility. Refusals can be divided into several relevant types (see Table 6-2). A person can prove innocence by using logical argument, physical evidence, or other means. Second, a person can refuse to offer an account by challenging the au-thority of the person asking for one: "We broke up months ago! I don't have to ex-plain to you what I do on weekends!" A third variation on refusals is to reject the definition of an offense—the accounter admits that the act took place but claims that it is wrong to label it an "offense": "Yes, I had lunch with my ex, but it was just a lunch. There is nothing wrong with having lunch!"

THE FUNCTIONS SERVED BY ACCOUNTS

Each type of account serves a specific function. By definition, an excuse attempts to exonerate the accounter of being held responsible for an offense, whereas a justification serves the function of making the action seem less negative (or even positive). When using a concession, the accounter accepts responsibility for the act and its consequences and claims, if appropriate forms of an apology are used, not to engage in the act again or to make restitution. In a refusal, however, the accounter asserts (or proves) innocence.

Table 6-2
SCHONBACH'S EXPANDED TYPOLOGY OF ACCOUNTS

Concessions

1.0	Explicit acknowledgment of own responsibility or guilt
1.1	Full confession of guilt, without reservations
1.2	Partial confession of guilt, with reservations
2.0	Explicit abstention from excuse or justification; concession of inappropriateness of excuses or justification in the present case
3.0	Expression of regret concerning the failure event (commission or omission)
3.1	Expression of regret concerning the consequences of the failure event
4.0	Restitution or compensation
4.1	Appeal to restitutions or compensations already performed
4.2	Offer of restitutions or compensations

Excuses

1.0	Appeal to own human shortcomings
1.1	Appeal to insufficient knowledge or skill
1.2	Appeal to will impairment
2.0	Reasons for the appeal to own shortcomings
2.1	Appeal to biological factors, such as arousal
2.2	Appeal to illness, addiction, drunkenness
2.3	Appeal to one's own negative past
2.4	Appeal to provocations by other persons
2.5	Appeal to duress by powerful agents
2.6	Appeal to loyalties
2.7	Appeal to the specific external circumstances of the situation
3.0	Appeal to own effort and care before and during the failure event
4.0	Appeal to shortcomings or misdeeds of other persons as frame of reference for the evaluation (hence a mild judgment is appropriate)
4.1	Appeal to shortcomings or misdeeds of the accuser as frame of reference for the evaluation of the failure event (hence a mild judgment is appropriate)
5.0	Appeal to participation of other persons in the failure event
5.1	Appeal to participation of the accuser in the failure event

Justifications

1.0 Denial of damage
2.0 Minimization of damage
2.1 Minimization of damage in view of the circumstances that provoked the failure event
2.2 Appeal to the positive consequences of the failure event
3.0 Appeal to the role of the victim
3.1 Justification of damage with qualities of the victim
3.2 Justification of damage with acts of the victim
4.0 Appeal to the right of self-fulfillment
4.1 Appeal to the right of self-fulfillment in view of one's own negative past
5.0 Appeal to loyalties
6.0 Appeal to positive intentions
7.0 Appeal to shortcomings or misdeeds of other persons as frame of reference for evaluation of the failure event (account giver's moderation should be acknowledged)
7.1 Appeal to shortcomings or misdeeds of the accuser as frame of reference for evaluation of the failure event (account giver's moderation should be acknowledged)

Refusals

1.0 Claiming that the failure event simply did not occur
2.0 Explicit refusal of a confession of guilt
3.0 Unrestricted attribution of guilt to other persons
3.1 Unrestricted attribution of guilt to the accuser
4.0 Denial of the right of reproach
4.1 Denial of the right of reproach on the basis of own identity or role in relation to the accuser
4.2 Denial of the right of reproach in view of the negative qualities or deeds of the accuser
5.0 Referral to other sources of information
6.0 Evasions or mystifications

Source: Adapted from Schonbach 1980. Reprinted by permission of John Wiley and Sons, Ltd. and the author.

144

In Chapter 5 we emphasized the importance of maintaining a positive image. Snyder and Higgins (1990) argue that there are two dimensions on which we are appraised (see Figure 6-1). The "enhancing processes" reflects the process in which we attempt to link ourselves to positive actions and behaviors. The "protective processes" involve either an attempt on our part to make a negative act appear to be less negative or to make it seem that we are not really linked to the act. The first dimension involves the perceived *linkage* of the accounter to a particular act or outcome (e.g., failing to make a complete stop at a stop sign). The accounter may have no link to the act in question (he believed that he did in fact come to a complete stop), and the accounter would probably use a refusal. Otherwise, the accounter may be fully or only partially linked to the act in question (he did in fact intend to hurry through the intersection, or his foot slipped off the brake pedal). An excuse serves the function of reducing the link or association between the accounter and the questionable act.

The second dimension is a *valence* dimension. We normally do not want to be associated with negative acts, so we naturally attempt to make questionable acts appear to be less negative (or even positive). To do this, we use justifications. Further, we use apologies to imply that we were bad only *temporarily*.

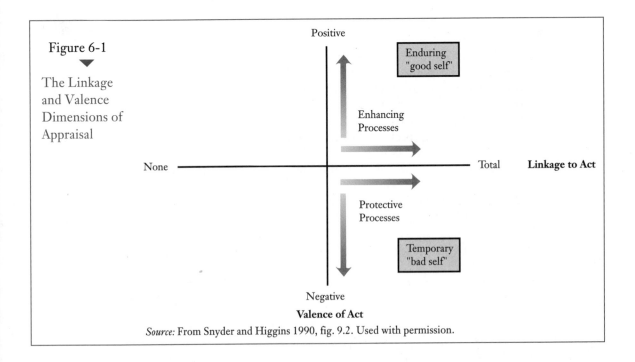

Figure 6-1

The Linkage and Valence Dimensions of Appraisal

Source: From Snyder and Higgins 1990, fig. 9.2. Used with permission.

In sum, excuses operate directly on the linkage dimension by making it appear that we are less directly or intentionally related to negative acts. A refusal operates to eliminate any link between ourselves and the act. A justification attempts to reduce the negativity of the act, and a concession (coupled with forms of an apology) places us temporarily in the role of the "bad self."

Goals Achieved through the Communication of Accounts

Accounts are used to achieve the general goal of defending the self. Accounts also are communicated to satisfy particular goals—to repair relationships, to control emotions, to avoid punishments, to create impressions, and to manage or avoid conflict. The following four sections each focus on a different goal pursued by communicators when employing accounts.

REPAIRING RELATIONSHIPS

Apologies and excuses are more likely to be perceived as polite, preferable, and effective than justifications and refusals. The reasoning is simple. When we ask for an account from someone, we prefer to hear an admission of guilt coupled with some form of apology. An apology containing some of the elements just listed (promise of restitution, expression of remorse, etc.) will be perceived as more polite, more preferred, and more useful than other accounts in solving disputes.

An excuse is the second most polite response because the accounter communicates a lack of intention to behave in an offensive manner. Justifications come third in politeness, preference, or usefulness. An accounter who justifies an offense is trying to show that there was some good reason for the offense, but often we don't like to hear this. The driver who justifies speeding by citing lateness for work, for example, is offering an account that police officers prefer not to hear. Refusals are the least preferred type of account to receive. No one likes to be challenged, proved wrong, or contradicted on matters of ethics.

Holtgraves (1989) demonstrated that apologies and excuses are preferable and more helpful than justifications (he did not study refusals). Students read the following scenario:

> James and Paul have known each other for several years and are good friends. They recently made plans to attend a concert together in a nearby city. On the night of the concert, James is supposed to pick up Paul and drive them to the concert. However, James arrives an hour and a half late, too late to go to the concert. When James arrives, Paul confronts him and tells him how upset he is.

They then read one of the following accounts offered by James:

Full-blown apology: "I apologize for making us miss the concert. It was a terrible thing to do, and I'm very sorry. It won't happen again. Please forgive me. Is there anything I can do to make it up to you?"

Apology: "I apologize for making us miss the concert."

Regret: "I'm sorry for making us miss the concert."

Regret plus excuse: "I'm sorry for making us miss the concert. I got so busy at work I forgot all about the concert."

Excuse: "I got so busy at work I forgot all about the concert."

Regret plus justification: "I'm sorry for making us miss the concert, but it's not that big a deal; it wasn't going to be that good a concert anyway."

Justification: "It's not that big a deal; it wasn't going to be that good a concert anyway."

After reading the scenario and one of the accounts, Holtgraves had the students complete a questionnaire asking them to rate the various accounts in terms of how satisfied the hearer would be with the account, how difficult it would be for the speaker to say the account, how helpful the account would be in solving the conflict, and how likely it is that the speaker would use the account.

Table 6-3 presents the students' perceptions. Justifications were rated as the least satisfying, followed in order by the regret plus justification and the excuse accounts. The full-blown apology was rated highest in hearers' satisfaction. Similarly, the justification, regret plus justification, and excuse were rated low in helping solve the conflict, followed by regret only, which was rater lower in helpfulness than regret plus excuse. The apology and full-blown apology were rated highest in helpfulness. Generally speaking, apologies were rated as more polite, preferred, and helpful, whereas justifications received low ratings on usefulness in repairing relationships.

Holtgraves' is not the only study to demonstrate that apologies and excuses are effective in repairing relationships. Cody and McLaughlin (1990) review a number of studies showing that apologies help reduce both the punishments that the accounter might receive and the anger that the victim might experience. Research also indicates that children know at quite a young age that apologies are required to resolve disputes when the rights of others are violated (Darby and Schlenker 1982; Schlenker and Darby 1981). Further, women are more likely to employ fuller apologies than men (Gonzales et al. 1990; Schonbach 1990).

COPING WITH EMBARRASSMENT

Few of us have escaped the situation of having spilled something at dinner, forgotten to bring something for a party, misplaced a checkbook, or the like. Metts and Cupach (1989) identify four common types of embarrassing situations:

Table 6-3

REACTIONS TO VARIOUS TYPES OF ACCOUNTS

Type of Account	Satisfaction	Difficulty	Helpfulness	Likelihood
Justification	1.18	2.85	1.33	3.44
Regret plus justification	1.68	3.00	2.03	3.38
Excuse	2.91	2.38	2.64	4.51
Regret plus excuse	3.95	3.09	3.96	4.63
Regret	3.53	3.18	3.54	4.77
Apology	3.91	3.59	4.12	4.72
Compensation	5.53	4.78	5.26	4.19

Note: Ratings were made on a 7-point scale. The higher the number, the higher the level of satisfaction, difficulty, helpfulness, or likelihood of use.
Source: Adapted from Holtgraves 1989. Copyright © 1989 by T. Holtgraves.

1. *Faux pas:* acts that are intentionally performed but prove to be inappropriate when the correct interpretation of the situation becomes clear (Example: Wearing informal attire to a formal function).

2. *Mistakes:* intentional acts that would be appropriate to the situation but are not because they are incorrectly or incompletely executed (Example: Attempting to purchase items at a department store using an expired credit card and having no checks to complete the transaction).

3. *Accidents:* unintentional acts that are inappropriate to the situation (Examples: Falling, tripping, spilling, tearing one's clothes).

4. *Recipient situations:* failure events that arise for the embarrassed person because of the behavior of others; the embarrassed person is made to feel conspicuous by the unexpected positive or negative attention of others or the unexpected intrusion of another person into the embarrassed person's personal or private activity (Examples: Being criticized in class, receiving excessive praise in public, having one's parents appear unexpectedly while one is only partly clothed in the living room with a friend).

We use accounts to reduce our feelings of embarrassment in situations such as these. We pursue goals when confronted by embarrassment: reducing our feelings of embarrassment, shame, and so on and controlling perceptions of our responsibility for the action.

Six-year-old Calvin resorts to scapegoating so that he won't be responsible for his actions.

Here, he struggles with the realization that he should apologize to Susie, but apologizing is hard to do.

Susie at first accepts Calvin's "perfunctory apology" and then realizes that she'd rather hear a "full blown" one.

Metts and Cupach (1989; Cupach and Metts 1990) were interested in what friends and roommates say to each other when they are embarrassed. Table 6-4 presents a summary of the types of messages used when they are embarrassed (top portion) and when they try to help others cope with embarrassment (bottom portion).

Table 6-4

METHODS FOR COPING WITH EMBARRASSMENT

Tactics for Coping with Embarrassment

Tactics	*Definition and Example*
Simple apology	Clichéd statements of regret and requests for pardon: "I'm sorry," "Please excuse me," "Please forgive me."
Excuse	Acknowledgment of a questionable act while claiming minimal or no responsibility: "I've had so much on my mind with exams and papers."
Justification	Acknowledgment of responsibility for an act while claiming minimal, no, or positive consequences: "Mom, this is not what it seems."
Humor	Laughter and joking. After falling down a flight of stairs in full skirt and high heels: "Hi, I just thought I'd drop in."
Remediation	Correcting the problem: Clean up spill, collect dropped packages, clean a stain.
Escape	Physically retreating from the scene.
Avoidance	Ignoring the problem: "Having spilled beer on my pants, I just smiled and acted like it didn't bother me."
Aggression	Physically or verbally attacking another person as retaliation.

Tactics Available to Others When Helping Persons Cope with Embarrassment

Tactics	*Definition and Example*
Simple apology	Expressions of regret offered by observers who feel responsible for the embarrassment of another: "I'm sorry" offered by a person who bumped a drink tray, causing the respondent's embarrassing incident.
Excuse	Acknowledgment of an untoward act but minimization of the embarrassed person's responsibility for its occurrence. When an embarrassed person fell while sweeping a floor at work, her boss offered: "The broom handle is rotten."

(continued)

(continued from previous page)

Tactics	Definition and Example
Justification	Acknowledgment of an untoward act but minimization of the offensiveness of the act: When an embarrassed person spilled gum and candy while restocking, a co-worker said: "Don't worry about it—it's just gum, not glassware."
Humor	Laughing along with the embarrassed person or making jokes. When a manager of a fast-food restaurant is sprayed with strawberry milkshake because the embarrassed person did not put a lid on the blender, she said: "Luckily, I look good in pink."
Remediation	Helping clean up messes, spills, dropped packages, and so on.
Avoidance	Acting as though no infraction has occurred. When an embarrassed person tripped in church after receiving communion, her family made room for her in the pew as if nothing had happened.
Empathy	Assuring the embarrassed person that his or her predicament or behavior is not unique and happens to others. When an embarrassed person found that he had been sitting in the wrong class for ten minutes, a classmate said: "The same thing happened to me last semester."
Support	Verbal and nonverbal assurances of continued positive regard for the embarrassed person. When the embarrassed person tripped in church, her mother patted her leg when she returned to her seat.

Source: Adapted from Metts and Cupach 1989. Copyright by the Speech Communication Association. Reprinted by permission of the publisher and authors.

Tactics for coping with embarrassment serve two purposes: to avoid a negative evaluation by others and to reduce the actual feelings of being embarrassed. The first of these goals is achieved primarily through the use of accounts. Apologies are used to accept responsibility and express regret over the occurrence of the failure event, excuses attempt to make it appear that the embarrassed person is not really to blame for the event, and justifications attempt to minimize the apparent harm involved in the event. Cupach and Metts also note that effective ways to cope with embarrassment entail sequences of tactics, usually involving apologies and humor. Common sequences include apology, remediation; apology, escape, remediation; humor, apology; humor, excuse; and humor, escape, remediation.

Although accounts (and humor) are critically important in our attempts to avoid a negative evaluation when we engage in embarrassing actions, accounts are not particularly useful in actually reducing our feelings of embarrassment. According to Cupach and Metts (1990), the actions of both the embarrassed person and the other are important for effectively handling embarrassment. Two conclusions can be cited. First, only a few of the tactics used by the embarrassed person were considered effective in reducing embarrassment. Second, many of the tactics used by the other person are effective in helping reduce the embarrassed person's uncomfortable feelings. We depend on our friends to help us overcome the emotional aspects of embarrassment.

Only humor, remediation, and excuses were rated as effective by the embarrassed party for reducing felt embarrassment—and humor was most effective. Escape from the scene was considered ineffective. By contrast, others can help the embarrassed person reduce feelings of discomfort by using nearly all of the tactics listed in the lower portion of Table 6-4. Remediation (helping) was most effective, followed by empathy, justification, support, avoidance, and humor.

What these studies show is that we can use accounts (and humor) effectively to reduce the likelihood that others will evaluate us negatively. However, our feelings of embarrassment can linger on after we use tactics such as apology plus remediation

Effective ways of coping with embarrassment include excuses, apologies, and humor.

(Alan Carey/The Image Works)

or humor plus remediation. The other person can help us feel better by using remediation, sympathy, empathy, justification, humor, and avoiding mention of our predicament.

IMPRESSION MANAGEMENT

An A student with perfect attendance who wrote a wonderful paper, topped the grading curve on the midterm, and holds a major scholarship enters the professor's office and says: "Sir, you won't believe it, but when I cleaned off my desk last weekend, I accidentally threw away my list of references and notes concerning my second paper. The paper won't be ready on time."

A C- student with a shoddy attendance record who turned in a poorly written paper (late), blaming a computer breakdown, and who had to make up a midterm because his car broke down on the day the test was scheduled enters the professor's office and says: "Sir, you won't believe it, but when I cleaned off my desk last weekend, I accidentally threw away my list of references and notes concerning my second paper. The paper won't be ready on time."

What is your impression of these two students? Who is more competent? dedicated? likable? Who is pathetic and helpless? Would you, as the professor, forgive each student equally? Would you lecture both of them on being more responsible? Would you penalize both papers for being late?

Two interrelated issues are important when we consider the relationship between accounts and impressions: The account a person uses has an impact on our impressions of that person, and our impression of an accounter has an impact on the credibility of an account the next time that person communicates one. The most obvious illustration of this is when a series of mistakes befalls a person, who always uses an excuse to deny personal responsibility: "I am late because my alarm didn't go off," "My car wouldn't start," "I can't stay because I misplaced my wallet and have to go find it or go to the lost and found," and so on.

An excuse may be believable for any one mistake. Why? Because an accident, by definition, could befall anyone at any time, and one cannot always control external circumstances. However, it is unusual and suspicious if a series of mistakes and errors occurs over time and the person involved persists in blaming fate, accidents, or others. Ultimately, we tell such communicators to take responsibility for their lives, to plan ahead and budget their time: buy a new alarm clock, leave for work earlier, don't wait until the last minute to cram for the test, join the car pool, always check the antifreeze, and so forth. Though some events occur without warning and cannot be controlled by anyone, hundreds of questionable acts occur every day that could have been prevented or avoided by planning ahead.

Communicators who rely too heavily on excuses will ultimately be perceived as incompetent, helpless, and irresponsible. Indeed, the **accounter's dilemma** relates to a basic problem: We would like to argue that we were not responsible for a questionable action by locating the cause external to ourselves (bad traffic, a faulty computer printer), but in doing so we admit to having little control over our surroundings. Too great a reliance on excuses will result in a tarnished public image. Thus an excuse may result in our being forgiven for a specific questionable act, but reliance on excuses does not create an image of competence.

By contrast, justifiers are perceived as more competent than excuse givers. Why? When we use a justification, we are admitting responsibility for an action but claiming that the action wasn't actually negative (or that the consequences were positive). As justifiers, then, we argue that we know what we are doing; that we are responsible, not helpless; and that we are competently working on certain goals. Although it is true that our goals may be different from those of the person asking for an account and that we may have a conflict over goals, as justifiers we are nonetheless still responsible and competent at pursuing our particular goals (even if they involve questionable behaviors).

One study that examined the impressions we make of different types of accounters had students read a scenario in which an employee new to a work unit failed to do a computer check on financial records at the close of the workday. The former supervisor, who had been training the new employee, noticed this error and asked why the "standard error detection" runs had not been done. The students then read one of nine versions of accounts:

Apologies

Full-blown apology: "Yes, I know I made an error. I'm terribly sorry about this. I'm solving it right now before I go home. I'll be more careful in the future!"

Perfunctory apology: "Yes, I know I made an error. I'm sorry."

Excuses

Appeal to accident: "The computer was down nearly all day. I couldn't finish the work today."

Denial of intent: "I didn't intend to be sloppy. I have been suffering with this stomach flu that has been going around. It is slowing me down and making me groggy."

Justifications

Minimizing harm: "Yes, there was an error. I was using some new software that presumably will do a faster job than our old software. It was faster, but obviously made at least one error."

Higher loyalty or involvement: "One of our major clients called in today with a crisis, and I spent well over an hour trying to trace down the paper trail to resolve it. Given my limited time, I decided it was more important to handle the emergency than to run the standard tests on schedule."

Refusals

Denial of offense: "No, you must have some other day-end statement, or perhaps you are reading it wrong. There is no error in my accounts for today."

Challenge to authority: "You are no longer my supervisor and no longer associated with this unit. I do not have to explain myself to you. I handle things here now."

Logical proof: "Yes, I saw that statement. I ran the checks. As you can tell from these printouts, the error does not originate from this office."

Students then rated their impressions of the accounter. Table 6-5 presents the results of whether the accounter was perceived as high, average, or low in ratings of the five common self-presentational styles discussed in Chapter 5.

Table 6-5

ACCOUNTS AND THE IMPRESSIONS THEY CONVEY

Accounts	Impression Styles (Image Desired)				
	Intimidation (strong, ruthless)	*Ingratiation (likable)*	*Supplication (helpless)*	*Exemplification (dedicated)*	*Self-promotion (competent)*
Apologies					
Full-blown	L	H*	A	H*	H*
Perfunctory	L*	H	H	A	L*
Excuses					
Accident	A	A	H*	A	L
Denial of intent	A	A	H	A	L
Justifications					
Minimizing harm	L	A	L	H	H
Higher loyalty	L	H	L	H	H
Refusals					
Denial of offense	H	L	L*	L	A
Challenge	H*	L*	L	L*	A
Logical proof	L	A	L	H	H

Note. Ratings: L = low; A = average; H = high.
* indicates lowest or highest rating for that particular style.
Source: Adapted from Braaten, Cody, and Bell–De Tiene 1993.

How are accounts related to our public images? Not surprisingly, a person who communicated a full-blown apology was rated as likable, dedicated, competent, and low on intimidation. The accounter who relied on a mere perfunctory apology, however, was rated as incompetent, helpless, weak (lowest in intimidation) but still likable. Accounters who relied on excuses were perceived as helpless and incompetent and were generally undistinguished on other perceptions. Accounters who relied on justifications were perceived as highly dedicated and competent and were rated low in intimidation and supplication—they were seen as neither ruthless nor helpless. Further, the higher loyalty message was especially effective; accounters who used it were perceived as highly likable, as well as highly dedicated and competent.

Accounters who challenged the authority of others were perceived as intimidating, unlikable, and lacking in dedication, as were accounters who denied their offense. Although such tactics might be viewed negatively by most of us, we should recognize that intimidators are probably not interested in resolving conflicts or in repairing relationships. Intimidators use these tactics to take control of their work area and to show off to others who possess authority and power. Logical proofs, however, operated much differently: people who proved their innocence by displaying physical evidence were perceived as dedicated and competent.

Earlier we had concluded that apologies and excuses were effective in repairing relationships when people communicated accounts for a single act (failing to pick up a friend for a concert). An accounter who focused on creating a public image of dedication and competence, however, should not rely on excuses. Rather, the perceptions of dedication and competence are best created and maintained when accounters employ full-blown apologies, justifications, and logical proofs.

A CASE STUDY: TRAFFIC COURT

We often have to communicate accounts to bureaucrats, and apologies and excuses may not be the most effective tactics in these more formal contexts. A study conducted in traffic court demonstrated this nicely. Cody and McLaughlin (1988) studied the accounts 375 drivers communicated in traffic court. Seventy-four of the drivers appeared in court and used concessions—admissions of guilt with or without apologies. In this particular setting, using an apology for engaging in a moving violation (speeding, running a red light) carried no weight. Ninety-seven percent of the drivers who used concessions or apologies were simply penalized and asked to pay the whole fine. Did any drivers find this type of account helpful? Yes. Nineteen of the seventy-four drivers who used concessions asked for an alternative and cost-free punishment, attendance at traffic school. They were allowed to attend traffic school if they were apologetic, were guilty of relatively minor offenses, and had good driving records.

Excuses were the most popular type of argument made in traffic court—over a third of the drivers used an excuse. However, only 25 percent of the excuse givers were actually effective in avoiding penalties or in getting penalties reduced. Why? Because the judge has the ability to reduce the fine and may do so only in certain circumstances. Different types of excuses varied widely in their effectiveness.

The least effective form of an excuse was scapegoating: "I had to drive on the shoulder of the freeway because other drivers wouldn't let me merge in." More than 80 percent of the drivers who tried to make "other drivers" the scapegoat for their offense were fully penalized. A second ineffective form of excuse was a lack of knowledge: "I didn't know that it was illegal to make a U turn in *any* business district in town. I thought 'No U Turn' signs had to be posted." Approximately 80 percent of the lack-of-knowledge drivers also were penalized fully. A third ineffective type of excuse was the impairment or illness claim that the driver's vision was impaired, the driver became ill, the road condition or lack of lighting impaired vision, or the like. Seventy percent of these drivers were penalized in full.

Only one type of excuse was helpful, a hybrid of apology plus denial of intent:

> "Your Honor, I'm really sorry that this had to occur. I didn't intend to do anything wrong. I picked up the kids from school and left through the back alley. The kids were screaming and singing because we were going Christmas shopping. I sped up and then the officer pulled me over even before I saw the flashing lights [at the school zone, indicating a reduction in speed when children are getting out of school]. I drive on this street every day, and usually there is no reduction in speed at noon, but this day was different because school was being let out early."

Only 30 percent of the drivers using such a combined argument were asked to pay the full penalty, but few relied on this approach.

Justifications were rarely used in traffic court (only 45 of the 375 drivers resorted to them). Why? It simply is not a good tactic to argue that the driver has "good reason" to violate the law:

> "Your Honor, it is true that I went through the light when it was yellow and it turned red. But there was good reason. It was raining, the streets were wet, and the driver behind me was tailgating me. I thought that if I slammed on my brakes, I would have been rear-ended. I thought it was safer simply to go through the intersection."

That is not an effective argument. Nor is this one: "I left my curling iron on and was hurrying home so that the house wouldn't burn down." Over 90 percent of the drivers who relied on justifications were penalized fully for their offenses.

There were three types of refusals or denials. Some drivers challenged the authority of the officer by questioning competence or integrity: "I am a good taxpaying citizen, and I should not be getting a ticket in this *speed trap!*" "I might have been going sixty, but I was not going anything like seventy. I think the officer added those extra miles on just to make me more upset." Over 90 percent of the drivers who used this type of account were penalized in full.

A second type of refusal or denial was denying the offense. Drivers usually recounted their story about what happened and accepted responsibility for what happened but claimed that what actually took place was not really an offense. For example, they might claim that the light had not yet turned red when they went through it or that they had, in their opinion, come to a complete stop. Over 80 percent of these drivers were penalized fully.

The only form of refusal or denial that was effective was logical proof. Drivers provided photographs of the scene to support the claim that the view of the stop sign was blocked, work orders from the city office to indicate that a curb had not been painted in years, or a sheaf of complaints about the site filed by other people. Certain drivers presented convincing logical arguments; for example, one driver had been ticketed for speeding in a residential area, but he was not ticketed for failing to stop at the stop signs on each corner. He claimed that he could not have accelerated to 45 miles per hour in his Volkswagen minivan in one city block and yet come to a complete stop. Only 25 percent of the drivers who attempted the logical proof claim were fined. However, not many drivers relied on this strategy.

Logical proof arguments were effective because they successfully raise a question of reasonable doubt about the driver's guilt. Apology plus denial of intent arguments were effective because the driver displayed remorse and made a credible claim concerning unintentional causes for the violation. However, simple apologies, most excuses, most refusals or denials, and all justifications were ineffective.

Attribution Theory and the Communication of Accounts

Attribution theory is an important theory of human cognition that is relevant to many aspects of interpersonal communication. It is important with reference to accounts for two reasons. First, attribution theory deals with our judgments concerning why people behave the way they do, and these judgments influence our evaluation of the accounts that are communicated. Second, excuses themselves suggest causes for questionable behavior, and certain types of excuses are effective in achieving remedial goals and in controlling emotions of the people with whom we speak.

Fritz Heider (1958) speculated that people act like "naive social scientists" who study other's actions in order to judge why people act the way they do. When we make observations about others, we search for causes that would explain why they behave the way they do.

One important distinction between causes is the distinction between situational (or external) causes of behavior and dispositional (or internal) causes. **Situational** or **external causes** are things in the environment that we believe account for a person's behavior. Statements that reflect situational or external causes include "Pat is ner-

IS MORLEY DRIVING SAFER?

There was Morley Safer, zipping through the Pennsylvania township of Tobyhanna, when a state trooper spotted him and pulled him over. What excuse would the "60 Minutes" correspondent give for doing 75 in a 55-mile-per-hour zone? His foot got stuck to the accelerator? He liked to feel the wind in his hair? Safer looked the trooper right in the eye and said that he was speeding because he was working on a story about, uh, speeding. The trooper didn't buy it, and Safer ended up paying a $134 fine.

If Safer had read this book, he would have known that justification is not a good tactic in this situation.

Based on story reported in the *Long Beach Press-Telegram*, May 31, 1992.

vous about multiple-choice tests," "Pat drinks at football games with his friends," "Pat is funny in class but serious in the library." **Dispositional** or **internal causes** of behavior are attributed to a person's personality, nature, or beliefs about the world. Statements that reflect dispositional or internal causes include "Amy is an anxious person" (all the time), "Amy loves beer" (all the time), and "Amy is a cutup" (funny in all settings).

What determines our attributions of actions to internal or external causes? Three features of observing others influence such judgments: distinctiveness, consistency, and consensus (see also Kelley 1973). **Distinctiveness** deals with whether or not a person's behavior is distinctly different in one situation than in other situations. For example, if a friend of ours obtained good grades in all of her classes but one, we are likely to make an external judgment: the one class is too difficult or is poorly taught. However, if the friend received poor grades in all her classes, we would make an internal attribution: she is inept, not very smart, or not very motivated to work hard. In this second instance, of low distinctiveness, we probably wouldn't believe the student if she used an excuse blaming her professors for the low grades. However, in the case of high distinctiveness—the first situation—we probably would believe the excuse that the one professor was to blame for the poor grade.

Consistency refers to the extent to which the student's behavior is the same over time. Highly consistent behavior means that our friend has always received high grades or has always received low grades. If she has always received low grades in high school and in college, we make the internal attribution that our friend is personally responsible for the grades she received, including the poor grades this semester. However, low consistency may mean that the student received high grades in the past but is currently receiving low grades this semester. Because our friend has in the past demonstrated the ability and motivation to obtain good grades, we would probably look for external causes for the recent bout of bad grades—perhaps this semester she has tough professors, or perhaps she is spending too much time on sports or dating. When this student uses an excuse blaming her professors, it may be believed.

Consensus deals with the perception of similar others in similar situations—for example, how well our friend is doing in one class relative to similar other students in the same class. High consensus means that all students in particular classes received poor grades. When all students receive poor grades, we tend to believe that external factors such as the professor's teaching, the professor's attitude, or the course content caused our friend's poor grades. Consensus is low, however, when other students are receiving good grades, but our friend is one of the few who are receiving poor grades. When consensus is low, we are not likely to believe our friend if she attempted to use an excuse blaming the professor for the poor grade.

Thus attribution theory deals with the fundamental issue of how we make *attributions* concerning why people behave the way they do. We are likely to believe that a person's behavior is caused by external factors when distinctiveness is high (receiving good grades in all classes but one), when consistency is high (receiving good grades consistently over time except in this one class), and when consensus is high (all students were performing poorly in this class). In such circumstances, we are likely to believe our friend's excuses for the poor grades. By contrast, if we perceive the friend as making poor grades in all classes, making poor grades consistently over time, and making poor grades when other students are making good grades, we judge the behavior as being caused by internal causes, and we are likely to view any excuse communicated by this person as unconvincing.

THE CREDIBILITY OF EXCUSES

We can claim several types of causes for events (Weiner 1986):

1. Causes can be *stable* or *unstable.* Stable causes are ones that recur consistently and predictably over time. Traffic is congested at 8 A.M. and at 5 P.M. and is especially bad on Monday mornings, Friday afternoons, and whenever it snows or rains. Unstable causes are ones that cannot be predicted—freezing rain in April, a truck that jackknifed, an insect bite, and so on. Stable causes are linked to the perception of *consistency.* The student who received poor grades is likely to be perceived as a poor student if she received poor grades consistently (stably over time).

2. Causes can be *internal* ("I didn't want to go to the concert because I don't like that group anymore") or *external* ("My car was hit by a hit-and-run driver, and I can't go because I have to wait for the insurance adjuster"). Such causes can also be referred to as *personal* ("*I* don't like Chinese food," "*I've* decided to change my ma-

jor") or *impersonal* ("My parents insist that I major in business," "Because of money problems at home, I have to drop out of school"). In our example of the student who received poor grades, the attribution of internal or external causes was strongly linked to the perception of distinctiveness.

3. Causes can be *controllable* or *uncontrollable.* For example, the claim "I ran out of gas" may be external and unintentional, but it is controllable—the amount of gas in the tank is under the driver's control. An uncontrollable cause is one outside our ability to alter or change: "The baseball game ended early because of the rain, and I unexpectedly got stuck in traffic." In our example of the student who received poor grades, the perception of consensus is relevant to the judgment of whether she can control the behavior: if *all* students received poor grades, it is likely that the students did not have much control over the grades they received.

4. Causes can be *intentional* ("I was in a hurry to get home because it was dark and I was in a high-crime area") or *unintentional* ("I didn't mean to spin my wheels and burn rubber when I accelerated").

The driver who told about the bee communicated an account in such a way as to increase the likelihood that he would not be ticketed. The driver claimed that the bee and its potential sting caused him to speed and to drive erratically. This explanation involves a cause that is *unintentional* (the bee's presence distracted him from driving), *uncontrollable* (the driver can control neither the bee nor his driving behavior when he tried to avoid the bee), *unstable* (he rarely has to confront a problem like this one), and *external* (the bee is an environmental feature that caused the driver's behavior). Thus the *communicated excuse* involved a cause that was uncontrollable, unintentional, unstable, and external. The *true* or *withheld* reason, however, is best characterized as *controllable, intentional, stable,* and *internal*—the driver controls his speed, intends to speed, speeds often, and is personally causing the speeding.

The central proposition concerning attributions and the credibility of excuses is simply this: Communicated excuses that cite causes that are unintentional, unstable, uncontrollable, and external are more effective in achieving interpersonal goals than excuses that are intentional, stable, controllable, and internal. A very simple study by Weiner and associates (1987) demonstrated this clearly.

Weiner and his colleagues had pairs of students show up for a study purportedly on first impressions, and one student in each pair of students was asked to wait for the partner to show up so that the study could begin. The other student, however, was asked to do a bit of acting by pretending that he or she was late and to give an excuse to the waiting student, one of four kinds of excuses. One group was told to communicate whatever they thought would be a bad excuse, one that would evoke anger. Another group was told to communicate whatever they thought would be a good excuse, and a third group was told to communicate any excuse they wanted to communicate. The fourth group of students were told not to communicate any reason for being late.

Weiner and his colleagues found that the excuses that the students believed to be good excuses involved causes that were uncontrollable, external, unintentional, and unstable; 83 percent of the good excuses involved claims that the student had a sudden, unexpected obligation ("I had to take my mother to the hospital"), a problem in transportation or arrival ("I could not find the room"), or a school demand that kept them from being prompt ("My midterm took longer than expected"). Students instructed to communicate any excuse communicated excuses that were similar to the good ones. This suggests that people normally try to communicate good excuses. However, students who constructed bad excuses used reasons that were internal, intentional, or controllable: "I ran into some friends and stayed to talk with them for a while," "I forgot," and the like.

The students rated each other in terms of emotions (angry, warm, irritated, etc.), interpersonal traits (dependable, sensitive, friendly, etc.), and social behavior (whether they liked the partner). Students who communicated good excuses were perceived as having a more favorable personality, being more likable, and having more positive feelings than students who communicated bad excuses or who failed to communicate any reason for being tardy.

CONTROL OF EMOTIONS

We do not want to hurt other people's feelings, and excuses are used strategically so that we do not make others feel rejected. Folkes (1982) demonstrated this in a study in which students were asked to report how they turned down offers for dates. Students were asked to recall encounters in which they asked others for dates but were rejected. They were asked to write what was said to them when the rejecting party declined the date offer. They were also asked to recall encounters in which they were asked for dates and rejected others. The students were also asked to write out two sets of reasons: reasons *privately* held for rejecting the date offer, and the *publicly* communicated reasons for rejecting the date offer. The central idea is that we have personal reasons for rejecting date offers but publicly communicate impersonal, uncontrollable, and unstable causes to others so that they will not feel personally rejected.

Folkes coded all the reasons written on three of the parameters of causes we discussed earlier: personal versus impersonal (internal versus external), controllable versus uncontrollable, and stable versus unstable. The results are presented in Table 6-6. Most reasons were privately held, and usually only one reason was communicated to the rejected person. Most reasons communicated to rejected parties involved impersonal causes for the rejection. First, when students recalled being rejected, the vast majority of reasons communicated to them were impersonal—the rejector had to study for finals, was seriously involved with someone else, or preferred an activity different from the one offered in the date.

Table 6-6
REASONS FOR REJECTING DATE OFFERS

Type of Reason	Public Reasons Reported by Rejected Persons (%)	Reasons Reported by Rejectors	
		Public (%)	Private (%)
Impersonal, uncontrollable, unstable (rejector had to study for finals)	59	64	30
Impersonal, uncontrollable, stable (rejector was seriously involved with someone)	9	8	7
Impersonal, controllable, unstable (rejector would rather go to a dance than to the movies)	22	15	12
Impersonal, controllable, stable (rejector did not want to jeopardize a relationship with someone they were currently dating)	1	3	4
Personal, uncontrollable, unstable (rejector was in a bad mood)	3	0	5
Personal, uncontrollable, stable (rejected person was too old)	1	8	26
Personal, controllable, unstable (rejected person had a lot of nerve asking the rejector out only hours in advance)	3	1	2
Personal, controllable, stable (rejector did not agree with the rejected person's religious beliefs)	1	1	14
Total number of reasons listed:	68	96	207

Source: Adapted from Folkes 1982, tab. 242. Reprinted with permission of Academic Press.

A similar conclusion is reached when we look at the publicly communicated reasons for why we reject dates. The most frequently used reasons are impersonal, uncontrollable, and unstable ones (64 percent of all publicly communicated reasons for rejection). When we tell others that we can't see them because we have to take a test, drive a friend to the airport, or visit a friend in the hospital, we try to avoid making the others feel personally rejected. In reality, our true, privately held reasons for rejecting date offers are personal, uncontrollable, and stable ("The guy was too old"), or personal, controllable, and stable ("We're of different religions. It just wouldn't work out").

Folkes demonstrated that we use excuses strategically to avoid hurting the feelings of rejected parties. It is easier, gentler, and less hurtful when we say that we have to spend the weekend visiting our grandparents than to tell a person that he or she is old, weird, or inadequate.

Chapter Summary

Verbal messages called accounts can be used to repair interpersonal relationships, cope with embarrassment, create public impressions, and assuage bureaucrats. Generally speaking, a full-blown apology produces more overall positive consequences, resolves interpersonal disputes as well as problems in embarrassing situations (along with humor), and helps create an image of competence, dedication, and likability. Excuses are also effective in repairing relationships but are linked to lower ratings of competence. Justifications are not as effective as apologies and excuses in improving interpersonal situations, but they are effective in promoting an image of competence, dedication, and, to a lesser degree, likability (much as logical proof accounts do). At the other extreme are refusals that deny the offense or challenge authority. These do not help mend interpersonal relationships or assuage bureaucrats, but they do give rise to perceptions of strength and power (the intimidation style of self-presentation).

Attribution theory seeks to explain the judgments that people make about the causes of behavior. Communicators withhold certain reasons for behaving and publicly communicate reasons in such a way as to maintain positive relationships with others and to reduce feelings of anger and rejection.

KEY TERMS

account	attribution theory
excuse	situational (external) causes
justification	dispositional (internal) causes
concession	distinctiveness
apology	consistency
refusal	consensus
accounter's dilemma	

EXERCISES FOR FURTHER DISCUSSION

▼

1. Think about a situation in which the excuse you gave for some action or behavior may have been less than honest. Write a short paragraph explaining why you gave the excuse that you did.
    a. What ethical principles do you think guided your choice about whether or not to tell the complete truth?
    b. Do you think that it is acceptable to use excuses that are somewhat dishonest with a parent? with a boyfriend or girlfriend? with a manager or employer? with someone you are trying to avoid?
    c. If you see a difference between these situations, what principles would you say guide your behavior?
2. Analyze your success or failure at providing accounts to your parents or to an authority figure at work. Try to think of some situations in which you were successful and some in which you were not.
    a. In the situations in which you were successful, why were you successful?
    b. In the situations in which you were unsuccessful, what do you think you could have done differently?
    c. How important is it to you that authority figures (parents or managers) have a good impression of you?
    d. Do you think that your authority figures react better to excuses or to justifications?
3. There are some types of accounts that we see almost every day in the newspaper—for example, coaches and players will use accounts to explain why they lost a game, and politicians will use accounts to explain why crime, inflation, or unemployment is increasing. Go through a newspaper and write down as many accounts as you can find, identifying each according to the types presented in this chapter.
    a. How many of each type of account did you find?
    b. Which accounts did you find most convincing or believable?
    c. Which accounts did you find least convincing or believable?
4. The following list asks you to think about a variety of situations in which you and a friend would need to offer accounts. Working with a good friend or a romantic partner, read each item, and write down the account you would use. When you are done, try to answer the questions that follow.
    A. You and a friend want to skip a wedding and wedding reception to do something that you would both find more enjoyable. You will need to offer an account to the groom, who is an acquaintance from work.
    B. You and a friend want to skip a dinner dance hosted by an organization you belong to (for example, your fraternity or sorority) in order to do something

that you would find more enjoyable. You will need to offer an account to the chairperson of the Social Committee.

C. You want to cancel a trip home that you planned for the end of the month. You had planned to take a new friend home to be introduced to your parents, but that person would rather put the meeting off for a while. You will need to offer an account to your parents.

D. You have made plans to spend the holidays skiing with a friend, but members of your family have called to ask when they can expect you to come home. You will need to offer an account for why you are not coming home.

E. You and a friend are asked to dinner by a friend whom you like but who is notoriously opinionated and overbearing. You need to provide an account for why the two of you are not able to come to dinner.

   a. Did the two of you give similar accounts?

   b. If there were differences in the types of accounts you gave, discuss your reasons for giving the different types of accounts, and try to decide which account would be more successful.

   c. What problems could you envision if you each provided different accounts to the same people?

   d. How important do you think it is that people who do things together have a common understanding of the types of accounts to use in different situations?

SUGGESTED READING

▼

ACCOUNTS

Cody, M. J., and McLaughlin, M. L. 1990. Interpersonal accounting. In *Handbook of language and social psychology*, ed. H. Giles and P. Robinson, 227–255. London: Wiley. This book chapter presents a general overview of research on accounts, including a historical overview, a discussion of various typologies of accounts, and an analysis of how accounts operate in interpersonal relationships, legal settings, and organizational settings.

McLaughlin, M. L.; Cody, M. J.; and Read, S. J., eds. 1992. *Explaining the self to others: Reason-giving in a social context*. Hillsdale, N.J.: Erlbaum. This volume contains a number of chapters devoted to how accounts, or, more generally, explanations, are used to pursue specific communicative functions. Special attention is given to (a) the psychological underpinnings of creating and communicating social explanations to various audience members and (b) the role of accounts in managing, or escalating, conflict in interpersonal, legal and managerial settings.

Schonbach, P. 1990. *Account episodes*. Cambridge: Cambridge University Press. This book devotes considerable attention to an extensive typology of accounts, and emphasizes the importance of reproaches in the communication of accounts and their evaluations. Reproaches are used by individuals when they ask for an account (i.e., "Son, why did you leave the car lights on all night?"), and Schonbach demonstrates that severely or harshly phrased accounts cause account-makers to behave defensively—communicating fewer apologies and excuses, and communicating more justifications and refusals.

Snyder, C. R.; Higgins, R. L.; and Stucky, R. J. 1983. *Excuses: Masquerades in search of grace*. New York: Wiley/Interscience. This volume focuses attention on how the "excuse" operates to protect the self from being viewed negatively.

ACCOUNTS IN MANAGER-WORKER RELATIONSHIPS

Bies, R. J., and Sitkin, S. B. 1992. Explanation as legitimization: Excuse-making in organizations. *Explaining the self to others: Reason-giving in a social context*, ed. M. L. McLaughlin; M. J. Cody; and S. J. Read, 183–198. Hillsdale, N.J.: Erlbaum. Bies and Sitkin offer an extensive overview of how accounts are used by corporations and by managers to resolve disputes and/or differences in perceptions. Of particular interest is how managers communicate accounts when communicating negative information to employees, concerning a decline to hire or promote, a decision to freeze budgets, etc.

Braaten, D. O.; Cody, M. J.; and Bell–DeTiene, K. 1993. Account episodes in organizations: Remedial work and impression management. *Management Communication Quarterly* 6, 219–250. Two studies are reviewed: one demonstrating the importance of using apologies and excuses in smoothing over interpersonal disputes on the job, the second assessing how hearers perceive communicators who employ different types of accounts.

ACCOUNTS AND EMBARRASSMENT

Cupach, W. R., and Metts, S. 1990. Remedial processes in embarrassing predicaments. In *Communication yearbook 13*, ed. J. A. Anderson, 323–352. Newbury Park, Calif.: Sage. Cupach and Metts thoroughly review the research on embarrassment, including what communicators say and do when they are embarrassed and what tactics are best for coping effectively with embarrassment.

REFERENCE LIST

Braaten, D. O.; Cody, M. J.; and Bell–De Tiene, K. 1993. Account episodes in organizations: Remedial work and impression management. *Management Communication Quarterly* 6: 219–250.

Cody, M. J., and McLaughlin, M. L. 1988. Accounts on trial: Oral arguments in traffic court. In *Analyzing everyday explanation: A casebook of methods*, ed. C. Antaki, 113–126. London: Sage.

———. 1990. Interpersonal accounting. In *Handbook of language and social psychology*, ed. H. Giles and P. Robinson, 227–255. London: Wiley.

Cupach, W. R., and Metts, S. 1990. Remedial processes in embarrassing predicaments. In *Communication yearbook 13*, ed. J. A. Anderson, 323–352. Newbury Park, Calif.: Sage.

Darby, B. W., and Schlenker, B. R. 1982. Children's reactions to apologies. *Journal of Personality and Social Psychology* 43:742–753.

Folkes, V. S. 1982. Communicating the causes of social rejection. *Journal of Experimental Social Psychology* 18:235–252.

Gonzales, M. H.; Pederson, J. H.; Manning, D. J.; and Wetter, D. W. 1990. Pardon my gaffe: Effects of sex, status, and consequence severity on accounts. *Journal of Personality and Social Psychology* 58:610–621.

Heider, F. 1958. *The psychology of interpersonal relations*. New York:Wiley.

Holtgraves, T. 1989. The form and function of remedial moves: Reported use, psychological reality, and perceived effectiveness. *Journal of Language and Social Psychology* 8:1–16.

Kelley, H. 1973. The processes of causal attribution. *American Psychologist* 28:107–128.

Metts, S., and Cupach, W. R. 1989. Situational influence on the use of remedial strategies in embarrassing predicaments. *Communication Monographs* 56:151–162.

Schlenker, B. R. 1980. *Impression management*. Pacific Grove, Calif.: Brooks/Cole.

Schlenker, B. R., and Darby, B. W. 1981. The use of apologies in social predicaments. *Social Psychology Quarterly* 44:271–278.

Schonbach, P. 1980. A category system for account phases. *European Journal of Social Psychology* 10:195–200.

———. 1990. *Account episodes*. Cambridge, England: Cambridge University Press.

Scott, M. B., and Lyman, S. M. 1968. Accounts. *American Sociological Review* 33:46–62.

Snyder, C. R., and Higgins, R. L. 1990. Reality negotiation and excuse-making: President Reagan's March 4, 1987, Iran arms speech and other literature. In *The psychology of tactical communication*, ed. M. J. Cody and M. L. McLaughlin, 207–228. Clevedon, England: Multilingual Matters.

Weiner, B. 1986. *An attribution theory of motivation and emotion*. New York: Springer-Verlag.

Weiner, B.; Amirkhan, J.; Folkes, V. S.; and Verette, J. A. 1987. An attributional analysis of excuse giving: Studies of a naive theory of emotion. *Journal of Personality and Social Psychology* 52:316–324.

C H A P T E R   7

DISCLOSING THE SELF

That Saturday night, John felt alone. Another weekend had come, and he couldn't get up the nerve to ask Julie for a date. She represented everything he wanted in a companion: she was positive, athletic, intelligent, and kind. But here he was again on a weekend night, hanging out with Dave. John liked to hang out with Dave, but not all the time. John felt that if he could talk about Julie, he might feel better and get some advice about what to do next. Dave had been pretty trustworthy so far. So when the conversation topic turned to women, John decided to tell Dave what was bothering him.

Self-disclosure is communication that offers information about oneself. Cozby (1973) defines self-disclosure as *any* information that one person offers another (p. 73). A more specific definition is offered by Pearce and associates (1974):

> Self-disclosing communication occurs when a person intentionally tells something about himself (herself) to another person. Thus defined, self-disclosure is best conceptualized as a subset of communication behavior involving specific types of speaker decisions about what and to whom to speak. (p. 5)

This chapter examines how people present themselves through self-disclosure.

Types of Self-disclosure

Gilbert and Horenstein (1975) observe that disclosure is not simply divided between people who do and do not disclose. Instead, there are several types. Berg and Archer (1982) distinguish three kinds of self-disclosure: *evaluative intimacy, topical intimacy,* and *descriptive intimacy*. **Evaluative intimacy** refers to disclosures that express an assessment about some thing, person, or event; for example, "I like Mozart," "He is a sexist pig," and "Florida beaches are better than California beaches" are evaluative disclosures. **Topical intimacy** refers to discussing a particular topic. You can talk a lot about a topic without necessarily disclosing intimate secrets about the topic ("The Bulls won a third championship. I can't remember the last time a team won three. Everyone out here seems to love the Bulls"). **Descriptive intimacy** refers to self-revelations, or personal information about yourself ("That's the first time she's broken a date with me," "I earned a letter in high school for wrestling"). The distinctions among types of disclosure can be important. For example, Berg and Archer found that evaluative disclosures were used when the communicator's goal was to create a favorable impression more than when the communicator's goal was to obtain information.

SOCIAL PENETRATION THEORY

Perhaps the most cited theory regarding self-disclosure is **social penetration theory** (Altman and Taylor 1973; see also Chapter 8). According to social penetration theory, each relationship is assessed in terms of its rewards and costs. If the rewards outweigh the costs, increases in intimacy are sought. For example, if an acquaintance has similar values, tells interesting stories, or can help you with your homework, you may want to learn more about this person and share more about yourself. If the costs outweigh the rewards, no further intimacy is sought. Moreover, if the forecast for rewards is low relative to costs, the relationship may be downplayed or even terminated.

Altman and Taylor predict that self-disclosure is most prevalent during the initial acquaintance stages and becomes less frequent in later stages once the partners have learned more about each other. In addition, disclosure occurs along two dimensions. The first dimension is *depth*, or the level of intimacy of the disclosure. The second dimension is *breadth*, or the number of topics that are discussed. According to Altman and Taylor (1973), people penetrate one another's individuality along various topics in different degrees of intimacy (hence, the expression *social penetration*), as the following scenario illustrates.

Kris Wilkins has many friends. Perhaps her best friend is John. John and Kris have known each other since the fifth grade. And although they thought about dating during high school, nothing serious ever came of that. Kris knows that John will support her, regardless of what she thinks or does. For example, last year Kris dated someone John thought was immature. Kris was being used and most people guessed that. Still, throughout that relationship, and afterward, Kris knew she could count on John. It was during this period that Kris often confided in John, relating things about herself she never thought she could tell anyone. Besides telling John all about her relationships with men, she also shared plans and dreams for the future and personal opinions about almost everything. Kris implicitly trusts John and believes that he would never use this information to hurt her.

Another friend of Kris's is Julie. Julie is new to the school, having just transferred there from a two-year college. Kris met Julie while taking the same aerobics class, and they hit it off right away. Now, Julie and Kris usually go to aerobics together and hang out on weekends. They talk about everything, but not at very deep levels. Kris's friend John has a crush on Julie. Julie knows that Kris and John are very close, so she doesn't want to say anything about John or her boyfriend back home. So whenever the talk about guys gets too personal, Julie changes the topic.

And then there's Beth. Beth and Kris are both communication majors, so they have had several classes together. Beth is very popular and was elected president of her sorority. Because she has so many other friends, Beth hasn't gotten to know Kris very well. Kris doesn't belong to a sorority, and she feels out of place at sorority parties. So Beth knows to a moderate degree how Kris feels about schoolwork and career goals.

Altman and Taylor (1973) liken the social penetration process to peeling an onion: penetration proceeds along breadth and depth dimensions, revealing various segments and layers of a person's personality. Figure 7-1 illustrates social penetration using the onion skin metaphor, with reference to Kris's relationship with her three friends, John, Julie, and Beth. More specifically, we illustrate how well each friend knows Kris in terms of depth and breadth in four topic areas: romantic relationships, college issues (such as grades), future plans and hopes, and personal opinions. These are common disclosure topics for college students (see Schmidt and Cornelius 1987).

As Figure 7-1 indicates, Kris allows three friends to penetrate her personality along different topics (breadth) and to different levels of intimacy (depth). For example, John knows all about Kris's relational life, future plans, and personal opinions; Julie has penetrated all four topic areas, but only superficially; and Beth knows Kris moderately well only in terms of college issues and future plans. As this example indicates, social penetration theory is useful for understanding how people become more intimate along the dimensions of breadth and depth.

DIMENSIONS OF SELF-DISCLOSURE

Two dimensions of self-disclosure, breadth and depth, have already been discussed. **Breadth** refers to the number of topics disclosed, and **depth** refers to the level of intimacy involved in the disclosure. Wheeless (1976) identifies five other important dimensions of self-disclosure: conscious intent; amount, or frequency; valence, or degree of positivity or negativity; control of depth; and honesty or accuracy. Wheeless refined a measure of these various dimensions of self-disclosure in the Revised Self-disclosure Scales. Table 7-1 (see page 174) reports sample items from Revised Self-disclosure Scales for each of these five dimensions.

Dimensions of self-disclosure can be used to assess how one's self-disclosure is associated with various relational features. Wheeless and Grotz (1977), for example, found that trust was related to control of depth and intent to disclose more than the other dimensions of self-disclosure.

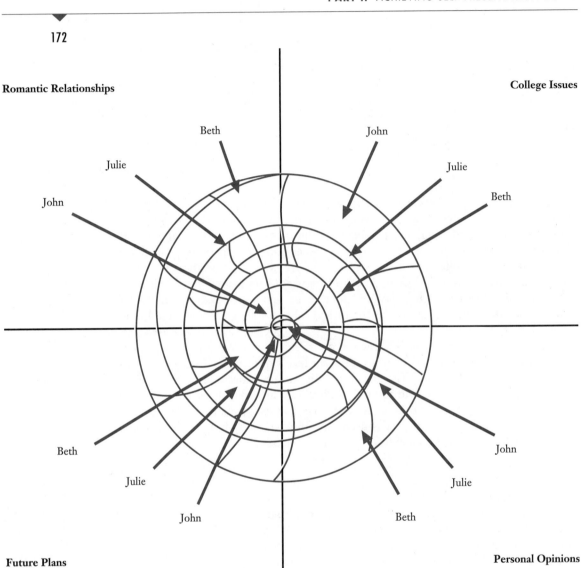

Romantic Relationships

College Issues

Future Plans

Personal Opinions

Figure 7-1 ▼ Social Penetration of Kris by Three Friends
Source: Adapted from Altman and Taylor 1973, 28.

Social penetration theory holds that we will become closer to individuals who are rewarding to be with. Over time, if the rewards continue to outweigh the costs, we tend to disclose more about ourselves.

(Joel Gordon)

Factors Affecting Self-disclosure Choices

People have many reasons to disclose. As Miller (1990) notes, an individual discloses to obtain various interpersonal goals. A person may disclose to get close to another person, to be the center of attention, to avoid rejection, to achieve acceptance, and to obtain other goals. These various reasons reflect the basic thesis of this book: that people disclose primarily to achieve interpersonal goals. Of course, people disclose for many reasons, but accompanying all these reasons is a concern for presenting an image of who they are.

Examination of the research uncovers specific kinds of interaction goals sought through self-disclosure in different relationships. For example, surveying married couples, Burke, Weir, and Harrison (1976) report that husbands and wives have similar reasons for disclosing and that 70 percent of the reasons were one of these four: unburdening oneself (catharsis), increasing the spouse's understanding of oneself, seeking advice or solutions to a problem, and seeking clarification and new perspectives (see also Derlega and Grezlak 1979).

Table 7-1

EXAMPLES FROM THE REVISED SELF-DISCLOSURE SCALES

Dimension	Examples
I. Intent	"When I wish, my self-disclosures are always accurate reflections of who I really am." "When I reveal my feelings about myself, I consciously intend to do so."
II. Amount (frequency)	"I usually talk about myself for fairly long periods at a time." "I often discuss my feelings about myself."
III. Valence	"I usually disclose positive things about myself." "On the whole, my disclosures about myself are more negative than positive."
IV. Control of depth	"I intimately disclose who I really am, openly and fully, in my conversation." "Once I get started, my self-disclosures last a long time."
V. Honesty (accuracy)	"I cannot reveal myself when I want to because I do not know myself thoroughly enough." "My self-disclosures are completely accurate reflections of who I really am."

Source: Adapted from Wheeless 1976, 57–58.

THE NORM OF RECIPROCITY

One of the most examined reasons for people's disclosure is the norm of reciprocity. A norm refers to a behavior so common that it is expected. The **norm of reciprocity** means offering a communicative response that matches the partner's previous communication. When applied to self-disclosure, the norm of reciprocity, or **dyadic effect**, as Jourard (1971) calls it, refers to the phenomenon of the communicator matching the partner's previous disclosure at a similar level of intimacy.

The norm of reciprocity is explained according to various theories, as Jones and Archer (1976) observe. First, you match disclosures because the other communicator cues you regarding what is appropriate in a particular context. Or you reciprocate behavior because you trust the other person, so you feel safe in risking a disclosure. Or you may feel compelled to exchange information so as not to be indebted. As Chaikin and Derlega (1974) indicate:

One of the most examined reasons for people's disclosure is the norm of reciprocity, or the dyadic effect. This means that one person will generally match a partner's disclosure at a similar level of depth.

(Jeffrey W. Myers/Stock, Boston)

The recipient to high disclosure who fails to reciprocate has put himself [or herself] and the discloser in an inequitable relationship. . . . Since inequity sets up tension which motivates behavior designed to reduce it, reciprocity in self-disclosure should be likely to occur. (p. 118)

But how strong is the reciprocity norm?

Much of the research indicates that the norm of reciprocity has a strong influence on our self-disclosure behaviors (for a thorough review, see Dindia 1982). Rosenberg and Mann (1986) found that children learn the norm of reciprocity for disclosure by the sixth grade. Ludwig, Franco, and Malloy (1986) found that reciprocation of high or low disclosure was a powerful predictor of the communicator's level of disclosure, regardless of people's predispositions to monitor themselves. In a similar vein, Shaffer and Ogden (1986) found that intimate disclosures lead to intimate disclosures and that participants had more invested emotionally in high-disclosure situations than in low-disclosure situations.

Other research has questioned the proposition that the norm of reciprocity leads to matching disclosure levels. Using an observational method and sequential analyses, Dindia (1982) found no evidence for the norm of reciprocity. Likewise, Schmidt

Reciprocating disclosures can be risky business

(From Berkeley Breathed, *Outland*. © 1990 Washington Post Writers Group. Reprinted with permission.)

and Cornelius (1987) report that participants rated the other's behavior as the least important influence on their own self-disclosing behavior. Pearce and colleagues (1974) also argue that self-disclosure is affected more by what people *perceive* as equivalent than what is actually equivalent: "From this perspective, we would expect persons to disclose in a way which is equivalent to what they think the other has disclosed to them rather than to the other's actual disclosure" (p. 8).

REASONS FOR NOT DISCLOSING

Rosenfeld (1979) investigated the reasons why college students avoid self-disclosure. Of the eighteen reasons examined, both male and female participants indicated that the most important reason was "If I disclose, I might project an image that I do not want to project." Clearly this reason concerns maintaining a positive self-presentation. Rosenfeld also explored the issue of whether sex differences affect reasons for not disclosing. For men, the next important reasons (following projecting a bad image) were "If I disclose, I might give information that makes me appear inconsistent," "Self-disclosure might threaten relationships I have with people other than the close acquaintance [the target of disclosure]," and "If I disclose, I might lose control over the other person." For women, the next important reasons (following projecting a bad image) were "If I disclose, I might be evaluating or judging the other person," "Self-disclosure is a sign of weakness," and "Self-disclosure might hurt our relationship." Rosenfeld concluded that men avoid disclosure primarily to maintain control over the social situation, and women avoid disclosure to prevent personal hurt and relational problems (pp. 72–73).

Examining married couples' reasons for not disclosing their problems to the spouse, Burke and associates (1976) also found gender differences. Forty-eight percent of the wives did not want to worry the spouse; only 18 percent of the husbands cited this motive. Twenty-two percent of the wives claimed that the husband was not responsive to their problems; only 15 percent of the husbands said that their wives were not responsive. Husbands did not disclose personal problems to their wives primarily because husbands tried to separate work problems from family life (25 percent of husbands said this, but none of the wives did). Finally, 20 percent of the husbands claimed that they did not disclose personal problems because the spouse lacked knowledge relevant to the issue (none of the wives claimed this).

SELF-DISCLOSURE AND PRIVACY
Cozby (1973) argued that disclosure should be viewed as a product of two competing forces, "one operating to increase disclosure, the other operating to decrease disclosure" (p. 88). According to Cozby, people who study self-disclosure typically focus on the positive aspects (e.g., therapeutic value). But Cozby warns that privacy must also be maintained so that the communicator can retain a sense of identity.

Ten years after Cozby argued that disclosure should be examined in light of privacy needs, Rawlins (1983) argued that people actually balance their disclosures with protecting themselves and others. Rawlins calls this a dialectical tension between expressiveness and protectiveness: *"self limits self's own vulnerability and strives to protect other while still expressing thoughts and feelings"* (p. 5). Two communicator considerations affect the degree of expression or protectiveness: *tolerance of vulnerability* and *likelihood of candor* (Rawlins 1983).

TOLERANCE OF VULNERABILITY
Tolerance of vulnerability arises because our disclosures make us susceptible to others. Accordingly, we must assess how vulnerable we will become. Rawlins (1983) reports that tolerance of vulnerability is a function of two factors: the need to be open and the degree of trust in the other. Figure 7-2 shows how the need to be open and trust in the other interact to affect tolerance of vulnerability.

According to the figure, you would feel most at ease disclosing personal information in situations where you trusted the other party and felt a need to be open. Spouses, psychologists, clergy, and best friends can reassure us they can be trusted with intimate disclosures more easily than strangers, co-workers, or acquaintances can. You are most likely to conceal information from others when your need to be open is low and you do not trust the other party. But in cases where either the need to be open or trust is low, you must judge the extent to which the disclosure is worth the risk. As Gilbert (1976b) postulates, security needs balance intimacy needs. Hence there are times when you wish to maintain the status quo and not disclose, and there are occasions when you risk your security in order to increase intimacy.

Figure 7-2

▼

Tolerance of
Vulnerability

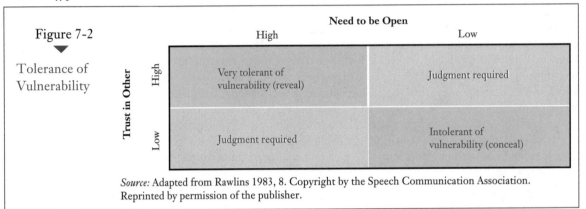

Source: Adapted from Rawlins 1983, 8. Copyright by the Speech Communication Association. Reprinted by permission of the publisher.

LIKELIHOOD OF CANDOR

Rawlins (1983) also observes that the expressiveness-protectiveness decision is made on the basis of the **likelihood of candor,** the probability that you will make personal observations about your communication partner. The likelihood of candor is comprised of two factors: your perceived need to be honest about the issue at hand and your restraint, or awareness that certain topics should be avoided. Figure 7-3 portrays how the need to be honest and restraint affect the likelihood of candor.

Figure 7-3 indicates that you are most likely to disclose if you have a high need to be honest with your partner about the issue and restraint is not appropriate. For example, imagine that you have a friend who drinks so much that it is affecting his work and his physical health. Because you are friends, you feel compelled to be honest with him. According to Figure 7-3, you are least likely to be candid with your partner when you have a low need to be honest and the issue is a sensitive one. For example, you have an in-law who idolizes a TV evangelist you do not like, but your need to express this opinion is low. Judgment regarding candor is required when either the need to be honest or topic appropriateness is low. For example, do you disclose your honest impressions to a friend whose new expensive haircut is definitely not flattering?

PRIVACY BOUNDARY COORDINATION

Petronio (1991) offers insight into how relational privacy is achieved. Petronio's theory concerns the manner in which married couples coordinate their boundaries of privacy. As Petronio, Martin, and Littlefield (1984) note, disclosure functions to define the boundaries of privacy (p. 269).

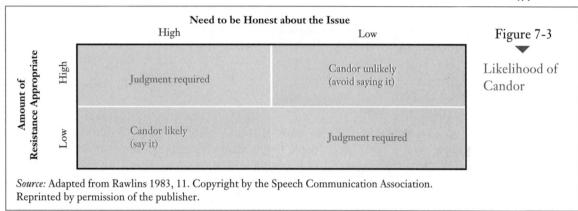

Need to be Honest about the Issue

	High	Low
High (Amount of Resistance Appropriate)	Judgment required	Candor unlikely (avoid saying it)
Low	Candor likely (say it)	Judgment required

Figure 7-3 ▼ Likelihood of Candor

Source: Adapted from Rawlins 1983, 11. Copyright by the Speech Communication Association. Reprinted by permission of the publisher.

According to Petronio (1991), **boundary coordination** refers to the degree to which the explicit or implicit demand within a disclosure is met by an explicit or implicit response. Petronio reports four ways in which disclosure demands and responses are coordinated in daily life. First, a *satisfactory fit* involves a disclosure with an explicit, direct message and a response that is also direct. For example, the husband discloses, "I don't care for such parties," to which the wife replies, "I agree—they are too formal." Both messages are clear and reflect satisfactory boundary coordination. Second, *overcompensation* occurs when the disclosure is implicit and the response is explicit. For example, the wife says, "I happen to have the day off tomorrow," to which the husband responds, "There is no way that I can take a weekend trip until the first of the month." Clearly, the second message provides more information than the first message demands. A *deficient fit* takes place when the disclosure is explicit and the response is implicit. For example, the wife notices, "You never surprise me with cards or flowers anymore," to which the husband responds, "I never thought of that before." In this example, the husband evades the implied demand of offering reasons for not sending cards or flowers. Finally, an *equivocal fit* takes place when both the disclosure and the response are implicit or indirect. For example, the husband confides, "It was quite a day today," to which the wife replies, "How about I take you out to dinner?" In this case, neither want to discuss the details of the husband's (rough) day, so both parties coordinate in an indirect manner the level at which the issue is discussed.

In sum, self-disclosure is understood in terms of pulls to express yourself versus desires to protect yourself. As Rawlins observes, needs for honesty and candor are balanced by how much you trust your partner and the sensitivity of the issues under discussion. In addition, Petronio's theory indicates that privacy boundary coordination involves four types of responses to disclosures: satisfactory, overcompensatory, deficient, and equivocal.

Factors Affecting the Manner of Self-disclosure

What are the various influences on self-disclosure? Do some people tend to disclose more than others? Are people more likely to communicate in some relationships more than others? In addressing these questions, we will discuss four factors that affect self-disclosure: gender differences, personality, relationship type, and culture.

GENDER DIFFERENCES

Much of the early research on self-disclosure found differences between men and women. Jourard (1971), for example, reported that women disclose for affection purposes whereas men disclose on the basis of what they know about the other. Derlega and colleagues (1981) state that men may use a *status-assertive* disclosure style, hiding weaknesses and emphasizing successes, but women use an *affiliative*, or status-neutralizing, disclosure style. This concept implies that "sex differences in disclosure may be partially understood in terms of divergent self-presentation strategies favored by men and women" (Derlega et al. 1981, 445). In short, during disclosure men prefer to present themselves as strong and independent, whereas women prefer to present themselves as kind and sensitive.

Although they may disclose more than men do, women may be more particular than men about the conditions surrounding the disclosure episode. Petronio and coworkers (1984) found that women place more importance on certain "prerequisites" for self-disclosure than men do. "Before women will disclose, they find it more important than do men that the receiver be discreet, trustworthy, sincere, liked, respected, a good listener, warm, and open" (p. 271). Why do women place more value on these prerequisites for disclosure? Petronio and colleagues reason that women are more attuned than men to "self-presentation and other's receptiveness to the communication" (p. 272).

Not all research on self-disclosure has found clear-cut sex differences. In an analysis of 205 studies on sex differences in self-disclosure, Dindia and Allen (1992) found that women tend to disclose more than men, but the differences were small. They also found that the sex of the target affected the differences due to the communicator's sex. Specifically, women are more likely to disclose to women and to members of the opposite sex (i.e., women are more likely to disclose to men than men are likely to disclose to women), but men are *just as likely* as women to disclose to other men. Thus it appears that when we discuss sex differences in self-disclosure, we

BROKEN PROMISES?

When their marriage of more than a decade ended in divorce, Anaheim, Calif., banker Robert Askew sued his ex-wife for fraud because she admittedly concealed the fact that she had never felt sexually attracted to him. An Orange County jury agreed, and ordered Bonette Askew to pay her ex-husband $242,000 in damages.

Such sexual tugs-of-war between couples are not uncommon, therapists and psychologists say. But the Askews' most intimate troubles were not confined to a private bedroom; they were divulged in a public courtroom, where they were analyzed by a jury rather than a marriage counselor.

Bonette Askew, 45, acknowledged in court that she had never been sexually attracted to her husband. But she said she always loved him and noted that their marriage was not sexless and that they had two children together.

She first admitted her lack of sexual desire for him during a joint therapy session in 1991. "I guess he confused sex with love," Bonette Askew said, adding that she concealed her lack of desire because she "didn't want to hurt his male ego."

But Ronald Askew, 50, said his lawsuit had more to do with honesty and integrity than sex. He felt deceived, especially because he said he repeatedly asked her before their marriage to be honest with him and disclose any important secrets.

"Broken Promises," by Marla Cone. Copyright 1993 *Los Angeles Times*. Reprinted with permission.

This story underscores the importance of deciding whether or not one should disclose personal thoughts and feelings. Should Bonette Askew have disclosed that she was not sexually attracted to Ronald Askew before they were married? Should she have remained quiet on the topic, even during marital counseling? If Ronald Askew thinks highly about honesty, why did he sue his ex-wife once she revealed that she was never attracted to him? If there is a moral regarding being honest that we can derive from this story, what would it be?

should recognize that these differences are small and dependent on the composition of the dyad.

PERSONALITY

Several personality factors may potentially affect self-disclosure (see Cozby 1973, 75–80). For example, reviewing studies on extroversion, Cozby found a positive relationship between extroversion and self-disclosure. In addition, varying one's disclosure to match the partner's is generally taken as a sign of a stable individual. Later in this book (Chapter 13) we review how select aspects of personality are linked to interpersonal communication behaviors. Here we will highlight one personality factor receiving recent attention: self-monitoring.

Self-monitoring refers to the degree that people monitor their emotional and behavioral responses to different social situations (see Snyder 1974, 1979; see also Chapter 13). High self-monitors adapt their responses to fit social norms, and low self-monitors maintain the same consistent manner across situations. In general, the research reveals that high self-monitors are more likely to reciprocate the level of disclosure than low self-monitors (see Ludwig et al. 1986).

NATURE OF RELATIONSHIP

The nature of the relationship between communicators affects their self-disclosure. Miller (1990) has demonstrated that we disclose to others because such disclosures are understood within the context of the relationship. She offers the following example: Mary may "respond with joy to Alice's teary-eyed disclosure [because] Alice's telling her this news fits with Mary's understanding that Alice has longed to see her beloved father again and has been worried about him" (p. 52). Relation-specific effects are gleaned from other studies. For example, Dickson-Markman (1986) found that the valence of disclosure becomes more negative as the age group of friends increases.

Married couples also have marked disclosure patterns. For example, Burke and colleagues (1976) reported that both husbands and wives most often selected their spouse as the person to whom they would disclose personal problems. These researchers also found that amount of disclosure was negatively associated with a person's age and length of marriage but that disclosing problems was positively associated with the spouse's helping (that is, as disclosure increased, so did actual helping behavior). Morton (1978) reports that married couples were likely to offer descriptive disclosures more than evaluative disclosures. Strangers, by contrast, were more likely to engage in evaluative disclosures. Overall, and remembering that spouses prefer to disclose to each other, the tendency in marriage is for the amount of disclosure to decrease, the valence of disclosure to become more negative, and the type of disclosure to become more descriptive (and less evaluative) over time.

CULTURAL GROUP

Gudykunst and Kim (1984, 181–183) review the limited research related to cultural influences on self-disclosure. Generally, Americans disclose more frequently than other cultural groups, with the exception of those in the Middle East (see also Gudykunst and Nishida 1984). Nakanishi's (1986) review of the literature also suggests that, in general, Americans tend to disclose more than Asians do. For example, the Japanese people are less dependent than Americans on explicit symbols to infer personal characteristics, such as status. Nakanishi also reports that in his Japanese sample, high disclosers were held to be less socially attractive and less communicatively competent than moderate or low disclosers.

Factors Affecting the Perception of Self-disclosure

Dave raised the topic first. He said, "You know, getting together like this every Saturday is OK, but I could really use some company from a member of the female persuasion. I'd like to ask Beth out, but then so would every guy in town. Besides, she is so busy with her sorority these days, I don't know if she would find time for me." John replied, "Yeah, I know what you mean. I've been thinking of asking out Julie, you know, the transfer student who's been exercising with Kris. She is the most positive woman I know. But something tells me she's seeing another guy, you know, 'cause she doesn't flirt or anything. It drives me crazy—I think about her all the time. Seriously, all I do is think about her."

When you disclose, the other person evaluates you as well as your message (Derlega et al. 1987). Your self-disclosure is viewed as appropriate or inappropriate in terms of its timeliness in the interaction, the overall communication episode, and the relationship. The exchange between Dave and John appears appropriate in terms of its timeliness, the episode, and their relationship. What and how you disclose to others can have a profound effect on your public image and your personal relationships. We will examine the consequences of self-disclosure in terms of its amount, reciprocity, valence, honesty, and timing.

AMOUNT OF DISCLOSURE

Does the amount of self-disclosure, in terms of depth and breadth, affect your public image or personal relationships? This question does not have a simple answer. As Chaikin and Derlega (1974) state, "No simple relationship between level of disclosure and evaluation of the discloser exists" (p. 117). There are at least two competing hypotheses.

One hypothesis is that there should be a positive and linear association between disclosure and liking the discloser because disclosures are a reward for the recipient and lead to relational intimacy. Indeed, several studies have reported a positive and linear association between amount of self-disclosure and liking or relational satisfaction (e.g., Hendrick 1981; Worthy, Gary, and Kahn 1969).

A second hypothesis, which has also received empirical support, is that there should be a curvilinear association between disclosure and liking the discloser (e.g., Cozby 1972; Gilbert 1976a). Liking rises with increased disclosures to a point; then liking decreases as disclosure continues to increase. Why would liking decrease if the communicator continues to disclose? One explanation is too much disclosure causes anxiety in the hearer (Cozby 1972). For example, according to Jones and Archer (1976), too much disclosure embarrasses the hearer without providing a means to cope with the embarrassment. Another explanation is that relationships function best when moderate disclosure, not total disclosure, is offered. In other words, total relational intimacy may be an ideal, but it is not functional or realistic (Gilbert 1976a).

One answer to these contradictory results may be found in the difference between *personalistic* and *general* self-disclosure. **Personalistic self-disclosure** involves messages expressed because the particular relationship between the communicator and the recipient permits deep disclosures (see Jones and Archer 1976; Miller 1990). **General self-disclosure** involves messages sent to almost anyone—the discloser offers personal information to friends, acquaintances, Mom and Dad, Cousin Jack, and the pizza man. When people believe that a disclosure they are hearing is not targeted specifically for them, they regard the discloser as less well adjusted and less likable than the person who reserves the disclosure for a particular person (Falk and Wagner 1985; Jones and Archer 1976).

A second reason for the unclear association between depth of disclosure and liking is that other dimensions, such as reciprocity and valence, must be considered as well (see Gilbert 1976a; Gilbert and Horenstein 1975). It is possible that reciprocation or valence, more than the sheer amount of disclosure, affects our impressions of the communicator.

RECIPROCITY

You will recall that one of the reasons why people disclose has to do with the norm of reciprocity. We feel compelled to match the level of disclosure initiated by our conversational partner. If the norm of reciprocity guides expectations for appropriate disclosure, then not reciprocating disclosures should lead to negative judgments about the communicator. This expectation has been tested in several experiments.

Chaikin and Derlega (1974) had participants watch a videotape of Sue as she offered either a high or a low disclosure in response to another person's initial high or low disclosure. That is, each participant was exposed to one treatment condition: a high or low disclosure followed by Sue's high or low response. Participants then rated Sue on several factors, including her perceived warmth, psychological adjustment, appropriateness, and desirability as a friend. According to the norm of reciprocity, participants should rate Sue most favorably in the condition where she offered a high disclosure in response to a high disclosure or when she offered a low

Table 7-2
RESULTS OF CHAIKIN AND DERLEGA'S (1974) STUDY

Initial Message	Sue's Response	Measures			
		Warmth	*Psychological Adjustment*	*Appropriateness*	*Desirability as a Friend*
Low	Low	6.12	5.85	5.92	5.66
Low	High	6.35	3.85	3.00	4.41
High	Low	5.10	6.15	5.62	5.50
High	High	6.35	5.31	5.62	5.65

NOTE: The higher the number, the greater the perceived rating on a 9-point scale.
Source: Adapted from Chaikin and Derlega 1974, 124–125.

disclosure in response to a low disclosure. Table 7-2 reports the relevant results of this experiment.

As the table reveals, when Sue offered high intimacy in response to low intimacy, participants rated her as warm but inappropriate, psychologically maladjusted, and undesirable as a friend. And when Sue offered a low-depth disclosure in response to a high-depth disclosure, participants rated her as psychologically well adjusted but cold. Finally, Table 7-2 reveals support for the expectation that people who match low disclosure levels are perceived favorably, compared to those who do not match low disclosure levels. Chaikin and Derlega (1974) concluded that people are guided by two social norms: the norm of reciprocity and a norm of appropriateness that prescribes that one should not disclose too much information in most situations.

Support for variations on the reciprocity norm has been reported in other studies. Hosman (1987) found that a combination of breadth reciprocity and depth reciprocity was judged as competent. For example, if the communicator disclosed information on the same *topic* as an initial highly personal message, the communicator was perceived as socially competent, understandable, involved, attentive, and so forth. Reciprocating the same depth of disclosure and topic in response to a low personal disclosure was also seen as socially competent (Hosman 1987). Hosman's study is important, for it suggests that we do not have to offer highly personal information to satisfy the reciprocity norm. Likewise, Bradac, Hosman, and Tardy (1978) found that the intensity of language affects how people view others who deviate from the norm of reciprocity. Language intensity refers to the use of language that connotes emotional involvement rather than neutrality ("I feel *fantastic*" instead of "I feel fine"). In this experiment, participants were exposed to high or low disclosures offered with high-intensity or low-intensity language. Each of these four types of messages was shown as a response to either a high- or low-intimacy disclosure.

Consistent with the Chaikin and Derlega (1974) study, Bradac and colleagues (1978) found that communicators who mismatched both intimacy and intensity levels of disclosures were judged least favorably. They also found that participants judged the intimate message *without* intense language most favorably of all message combinations when the message responded to a low-intimacy, low-intensity message. It is easy to imagine how a friend can tell you something very personal in a low-key manner ("Yeah, I was once in a mental hospital"). In doing so, the intensity of the disclosure is minimized.

VALENCE

Valence refers to the positive or negative elements in a message. Research reveals that valence has a strong effect on perceptions of the communicator. More precisely, it indicates that communicators who offer negative disclosures ("I am so depressed," "I can't stand people like that") are seen in a negative light.

Negative disclosures taint the conversation and the image of the communicator. Gilbert and Horenstein (1975) report that attraction for an individual was higher when that person offered a positive disclosure than when the person offered a negative disclosure, and intimacy level did not affect communicator attraction. Similarly, Hecht, Shepard, and Hall (1979) found that both positive and neutral messages, more than negative messages, were rated as satisfying to the receiver. For example, positive messages such as "I like working in groups" or neutral messages such as "Working in groups is sometimes kind of interesting" are more satisfying to hear than such messages as "I don't like working in groups" or "I get furious with people who don't show up for meetings."

HONESTY

Honesty in self-disclosure refers to offering information that accurately reflects your thoughts and feelings. Is honesty the best policy? Not always, according to the research. It appears that honesty about personal experiences may at times hurt your public image. Derlega, Harris, and Chaikin (1973) found people who disclosed personal deviant information were less liked than those who disclosed nonintimate information. Regardless of the value one places on honesty, some disclosures are viewed negatively (e.g., that you steal money from your parents, etc.).

Recall from Chapter 5 that too much self-promotion by disclosing accomplishments and successes may adversely affect others' impressions and choices of companions. Schlenker and Leary (1982) found that *accurate* communicators were seen as more competent and sincere than boastful communicators when the participants knew of the communicators' performance. The implication of this study is that people should be honest when disclosing information if a conversational partner has potential knowledge of that information.

TIMING

Is it better to offer a personal disclosure early in the conversation or later in the conversation? Research indicates that people who immediately offer a personal disclosure are seen as more immature, phony, maladjusted, and insecure than those who wait several minutes (Wortman et al. 1976). As Wortman and colleagues explain:

> If an individual makes a highly personal remark to us early in a conversation, we may conclude that this remark has little to do with his or her feelings for us. Instead, we may infer that he or she is the kind of person who is disclosing to everyone. If someone makes a disclosing remark after he or she has been talking to us for a while, we may be more likely to take the remark personally and infer that it has positive implications for the relationship. (p. 185)

But there may be some occasions when a disclosure should be offered right away. One instance may be when accepting responsibility for an action. For example, Archer and Burleson (1980) found that accepting responsibility for a *negative* event early in the conversation rather than later in the conversation led to social attraction. But in other circumstances, later disclosers were seen as more socially attractive than early disclosers. Imagine that you severely scratched your friend's car while attempting to park it. You suspect that she will discover that you are the responsible party. Because you are honest with your friends, you decide to relate the fact that you scratched the car. Archer and Burleson's study suggests that you should confess earlier rather than later.

In sum, the association between self-disclosure and liking for the communicator is not a simple one. Some observers have hypothesized a linear association, while others have hypothesized a curvilinear one. Perhaps more important than the amount of disclosure is how it is offered. Research reveals that people who reciprocate at the same level of depth or breadth are judged more favorably than those who do not reciprocate at the same level. The study by Bradac and co-workers suggests that how intensely you offer a disclosure affects how intimately it is perceived. In addition, the valence of the message affects the impression people have of the communicator: positive messages lead to positive evaluations. Finally, in general, disclosures that are offered late (rather than early) in a conversation reflect more positively on the discloser.

Chapter Summary

For several years it was believed that disclosure was necessary for a person's mental health and relational satisfaction. An underlying value assumption was that intimacy is the most important dimension of individual growth and interpersonal relationships. But as early as 1973, Cozby advised that "it is hoped that the peculiar value orientation that has occupied much of the written discussion of self-disclosure can be dispensed with. It seems far more important that the research be conducted" (p. 88). As this chapter has shown, the research indicates that deep, honest, and negative self-disclosure may generate poor impressions and harm relationships. Parks (1982) likewise argues against the assumption that self-disclosure and resulting intimacy represent effective interpersonal communication. Parks notes that "not all interpersonal communication scholars march to the beat of the ideology of intimacy" (p. 80). In addition, some recent research also suggests that self-disclosure does not occur as frequently as once believed (Duck et al. 1991).

Self-disclosure is an important communication activity, although it may not occur as much as other types of communication. It is the most controllable method you have of indicating to others just who you are. You can present yourself as wise or foolish in the ways you disclose your feelings, attitudes, and behaviors. The research suggests that high self-disclosure should be reserved for particular situations with people you know and trust. Reciprocity should mark the disclosure (do not disclose if the other person withholds information). In addition, negative disclosures can adversely affect your public image. As the old song prescribes, you may want to "accentuate the positive and eliminate the negative" when disclosing information about yourself.

These concluding remarks, however, are not absolute. There may be times when you should disclose a lot at once, trust people who could be manipulating you into disclosing, and present negative thoughts, feelings, and reports of behavior. Of course, judgment is required in all disclosure situations. Inappropriate use of self-disclosure can handicap you in achieving your interpersonal goals. Wise use of self-disclosure can help you obtain your self-presentation, relational, and instrumental goals.

KEY TERMS

self-disclosure   dyadic effect
evaluative intimacy   tolerance of vulnerability
topical intimacy   likelihood of candor

descriptive intimacy
social penetration theory
breadth
depth
norm of reciprocity

boundary coordination
self-monitoring
personalistic self-disclosure
general self-disclosure

EXERCISES FOR FURTHER DISCUSSION

▼

1. Think back to the last time you disclosed to someone. Try to recall the event as specifically as possible: Who was it? Where did it take place? When did it take place? What was the self-disclosure about? Now look again at the items in Table 7-1 and try to evaluate your self-disclosure. Was your self-disclosure an accurate reflection of who you are?

2. Write down a list of five people to whom you recently disclosed or who disclosed to you.
    a. How many men are on the list? How many women are on the list?
    b. In your experience, do men or women disclose more?
    c. In your experience, do you find it easier to disclose to men or to women?

3. Look back to the list you created for exercise 2. Write down a sentence or two for each disclosure, describing as precisely as possible how the disclosure was communicated.
    a. What were the differences in communication behavior?
    b. Were there any difference between how men and women disclosed?
    c. Did you find that you preferred some types of self-disclosure over other types?

4. Try to think of a situation you have been in where you thought someone was trying to use the norm of reciprocity to get you to disclose.
    a. What do you think the person's motives were? Did the person genuinely want to be intimate with you, or was the person trying to find out something from you?
    b. What was your reaction to the person's self-disclosure? Was it different from your reaction to other people's self-disclosures?
    c. What do you think would be a good strategy to handle a situation in which you feel pressure to disclose but don't really want to?

5. Review the section on perceptions of self-disclosure and the dimensions of depth, breadth, reciprocity, valence, honesty, and timing.
    a. Which of these dimensions has had the most profound effect on the way others view you?
    b. Do your disclosures take on different characteristics with different people?

   c. Do you think that these different characteristics lead to different impressions of you?

6. List three suggestions you would give to someone regarding self-preservation through self-disclosure, based on the information in this chapter.

SUGGESTED READING

SELF-DISCLOSURE THEORY

Altman, I., and Taylor, D. A. 1973. *Social penetration: The development of interpersonal relationships.* Austin, Texas: Holt, Rinehart and Winston. This classic book links self-disclosure to relational development, showing how intimacy increases along the dimensions of breadth and depth. The authors specify propositions that predict when a relationship will escalate or de-escalate.

Gilbert, S. J. 1976. Empirical and theoretical extensions of self-disclosure. In *Explorations in interpersonal communication*, ed. G. R. Miller, 197–215. Newbury Park, Calif.: Sage. Gilbert explores the premise that self-disclosure is related to liking in a linear fashion. She presents the hypothesis that the relationship between disclosure and liking is, instead, curvilinear.

REVIEWS

Cozby, P. C. 1973. Self-disclosure: A literature review. *Psychological Bulletin*, 79:73–91. Few reviews on self-disclosure are as comprehensive as this one. Although much research on the topic has been presented since 1973, this review still discusses many current issues.

RECIPROCITY

Dindia, K. 1982. Reciprocity of self-disclosure: A sequential analysis. In *Communication yearbook 6*, ed. M. Burgoon, 506–528. Newbury Park, Calif.: Sage. Dindia does an excellent job of reviewing the literature on reciprocity of disclosure. In addition, this article examines reciprocity using observational data.

SEX DIFFERENCES

Dindia, K., and Allen, M. 1992. Sex differences in self-disclosure: A meta-analysis. *Psychological Bulletin*, 112:106–124. This review examines how sex differences affect disclosure. Over two hundred articles are included in this statistical analysis.

REFERENCE LIST

▼

Altman, I., and Taylor, D. A. 1973. *Social penetration: The development of interpersonal relationships.* Austin, Texas: Holt, Rinehart and Winston.

Archer, R. L., and Burleson, J. A. 1980. The effects of timing of self-disclosure on attraction and reciprocity. *Journal of Personality and Social Psychology* 38:120–130.

Berg, J. H., and Archer, R. L. 1982. Responses to self-disclosure and interaction goals. *Journal of Experimental Social Psychology* 18:501–512.

Bradac, J. J.; Hosman, L. A.; and Tardy, C. H. 1978. Reciprocal disclosures and language intensity: Attributional consequences. *Communication Monographs* 45:1–17.

Burke, R. J.; Weir, T.; and Harrison, D. 1976. Disclosure of problems and tensions experienced by marital partners. *Psychological Reports* 38:531–542.

Chaikin, A. L., and Derlega, V. J. 1974. Liking for the norm breaker in self-disclosure. *Journal of Personality* 42:117–129.

———. 1973. Self-disclosure: A literature review. *Psychological Bulletin* 79:73–91.

Derlega, V. J.; Durham, B.; Gockel, B.; and Sholis, D. 1981. Sex differences in self-disclosure: Effects of topic content, friendship, and partner's sex. *Sex Roles* 7:433–447.

Derlega, V. J., and Grezlak, J. 1979. Appropriateness of self-disclosure. In *Self-disclosure: Origins, patterns, and implications of openness in interpersonal relationships*, ed. G. J. Chelune, 151–176. San Francisco: Jossey-Bass.

Derlega, V. J.; Harris, M. S.; and Chaikin, A. L. 1973. Self-disclosure reciprocity, liking, and the deviant. *Journal of Experimental Social Psychology* 9:277–284.

Derlega, V. J.; Winstead, B. A.; Wong, P. T. P.; and Greenspan, M. 1987. Self-disclosure and relationship development: An attributional analysis. In *Interpersonal processes: New directions in communication research*, ed. M. E. Roloff and G. R. Miller, 172–187. Newbury Park, Calif.: Sage.

Dickson-Markman, F. 1986. Self-disclosure with friends across the life cycles. *Journal of Social and Personal Relationships* 3:259–264.

Dindia, K. 1982. Reciprocity of self-disclosure: A sequential analysis. In *Communication yearbook 6*, ed. M. Burgoon, 506–528. Newbury Park, Calif.: Sage.

Dindia, K., and Allen, M. 1992. Sex differences in self-disclosure: A metaanalysis. *Psychological Bulletin* 112:106–124.

Duck, S. W.; Rutt, D. J.; Hurst, M. H.; and Strejc, H. 1991. Some evident truths about conversation in everyday relationships: All communications are not created equal. *Human Communication Research* 18:228–268.

Falk, D. R., and Wagner, F. N. 1985. Intimacy of self-disclosure and response processes as factors affecting the development of interpersonal relationships. *Journal of Social Psychology* 125:557–570.

Gilbert, S. J. 1976a. Empirical and theoretical extensions of self-disclosure. In *Explorations in interpersonal communication*, ed. G. R. Miller, 197–215. Newbury Park, Calif.: Sage.

————. 1976b. Self-disclosure, intimacy, and communication in families. *Family Coordinator* 25:221–231.

Gilbert, S. J., and Horenstein, D. 1975. The communication of self-disclosure: Level versus valence. *Human Communication Research* 1:316–322.

Gudykunst, W. B., and Kim, Y. Y. 1984. *Communicating with strangers: An approach to intercultural communication.* Reading, Mass.: Addison-Wesley.

Gudykunst, W. B., and Nishida, T. 1984. Individual and cultural influences on uncertainty reduction. *Communication Monographs* 51:23–56.

Hecht, M.; Shepard, T.; and Hall, T. J. 1979. Multivariate indices of the effects of self-disclosure. *Western Journal of Speech Communication* 43:235–245.

Hendrick, S. S. 1981. Self-disclosure and marital satisfaction. *Journal of Personality and Social Psychology* 40:1150–1159.

Hosman, L. A. (1987). The evaluational consequences of topic reciprocity and self-disclosure reciprocity. *Communication Monographs* 54:420–435.

Jones, E. E., and Archer, R. L. 1976. Are there special effects of personalistic self-disclosure? *Journal of Experimental Social Psychology* 12:180–193.

Jourard, S. M. 1971. *The transparent self,* 2d ed. New York: Van Nostrand.

Ludwig, D.; Franco, J. N.; and Malloy, T. E. 1986. Effects of reciprocity and self-monitoring on self-disclosure with a new acquaintance. *Journal of Personality and Social Psychology* 50: 1077–1082.

Miller, L. C. 1990. Intimacy and liking: Mutual influence and the role of unique relationships. *Journal of Personality and Social Psychology* 59:50–60.

Morton, T. L. 1978. Intimacy and reciprocity exchange: A comparison of spouses and strangers. *Journal of Personality and Social Psychology* 36:72–81.

Nakanishi, M. 1986. Perceptions of self-disclosure in initial interaction: A Japanese sample. *Human Communication Research* 13:167–190.

Parks, M. 1982. Ideology in interpersonal communication: Off the couch and into the world. In *Communication Yearbook 6,* ed. M. Burgoon, 79–107. Newbury Park, Calif.: Sage.

Pearce, W. B.; Sharp, S. M.; Wright, P. H.; and Slama, K. M. 1974. Affection and reciprocity in self-disclosing communication. *Human Communication Research* 1:5–14.

Petronio, S. 1991. Communication boundary management: A theoretical model of managing disclosure of private information between marital couples. *Communication Theory* 1:311–335.

Petronio, S.; Martin, J.; and Littlefield, R. 1984. Prerequisite conditions for self-disclosure: A gender issue. *Communication Monographs* 51:268–273.

Rawlins, W. R. 1983. Openness as problematic in ongoing friendships: Two conversational dilemmas. *Communication Monographs* 50:1–13.

Rosenberg, K. J., and Mann, L. 1986. The development of the norm of reciprocity of self-disclosure and its function in children's attraction to peers. *Child Development* 57:1349–1357.

Rosenfeld, L. 1979. Self-disclosure avoidance: Why I am afraid to tell you who I am. *Communication Monographs* 46:63–74.

Schlenker, B. R., and Leary, M. R. 1982. Audiences' reactions to self-enhancing, self-denigrating, and accurate self-presentations. *Journal of Experimental Social Psychology* 18:89–104.

Schmidt, T. O., and Cornelius, P. R. 1987. Self-disclosure in everyday life. *Journal of Social and Personal Relationships* 4:365–373.

Shaffer, D. R., and Ogden, J. K. 1986. On sex differences in self-disclosure during the acquaintance process: The role of anticipated future interaction. *Journal of Personality and Social Psychology* 51:92–101.

Snyder, M. 1974. The self-monitoring of expressive behavior. *Journal of Personality and Social Psychology* 30:526–537.

———. 1979. Self-monitoring processes. In *Advances in experimental social psychology*, vol. 12, ed. L. Berkowitz, 85–128. Orlando, Fla.: Academic Press.

Wheeless, L. R. 1976. Self-disclosure and interpersonal solidarity: Measurement, validation, and relationships. *Human Communication Research* 3:47–61.

Wheeless, L. R., and Grotz, L. 1977. The measurement of trust and its relationship to self-disclosure. *Human Communication Research* 3:250–257.

Worthy, W.; Gary, A. L.; and Kahn, G. M. 1969. Self-disclosure as an exchange process. *Journal of Personality and Social Psychology* 13:59–63.

Wortman, C. B.; Adesman, P.; Herman, E.; and Greenberg, R. 1976. Self-disclosure: An attributional perspective. *Journal of Personality and Social Psychology* 33:184–191.

P A R T   I I I

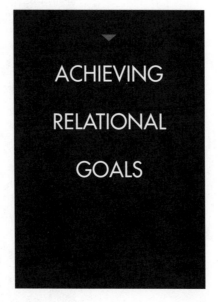

ACHIEVING

RELATIONAL

GOALS

In Part III, we take a closer look at relational goals, specifically relational escalation, maintenance, and de-escalation. Chapter 8 discusses relational escalation: the advantages and disadvantages of involvement, the emotional processes of attraction and intimacy, and some current research on relational escalation—including a word about love. Chapter 9 centers on relational maintenance: the reasons why people choose to maintain relationships, the strategies they use, and the different forms long-term relationships can take. Chapter 10 discusses why and how relationships end or de-escalate. We look at the four phases of disengagement, the methods people use to break up, and the emotional consequences of ending a relationship.

CHAPTER 8

ESCALATING

RELATIONSHIPS

Tracy worked part time at a video store, supporting herself while she finished her B.A. It was ironic that she worked in a video store because she was an English literature major who did not spend much time watching videos at home. Occasionally, she would recognize people from school—fellow students, teachers, and others—and they would recognize her. Tracy took good care of herself, was very helpful to customers, and had a very pleasant voice. Men were attracted to her.

One was Brad, a graduate student. Although he never went out of his way to talk with Tracy, Brad showed interest. He would compliment her on her appearance, ask how her day had gone, and be attentive to her responses. Tracy was also attracted to Brad, so she smiled and asked him about his interests. When she discovered that Brad didn't have a girlfriend, Tracy hinted that she was available for a date.

Recall that the three primary interpersonal goals are self-presentation, relational, and instrumental. At this juncture we turn our attention to the associations between communication and relationship development. The chapters in Part III discuss the relationship of communication to the goals of relational escalation, maintenance, and de-escalation or termination. This chapter focuses specifically on how people escalate relationships.

What Is Relational Escalation?

What does it mean to escalate a relationship? Most people would point to increases in intimacy. Perlman and Fehr (1987) identify seven qualities of intimate relationships:

1. Interaction increases in terms of frequency, duration, and number of social contacts.
2. Partners gain knowledge of one another's innermost levels of being. Topics for discussion and level of personalness of topics increase, and partners develop personal communication modes (or idiosyncratic messages).
3. Partners become more skilled at tracing and predicting each other's behavior.
4. Partners increase their own investments (time, money, emotional energies, etc.) in the relationship.

5. Interdependence and a sense of "we-ness" increase.

6. Partners feel that their separate interests are linked to the well-being of the relationship.

7. Positive affect (warmth, liking, loving, etc.) and sense of caring, commitment, and trust increase.

From this list and other research (e.g., Burgoon and Hale 1984; Kelley 1979; Morton, Alexander, and Altman 1976), we can make three general observations. First, escalation of relationships means the successful "negotiation" of both intimacy and control. Not only do partners learn more about each other cognitively and emotionally, but they must also learn how to respond to each other behaviorally by coordinating actions and activities. Second, relational escalation moves partners from social relationships to personal involvements. Broadly speaking, social relationships are role relationships in which participants can be replaced by other people; personal relationships are unique insofar as you cannot replace the other person yet have the relationship continue (see Duck et al. 1984). Finally, it is impossible to discuss relational initiation and escalation without discussing communication behavior. Communication is the primary instrument used for relational initiation and escalation.

ADVANTAGES OF ESCALATING RELATIONSHIPS

The first advantage of escalating a relationship is that you become more interdependent with the other person as the relationship matures, and this helps you achieve desired personal outcomes (Kelley 1979). That is, the closer you become to someone, the more you affect each other's goals. Making dinner while your friend helps you type a paper, pooling money for a long road trip, and borrowing each other's clothes are examples of achieving personal goals together.

The second advantage is the satisfaction of particular interpersonal needs. As you may recall from Chapter 2, Schutz (1966) identifies three fundamental interpersonal needs: *inclusion*, *control*, and *affection*. According to Schutz, you need to include others as part of your world or to be included. Once the inclusion need is met, you may have a need to direct others or to be directed. Finally, you may have a need to express or receive affection. Relational escalation involves meeting these particular needs. This translates into sharing with another person things like art, the seasons, and music (inclusion); greater coordination about how to get to school, where to look for a job, and how much money to save (control); and giving hugs, sending birthday cards, and complimenting each other (affection).

A third advantage to escalating relationships is achieving an understanding of your partner, whether that person be a friend, relative, or lover. Miller and Steinberg (1975) argue that a truly interpersonal relationship is based on unique knowledge of the other person. Andersen (1989) observes that "interpersonal relationships are characterized by relational uniqueness and a psychological understanding of one's relational partner rather than stereotyping and purely functional orientation toward the other" (p. 5). In short, knowing another person is an important outcome of relational escalation, one that most people view as positive.

The last advantage is that relational escalation helps reduce uncertainty about the other person (Berger and Calabrese 1975). Berger and Calabrese posit that uncertainty is generally an anxious experience and that information about another person helps reduce uncertainty. Such information is obtained by interacting with the individual as well as by observing the other person in various social settings. Over time, this store of information helps reduce uncertainty about the person and the relationship (Miell and Duck 1986).

DISADVANTAGES OF ESCALATING RELATIONSHIPS

Hatfield (1984) presents five disadvantages of pursuing closer involvements with others. First, you may be exposed. Your private feelings and dreams are revealed, and many of these may be very personal or painful, so communicating them makes you vulnerable. Second, you may be abandoned. Many of us have experienced the heartache of losing someone we loved and trusted. For many people, the fear of abandonment is reason enough for not seeking new relationships. Third, you may fear angry attacks by your partner. In close relationships, people can be more malicious and hurtful than in social relationships. Knowing another intimately also means knowing how to hurt that person. Fourth, you may lose control over the situation. It is often easier to control your life alone. It is especially easier to control yourself when emotions are not rampaging through your thoughts. Finally, you may fear your own destructive impulses. Some people believe that they cannot make a commitment to someone, so they hold people at a safe distance to protect them. Others know that they have a quick temper, a jealous mind, or abusive tendencies. Because these destructive impulses could harm others, people may choose to keep others at a distance.

Interpersonal Attraction: The Catalyst of Escalation

Interpersonal attraction refers to the various forces that draw people together. As Huston (1974) notes, attraction involves emotional responses toward another person, as well as beliefs, evaluations, and behaviors regarding that person. In other words, there are a variety of forces that draw people together, and there are different responses to attraction.

Research has uncovered various dimensions of interpersonal attraction. McCroskey and McCain (1974) report three dimensions: *social, task,* and *physical.* A person can be socially adept, good at doing a particular job, and/or physically beautiful.

Berger and co-workers (1977) offer a different set of dimensions: *supportiveness, character*, and *sociability*. Supportiveness is reflected in the extent to which someone understands you, likes you, and is interested in your welfare; character refers to how sincere, dependable, and ethical that person is; and sociability concerns how outgoing, popular, and pleasant that person is. Berger and colleagues found that these dimensions changed in importance across relationships. For example, close friends and lovers rated supportiveness as more important than acquaintances did. The Berger study reveals that the bases for attraction vary across relationships and that these bases may actually shift in importance as a particular relationship develops.

Clatterbuck (1980) provides an effective scheme for organizing the research on interpersonal attraction. He separates the attraction research into four classes: *anthropological, reinforcement, cognitive*, and *structural*. The anthropological class includes studies that have examined attraction on a social level, for example, the relationship between physical beauty and liking. The reinforcement class refers to studies of interpersonal attraction as a learned response to reinforcements (see Byrne 1971). The cognitive class concerns how people's similarities in cognitions lead to liking. The structural class refers to how people structure their communication in order to be seen as attractive. Although it is impossible to review all of the research regarding interpersonal attraction, let us look at some of the most important findings in each of the four classes referenced by Clatterbuck.

ANTHROPOLOGICAL CLASS: PHYSICAL BEAUTY

When we hear the term *attractive*, most of us think of physical beauty. And research reveals that a person's physical appearance can dramatically affect our response to that person. Bull and Rumsey (1988) document several correlates of physical beauty. These include favorable attributions about the person, such as kindness, warmth, intelligence, and honesty; sexual experiences, where more physically appealing people experience more opportunities; earlier romantic involvements and marriage; and perceived similarity (in beliefs and values). In addition, Bull and Rumsey review several studies indicating that people who are unusual-looking may be stigmatized. For example, people with cleft palates have difficulty meeting new people, and they marry less frequently and have fewer children than those without cleft palates. Hatfield and Sprecher (1986) offer a similar view when they conclude, "These studies actually demonstrated that '*what is beautiful is good; what is ugly is bad*'" (p. 356).

Clearly, people are drawn to those who are physically attractive. After all, physical characteristics offer a lot of initial information about a person. Two observations about the effects of physical beauty should be made. First, physical beauty is often defined by cultural standards. For example, Hatfield and Sprecher (1986) note that "in some societies (like our own), a slim woman is the ideal. The opposite, however, is true in most other societies—the fatter the better" (p. 7). Second, the manner in which a person communicates affects whether that person is seen as beautiful. Levinger (1974) notes the possibility of how "initial impressions of a 'beautiful person' are outweighed by subsequent interaction with him or her; or how an 'ugly' person may gradually or suddenly become attractive for reasons other than a change in physical appearance" (p. 105). Our point is that we should not dismiss the effects of physical beauty on relational development; rather, we should observe for ourselves how physical beauty and communication behavior combine to affect relational growth.

REINFORCEMENT CLASS: SUPPORTIVENESS

The reinforcement class of studies regards interpersonal attraction as a learned response. Byrne and Krivonos (1976) explain that communication and other social activities can be classified as either rewarding or punishing. The rewarding messages and activities lead to positive feelings, which are linked to the source of those messages and activities. Hence "we like others who reward us because they elicit our good feelings" (p. 1).

How do we reward others and thereby increase our own attractiveness? There are numerous ways, of which four are most salient. First, showing that we have similar attitudes and values increases attraction because this indicates to the other person that his or her way of thinking about the world is correct (Byrne and Clore 1970). Second, we reward others by being supportive of their goals and interests, as the Berger and colleagues (1977) study found. Third, as mentioned in Chapter 3, we can confirm the other by responding in direct and affirmative ways. Finally, complimenting the other can be highly reinforcing (but see Chapter 5 on ingratiation).

COGNITIVE CLASS: ATTITUDE SIMILARITY

According to the cognitive approach, attitude similarity increases interpersonal attraction because people like to remain consistent in their beliefs, values, and behaviors. And because it is easier to retain consistency in a relationship with someone who agrees (rather than disagrees) with us, we are drawn to others who have beliefs,

The initial phases of a relationship are often exciting and charged with energy.

values, and behaviors similar to our own. This tendency to be attracted to others who have similar cognitions is called **homogamy** (Kerckhoff 1974), the principle behind the saying "birds of a feather flock together."

If you are tempted to counter with the adage "opposites attract," you would be right to do so; in a fundamental way, both truisms are correct. You will recall that according to Schutz's postulate of compatibility, one person's needs must be "balanced" by his or her partner's needs. So, for example, if one person has a high need to receive affection, the partner should have a high need to give affection in order for the couple to be compatible. Finding support for this postulate, Kerckhoff and Davis (1962) found that couples in long-term romantic relationships had higher need compatibility than couples in short-term relationships. In addition, the long-term couples had higher similarity of values. Given this study and many others on attitude similarity and attraction, we conclude that "birds of a feather flock together" is true regarding attitudes, beliefs, and values, whereas "opposites attract" holds true when discussing interpersonal needs.

Sunnafrank (1991; see also Sunnafrank and Miller 1981) points out that the link between attitude similarity and attraction can be understood only as a function of partners' communicating their similarities. The lion's share of the research regarding attitude similarity and attraction ignores communicative influences, although other studies show that how people communicate with one another filters the effects of attitude similarity on attraction (e.g., Sunnafrank and Miller 1981). Likewise, Duck and Miell (1984; see also Duck 1976) note that during the development of relationships, people obtain different kinds of information through communication. At the acquaintance stage, global assessments of attitudes and personality are obtained and act as filters for further acquaintance. More precise information about the partner's personality and world view become important as the relationship progresses.

STRUCTURAL CLASS: COMMUNICATION

Clatterbuck (1980) laments that relatively few studies have examined the manner in which interpersonal communication functions as a basis of attraction. Cappella (1984) further argues that attraction should be understood as the meshing of interaction styles. Wallace (1992) examined the research in order to discover specific interaction behaviors tied to interpersonal attraction. She uncovered eighty-five behaviors and through factor analysis identified four underlying factors: *sensitivity*, *confidence*, *talkativeness*, and *flirtatiousness* or *immediacy*. Table 8-1 presents sample items from these factors and reports the correlations between these factors and liking.

As Table 8-1 reveals, communicator use of sensitivity and confidence were strongly and positively correlated with liking the communicator. Being talkative was negatively correlated with liking. Wallace (1992) also found that communicator use of sensitivity and confidence behaviors were associated with attraction, regardless of

Table 8-1

COMMUNICATION-BASED ATTRACTION FACTORS
AND THEIR ASSOCIATIONS WITH LIKING

Factor	Examples	Correlation with Liking
Sensitivity	This person conveys a sensitive attitude, communicates feeling of trust, encourages my ideas, displays sincerity, asks for my opinions.	.84
Confidence	This person expresses himself or herself well verbally, tends to be a leader, is committed to his or her beliefs, is confident around the opposite sex, appears motivated.	.54
Talkativeness	This person talks a lot, tells numerous stories, talks about himself or herself, dominates the conversation, speaks in a loud voice.	−.41
Flirtatiousness/ Immediacy	This person flirts with me, physically touches me, stands very close to me, stares at me, hugs me or others.	.39

Source: Adapted from Wallace 1992.

perceptions of physical beauty, but flirtatious behavior varied with physical attractiveness and type of relationship.

In sum, four important factors of interpersonal attraction are physical beauty, reinforcement, attitude similarity, and communication. One prevailing notion is that these attraction factors are partly or entirely dependent on interaction behaviors.

Increasing Intimacy during Interaction

We will now examine how people attempt to increase the level of intimacy during interaction. First, we will note some of the communication behaviors associated with increased intimacy. Then we will describe a theory used to assess people's reactions to those communication behaviors.

COMMUNICATION BEHAVIORS ASSOCIATED WITH INCREASED INTIMACY
Researchers have provided lists of communication behaviors that indicate an increase in intimacy (e.g., Cappella 1984; Guerrero and Andersen 1991; Knapp 1984; Levinger 1974). These behaviors are often initiated by one person. They fall into verbal and nonverbal categories.

Several verbal messages are associated with increased intimacy:

1. *New topics* can be initiated, either by offering them yourself or by asking your partner to discuss something that has not been discussed before.
2. *Inclusive language* creates a sense of belonging, as when using the first person plural *we* instead of *I* and *you*.
3. *Personal idioms* include nicknames, expressions of affection, and references to sex that only the couple understand.
4. *Positive messages* refers to offering upbeat content and responses.
5. *Compliments* paid to the other identify aspects of the person that you appreciate.
6. *Constructive conflict* using cooperative tactics helps escalate the relationship more than using competitive tactics (see also Chapter 12).
7. *Metarelational talk* is talk about the nature of the relationship as an entity.

Several nonverbal behaviors also accompany increases in intimacy (also see Chapter 4).

1. *Gazes* last longer between intimate relational partners than between others.
2. *Direct body orientation* involves squarely facing the partner instead of interacting from the side.
3. *Shoulder orientation* refers to avoiding excluding the other by "turning a cold shoulder."
4. *Facial expressiveness* indicates greater interaction involvement.
5. *Proximity* reflects emotional closeness: less distance indicates a closer relationship.
6. *Touching* is one of the most sensitive barometers of intimacy; touching the other in particular places (e.g., neck, knees) indicates intimate involvement.
7. *Vocal affiliation*—warmth and pleasantness of voice—is an indicator of intimacy.
8. *Common possessions*, shared or jointly owned, indicate an intimate relationship.

Imagine that you have a friend who enacts a few of the behaviors just enumerated to show that he or she wants to escalate the relationship. What would you do? How

The behaviors associated with close romantic involvement can be obvious, such as increased touching and eye gaze. Increases in intimacy are also associated with verbal behaviors, such as use of inclusive language, nicknames, and meta-relational talk.

(Joel Gordon)

you respond during interaction depends on a number of factors, such as where you were at that moment, rules the two of you had established, and how you felt physically. Cognitive valence theory accounts for such factors.

COGNITIVE VALENCE THEORY

Andersen (1989, 1985; see also Andersen and Andersen 1984) has developed **cognitive valence theory** to explain how people respond to messages that signal increased intimacy. This theory "begins when the behavioral intimacy of a relational partner increases above the typical level that has been manifested previously in the relationship" (Andersen 1989, 5). To illustrate this theory, we refer to the character in the story at the beginning of this chapter. According to cognitive valence theory, if during interaction, Brad attempts to increase intimacy and those attempts are perceived by Tracy, several factors are considered. As Figure 8-1 indicates, if Tracy experiences low arousal as a result of Brad's intimacy gestures, she will not respond to Brad's change in intimacy. If Tracy experiences high arousal (increase in heart rate or fear), she will *compensate* for Brad's attempt to increase intimacy. Such compensation could include many behaviors: averting a gaze, increasing distance, not talking, or perhaps demanding that he leave her alone. It is at the moderate levels of arousal (heightened interest without fear) that cognitive valence theory predicts interesting variations.

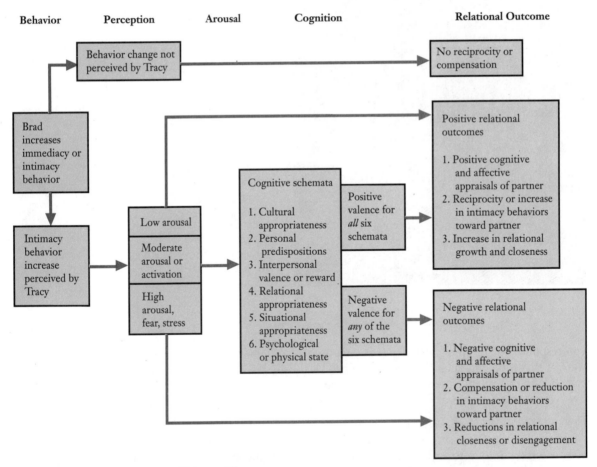

Figure 8-1 ▼ Cognitive Valence Theory
Source: Adapted from Andersen 1989.

If Tracy experiences moderate arousal (heightened interest without fear), she would cognitively assess Brad's attempt at intimacy according to six "cognitive schemata."

1. *Cultural appropriateness* asks whether Brad's behavior conforms to expected behaviors given the culture's rules and norms.
2. *Personal predispositions* are Tracy's tendencies to affiliate with other people. If she is affiliative generally, she is more likely to reciprocate Brad's intimacy behaviors.
3. *Interpersonal valence or reward* concerns Brad's reward value—is he rewarding?
4. *Relational appropriateness* asks whether Brad's behavior is understandable given the nature and expectations developed between him and Tracy.
5. *Situational appropriateness* refers to whether or not this kind of behavior is appropriate to the context (e.g., flirting at work is often inappropriate).
6. *Psychological or physical state* refers to internal feelings. If Tracy has the flu, for example, she may not feel up to reciprocating Brad's interactional intimacy.

According to Andersen's cognitive valence theory, if all six of the schemata are positive, positive relational outcomes will occur; that is, Brad will be viewed in a favorable light, Tracy will reciprocate his communication, and there will be an increase in intimacy. If, however, any of the six schemata is negative, negative relational outcomes are predicted; that is, Brad will be seen less favorably, Tracy will compensate for Brad's gestures of intimacy, and the relationship may de-escalate. As Andersen (1989) notes, "This model has suggested that movement toward intimacy is a fragile, perilous process. Behavioral intimacy increases must undergo positive schematic analysis across at least six relational schemata" (p. 41).

Relational Escalation Processes

Brad asked Tracy out for coffee after work. Within a couple of hours, Brad learned that Tracy likes jazz dancing and painting, and Tracy learned about Brad's writing poetry and his thesis on the French existential movement following World War II. Both were infatuated before the caffeine wore off, and each had trouble sleeping that night.

Soon they became inseparable. It was amazing that they could find the extra energy it took to see each other. They gradually learned a lot about each other's pasts and plans for the future. Tracy read to Brad and painted a lovely landscape for him. He bought her a custom-made music box that played a song they both liked.

After a few months, they had truly become a couple. They no longer talked for hours and hours about really personal issues. They instead focused on what they ate for dinner, which videos to see, road trips, and different card games. Every now and then they had deep talks, like before. They also began to have conflicts, but these also somehow seemed normal.

We will now discuss the general progression of relationship intimacy. We will examine properties of communication that change, stages of relational escalation, research on escalation, turning points, and love. This material emphasizes that relationships develop in different ways.

SOCIAL PENETRATION REVISITED

We turn again to social penetration theory to examine relational escalation processes because it has guided much theory and research on relational escalation. You may recall from Chapter 7 that social penetration theory concerns how individuals reveal information about themselves according to the dimensions of breadth (number of topics) and depth (how personal the disclosure is). Moreover, relational rewards are compared against costs, such that if the relationship is rewarding, it is pursued; if the relationship is more costly than rewarding, it is not pursued. Such bookkeeping takes into account the present status of the relationship as well as forecasts for the future (e.g., "Once she moves back home, this relationship won't be so frustrating"). According to Taylor and Altman (1987), "Social penetration processes proceed in a gradual and orderly fashion from superficial to intimate levels of exchange as a function of both immediate and forecast outcomes" (p. 259).

Altman and Taylor (1973) identify eight dimensions of communication that increase as the relationship escalates (see also Knapp 1984). These dimensions are (1) *richness,* or breadth of interaction along various topics; (2) *uniqueness of interaction,* where the couple exchange verbal and nonverbal messages known only to them; (3) *efficiency of exchange,* or the accuracy and sensitivity of message exchange that does not require elaboration; (4) *substitutability and equivalency,* which means that "more ways become available to communicate the same feeling in a substitutable and equivalent fashion" (p. 132); (5) *synchronization and pacing,* which refers to spontaneous coordinating and interweaving of behaviors (e.g., washing dishes together, agreeing quickly, sharing the bathroom without conflict); (6) *permeability and openness,* which refers to verbal and nonverbal exchanges of intimacy, including sexual closeness; (7) *voluntariness and spontaneity of change,* which refers to the couple's ability to be creative and spontaneous in their communicating with each other; and (8) *evaluation,* or the increased tendency to point out the negative and positive aspects of the other.

Research offers some support for the claim that these dimensions increase as the relationship matures. Knapp, Ellis, and Williams (1980) found that *personalized* messages (e.g., sharing secrets, using greater numbers of channels, using messages only the dyad understands) were perceived more in relationships having greater intimacy. The researchers also found that *synchronized* messages (messages that are smooth-flowing and spontaneous) were also perceived more in intimate relationships. Interestingly, and contrary to theory, *difficulty* (awkwardness, inability to understand) of communication did not differ among relationships that varied in intimacy. These findings indicate that communication generally becomes more personal and spontaneous, but not less difficult, as the relationship progresses. Using student diaries, Baxter and Wilmot (1983) also found that communication personalness increased as social penetration theory predicts. But, these authors also reported that frequency of contact and breadth of topics discussed did not increase over time.

STAGES OF RELATIONAL ESCALATION

Altman and Taylor (1973) identify four stages of relational escalation, based on changes in the eight dimensions just discussed. Stage 1 is **orientation.** Responses are very general, stereotyped, and typically sensitive to the norms of social appropriateness. There is little richness, no uniqueness, little efficiency, and no substitutability or open evaluation of the other. Only superficial information is discussed. Synchronicity is limited to normative behaviors (e.g., greeting with a handshake, holding a door open).

The second stage is **exploratory affect exchange.** Because there is some penetration of the personality, increases in richness, uniqueness, and efficiency in the outer areas of the personality occur. Nonverbal behaviors are smoother and more synchronized. Open evaluations begin regarding superficial topics. Many relationships do not escalate beyond this stage.

The third stage is **affective exchange.** This stage reflects communication that is rich and "freewheeling." There is increased efficiency and substitutability (e.g., a particular glance is understood to mean "It's time to go"). Interaction is spontaneous. Many barriers are broken down in this stage to permit greater permeability of exchange.

The final stage is **stable exchange.** At this point, all dimensions of communication are at their maximum. Communication is very efficient, and there are a multitude of ways for saying the same thing. Perhaps for the first time, there is richness in exploring the deepest parts of the personality.

Knapp (1984) also offers an account of how communication is associated with relational escalation. **Initiating** is the first stage. Initiating refers to the processes and behaviors involved in coming into contact with someone. People ask themselves questions such as "How do I meet this person?" and "Is this person open to meeting me?" According to Wilmot (1987), initiating actually begins when you become aware of someone who is aware of you. Many relationships never escalate past the initiating stage. Although we may meet many people in a given day, nothing more than recognition or greetings are exchanged.

Knapp's next stage is **experimenting.** In this stage, "name, rank, and serial number" are offered ("So, what's your middle name?" "I am the firstborn," "My astrological sign is Leo—what's yours?"). In other words, during the experimenting stage, people engage in small talk. The objective in this stage is not to discover immediately another's core self; it is instead to present oneself as socially competent and to experiment with possible avenues for future interaction ("Do you like to ski?" "Does your son like preschool?" "Are you involved with anyone?"). People can become frustrated at making small talk, especially if none of their relationships seem to progress beyond that stage. Nevertheless, as Knapp points out, small talk functions to maintain most of our relationships and to serve as a springboard for escalating others.

Intensifying occurs when people move beyond superficial knowledge of one another to explore more intimate aspects. Knapp offers several communication behaviors that accompany intensifying. These include increases in personal self-disclosure, informal forms of address ("Bro," "Sweetie"), use of the first person plural ("*Let's* go to a movie," "What are *we* doing Friday?"), direct expressions of affection that may be reciprocated ("I think you're great," "Well, I think you're fantastic"), verbal shortcuts that both people understand to replace full sentences ("Seatbelt" instead of "Please fasten your seatbelt"), and a clearer understanding of nonverbal messages (e.g., a sigh does not necessarily mean frustration).

Knapp (1984) refers to the **integrating** stage as "a point where the two individual personalities almost seem to fuse or coalesce, certainly more than at any previous stage" (p. 38). Specific communication behaviors accompanying this stage: intimacy "trophies" (such as rings and pictures) are exchanged; both persons' social networks merge, or one person's friends are adopted; particular attitudes, beliefs, and activities are developed together (e.g., going to church together, taking classes together, changing political positions); nonverbally, the dyad becomes synchronized, so the two act in unison; the couple identify with particular events or places (our song, our favorite Italian restaurant, the day we met, etc.); and similarities in dress, speech, and mannerisms occur (e.g., matching outfits, adjusting speaking speed to accommodate the partner).

Knapp's final stage of relational escalation is **bonding.** This refers to a public announcement of sorts that the relationship is indeed unique and should be respected. The wedding ritual is the prototype of bonding. It communicates clearly that a particular relationship is treasured by the couple and legally sanctioned by society. Similar romantic bonding rituals are going steady and getting engaged. Knapp notes that few bonding rituals have been institutionalized by society for nonromantic relationships.

The discussion regarding stages focuses our attention on several ways in which communication behavior is tied to the development of personal relationships. This discussion might also imply that all relationships develop in a relatively simple and linear manner, graduating to higher levels of intimacy, and that each stage must include the behaviors we described. But this is not the case. The process for many is not simple or linear. Instead, relational escalation probably involves cycles of growing together as well as periods of stability and stagnation, as theorists such as Altman and Taylor (1973) and Knapp (1984) have recognized.

RESEARCH ON RELATIONAL ESCALATION

Research indicates that relationships do not progress in a linear manner. That is, as the relationship grows, partners reveal more about each other, display more immediate nonverbal cues, and become more efficient in their use of messages, to a point. But such disclosures, displays of affection, and efficiency are not continual. After a period of time, they subside. In addition, the communication behaviors that signal increased intimacy alternate with talk about routine and mundane topics and periods of lack of affection, conflict, and awkward or inefficient communication.

Recent research suggests that relationships grow in intimacy to a point, then subside as the relationship becomes stable. Van Lear (1987) found that as the relationships progressed, private and personal disclosures increased until they reached a peak in personalness, after which the number of such messages declined. Likewise, Hays (1984) studied the development of friendships and found that intimate communication was highest in the six- to nine-week range, and intimate messages decreased at twelve weeks. However, participants who were not close experienced a steady decline in intimacy of communication almost from the outset of the study. Guerrero and Andersen (1991) found that seriously dating and marriage-bound participants touched each other more than either married people, casual daters, or couples just beginning to date. Guerrero and Andersen noted that once the feelings of attachment have been secured, there is less need for personal disclosures and displays of affection. Van Lear (1992) found that during a given conversation or between conversations, acquaintances cycle back and forth between personal and superficial issues. But overall the discussions became more intimate to a point.

Huston, McHale, and Crouter (1986) interviewed married couples at the beginning of the marriage and then a year later. In general, they found that couples became less satisfied with their relationship and with the *quantity* of various kinds of communication during their first year of marriage. Behaviors that were less frequent after one year of marriage were approving or complimenting the spouse, making the partner laugh, expressions of love, initiating sex, doing something nice for the partner, sharing physical affection (besides sex), and sharing emotions, feelings, or problems. The most harmful communication behavior was being negative (criticism, sarcasm, etc.). This study provides further evidence that intimate messages subside toward the end of the relational escalation process.

Research indicates that relational escalation is marked by ebbs and flows of messages that signal increased involvement. A couple's interpersonal communication will tend toward a level of intimacy that can be sustained over time.

(Cynthia Benjamins/Black Star)

In sum, research indicates that relational escalation is marked by ebbs and flows of increased involvement. After a period of time, communication decreases to a level of intimacy fluctuation that can be sustained over time. Figure 8-2 contrasts how some people think relationships should escalate—in a straight line over time—with how the research suggests relationships actually do progress—in cycles to a high point of intimate exchange and then down to a point of stable exchange.

Do couples escalate their relationships at the same rate? Associated with this question is the issue of what events, if any, mark the escalation of relationships. An examination of romantic couples' turning points addresses both of these issues.

TURNING POINTS

Baxter and Bullis (1986) define the **turning point** as "any event or occurrence that is associated with change in a relationship" (p. 470). When you recall a friendship or a romantic involvement, you can pinpoint particular events where the relationship changed. Such events as deciding to be committed to each other, a death in the family, or making up after a separation can significantly affect the escalation of the relationship.

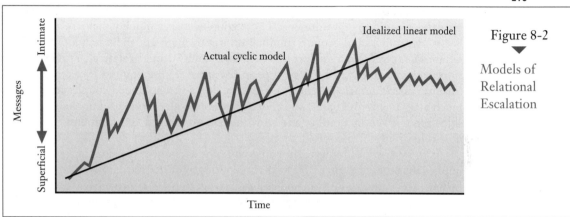

Figure 8-2

Models of Relational Escalation

One method of demarcating turning points is the Retrospective Interview Technique (RIT) (Huston et al. 1981). Using RIT, researchers can locate turning points of relationships on a grid. The points can be plotted by using the x axis to represent time and the y axis to represent degree of commitment (from no commitment to 100 percent). Figure 8-3 illustrates the escalation of a hypothetical relationship using this method.

Using this type of method, Huston and colleagues (1981) reported on two studies on courtship that revealed three couple types that vary in their escalation toward

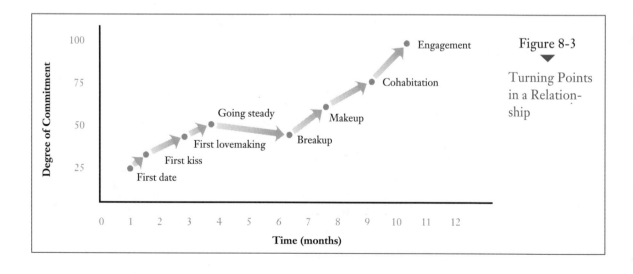

Figure 8-3

Turning Points in a Relationship

commitment (marriage). According to Huston and co-workers, *accelerated* courtship escalates rapidly to commitment. These couples marry quickly, have relatively low levels of conflict, and require minimal efforts to maintain their relationships. The *intermediate* courtship type involves high levels of love and a relatively rapid progression to commitment. The third type is *prolonged*. These couples escalate the relationship in a "gradual and uncertain fashion" (p. 72). Prolonged couples have just as much love as intermediates, and more than accelerated couples, but their relationships are marked by conflict and slow movement toward commitment. Figure 8-4 illustrates these three courtship types.

As these analyses indicate, not all courtships escalate at the same rates. This also implies that these couples vary in their experience of the escalation stages reviewed earlier. According to Huston and colleagues, accelerated courtships moved from 25 percent commitment to 75 percent commitment in about three months; intermediate couples moved from 25 percent commitment to 75 percent commitment from six to nine months; prolonged courtships required between 17 and 28 months to move from 25 percent commitment to 75 percent commitment. In addition, these couples differed in the number of turning points they experienced. As would be expected, the prolonged couples experienced the most turning points (an average of 11.4) than the accelerated (5.4) or intermediate courtship types (5.3).

Baxter and Bullis (1986) wanted to uncover the specific content of turning points, to explore precisely what was altering the trajectory of romantic relationships. They uncovered twenty-five different types of turning points, which were collapsed into thirteen categories. Table 8-2 presents the thirteen turning point types and the percentage change in commitment associated with each type.

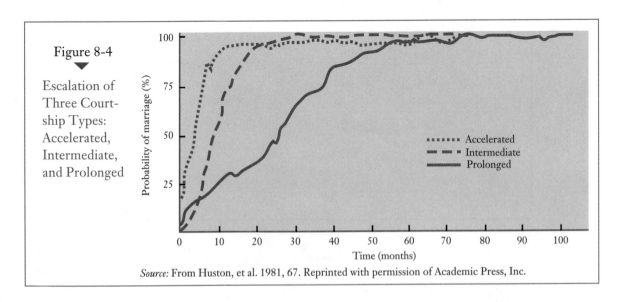

Figure 8-4

Escalation of Three Courtship Types: Accelerated, Intermediate, and Prolonged

Source: From Huston, et al. 1981, 67. Reprinted with permission of Academic Press, Inc.

Table 8-2
TURNING POINT TYPES AND COMMITMENT SCORES

Turning Point Type	Description	Example	Commitment Score* (%)
"Getting to know you" time	Events that help the parties get to know each other	Studying together	21.13
Quality time	Time spent enjoying each other's company for its own sake	Getting away together	15.18
Physical separation	Time spent apart, but not breakups	School break, vacation	−.30
External competition	Another person or demand competing with the relationship	Return of an old flame	−13.44
Reunion	Reunion after a physical separation	First night together after six weeks apart	10.72
Passion	Physical or emotional affection acutely experienced	Love at first sight, first kiss	20.35
Disengagement	Breakup initiated by one or both parties	Trial separation	−23.28
Positive psychic change	Change of attitude to feel more positive about the relationship	Realization of intensity of partner's feelings	18.98
Exclusivity	Agreement not to date others	Going steady, avoiding former romantic partners	19.21
Negative psychic change	Change of attitude to feel less positive about the relationship	Realization that both parties are unhappy	−9.00
Making up	Repair of the relationship after a breakup or fight	Agreeing to give the relationship one more try	21.60
Serious commitment	Event committing the partners for the future	Moving in together, engagement	23.26
Sacrifice	One person's giving of self on the partner's behalf	Help in a time of crisis, giving a gift	17.61

*Change in degree of commitment following the turning point.
Source: Adapted from Baxter and Bullis 1986. Reprinted by permission of Sage Publications, Inc.

TURNING POINTS IN *ANNIE HALL*

Have you ever looked back on a relationship's significant events, its turning points? That's what Woody Allen does in *Annie Hall*, a perceptive film about his real-life love relationship with Diane Keaton, cast in the title role.

The development of that relationship is not presented chronologically. We learn the details of how the two met and their key encounters much as real remembrances occur, in sharply recalled vignettes. At the end of the film, when the couple meet for lunch to "kick around old times," we see about a dozen brief flashbacks of scenes in the film, each a significant event in the relationship.

Among these turning points, of course, is the day they met, when Annie Hall gives Alvie Singer (Woody Allen) a ride home. Alvie comments on Annie's terrible driving; nevertheless, she invites him up to her apartment for a drink. Alvie thinks Annie is beautiful; she hopes that he's not a flake. Alvie invites himself to hear her sing, and she agrees. That is how they begin dating.

Another turning point is the famous lobster scene. As Alvie and Annie cook a lobster meal together, the lobsters get loose, and Alvie pretends to panic. One lobster supposedly hides behind the refrigerator, and Alvie proposes flushing it out with a dish of melted butter. Laughing at his mock hysteria, Annie takes pictures of Alvie holding a lobster. These shared moments clearly increase their intimacy and serve to move their relationship into the phase of exploratory affective exchange.

A truly significant turning point is illustrated in the spider episode. They had broken up, but Annie calls Alvie to help her kill a spider "as big as a Buick" in her bathroom. After she swats at the spider a few times with her tennis racket, she breaks into tears, and they talk about how much they miss each other. They decide to make up. In many relationships, such a reconciliation can increase a couple's commitment, as it apparently does for Alvie and Annie.

Many other important turning points in relationships are portrayed in *Annie Hall*. In one scene, Alvie makes a telling comment about relationship development: "A relationship is like a shark, you know. It has to constantly move forward, or else it dies." In *Annie Hall*, through recollections of a relationship's significant events, we get that sense of moving forward into uncharted and ever-changing waters.

As the table indicates, most turning points helped the couple escalate toward commitment. As might be expected, a few of the turning points—external competition, disengagement, and negative psychic change—impeded movement toward commitment. The researchers also found that many of the turning points involved relational talk, or messages about the nature of the relationship.

A WORD ABOUT LOVE

Many people would argue that the highest, most meaningful relational experience is love. But love is easier to want than to understand.

There are many views on love. Rubin (1973) defines love as giving and caring without needing attachment (pp. 213-215). Fromm (1956) sees love as an art, requiring discipline and commitment. Based on years of clinical work as well as research, Lasswell and Lasswell (1976) identified six types of love (agape, eros, etc.). Marston, Hecht, and Robers (1987) recognize that love encompasses many experiences. These authors conceptualize love as an experience of "polyvalent" and interdependent thoughts, feelings, and behaviors. In their words, love "involves the individual in all aspects of his or her being: thought, . . . action, . . . and feelings" (p. 391).

Marston and colleagues investigated experiences of love by having people describe their attitudes, feelings, and physiological responses to love. Using this open-ended method, these researchers discovered six types of **love ways.** *Collaborative* love is marked by feelings of energy and heightened emotions. Collaborative lovers communicate their love by showing support for their partner. *Active* lovers do things together. Active love is characterized by feelings of strength. It is communicated in talks about one's feelings. *Secure* love is defined by the feelings of security it offers the couple. It is communicated when the partner discusses personal, intimate topics and when one partner does favors for the other. *Intuitive* lovers do not have to say anything because their love is communicated primarily through nonverbal means. Intuitive love involves feelings of warmth, nervousness, and loss of appetite. *Committed* love is defined as togetherness. It is communicated in messages about being together now and in the future. *Traditional romantic* love is experienced with feelings of being beautiful and confident. These lovers also express their love openly.

Marston and associates found that most of their participants reported more than one love way for the same relationship (usually two). Not only are there several types of love experiences, but this study indicates that a relationship is likely to involve a plurality of love experiences. That is, one person may experience intuitive and committed love ways, whereas the partner may experience secure and traditional romantic love ways. The Marston study draws our attention to the various experiences people associate with love, and it suggests that people are experiencing a variety of relational realities.

Chapter Summary

Much has been said about the ways in which relationships escalate. A majority of the research has focused on the relational property of intimacy and how couples achieve intimacy. Our review reflects this research bias. At the same time, we have noted that relationships are not comprised only of intimacy. Other important relational features must be considered—control and trust, for example. Clearly, more needs to be done to research how friends and romantic couples develop these other relational characteristics.

Certain bases of attraction, such as attitude similarity and reinforcement, cannot be brought about without communication. In other words, you use communication to make your attitudes and values known, to reveal your personality, to compliment your acquaintance, and to achieve other goals. These observations are not new (see, for example, Duck 1976).

People also use communication to increase intimacy during interaction. Cognitive valence theory serves a useful purpose in discussing how people respond to increases in intimacy behaviors. The six schemata presented by Andersen appear quite reasonable as those that most people would use in a relatively brief period.

Concerning relational escalation processes, social penetration theory provides the background for much of the thinking and research on the topic, as reflected in the general cyclic model appearing in Figure 8-2. Relationships escalate in cycles, and communication becomes less personal at particular points of escalation, with the most stable relationships reporting less intimacy over time. Relational turning points are excellent benchmarks for noting how a relationship escalates. Research on the topic reveals that there are about thirteen turning point types and that accelerated, intermediate, and prolonged courtships vary in length and in number of turning points. The variety of love ways underscores the complexity of relational life: not only is there more than one type of love, but a person can experience more than one love way in a given relationship.

In short, in terms of intimacy, relationships begin and develop in various ways. Reading about these differences and noting the role of communication in various patterns of relational escalation should enable us to understand better how people achieve their relational escalation goals.

KEY TERMS

▼

interpersonal attraction	initiating
homogamy	experimenting
cognitive valence theory	intensifying
orientation	integrating
exploratory affect exchange	bonding
affective exchange	turning point
stable exchange	love ways

EXERCISES FOR FURTHER DISCUSSION

▼

1. Review the factors contributing to interpersonal attraction: physical beauty, supportiveness, attitude similarity, and communication. Now consider how these factors have affected your own interpersonal relationships.
   a. Which of these factors do you find most important in your relationships?
   b. Are some of these factors more important in one kind of relationship than in others? Which ones are most important in which relationships?
   c. Are some factors more important in earlier stages of a relationship and others more important in later stages?
2. Write a short paragraph in which you describe a situation in which someone tried to increase intimacy through interaction behaviors.
   a. What did you do at the time?
   b. Did your reactions correspond to what cognitive valence theory predicts?
3. Compare Altman and Taylor's model of relational escalation with Knapp's model.
   a. If you were to analyze relational escalation, which set of stages would you use? Why?
   b. Does one of the models work better to describe certain types of relationships (for example, friendships, romantic relationships)?
4. Interview someone you know who is married or engaged. Ask this person to relate the story of his or her relationship, beginning when they first met. Try to get the person to be as specific as possible about any critical events that affected the relationship. Then try to construct a graph similar to the one in Figure 8-3, noting where the critical events took place. Discuss with the person you worked with whether or not the graph provides an accurate reflection of that person's relational escalation. If it does not, what would that person include or exclude?
5. Review the various types of love ways.
   a. In your experience, do people usually think of only one type of love way? If so, which type?
   b. Which of these types have you experienced in your romantic relationships?
   c. Do you think there is an ideal way of love?

SUGGESTED READING

▼

INTERPERSONAL ATTRACTION

Clatterbuck, G. W. 1980. A metatheoretical perspective on interpersonal attraction: The role of communication constructs. In *Interpersonal communication: A relational perspective*, ed. B. W. Morse and L. A. Phelps, 119–131. Minneapolis: Burgess. This review of the attraction literature analyzes four major approaches. Clatterbuck emphasizes the need to study the communication foundations of interpersonal attraction.

Hatfield, E., and Sprecher, S. 1986. *Mirror, mirror . . . : The importance of looks in everyday life*. Albany: State University of New York Press. A very readable book and an excellent review of research on physical beauty. Individual and cultural standards for attractiveness are discussed.

ESCALATION PROCESSES

Altman, I., and Taylor, D. A. 1973. *Social penetration: The development of interpersonal relationships*. Austin, Texas: Holt, Rinehart and Winston. This book discusses dimensions of intimate relationships and stages of intimacy.

Knapp, M. L., and Vangelisti, A. 1992. *Interpersonal communication and human relationships*, 2d ed. Needham Heights, Mass.: Allyn & Bacon. This book analyzes different stages of relational growth and decay. The discussion of how communication is linked to these various stages is one of the major strengths of this text.

TURNING POINTS

Baxter, L. A., and Bullis, C. 1986. Turning points in developing romantic relationships. *Human Communication Research* 12:469–493. This study examines the various turning points in romantic relationships. Both positive and negative turning points are associated with relational satisfaction.

LOVE

Hendrick, C., and Hendrick, S. 1991. *Romantic love*. Newbury Park, Calif.: Sage. The Hendricks provide an excellent summary of research on love. Various types of romantic love are explored.

REFERENCE LIST

Altman, I., and Taylor, D. A. 1973. *Social penetration: The development of interpersonal relationships*. Austin, Texas: Holt, Rinehart and Winston.

Andersen, P. A. 1985. Nonverbal immediacy in interpersonal communication. In *Multichannel integrations of nonverbal behavior*, ed. A. W. Siegman and S. Feldstein, 1–36. Hillsdale, N.J.: Erlbaum.

———. 1989. *A cognitive valence theory of intimate communication*. Paper presented at the conference of the International Network on Personal Relationships, Iowa City, Iowa.

Andersen, P. A., and Andersen, J. F. 1984. The exchange of nonverbal intimacy: A critical review of dyadic models. *Journal of Nonverbal Behavior* 8:327–349.

Baxter, L. A., and Bullis, C. 1986. Turning points in developing romantic relationships. *Human Communication Research* 12:469–493.

Baxter, L. A., and Wilmot, W. W. 1983. Communication characteristics of relationships with differential growth rates. *Communication Monographs* 50:264–272.

Berger, C. R., and Calabrese, R. J. 1975. Some explorations in initial interaction and beyond: Toward a developmental theory of interpersonal communication. *Human Communication Theory* 1:99–112.

Berger, C. R.; Weber, M. D.; Munley, M. E.; and Dixon, J. T. 1977. Interpersonal relationship levels and interpersonal attraction. In *Communication Yearbook 1*, ed. B. D. Ruben, 245–262. New Brunswick, N.J.: Transaction Books.

Bull, R., and Rumsey, N. 1988. *The social psychology of facial appearance*. New York: Springer-Verlag.

Burgoon, J. K., and Hale, J. L. 1984. The fundamental topoi of relational communication. *Communication Monographs* 51:193–214.

Byrne, D. 1971. *The attraction paradigm*. Orlando, Fla.: Academic Press.

Byrne, D., and Clore, G. L. 1970. A reinforcement model of evaluative responses. *Personality* 1:103–127.

Byrne, D., and Krivonos, P. D. 1976. *A reinforcement-affect theory of interpersonal communication*. Paper presented at the Speech Communication Association convention, San Francisco.

Cappella, J. 1984. The relevance of microstructure interaction to relationship change. *Journal of Social and Personal Relationships* 2:239–264.

Clatterbuck, G. W. 1980. A metatheoretical perspective on interpersonal attraction: The role of communication constructs. In *Interpersonal communication: A relational perspective*, ed. B. W. Morse and L. A. Phelps, 119–131. Minneapolis: Burgess.

Duck, S. W. 1976. Interpersonal communication in the acquaintance process. In *Explorations in interpersonal communication*, ed. G. R. Miller, 127–149. Newbury Park, Calif.: Sage.

Duck, S. W.; Lock, A.; McCall, G.; Fitzpatrick, M. A.; and Coyne, J. C. 1984. Social and personal relationships: A joint editorial. *Journal of Social and Personal Relationships* 1:1–10.

Duck, S. W., and Miell, D. 1984. Towards a comprehension of friendship development and breakdown. In *The social dimension: European perspectives on social psychology*, ed. H. Teifel, C. Fraser, and C. Jaspers, 228–248. Cambridge, UK: Cambridge University Press.

Fromm, E. 1956. *The art of loving*. New York: Harper Collins.

Guerrero, L. K., and Andersen, P. A. 1991. The waxing and waning of relational intimacy: Touch as a function of relational stage, gender, and touch avoidance. *Journal of Social and Personal Relationships* 8:147–165.

Hatfield, E. 1984. Epilogue: The dangers of intimacy. In *Communication, intimacy, and close relationships*, ed. V. J. Derlega, 207–220. Austin, Texas: Academic Press.

Hatfield, E., and Sprecher, S. 1986. *Mirror, mirror . . . : The importance of looks in everyday life.* Albany: State University of New York Press.

Hays, R. 1984. The development and maintenance of friendship. *Journal of Social and Personal Relationships* 1:75–98.

Huston, T. L. 1974. A perspective on interpersonal attraction. In *Foundations of interpersonal attraction*, ed. T. L. Huston, 3–28. Orlando, Fla.: Academic Press.

Huston, T. L.; McHale, S. M.; and Crouter, A. C. 1986. When the honeymoon's over: Changes in the marriage relationship over the first year. In *The emerging field of personal relationships*, ed. R. Gilmour and S. W. Duck, 109–132. Hillsdale, N.J.: Erlbaum.

Huston, T. L.; Surra, C.; Fitzgerald, N. M.; and Cate, R. 1981. From courtship to marriage: Mate selection as an interpersonal process. In *Personal relationships 2: Developing personal relationships*, ed. S. W. Duck and R. Gilmour, 53–88. Orlando, Fla.: Academic Press.

Kelley, H. H. 1979. *Personal relationships: Their structure and processes.* Hillsdale, N.J.: Erlbaum.

Kerckhoff, A. C. 1974. The social context of interpersonal attraction. In *Foundations of interpersonal attraction*, ed. T. L. Huston, 61–78. Orlando, Fla.: Academic Press.

Kerckhoff, A. C., and Davis, K. E. 1962. Value consensus and need complementarity in mate selection. *American Sociological Review* 27:295–303.

Knapp, M. L. 1984. *Interpersonal communication and human relationships.* Newton, Mass.: Allyn & Bacon.

Knapp, M. L.; Ellis, D. G.; and Williams, B. A. 1980. Perceptions of communication behavior associated with relationship terms. *Communication Monographs* 47:262–278.

Lasswell, T. E., and Lasswell, M. E. 1976. I love you, but I'm not in love with you. *Journal of Marriage and Family Counseling* 2:211–224.

Levinger, G. 1974. A three-level approach to attraction: Toward an understanding of pair relatedness. In *Foundations of interpersonal attraction*, ed. T. L. Huston, 99–120. Orlando, Fla.: Academic Press.

Marston, P. J.; Hecht, M. L.; and Robers, T. 1987. "True love ways": The subjective experience and communication of romantic love. *Journal of Social and Personal Relationships* 4: 387–407.

McCroskey, J. C., and McCain, T. A. 1974. The measurement of interpersonal attraction. *Speech Monographs* 41:261–266.

Miell, D., and Duck, S. W. 1986. Strategies in developing friendships. In *Friendships and social interaction*, ed. V. J. Derlega and B. A. Winstead, 129–143. New York: Springer-Verlag.

Miller, G. R., and Steinberg, M. 1975. *Between people.* Chicago: Science Research.

Morton, T. L.; Alexander, J. F.; and Altman, I. 1976. Communication and relationship definition. In *Explorations in interpersonal communication*, ed. G. R. Miller, 105–125. Newbury Park, Calif.: Sage.

Perlman, D., and Fehr, B. 1987. The development of intimate relationships. In *Intimate relationships*, ed. D. Perlman & S. W. Duck, 13–42. Newbury Park, Calif.: Sage.

Rubin, Z. 1973. *Liking and loving: An invitation to social psychology.* Austin, Texas: Holt, Rinehart and Winston.

Schutz, W. C. 1966. *The interpersonal underworld*, reprint ed. Palo Alto, Calif.: Science and Behavior Books.

Sunnafrank, M. 1991. Interpersonal attraction and attitude similarity: A communication-based assessment. In *Communication yearbook 14*, ed. J. A. Anderson, 451–483. Newbury Park, Calif.: Sage.

Sunnafrank, M., and Miller, G. R. 1981. The role of initial conversations in determining attraction to similar and dissimilar strangers. *Human Communication Research* 8:16–25.

Taylor, D. A., and Altman, I. 1987. Communication in interpersonal relationships: Social penetration processes. In *Interpersonal processes: New directions in communication research*, ed. M. E. Roloff and G. R. Miller, 257–277. Newbury Park, Calif.: Sage.

Van Lear, C. A. 1987. The formation of social relationships: A longitudinal study. *Human Communication Research* 13:279–322.

———. 1992. Testing a cyclical model of relational development: Two longitudinal studies. *Communication Monographs* 58:337–361.

Wallace, L. A. 1992. *Interpersonal attraction and communication: Development of the Communication Based Measure of Attraction*. M.A. thesis, Ohio University, Athens.

Wilmot, W. W. 1987. *Dyadic communication*, 3d ed. New York: Random House.

CHAPTER 9

MAINTAINING

RELATIONSHIPS

There was one ritual we developed when we were very small that we revealed to not another living soul. Whenever we were hurting or damaged or sad, whenever our parents had punished or beaten us, the three of us would go to the end of the floating dock, dive into the sun-sweet water, then swim out ten yards into the channel and form a circle together by holding hands. We floated together, our hands clasped in a perfect unbreakable circle. I held Savannah's hand and I held Luke's. All of us touched, bound in a ring of flesh and blood and water. Luke would give a signal and all of us would inhale and sink to the bottom of the river, our hands still tightly joined. We would remain on the bottom of the river until one of us squeezed the hands of the others and we would rise together and break the surface in an explosion of sunlight and breath.

From Pat Conroy, *The Prince of Tides*, pp. 442–443

The Prince of Tides relates how three children—Luke, Savannah, and Tom—survive the cruel lessons of an abusive father and a manipulative mother. We see how the children bond together, protect one another, and engage in activities that mark their special relationships. Their childhood ritual of holding hands and sinking to the bottom of the river symbolizes their connection and support for one another. As the children mature, they develop their own lives. And although their communication is periodic, it is clear that Luke, Savannah, and Tom maintain their deep affection and unfaltering support for one another in adulthood.

This chapter is about how we maintain our personal relationships. Friendships fade, romances die, and family ties wither unless we make efforts to ensure their continuance. What are the various factors that influence maintenance behaviors? What are the communication strategies that people use to maintain their relationships? Are there tensions that are just part of having relationships? This chapter addresses these questions in examining how actors attempt to maintain their relationships.

Duck (1988) noted that there are at least three situations in which people seek the goal of relational maintenance: to sustain the existence of a relationship, to keep the relationship from becoming more intimate, and to stabilize a rocky relationship (see also Dindia and Baxter, 1987). From experience, we all can relate to these types of situations. Moreover, we recognize in these types of situations that the goal of maintaining relationships is not an easy task.

226

Why we even try to maintain our relationships can be at times a tricky question. According to Wilmot (1987), there are three reasons why people maintain a relationship: because the relationship serves its functions well (e.g., your romantic partner is affectionate, your father is supportive), because it provides security and support in a changing world and during crises, and because it offers a sense of pride in being in the relationship. Rusbult (1987) adds other reasons perhaps more specific to romantic relationships. She holds that people are committed to maintain their relationships due to the amount of satisfaction, investment (for example, time, money, and emotional energy), and lack of potential alternative relationships or activities.

Relational Maintenance and Equity

Steve and Jennifer began dating when Jennifer was in law school, and they married just before her bar exam. Steve is a real estate agent and earns decent money, though he will never be wealthy. He is also responsible and faithful. Jennifer is intelligent and exciting, and she introduces Steve to different ideas and new, cultural things to do. Jennifer knows that Steve isn't deeply committed to his career, but she appreciates his responsibility and how he supported her during law school.

Jennifer passes her bar exam and accepts a position in a respected law firm. Within a year, Jennifer earns twice as much money as Steve does, and she has much potential for career advancement. Typically, the junior members of the firm go out for drinks after work. But Steve disapproves of Jennifer socializing with her associates after work hours, and he wants her to spend more time at home, as she did before.

Jennifer has become tired of being constrained and being the one who plans for special activities. She feels that the fun has disappeared from the marriage. Jennifer also believes that she needs someone smarter to share her ideas with. In short, Jennifer resents that she now pays most of their bills and feels restricted in her activities by Steve. Steve feels a bit guilty for not pulling his share, but he recalls how he helped put Jennifer through school. Still, he thinks that it's only fair that she stick it out. Mostly, Steve is anxious that Jennifer will leave him because she has so much else going for her.

As this story illustrates, people stay in relationships to the extent that they are rewarding and equitable. Research by Hatfield and colleagues (1985; see also Utne et al. 1984) reports that maintaining relationships is strongly linked to the amount of rewards and equity in the relationship. The most satisfying relationships are those that are rewarding and fair. Hatfield and associates (1985; see also Hatfield, Walster, and Berscheid 1978) also specify the main propositions of equity theory:

Proposition 1: Individuals try to increase their rewards and minimize their punishments.

Proposition 2a: Groups, including relationships, can maximize their rewards by developing systems of equity and influencing others to adopt those systems of equity.

Proposition 2b: Groups will usually reward persons who treat others equitably and will punish those who do not treat others equitably.

Proposition 3: People become distressed when they see their relationships as inequitable. The more inequitable the relationship, the greater the distress.

Proposition 4: People who perceive inequity will try to restore equity. The greater the inequity, and the accompanying distress, the harder people try to restore equity.

Equity specifically refers to the principle of fairness that is based on a comparison of what two people put in (inputs) and obtain (outputs) from each other. If the input-outcome ratios are equal, then the relationship is equitable. Of course, some relationships suffer from inequity. People who receive fewer rewards relative to their partners are *underbenefited*. Those who receive greater rewards relative to their partners are *overbenefited*. Research shows that underbenefited partners are less satisfied because they are in inequitable arrangements and derive relatively few rewards; overbenefited people still obtain more rewards than their partners. Sprecher (1986) found that underbenefitedness was strongly associated with negative emotional responses to the partner (such as anger, resentment, and depression). These negative emotional reactions to underbenefitedness may contribute to lack of effort to maintain the relationship. For example, Canary and Stafford (1992) found that underbenefited people do not expend as much effort as equitably treated people to maintain their marriages.

Research has shown that underbenefited persons are less content in their relationships and are angry at the partner, whereas highly overbenefited persons feel guilty (Hatfield et al. 1985). One study (cited in Hatfield et al. 1985) found that people who felt underbenefited sought extramarital affairs much earlier than those who felt overbenefited. The most satisfying relationships are those where both partners feel rewarded on an equal basis. Figure 9-1 illustrates the connection between relational contentment and equity.

Equity also operates in people's attributions of how much the other tries to maintain the relationship. For example, in a study of how dating partners maintain their relationships, Fletcher and colleagues (1987) found that relational commitment, happiness, and love were highest when efforts to maintain the relationship were seen as equal. But people reporting much greater or lesser degrees of effort at maintaining the relationship, relative to perceptions of the partner's efforts, were

Figure 9–1

The Relation-
ship between
Equity and
Contentment

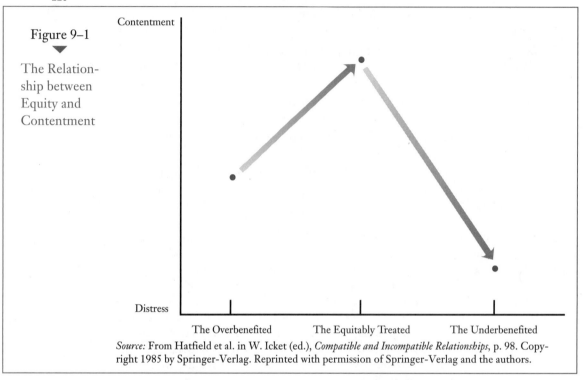

Source: From Hatfield et al. in W. Icket (ed.), *Compatible and Incompatible Relationships*, p. 98. Copyright 1985 by Springer-Verlag. Reprinted with permission of Springer-Verlag and the authors.

dissatisfied with their relationships. Imagine if your attempts to keep a relationship going are not reciprocated (you write letters and cards, but your partner does not; you try to be upbeat, but your partner only complains about your behavior; your partner doesn't help you at all with the household chores).

In sum, satisfaction and equity affect your motivation to maintain your relationships. If you feel underbenefited or overbenefited, you will probably expend less effort to maintain the relationship than if you are in a rewarding and equitable relationship.

Relational Maintenance Strategies

There are several noninteractive and interactive methods for maintaining your relationships. For example, Rusbult, Drigotas, and Verette (1994) show how people maintain their marriages noninteractively by derogating alternative relational partners, by sacrificing personal rewards for the sake of the relationship, and by believing in the perceived superiority of the marriage over other marriages. This book, however, focuses on how interpersonal communication functions to achieve desired goals. Hence we will discuss various interactive strategies that people use to maintain their relationships.

These various maintenance strategies are successful in some, but not all, relationships. The list of strategies is adapted from research on relational maintenance by Stafford and Canary (1991). These authors examined the literature, asked open-ended questions about how couples maintained their relationships, and statistically revealed five strategies: positivity, openness, assurances, social networks, and sharing tasks.

POSITIVITY

Positivity involves such behaviors as acting cheerful, being courteous, and refraining from criticism. Positivity can be an effective means of maintaining a relationship because being positive can increase the reward level of the partner. We all know people who are genuinely positive and rewarding to be with; they smile when they see us, tell us how appreciative of us they are, and never complain about the relationship.

Sampling romantic relationships, Canary and Stafford (1992) and Stafford and Canary (1991) found that positivity was strongly associated with liking the partner. Another way of being positive in romantic relationships is to use what Dindia (1989) calls romantic tactics—showing affection, being fun and spontaneous, and so on.

Positivity is similar to Bell, Daly, and Gonzalez's (1987) idea that relational maintenance is achieved through affinity-seeking behaviors. Recall from Chapter 5 that affinity seeking refers to a person's attempt to get another to like him or her. Bell and co-workers found that wives reported that their husbands' most effective affinity-maintenance tactics were honesty, physical affection, self-inclusion (husbands including themselves in the wives' activities), sensitivity, and shared spirituality.

Perhaps the opposite of positivity is using **antisocial tactics** (Dindia 1989). Antisocial tactics "represent people's attempts to obtain relational rewards by imposing their position on another through force or deception" (Roloff 1976, 181). Dindia (1989) found that husbands' use of antisocial tactics was negatively associated with wives' satisfaction. People may use antisocial strategies to limit a relationship's intimacy or to assert control over the partner. Sometimes people act rude to discourage their partners from escalating the relationship (not returning phone messages, lying about plans for the weekend, threatening or intimidating the partner, etc.).

OPENNESS

The strategy of **openness** reflects the extent to which partners explicitly discuss the nature of their relationship. (This strategy has also been called *directness* by Ayres [1983] and Shea and Pearson [1984].) Using openness, people attempt to maintain their relationships by disclosing their feelings about the relationship, asking how their partner feels about the relationship, discussing relational goals, and having periodic talks about the relationship.

Openness helps maintain the relationship by discussing topics crucial to the relationship (such as the agreement to have an exclusive sexual relationship). In addition, being open about successes and confiding in each other are two important ways in which friendships are maintained (Argyle and Henderson 1984). It is often difficult to maintain a relationship at a satisfactory level without being open about what you want.

Though openness can be effective, research indicates that being too open (and especially being negative) may harm the relationship (see, for example, Hecht, Shepard, and Hall 1979; see also Chapter 7). In addition, Ayres (1983) found that openness was not a preferred strategy if the communicator thought the partner wanted to change the level of intimacy in the relationship but the communicator did not. Instead, actors preferred avoidance (ignoring the person) when the partner wanted to increase the level of intimacy and balance (keeping emotions constant) if they wanted to maintain their relationship when the other person wanted to de-escalate the relationship.

Baxter and Wilmot (1985) report that couples shy away from discussing *taboo topics*, or topics seen by either or both partners as "off limits." Sampling opposite-sex friendships and romantic involvements, Baxter and Wilmot found that the following were common taboo topics: state of the relationship, extrarelationship activity (such as other romantic parties), relationship norms (discussion of the relational rules), prior relationships, conflict-inducing topics, and negatively valenced disclosure. These researchers also examined the motives for various taboo topics. For example, discussing the state of the relationship could possibly destroy the relationship if there were large differences in commitment levels.

ASSURANCES

A third approach to maintaining relationships is to use **assurances.** Using this strategy, communicators show that they are faithful, stress their commitment to the relationship, and clearly imply that the relationship has a future (Stafford and Canary 1991). Friends engage in assurances by demonstrating emotional support, trusting one another, and offering to help in time of need (Argyle and Henderson 1984). Assurances show that you are committed to the relationship in both word and deed.

Assuring the partner through various actions maintains the relationship by reinforcing the assumption that the other will be there indefinitely. If the partner feels insecure about the future of the relationship, the communicator can maintain the relationship by seeking or offering assurances. Or, on the contrary, to maintain a low commitment level, one could avoid offering assurances about the future.

It is sometimes difficult to maintain your relationships unless you are open about what you want from them.

(*Cathy* copyright Cathy Guisewite. Reprinted with permission of Universal Press Syndicate. All rights reserved.)

Related to the strategy of assurances is the communication activity of comforting your partner. Burleson and Samter (1985; Samter and Burleson 1984) have shown that the more effective comforting tactics are those that focus on and offer information about the other person's needs (they take the perspective of the other person; see Chapter 13). A sampling of effective comforting messages is presented in Table 9-1.

Table 9-1
COMFORTING BEHAVIORS

Behavior Type	Description	Example[a]
Responsive acknowledgment	Utterances that offer emotional support	"Really? I'm sorry to hear that."
Psychological information	Questions about state of mind	"Do you still like him?"
Applied disclosure	Topical responses with relevant reference	"The same thing happened to me a couple of years ago. What a bummer!"
Emotional advice	Utterances that suggest methods of emotional coping	"Give yourself some time to think about things."
Explicit recognition	Utterances that show clear understanding of the suffering	"I know that this is a very difficult time for you."
Elaborated acknowledgment	Statements of recognition, explanation, and understanding	"I know that it hurts a lot now, but after a while the pain subsides, and soon you won't even remember his name."
Perspective	Statements offering a perspective on the problem	"You're young and have many opportunities. That may not be what you want to hear right now, but it's true. There are lots of other fish in the sea."

[a]Responses to the statement "My boyfriend broke up with me last night, and I don't know what to do. I feel so hurt!"
Source: Adapted from Samter and Burleson 1984, 244–246.

SOCIAL NETWORKS

A fourth strategy that people use to maintain their relationships is to rely on their **social networks,** their friends and family.

Milardo (1986) has argued that couples, and friends in particular, are bound together in sharing their networks. Furthermore, Stafford and Canary (1991) found that more use of social networks was made by married couples than by dating couples. The reason for this is that marriage involves increased shared activities and common social circles (e.g., having dinner at the in-laws every Sunday, having parties with other couples), whereas dating may be a time of redefining friendship ties.

The support of family and friends can be an important factor in the ability to maintain a long-term relationship. Friends and family members who support the relationship make it easier to sustain.

(Eugene Richards/Magnum Photos)

People who have established common social networks are more likely to use them to maintain their relationships than people who do not share social networks.

Relationships with social support appear to be more stable than those without such support. Parks and Adelman (1983) found that social networks help us reduce uncertainty about the partner. Also, Milardo (1986) has argued that relationship stability increases when the social networks of friends are close and interconnected. How many times have we relied on "a friend of a friend" to help us understand a relationship or had a party to reinforce the relationship? Indeed, lack of social support (among other reasons) may actually speed up the termination of the relationship (see Chapter 10).

SHARING TASKS

The fifth maintenance strategy Stafford and Canary (1991) found was **sharing tasks,** performing one's "fair share" of the work in the relationship. For example, one person may prepare dinner while the other cleans the kitchen, or one may wash the dishes if the partner folds the laundry. On another level, sharing tasks may refer to one person working overtime to relieve the burden of certain personal expenses on the partner (e.g., working extra hours to afford the vacation you both want to take).

Showing the partner that you shoulder your responsibilities illustrates equity in operation. Clearly, one way to maintain relational harmony and demonstrate an equitable relationship is to perform specific jobs and expectations. In other words, sharing tasks can be symbolic. For example, cleaning the house when your partner is very tired demonstrates your care for that person and your willingness to be interdependent.

Patterns in Relational Maintenance

SPIRALS
Steve and Jennifer have to settle a few issues. Jennifer likes to socialize with her friends from work. They often go out after a busy day to unwind. Steve really dislikes Jennifer spending so much time with others, especially one person who, Steve suspects, is attracted to Jennifer. Jennifer assures Steve that this socializing is necessary for her job and that he has nothing to worry about. Sometimes, especially when Jennifer gets home late, Steve questions her about who was there, what they discussed, whom she sat next to, why she was so late, and so forth. Steve also started calling her at the office to check up on her. The more Steve monitored her actions, the less Jennifer respected him. The less Jennifer respected Steve, the more she went out. They would eventually spiral into a big fight, feel bad about it, and then promise each other to "go back to the way things were." But the same cycle would repeat itself after a few weeks.

Wilmot (1987) discusses **spirals** that dyads experience. In a spiral, the actor's definition of the situation is intensified by the partner's response, which then prompts the actor to intensify his or her behavior, and so on. There are two types of spirals, *progressive* and *regressive*.

Progressive spirals occur when two people reinforce each other's positive behaviors. For example, you may smile at a joke, to which your friend laughs. You now find the joke even funnier, so you laugh too. Your friend recalls a similar joke, which you both find hilarious. Next you tell a joke and the two of you almost fall on the floor. Or a romantic relationship may involve one person saying with much sincerity, "I care about you very much." The partner reciprocates this message and adds "more than you know." This exchange opens the door for someone to risk saying "I love you." If the "I love you" is reciprocated, both people may feel free to say those words again later, which may also lead to other statements of increased involvement and commitment.

Regressive spirals occur when not understanding each other or having discrepant goals leads to further misunderstanding and differences. For example, recall Steve and Jennifer. Steve is worried that he is losing Jennifer and becomes more concerned when she goes out with her work associates. To reduce his uncertainty, Steve engages in detective strategies. Jennifer then feels even more constrained by Steve than before and looks forward to times to get out of the house. Of course, this independence makes Steve crazier and increases his need to gain control.

Wilmot (1987) points out that dyads maintain their relationships by fluctuating between progressive and regressive spirals. But too much regression or progression is difficult to sustain. Accordingly, partners stop their spirals before they hit the critical points; otherwise the relationship is jeopardized. Finally, the manner in which relationships are maintained can be portrayed by charting how spirals progress. Figures 9-2 and 9-3 portray two different dyads. The first dyad tends to maintain their relationship with moderate fluctuation. The second dyad, by comparison, is on a roller coaster. Such radical fluctuation can dismay and discourage the partners, and too much regressive spiraling saps the relationship (Wilmot 1987).

Wilmot (1987) suggests a plan for dealing with regressive spirals. First, recognize them when you are participating in a regressive spiral. Next, do not reciprocate negative behaviors. Reciprocation of negative communication behaviors is perhaps the most relationally damaging form of message exchange. For example, instead of trading insults, you could ask what is making the other person so upset, or you could simply not reply at all. Third, you could make clear your desire to maintain the relationship. Finally, you could rely on the more positive maintenance strategies reviewed earlier in this chapter. For example, again using the story of Steve and Jennifer, Steve could refrain from monitoring her actions and try an alternative maintenance strategy, such as positivity or use of her social networks (e.g., inviting her associates over for dinner).

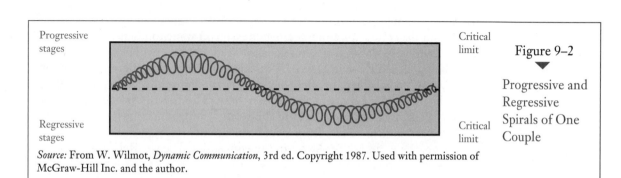

Figure 9–2

▼

Progressive and Regressive Spirals of One Couple

Source: From W. Wilmot, *Dynamic Communication*, 3rd ed. Copyright 1987. Used with permission of McGraw-Hill Inc. and the author.

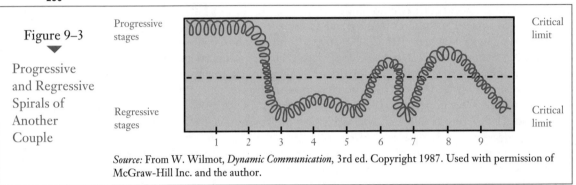

Figure 9–3

Progressive
and Regressive
Spirals of
Another
Couple

Progressive stages

Regressive stages

Critical limit

Critical limit

Source: From W. Wilmot, *Dynamic Communication*, 3rd ed. Copyright 1987. Used with permission of McGraw-Hill Inc. and the author.

DIALECTICS

So far we have based our discussion of relational maintenance on research related to how individuals maintain their relationships to restore rewards and equity. Now we take a different approach. It is based on three important assumptions about relationships and how people maintain them. The first assumption is that people in relationships experience tensions that reflect the presence of polar opposites that coexist in any relationship. The second assumption is that one such polar experience becomes meaningful only if its opposite is present. In other words, both conditions must occur if either is to have meaning. The interplay between polar opposites is called relational **dialectics** (see Baxter 1993; Baxter and Dindia 1990; Cupach and Metts 1988; Montgomery 1993; Wilmot 1987). Third, as Montgomery notes, "The presence of inherent, oppositional forces in a relationship results in constant change" (p. 208). Accordingly, relational dialectics are tensions that constantly ebb and flow.

Research reveals that there are at least four dialectical tensions (Cupach and Metts 1988; see also Baxter 1990). The first dialectic is **interdependence–autonomy.** You experience the pull of wanting to be connected with someone and share activities with someone, but you also want to assert your own individuality and separateness. The second dialectic is **openness–closedness.** You want to open yourself to your partner, to disclose who you are, but you also need to protect yourself and your partner by being closed (Rawlins 1983). The third dialectic is **predictability–novelty.** You may want to be able to predict your partner and know how to respond with that person, but you may also want new experiences. The fourth dialectic is **passion–stability.** Passion is emotional heat in the relationship, which must be balanced by stability to prevent the relationship from burning out.

At issue, then, are not problems in the conventional sense. Relational dialectics are an aspect of relationship life itself. Relational partners must learn how to respond to these dialectical tensions in order to maintain their relationships. Cupach and Metts (1988) indicate that when people have trouble managing their relational dialectics, they experience relational conflict and personal anxiety.

MAINTAINING A FRIENDSHIP IN *DRIVING MISS DAISY*

Driving Miss Daisy is a film about maintaining a friendship over many years as well as overcoming prejudice. Miss Daisy (Jessica Tandy) is an elderly Jewish woman who can no longer drive herself. Her son (Dan Ackroyd) hires an older black man, whose name is Houk (Morgan Freeman), to drive her car. Although Miss Daisy claims she holds no prejudices against black people, she actually does. Miss Daisy complains to her son about "those people," about how they like to meddle in her affairs, and about how they cannot be "trusted."

Houk finally wins the trust of Miss Daisy, and he drives her wherever she needs to go. And Miss Daisy, a retired teacher, teaches Houk to read and write. On one extraordinary long trip, they travel to Mobile, Alabama, from Atlanta, Georgia. We see how dependent she has become on Houk at this point: when he leaves the car for a few minutes, she cries out for him, apparently frightened to be alone. And at first she is very picky about his behaviors. He is not allowed to drive at the speed limit, he is not to park close to the front door of the synagogue, and he can't use the air conditioner. But later she stops criticizing him.

Houk manages to find a balance between being an employee and being a friend. One morning there is an ice storm, and Houk brings Miss Daisy some coffee. The following dialogue illustrates their friendship:

Houk:	I figured your stove was out, so I stopped by the Crispy Cream—I know how you got to have your coffee in the morning.
Miss Daisy:	How sweet of you, Houk.
Houk:	Yes'um. Shoot, we ain't had no good coffee since Ardella passed away.
Miss Daisy:	I can fix her biscuits and we both know how to make her fried chicken, but nobody can make Ardella's coffee.
Houk:	Ain't that the truth.
Miss Daisy:	Ardella was lucky.
Houk:	Yes'um, I expect she was. Well . . . (*he picks his things up*).
Miss Daisy:	Were you going?
Houk:	Just goin' to go out here, take these things.
Miss Daisy:	I don't know what you can do here today except keep me company.
Houk:	I might see if I can make us some fire.

But things are still not entirely smooth. When Martin Luther King, Jr., comes to Atlanta, Miss Daisy obtains tickets for a dinner where King will speak. She doesn't feel comfortable inviting Houk, although her son suggested it. Finally, on the way to the dinner, Miss Daisy indirectly asks Houk if he is interested in attending the dinner.

(continued)

(continued from previous page)

Houk:	Now, what do you think I am, Miss Daisy?
Miss Daisy:	What do you mean?
Houk:	This invitation to this here dinner come a month ago. Now, it be you want me to go with you, how come you wait 'til we're in the car and on the way before you ask me?
Miss Daisy:	What? All I said is [my son] said you wanted to go.
Houk:	Well, next time you want me to go somewhere, you ask me regular.
Miss Daisy:	You don't have to carry on so much.
Houk:	Well, now let's just leave it alone.
Miss Daisy:	Honestly.
Houk:	*(to himself)* Talk about things changing—ain't changin' all that much.

But by the end of the film, we see that most of the prejudice has been replaced by genuine friendship. The two confide in each other, depend on each other, and look forward to seeing each other. Miss Daisy shows her affection for Houk in the following scene:

Miss Daisy:	You ought not to be driving anything, the way you can see.
Houk:	How'd you know how I can see, 'less'n you can look out my eyes, hmm?
Miss Daisy:	Houk, you are my best friend.
Houk:	No, Miss Daisy.
Miss Daisy:	*(she reaches for and holds his hand)* You are. You are.
Houk:	Yes'um.

Soon after that, Miss Daisy must receive care at a nursing home. Houk continues the effort to maintain their relationship. Although he has stopped driving due to his failing vision, he still visits her by taking a taxi or having his daughter drive him. The final scene symbolizes their friendship: Houk feeds Miss Daisy bites of her Thanksgiving pie, which she eats joyfully.

Driving Miss Daisy shows that relationships require effort, or else they deteriorate. Houk works hard at establishing a good working relationship and then a friendship with Miss Daisy. Houk continues to work at the relationship by being positive and complimentary and by doing favors for Miss Daisy. *Driving Miss Daisy* is an excellent film for the analysis of how friendships are maintained as well as how prejudice can be overcome.

Excerpts from *Driving Miss Daisy* by Alfred Uhry. By permission of The Zanuck Company.

RESPONDING TO DIALECTICAL TENSIONS

Recently, researchers have uncovered ways in which people respond to dialectical tensions (Baxter 1990; Cupach and Metts 1988). The first response is called **selection.** The couple might select one dialectical term over the other. For example, some people decide to avoid the partner when their needs for privacy outweigh their needs to be with the partner. A second response is **separation.** Couples deny the presence of the dialectic by somehow separating the opposite tensions from one another. For example, you might have a "women's night out" in order to secure some time away from your partner every week. **Neutralization** refers to compromising the opposite tensions. One way to do this is to avoid the issue or handle the topics ambiguously (e.g., "We don't have to have affection to show affection"). The alternative approach to neutralization is discussion, where partners talk openly about the tension. **Revitalization** refers to a proactive but indirect response to the dialectics. For example, to revitalize passion, you might arrange to meet your partner in a new, romantic place (such as a restaurant at the top of a skyscraper).

Perhaps the most difficult response is **reframing** (see also Baxter 1990). Reframing involves placing your dialectical tensions in a different light so that the experience of both tensions is no longer contradictory. If you can accept that dialectics are a natural aspect of relationships, you may rise above the tension you feel. For example, you feel smothered by your child. But you realize that this is a common phenomenon between parents and their children, so you redefine the issue ("My child isn't really smothering me, it's just that I need some time alone and can't get away right now").

Some people give in to a particular dialectical pole. **Acquiescence** refers to giving in to a relational feature, not wishing to solve the dialectical problem. For example, you might accept that being married involves a higher degree of stability and less passion than you want. So you give in to the dialectic of stability saying, "No marriage has unbridled passion because people just cannot sustain that kind of emotion over the long haul."

As you might imagine, the effectiveness of these responses varies according to the dialectical tensions. For example, when used as a response to the dialectical tensions of interdependence–autonomy or predictability–novelty, reframing was positively correlated with relational satisfaction (Baxter 1990). Although reframing is a sophisticated strategy, it appears to help couples resolve issues concerning togetherness and predictability. But when faced with the tension of openness–closedness, use of neutralization (by being ambiguous) was negatively associated with relational satisfaction (Baxter 1990). It appears that being unclear about the issue does not help a couple manage the need to balance openness and closedness.

In sum, relational partners experience progressive and regressive spirals. Radical shifts and regressive spirals tend to wear down the relationship. Relational dialectics are tensions that dyads experience when they feel the pull of opposite but unavoidable elements of relational life. Effective responses for dealing with dialectics function to maintain the relationship.

Maintaining Different Types of Marriages

FITZPATRICK'S MARITAL TYPOLOGY

Fitzpatrick (1988) has presented research on the question, "What does marriage look like in the latter half of the twentieth century?" Her answer reveals that people have different types of marriages and that these marriage types differ in their communication behavior. This research has important implications for people who seek to maintain their marriages. The most obvious implication is that people should know what type of relationship they are in so that they can better understand their communication behaviors.

Fitzpatrick (1988) identifies three primary types of marriages. **Traditional couples** adopt an "ideology of traditionalism." Traditionals believe that society should have faith in its social institutions, that the woman should take the man's last name when they are married, and so on. Traditionals also are interdependent (they share in activities) and have conflict over major issues. **Separate couples** are similar to traditionals in their ideology of traditionalism, but separates are autonomous and avoid conflict of all kinds. **Independent couples** do not have traditional beliefs

People have different types of marriages and the manner in which they communicate with each other varies according to these types. That there are different marital types is clearly exemplified in the marriages of the Clintons and the Bushes.

(Rick Friedman/Black Star)

about the relationship, so they must negotiate many issues. Independents must negotiate answers to questions already decided by traditional norms, such as "Should we attend church?" "Who cooks tonight?" and "Which days are you getting the children?" Independents also tend to be interdependent and have conflict over anything. Finally, Fitzpatrick reports that about half of the marriages she has studied consist of **mixed couples,** in which the husband and the wife have different definitions for their marriage. The most common mixed type is the traditional wife and the separate husband.

Fitzpatrick (1988) argues that people enter and maintain their marriages through reliance on "marital schemata," which she defines as "knowledge structures that represent the external world of marriage and provide guidelines about how to interpret incoming data" (p. 255). Accordingly, traditionals view marriage in terms of traditional role behaviors. Knowing how to enact such behaviors, traditionals experience routine interactions and little discord. Separates, who essentially want little involvement with each other, have few interactions. Independents see marriage as the coordination of two individuals' goals. Accordingly, independents view interruptions of their individual goals more intensely than do traditionals or separates.

(David Burnett/Contact Press Images)

DIFFERENCES IN COMMUNICATION AMONG MARITAL TYPES

How do these couples communicate? Traditionals are more attuned to each other's needs. For example, traditional wives are the most accurate in perceiving their husbands' signs of affection and sexual interest. Traditionals appeal to the nature of their relationship and are honest when trying to persuade each other (Witteman and Fitzpatrick 1986).

As Fitzpatrick and Best (1979) put it, separates are "emotionally divorced" from each other. Separates are the least accurate in gauging each other's feelings, and they maintain their distance by vigilantly keeping information and emotions from surfacing in their conversations. In one study on conflict, separates used "blatant" forms of avoiding the issues, such as explicitly denying to each other that there was a problem, even after having told the researchers that a problem did indeed exist (Sillars et al. 1983). Likewise, Witteman and Fitzpatrick (1986) found that separates used "guerrilla-like" communication to persuade their partner; that is, they constrained the other person's behaviors, did not seek information from the other person, but appealed to their partner's sense of values.

Unlike separates, independent couples tend to share information and become emotionally involved in their conversations. Independents are likely to engage in refutation, to discount the other person's arguments, and to seek information more than the other types do (Witteman and Fitzpatrick 1986). Also, independents counter dominant actions of the spouse with dominant actions of their own (Williamson and Fitzpatrick 1985). Interestingly, Sillars and colleagues (1983) found that independents' relational satisfaction scores are *positively* associated with negative emotional displays (e.g., raising the voice), but their satisfaction scores are *inversely* correlated with neutral emotional signals. Independents are also relatively accurate in assessing their partners' nonverbal cues of pleasure and affection (Fitzpatrick 1988).

Chapter Summary

This chapter reviewed why and how people maintain their relationships. People are motivated to maintain relationships to the extent that the relationships are rewarding and equitable. But what may be rewarding and equitable in one relationship may result in dissatisfaction and inequity in another relationship. Accordingly, the various strategies for maintaining one's relationship will affect relationships differently. The five maintenance strategies reviewed in the first half of this chapter tend to help most relationships stay on an even keel.

It is also evident that different relationships experience spirals and dialectics, abstract sorts of problems. Dyads must learn to manage these spirals and dialectical tensions in order to maintain their relationships.

One relational type is not superior to any other. Nor are the communication behaviors that are used to maintain a particular type of relationship superior in quality to those used to manage others. The issue is whether the communication functions so that both members of the dyad can achieve their goal of maintaining their relationships as they want them.

KEY TERMS

▼

equity	passion–stability
positivity	selection
antisocial tactics	separation
openness	neutralization
assurances	revitalization
social networks	reframing
sharing tasks	acquiescence
spirals	traditional couples
dialectics	separate couples
interdependence–autonomy	independent couples
openness–closedness	mixed couples
predictability–novelty	

EXERCISES FOR FURTHER DISCUSSION

▼

1. Review Duck's three situations involving relational maintenance activities: to sustain the existence of a relationship, to keep the relationship from becoming more intimate, and to stabilize an unstable relationship. Now try to think of an example from your own life for each of these situations.
   a. What was the situation? Try to describe it as precisely as possible.
   b. Which person in the relationship was more active in maintaining it at the same level?
   c. What types of communication behaviors were used to maintain the relationship?
2. The Stafford and Canary typology was derived primarily from romantic couples' responses. Consider whether these strategies accurately describe other types of relationships.
   a. Do they accurately describe how family relationships are maintained? Why or why not?

b.   Do they accurately describe how friendships are maintained? Why or why not?

c.   What other strategies would you include in a list of ways in which people maintain their relationships?

3.   List five of the most important relationships in your life. Now try to think of situations in which you share tasks with the people you listed.

a.   What types of tasks do you share with people?

b.   Are there some tasks that you do with some people and other tasks that you do with other people?

c.   What do you think is the symbolic significance of the tasks you share with other people?

d.   Can you think of a situation in which someone expressed unhappiness in a relationship by not sharing in a task?

4.   Look again at the spirals depicted in Figures 9-2 and 9-3. Try to plot the spirals of two relationships you are in.

a.   Based on the spirals you have drawn, which of the two relationships is the more stable one?

b.   Does the stability of the relationships correspond to the fluctuation of progressive and regressive spirals?

c.   Do you think that Wilmot's prescriptions for managing regressive spirals would be effective in your relationships?

5.   List three dialectical tensions that you think cause problems in your relationships.

a.   In what types of relationships do you experience these tensions?

b.   In what ways do you handle these tensions?

c.   Can you think of some new ways to handle these tensions, based on the ideas presented in this chapter?

6.   Consider Fitzpatrick's three types of married couples: traditional, independent, and separate.

a.   What type of marriage do you think your parents have?

b.   What type of marriage do you think you are in or would choose?

c.   In what ways does the type of marriage your parents have influence your own relationships?

SUGGESTED READING

APPROACHES TO RELATIONAL MAINTENANCE

Canary, D. J., and Stafford, L. 1994. *Communication and relational maintenance.* New York: Academic Press. This book examines how relationships are maintained.

Noted scholars from communication and psychology emphasize different aspects of maintaining relationships.

EQUITY

Hatfield, E.; Traupmann, J.; Sprecher, S.; Utne, M.; and Hay, J. 1985. Equity and intimate relationships: Recent research. In *Compatible and incompatible relationships*, ed. W. Ickes, 91–117. New York: Springer-Verlag. Theoretical propositions, supporting research, and future extensions are covered in this review of equity theory.

RELATIONAL DIALECTICS

Montgomery, B. M. 1993. Relationship maintenance versus relationship change: A dialectical dilemma. *Journal of Social and Personal Relationships* 10:205–224. Montgomery argues that change is fundamental to stable relationships. Implications for the study of relational maintenance are examined.

MARITAL TYPES

Fitzpatrick, M. A. 1988. *Between husbands and wives: Communication in marriage.* Newbury Park, Calif.: Sage. Fitzpatrick presents an interesting review of her research on different types of marriage, including a first-rate discussion of couple types.

REFERENCE LIST

Argyle, M., and Henderson, M. 1984. The rules of friendship. *Journal of Social and Personal Relationships* 1:211–237.

Ayres, J. 1983. Strategies to maintain relationships: Their identification and perceived usage. *Communication Quarterly* 31:62–67.

Baxter, L. A. 1990. Dialectical contradictions in relationship development. *Journal of Social and Personal Relationships* 7:69–88.

———. (in press). A dialogic approach to relationship maintenance. In *Communication and relational maintenance*, ed. D. J. Canary and L. Stafford, Orlando, Fla.: Academic Press.

Baxter, L. A., and Dindia, K. 1990. Marital partners' perceptions of marital maintenance strategies. *Journal of Social and Personal Relationships* 7:187–208.

Baxter, L. A., and Wilmot, W. W. 1985. Taboo topics in close relationships. *Journal of Social and Personal Relationships* 2:253–269.

Bell, R. A.; Daly, J. A.; and Gonzalez, C. 1987. Affinity maintenance in marriage and its relationship to women's marital satisfaction. *Journal of Marriage and the Family* 49:445–454.

Burleson, B. R., and Samter, W. 1985. Consistencies in theoretical and naive evaluations of comforting messages. *Communication Monographs* 52:103–123.

Canary, D. J., and Stafford, L. 1992. Relational maintenance strategies and equity in marriage. *Communication Monographs* 59:243–268.

Cupach, W. R., and Metts, S. 1988. *Perceptions of the occurrence and management of dialectics in romantic relationships.* Paper presented at the Fourth International Conference on Personal Relationships, Vancouver, Canada.

Dindia, K. 1989. *Toward the development of a measure of marital maintenance strategies.* Paper presented at the International Communication Association Conference, San Francisco.

Dindia, K., and Baxter, L. A. 1987. Strategies for maintaining and repairing marital relationships. *Journal of Social and Personal Relationships* 4:143–158.

Duck, S. W. 1988. *Relating to others.* Milton Keynes, England: Open University Press.

Fitzpatrick, M. A. 1988. *Between husbands and wives: Communication in marriage.* Newbury Park, Calif.: Sage.

Fitzpatrick, M. A., and Best, P. 1979. Dyadic adjustment in relational types: Consensus, cohesion, affectional expression, and satisfaction in enduring relationships. *Communication Monographs* 46:165–178.

Fletcher, G. J. O.; Fincham, F. D.; Cramer, L.; and Heron, N. 1987. The role of attributions in the development of dating relationships. *Journal of Personality and Social Psychology* 53: 510–517.

Hatfield, E.; Traupmann, J.; Sprecher, S.; Utne, M. K.; and Hay, J. 1985. Equity and intimate relationships: Recent research. In *Compatible and incompatible relationships*, ed. W. Ickes, 91–117. New York: Springer-Verlag.

Hatfield, E.; Walster, G. W.; and Berscheid, E. 1978. *Equity: Theory and research.* Needham, Mass.: Allyn & Bacon.

Hecht, M.; Shepard, T.; and Hall, M. J. 1979. Multivariate indices of the effects of self-disclosure. *Western Journal of Speech Communication* 43:235–245.

Milardo, R. M. 1986. Personal choice and social constraint in close relationships: Application of network analysis. In *Friendship and social interaction*, ed. V. J. Derlega and B. A. Winstead, 145–166. New York: Springer-Verlag.

Montgomery, B. M. 1993. Relationship maintenance versus relationship change: A dialectical dilemma. *Journal of Social and Personal Relationships* 10:205–224.

Parks, M. R., and Adelman, M. B. 1983. Communication networks and the development of romantic relationships: An expansion of uncertainty reduction theory. *Human Communication Research* 10:55–79.

Rawlins, W. K. 1983. Openness as problematic in ongoing friendships: Two conversational dilemmas. *Communication Monographs* 50:1–13.

Roloff, M. E. 1976. Communication strategies, relationships, and relational change. In *Explorations in interpersonal communication*, ed. G. R. Miller, 173–196. Newbury Park, Calif.: Sage.

Rusbult, C. E. 1987. Responses to dissatisfaction in close relationships: The "exit-voice-loyalty-neglect" model. In *Intimate relationships: Development, dynamics, and deterioration*, ed. D. Perlman and S. W. Duck, 209–237. Newbury Park, Calif.: Sage.

Rusbult, C. E.; Drigotas, S. M.; and Verette, J. 1994. The investment model: An interdependence analysis of commitment processes and relationship maintenance phenomena. In *Communication and relational maintenance*, ed. D. J. Canary and L. Stafford. Orlando, Fla.: Academic Press.

Samter, W., and Burleson, B. R. 1984. Cognitive and motivational influences on spontaneous comforting behavior. *Human Communication Research* 11:231–260.

Shea, B. C., and Pearson, J. C. 1986. The effects of relationship type, partner intent, and gender on the selection of relationship maintenance strategies. *Communication Monographs* 53: 354–364.

Sillars, A. L.; Pike, G. R.; Jones, T. S.; and Redmon, K. 1983. Communication and conflict in marriage. In *Communication yearbook* 7, ed. R. N. Bostrom, 414–429. Newbury Park, Calif.: Sage.

Sprecher, S. 1986. The relation between inequity and emotions in close relationships. *Social Psychology Quarterly* 49:309–321.

Stafford, L., and Canary, D. J. 1991. Maintenance strategies and romantic relationship type, gender, and relational characteristics. *Journal of Social and Personal Relationships* 8:217–242.

Utne, M. K.; Hatfield, E.; Traupmann, J.; and Greenberger, D. 1984. Equity, marital satisfaction, and stability. *Journal of Social and Personal Relationships* 1:323–332.

Williamson, R. N., and Fitzpatrick, M. A. 1985. Two approaches to marital interaction: Relational control patterns in marital types. *Communication Monographs* 52:236–252.

Wilmot, W. W. 1987. *Dyadic communication*, 3d ed. New York: Random House.

Witteman, H., and Fitzpatrick, M. A. 1986. Compliance-gaining in marital interaction: Power bases, processes, and outcomes. *Communication Monographs* 53:130–143.

CHAPTER 10

DE-ESCALATING

RELATIONSHIPS

ILSA: You're saying this only to make me go.

RICK: I'm saying it because it's true. Inside us we both know you belong with Victor. You're part of his work—the thing that keeps him going. If that plane leaves the ground and you're not with him, you will regret it. Maybe not today. Maybe not tomorrow. But soon, and for the rest of your life.

ILSA: But what about us?

Rick: We'll always have Paris. We didn't have . . . We, we lost it until you came to Casablanca. We got it back last night.

ILSA: And I said I'd never leave you.

RICK: And you never will. But I have a job to do too, and where I'm going you can't follow. What I've got to do, you can't be any part of. Ilsa, I'm not good at being noble. But it doesn't take much to see that the problems of three little people don't amount to a hill of beans in this crazy world. Someday you'll understand that. . . . Now, now. . . . Here's looking at you, kid.

From *Casablanca*

Few relationships last a lifetime. Most simply deteriorate over time as we make new friends or move to new towns. Sometimes we do not simply drift apart but rather decide that a relationship isn't working out and decide to withdraw from it. **De-escalation** involves reducing the level of intimacy in the relationship; the brusquer option is **termination**—abandoning the relationship entirely. We often feel obligated to communicate our intentions to our partners. We talk about our feelings, the reasons for change, and our hopes for the future. This chapter focuses on why and how we break up and the consequences of doing so.

Why Break Up?

The first major study of disengagement was done by Hill, Rubin, and Peplau in 1976. The study was significant because it studied the same people over a two-year period, and the researchers managed to keep records of both partners in each relationship. Of 231 couples studied, 43 percent broke up over two years. Why did people break up? Who initiated the breakup, when, and with what consequences? This early study provided some answers:

1. *The more "in love" you are, the more likely you are to stay together.* Hill and colleagues looked at a number of measures of intimacy and found that couples were more likely to stay together when both partners were "in love," had thought of marriage, rated the relationship high in closeness, dated each other exclusively, and had dated for a longer period of time (about a year).

2. *Couples who were equally involved in the relationship were more likely to stay together than couples who were in inequitable relationships.* Of partners who indicated that they were equally involved, only 23 percent broke up. However, 54 percent of the couples involved in inequitable relationships broke up (see Chapter 9 concerning equity theory).

3. *Couples with similar characteristics and attitudes were more likely to stay together than dissimilar couples.* All couples in the study were matched in height, religion, and attitudes toward women's rights, religiosity, and number of children desired.

The classic movie *Casablanca* contains memorable scenes of love and relational disengagement. The more recent *When Harry Met Sally . . .* also focused on love and relational decay and disengagement. Harry and Sally were even shown reflecting on the choices made by the stars of the earlier film and the communication between them.

(© 1943 Turner Entertainment Co.)

The typical couple had been dating for eight months when the study began, so it is possible that pairs work out such matters fairly early on. What predicted staying together over the next two years? People who stayed together were also matched in SAT scores, educational aspirations, beauty, and age. It appears that people can cope with discrepancies (or mismatches; recall Chapter 4) in these areas for months but that these discrepancies do eventually pose problems.

4. *People break up seasonally.* People take advantage of vacations to separate from their partners and "get away from it all." Fully 71.1 percent of breakups occur during the summer months (April to September). Involvement also played an important role: the less involved partner took the opportunity to break off the relationship during a vacation, whereas the more involved partner indicated that things fell apart during the school year. Because it is sometimes difficult to say precisely when any relationship began to decay and fall apart, these results imply that the less involved person may have given up much earlier than the more involved partner, who continued to work on the relationship for weeks or even months.

5. *Both people claim credit for initiating the breakup.* Women indicated that they initiated the breakup 51.3 percent of the time, that the man did so in 35.5 percent of the relationships, and that it was mutual in 13 percent of the cases. Among men, 46.1 percent indicated that they had initiated the breakup, 39.5 percent reported that the woman had done so, and 15 percent said the decision was mutual. Because people prefer to be the initiator rather than the rejected party, most people recall being the initiator.

6. *Women list more relational problems than men do.* Table 10-1 provides a list of factors that contributed to the decision to break up. The most frequently cited reasons included boredom, differences in interests and backgrounds, desire to be independent, and conflicting attitudes on sex and marriage. Women provided more reasons for breaking off relationships than men did, citing differences in interests, differences in intelligence, conflicting ideas about marriage, independence, and interest in seeing someone else. Women were more sensitive to problem areas in the relationship and compared it with alternatives that appeared to be more promising.

The value of this study is that it provided a good deal of information concerning the disengagement process, and this information is useful for making comparisons between our own experiences and those of others who broke up or stayed together. Later studies, which examined only part of the overall process, nonetheless support the conclusions cited: People stay together when they are in equitable relationships, are committed to each other, and have many similarities and matching interests. Further, women display a greater preoccupation with relational quality and spend more time thinking about relational problems.

What precipitates the decision to leave a relationship?

Table 10-1
FACTORS CONTRIBUTING TO THE ENDING OF A RELATIONSHIP

	Women's Reports (%)	Men's Reports (%)	Agreement that Cause Contributed to Breakup
Dyadic factors			
Bored with relationship	76.7	76.7	Yes
Differences in interests	72.8	61.1	No
Differences in backgrounds	44.2	46.8	No
Differences in intelligence	19.5	10.4	No
Conflicting sexual attitudes	48.1	42.9	Yes
Conflicting marriage ideas	43.4	28.9	Yes
Nondyadic factors			
Woman's independence	73.7	50.0	Yes
Man's independence	46.8	61.1	Yes
Woman's interest in another man	40.3	31.2	Yes
Man's interest in another woman	18.2	28.6	Yes
Living too far apart	28.2	41.0	Yes
Pressure from woman's parents	18.2	13.0	Yes
Pressure from man's parents	10.4	9.1	Yes

Source: Adapted from Hill, Rubin, and Peplau 1976. Used with permission of the authors and the Society for the Psychological Study of Social Issues.

CONFRONTING RELATIONAL UNHAPPINESS:
THE FOUR PHASES OF DISENGAGEMENT

Partners become bored, develop different interests, and have conflicting ideas about marriage and sex. Every relationship will have problems. Why are people able to cope with certain problems but not with others?

According to Duck (1982), a person can proceed through four phases when deciding what to do about a relationship (see Figure 10-1): the **intrapsychic phase,** the **dyadic phase,** the **social phase,** and the **grave-dressing phase.** (The grave-dressing phase deals with the final phase of disengagement, explaining why a relationship decayed and ended. It is called "grave dressing" because after a relationship is "dead," each participant is likely to "dress up" the grave by promoting a positive image of their role in the relationship. Grave dressing will be discussed later in the

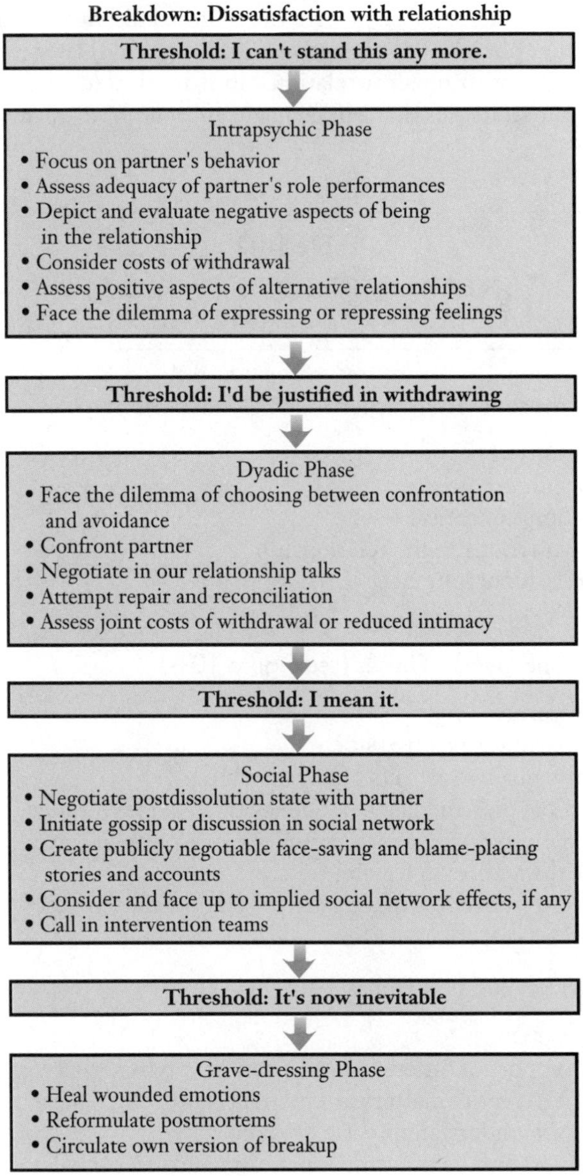

Breakdown: Dissatisfaction with relationship

| Threshold: I can't stand this any more. |

Intrapsychic Phase
- Focus on partner's behavior
- Assess adequacy of partner's role performances
- Depict and evaluate negative aspects of being in the relationship
- Consider costs of withdrawal
- Assess positive aspects of alternative relationships
- Face the dilemma of expressing or repressing feelings

| Threshold: I'd be justified in withdrawing |

Dyadic Phase
- Face the dilemma of choosing between confrontation and avoidance
- Confront partner
- Negotiate in our relationship talks
- Attempt repair and reconciliation
- Assess joint costs of withdrawal or reduced intimacy

| Threshold: I mean it. |

Social Phase
- Negotiate postdissolution state with partner
- Initiate gossip or discussion in social network
- Create publicly negotiable face-saving and blame-placing stories and accounts
- Consider and face up to implied social network effects, if any
- Call in intervention teams

| Threshold: It's now inevitable |

Grave-dressing Phase
- Heal wounded emotions
- Reformulate postmortems
- Circulate own version of breakup

Figure 10–1

Steps and
Decisions in
Relationship
Development
and Decline

Source: Adapted
from Duck 1982.
Reprinted with
permission of
Academic Press, Inc.,
and the author.

chapter, when we look at the consequences of relational disengagement; here we will emphasize the earlier phases of disengagement.) Duck (1984) later raised the issue of how a person might try to repair a relationship if motivated to do so. Table 10-2 outlines some repair strategies that can be made at each phase of the disengagement process.

Table 10-2
GENERAL METHODS EMPLOYED TO REPAIR RELATIONSHIPS

The Breakdown Phase: Dissatisfaction with the Relationship

Major repair concerns:
- To reduce turbulence in interactions
- To improve communication
- To focus on attractions in the relationship
- To increase relational intimacy

The Intrapsychic and Dyadic Phases (see Figure 10-1)

Major repair concerns:
- To bring out partner's positive side
- To focus on the positive aspects of relationship
- To reinterpret partner and partner's behavior as positive and well intentioned
- To reduce negativity toward partner and strike a more balanced view
- To reevaluate difficulties in leaving
- To reevaluate attractiveness of alternative relationships and partners

Social Phase and Beyond (see Figure 10-1)

Major repair concerns:
- To enlist the support of others to hold relationship together
- To obtain help to rectify matters or end the relationship
- To obtain help in understanding the breakup
- To obtain support and help during separation and after breakup
- To create acceptable public and private accounts of breakup
- To save face and justify breakup to self
- To circulate own version of breakup

Source: Adapted from Duck 1984.

During the *intrapsychic phase* a person reflects on the quality of the relationship, possibly comparing the relationship to others, and comparing the relational partners to potential partners. *Intrapsychic* conflict takes place when the individual weighs many issues in an internal struggle. There are six major concerns: To size up the partner's behavior, to assess the internal dynamics of the relationship, to express discomfort (but not directly to partner), to question one's relationship judgments, to find ways to modify the partner's behavior and change relationship outcomes, and to convince oneself that leaving could be better than staying. During this phase, the person who scrutinizes the relationship identifies the reasons or the causes of dissatisfaction and decides whether the problems can be solved and whether he or she is sufficiently motivated to continue to work in the relationship.

With regard to repairing relationships, Duck (1984) argues that when we first see signs of distress in a relationship, we may try to attempt to reestablish liking and attraction in the relationship by focusing on several communication-related activities (see Table 10-2). First, to reduce turbulence in interactions, the partner (or both partners) can attend workshops on social skills training and on specific skill acquisitions. Communicators have to eliminate or reduce the cause of the unhappiness in the relationship, and the unhappiness may stem from inappropriately communicated anger, frustrations from one's job that affect the relationship, difficulty in confiding one's emotions and feelings in the partner, and so on. Some of the changes partners have to make involve basic communication skills. Some communication skills programs, however, only teach participants how to identify the problems they have in the relationship and how to avoid turbulence. However, improved communication must occur in reality—actually engaging in improved listening skills and increased time allocated to metacommunicating—and must occur on a regular basis.

Another element of repair is to focus on rekindling the attractions that were once prominent in the relationship—perhaps returning to the activities the partners shared at one time. Another repair strategy includes reintroducing intimacy into the relationship. Increased self-disclosure, engaging in trust-building exercises and couple enrichment programs, and increasing quality time together in new activities are some important ways to increase intimacy.

The *dyadic phase* involves confronting the partner with the dissatisfaction (Figure 10-1). There are nine major concerns at this phase: to confront the partner with our dissatisfaction; to present our view of the relationship; to express discomfort directly to the partner; to assess the costs of being in the relationship and how to deal with the dissatisfaction; to evaluate the partner's views of the relationship; to cope with the partner's rejoinders, excuses, or apologies; to size up the relationship together; to consider alternatives; and to choose to repair or dissolve the relationship.

In the *social phase*, the individual basically tells the partner: "I am serious. I mean it." The individual goes public with his or her unhappiness with the relationship, seeking advice and support from others, perhaps asking for intervention from others. Concerns include creating an agreed-on postdissolution state of the relationship (for example, agreements might be reached concerning how much emotional and physical withdrawal will take place, as well as a statement concerning possible reconciliation), creating acceptable definitions for the partners ("friends," "acquaintances," etc.), considering implied status changes in terms of roles (for example, will both partners stay in the church choir?), evaluating the consequences of dissolution (who stays friends with the couple's friends?), placing blame, saving face, and obtaining acceptance of the dissolution from others (friends say, "You deserve someone better").

It is during the dyadic and social phases that others notice that "something is wrong." The nonverbal bonding behaviors outlined in Chapter 4 are no longer exhibited in public, and others notice their absence. Communication is problematic: channel discrepancy is noted in sarcastic comments (smiling face, negative tone of voice), or the couple use a tone of voice that lacks warmth and friendliness. Channel discrepancy may make it more difficult for distressed couples to talk openly with each other because mixed messages are more difficult to respond to and are basically unpleasant to view (see Leathers 1992). Nonetheless, distressed couples sit farther apart, refrain from touching, look less often at each other, lean away from each other, and fail to communicate many of the behaviors that indicate affiliation, liking, and intimacy.

A number of repair tactics are available during both these phases (see Table 10-2): Repair makers want to reestablish the partner's attraction to each other and their liking for each other as persons (but no longer as a couple, which was a motive at the breakdown phase). Four tactics are accentuating the partner's positive qualities while downplaying the negative, accentuating the positive outcomes from the relationship, reinterpreting the causes of the partner's unacceptable or annoying behaviors in positive ways, and finding fewer faults that can be blamed solely on the partner. The first two tactics generally deal with the attempt to perceive that one is in fact in an equitable relationship (introduced in Chapter 9). The reestablishment of equity as a repair strategy is discussed in the next section of this chapter.

The third and fourth tactics deal with the *attributions* the repair maker makes concerning the causes of the relational problems. We outlined attribution theory in Chapter 6, and we will have more to say about it shortly; basically, whether repairing relationships is judged as easy or difficult reflects the partner's assessment of the underlying causes—if the causes of the unhappiness are perceived to be stable, internal, intentional, and controllable (the partner has become extremely possessive), the partner is likely to believe that repair is difficult or even impossible to achieve and is likely to exit the relationship.

Repair tactics available during the final stages of the disengagement process are listed at the bottom of Table 10-2. First, a person might try to enlist the assistance of friends in holding the relationship together or removing obstacles that block relational growth (e.g., to stop in-laws from interfering in the relationship). Second, a person may seek social support from friends during the breakup period. Third, if the two continue toward breakup and dissolve the relationship, both will be motivated

When confronting relational unhappiness, individuals often progress through four phases of disengagement: the intrapsychic, dyadic, social, and grave-dressing phases.

(Joan Liftin/Actuality)

to portray themselves in a positive light and to protect a threatened esteem. Both will then begin to circulate stories or narratives ("accounts") concerning what happened, who was to blame, and so on.

In sum, as individuals confront relational unhappiness, they often (though not always) progress through four phases of disengagement, and there are a number of ways to try to repair the relationship. Progressing through these phases, the motivation necessary to work on relational repairs depends on how committed the partner was or is, how much in love the partners were at one time, the type of problems confronted, and the personalities of the individuals involved. (We will have more to say about personalities in Chapter 13.)

THE IMPORTANCE OF EQUITY

As noted, one way to look at repairing relationships focuses on how people restore equity in the relationship. Equity theory was outlined in Chapter 9, and there is considerable evidence to suggest that people who are not in an equitable, fair relationship will break up eventually. We all prefer to be in equitable relationships, and the lack of equity is a major reason for changing our behavior or deciding to terminate a relationship. Equity theory also outlines a number of tactics that individuals can use to restore equity. Tactics used to restore **psychological equity** create a perception of equity when in fact the relationship is not equitable. Other tactics can be used to restore **actual equity**—one person in the relationship takes a specific action to make sure that resources (inputs and outcomes) are distributed fairly between the partners. Both the underbenefited and the overbenefited partner may use a number of tactics to restore actual or psychological equity. However, we will focus on the options available to the underbenefited partner.

Underbenefited partners may engage in a number of actions to restore perceived psychological equity: distort inputs and outcomes, hope that the future will be better, compare the relationship to ones that are even less equitable, resign themselves to a higher order of "justice," and devalue themselves. During early episodes on the TV series "M.A.S.H.," "Hot Lips" Houlihan was in an inequitable relationship with Frank Burns—she supported him, loved him, did favors for him, and bought him things. Frank did virtually nothing for her. "Hot Lips" distorted her inputs and his inputs; she convinced herself that she enjoyed giving things to Frank, and she emphasized the fact that he was a doctor, and marrying a doctor was important to her. She tried to convince herself that she really wasn't in a terribly inequitable relationship, and she kept hoping that the future would be better. The inequity lasted for years, but as time passed it became obvious that Frank was not going to divorce his wife or even increase his contributions to the relationship. Hot Lips later found a more equitable relationship and got married. When Frank finally changed, it was too late; Hot Lips was happily married.

Sometimes victims admit to themselves that they are in inequitable relationships, but they might believe that they cannot really do anything about it (for example, they are against divorce) or that they do not have the power to change things. One way to cope with inequity is to compare one's level of inequity with other relationships that are even more inequitable, a consoling strategy that makes the victims feel better.

Another tactic is to convince oneself that a higher sense of justice will prevail; for example, victims may believe that they worked hard in their relationship but have nothing to show for it. Victims may come to believe that God, the IRS, or some other "higher" authority will intervene at some time ("People get what they deserve").

Finally, victims may come to devalue themselves. They may admit that they are in an inequitable relationship and recall that they have been in similar relationships in the past. A history of getting into inequitable relationships may result in the victims' coming to believe that it is their fate to be in such relationships and that they can expect no better. Having low expectations in relationships can help victims cope with inequity, at least temporarily.

How can the underbenefited partner restore actual equity? Three alternatives are to seek compensation (or restitution), retaliate, and withdraw. First, the underbenefited person may confront (or have a third party confront) the overbenefited partner with the inequity. By talking over the issue of involvements, the future of the relationship, and both partners' perceptions of the relationship, the person may elicit a change in inputs and a promise to maintain equity in the future.

People may not like to confront partners openly, and so they may act in indirect ways to prompt others to increase inputs into the relationship. For example, White (1980) asked student subjects if they had ever intentionally attempted to make their dating partners jealous. White identified five motivations for causing intentional jealousy: to get the partner to increase rewards or inputs into the relationship (indicated by 30.1 percent of the subjects), to test the relationship (39.7 percent), to seek revenge on the partner (9.7 percent), to bolster self-esteem (8.4 percent), and to punish the partner (1.4 percent). There were gender differences for only one of these motives: women were more likely to attempt to induce jealousy for the purpose of increasing rewards. Table 10-3 presents the results on inducing jealousy intentionally. The results are quite clear: Women who believed that they were the more involved partner were much more likely to try to make their partners jealous.

Another indirect way to establish actual equity seems, at first glance, to be counterproductive: some victims may temporarily increase their inputs even more in the hope that partners will notice the extra attention and increase their inputs as well. Once partners have increased their contributions, the victims can reduce some of the new special favors, and with luck, the partners will continue to provide the new inputs, thus leaving the relationship more equitable than it had been in the past.

Another way to restore actual equity is to retaliate against the overbenefited partner. The underbenefited partner can increase costs for the harmdoer (and derive some personal satisfaction), thereby making the relationship more equitable. What people do to retaliate may depend on the relationship and on the likes and dislikes of

Table 10-3
PARTNERS WHO ATTEMPT TO INDUCE JEALOUSY, AS A FUNCTION OF GENDER AND LEVEL OF INVOLVEMENT

	Level of Relative Involvement (% of subjects)		
	Less Involved	*Equally Involved*	*More Involved*
Men	14.6	17.3	22.2
Women	22.7	25.4	50.0

Source: Adapted from White 1980. Reprinted with permission of Sage Publications, Inc.

the partner (fail to have a term paper printed on time, do a poor job in word processing, invite the in-laws to visit on Super Bowl weekend, etc.).

Finally, partners can withdraw some or all inputs. If the underbenefited partners had done most of the work, they can pull out some of the involvement so as to make the contributions to the relationship more equal. Later, the underbenefited partners may withdraw all inputs, and no relationship will exist.

REASONS FOR DISENGAGEMENT

People give many specific reasons for disengagement besides the importance of equity. Knapp and Vangelisti (1992) cite Safran (1979) as identifying ten common trouble areas: (1) a breakdown in communication, (2) the loss of shared goals or interests, (3) sexual incompatibility, (4) infidelity, (5) diminution of excitement or fun, (6) money, (7) conflicts about children, (8) alcohol or drug abuse, (9) women's equality issues, and (10) in-laws.

Cody (1982) had students rate the importance of twenty-four potential reasons for disengagement and found that the reasons can be grouped into three general types: *faults*, *refusals to compromise*, and *constraints* (see Table 10-4). By *faults*, we mean that the initiator believed that some aspect of the partner's personality was at fault and clearly placed the blame for the disengagement on the partner. *Refusals to compromise* reflect the belief that the partner was unwilling to compromise for the good of the relationship, took the partner for granted, stopped being romantic, and so forth. The third category of reasons, *constraints*, reflects the belief that the partner wanted a far more intimate relationship than the respondent wanted to have. Both refusals to compromise and constraints tap into a person's level of commitment to a relationship. When you conclude that your partner refuses to compromise, you believe that you are putting more work into the relationship; you are more committed and involved. By contrast, when you feel that your partner constrains you, you believe that too much is expected of you; the partner is more involved in the relationship than you want to be. Unequal commitments and investments are strongly related to disengagement, and all three categories of problems (faults, refusals to compromise, constraints) affect communication during disengagement.

Metts and Cupach (1986) identified ten themes that characterize disengagements (see Table 10-5, p. 263). The three most common reasons given for opposite-sex relationship decay, for women, were drifting apart, rule violation, and third-party involvement; for men they were drifting apart, rule violation, and a critical event.

Listing problems, however, provides only limited information concerning why or how people break up. A number of theories discuss why certain problems result in decay. One of these, discussed in Chapter 9, focuses on the fact that certain problems cause increases in uncertainty, and because we neither like nor tolerate high levels of uncertainty, we dissociate ourselves from others who cause it. Here we will outline two other approaches to disengagement: attribution theory and valence of relational problems.

Table 10-4

REASONS CITED AS PRECIPITATING RELATIONAL DISENGAGEMENT

Type of Reason	Examples
Faults	My partner had too many faults.
	My partner's personality was incompatible with mine.
	My partner was too demanding.
	My partner behaved in ways that embarrassed me.
	My partner's behavior or personality was more to blame for the breakup than anything else.
Refusals to compromise	My partner was unwilling to contribute enough to the relationship.
	My partner no longer behaved as romantically toward me as before.
	My partner took me for granted.
	My partner wasn't willing to compromise for the good of the relationship.
Constraints	The relationship was beginning to constrain me; I felt a lack of freedom.
	Although I still cared for my partner, I wanted to start dating others.
	Although the relationship was a good one, I was getting bored with it.
	My partner contributed too much, and I started to feel suffocated.
	My partner was becoming too possessive of me.
Miscellaneous	Although I still liked my partner, the romance had gone out of the relationship.
	I was primarily interested in having a good time, not committing to a relationship.
	My partner was too dependent on me.
	The two of us developed different interests and had less in common.
	I couldn't trust my partner.
	One of us moved away, and we couldn't see each other very much anymore.

(continued)

Type of Reason	Examples
	(continued from previous page)
Miscellaneous	Most of my friends didn't like my partner (or most of my partner's friends didn't like me), causing problems that detracted from the relationship.
	The relationship itself didn't seem right, and its failings can't be blamed on one person or the other.
	My parents didn't approve of my partner (or my partner's parents didn't approve of me).
	My partner showed too much physical affection (or was too aggressive).

Source: Adapted from Cody 1982.

ATTRIBUTION THEORY

Communicators often focus on the underlying causes for why people behave the way they do (as discussed in Chapter 6). A potential disengager can identify the underlying causes for relational problems along four dimensions: *intentionality, controllability, internality,* and *stability.* Imagine, for example, that a relational partner doesn't open up to you and doesn't confide in you, and you want the partner to express what is on his or her mind and to disclose more information of a personal nature. Or you may scrutinize your relationship and conclude that your partner is too possessive. Are the underlying causes to these problems *stable* (recurring over time), *controllable, internal* (caused by the person's personality or caused by external factors like pressure from the job, school, and so forth), and *intentional?* After we make attributions concerning why the relational partner is behaving that way, we can make plans to change the behavior or, if the problem is *stable, intentional,* and *internally* caused, to disengage.

Cody and co-workers (1992) demonstrated how strongly attributed causes are related to the disengagement process. Six common problems were examined: lack of confiding (the partner failed to confide feelings and thoughts to a dating partner), lack of shared time (the partner failed to share quality time and to make time with the partner), rudeness (the partner was rude in public and embarrassed the dating partner), presentability (the partner failed to be presentable and well groomed in public), possessiveness, and jealousy. How do people perceive the underlying causes of these problems?

Students indicated that public rudeness and possessiveness are caused both intentionally and by internal causes. Further, these two relational problems were rated

Table 10-5
DISENGAGEMENT THEMES

Theme	Description
Drifting apart	The relationship erodes naturally over time, due primarily to increased interaction distance, decreased quantity and quality of communication, changing interests and values, or mutual diminished efforts to maintain the relationship.
Critical event	A single event, fight, argument, or confrontation alters the relationship permanently.
Rule violation	One partner engages in behavior deemed inappropriate to the relationship.
Third-party involvement	One or both relational partners put considerable time and effort into a new relationship, at the expense of their own.
Network involvement	One or both relational partners develop a new network of friends that displaces their own friendship or causes friction.
General incompatibility	Problematic personality differences or a basic lack of commonality.
Value difference	One person expresses values extremely different from those of the partner.
Overconsumption	Individuals spend too much time together, leading them to get tired of each other.
Relational or role definition	The partners clash over their roles in the relationship and their definition of intimacy.
Nonmutuality of effort	One partner puts in more work than the other.

Source: Adapted from Metts and Cupach 1986. Used by permission of the authors.

as more stable than problems like lack of confiding and lack of shared time. Jealousy was also perceived as an internally caused problem (but ratings on intentionality were only average, indicating, perhaps, that some people believed that jealousy is used intentionally, as White found in his 1980 study). Of these three problems, possessiveness and jealousy were rated as difficult to control, whereas it was thought that partners should be able to exert some control over rudeness.

By contrast, problems of presentability were rated as easily controllable, as were the problems of lack of shared time and, to a lesser degree, lack of confiding. These three problems were also rated as unintentional (especially lack of confiding and problems of presentability). Both problems of presentability and lack of shared time were rated as problems that were caused externally, and lack of confiding received average ratings on internality–externality, suggesting, perhaps, that some people believe this to be caused internally by the person's shyness and reticence or by a lack of trust in the partner.

The underlying attributional causes were related to the decision to break up in three ways. First, the students indicated that they were likely to withdraw from the relationship and were less likely to work on salvaging the relationship when the relational problems were caused by intentional, internal, and stable causes. The problems of possessiveness and rudeness are the result of a person who is internally motivated by personality (or by a need to dominate) to act intentionally and to do so consistently over time. Such a relational problem significantly reduced the attractiveness of the relationship, as well as the motivation to work hard to change the partner.

Second, the researchers had students rate the extent to which problems were easy to solve. Problems that were easy to control and occurred unintentionally (problems of presentability and lack of shared time) were perceived as easier to solve than problems that are less controllable and occur intentionally (possessiveness, jealousy). Third, Cody and associates (1992) asked students to indicate the extent to which they would accept a full-blown apology as a believable remedial tactic and wait to give the partner the chance to change his or her behavior, eliminate the problem, and salvage the relationship. (Recall the material on repairing relationships and apologies from Chapter 6.) Students indicated that only when the problem was not caused intentionally by the partner, under the partner's control, and solvable would a full-blown apology effectively help patch up the differences and prompt the granting of a second chance. That is, apologies were considered effective for problems of presentability and lack of shared time but ineffective for the problems of possessiveness and jealousy.

Although this project looked at only six relational problems, it is easy to see that these underlying factors apply to other problems you might experience. Are you and your partner fighting and arguing? What are the underlying causes? If the partner is trying to control you, the pressure placed on you is undeniably intentional and internal and may (as you date over months) become a stable, recurring problem. You may seriously question if you want to continue such a relationship. Alternatively, if the fighting and arguing was caused by your partner's being under a lot of pressure because of taking the Law School Admissions Test, you might perceive the causes as external, unstable, and unintentional (the person didn't *intend* to be bossy). You might stay in the relationship, work on a solution, and perceive a full-blown apology as a believable remedial tactic.

THE VALENCE AND FREQUENCY OF PROBLEMS
Vangelisti (1992) offered a somewhat different view of the link between relational problems and relational dissatisfaction. She argued that for a behavior to be judged as problematic, at least two of the following criteria must be fulfilled: The behavior must be negatively valenced (judged to be very negative in its impact on the relationship), and it must occur with some degree of frequency. If it does not occur with some degree of frequency, it must be salient enough for one or both partners to remember it and identify it as a continuing source of displeasure or difficulty.

Vangelisti (1992) interviewed couples that had been dating for an average of six years, identified common serious problems, and assessed the relationship between the frequency of occurrence of the problems, relational satisfaction, and underlying attributed causes for the problems. The most frequently cited problem was withholding expression of negative feelings (listed three times more frequently than any other problem), followed by not taking the other person's perspective when listening, withholding expression of feelings, and needing more time together to communicate. Vangelisti also found that relational problems occur fairly frequently: 16 percent of her respondents said that they occur more than once a week, 21 percent said they occur once a week, 19 percent said they occur every two weeks, and 16 percent said they occur every two months.

Vangelisti (1992) found no significant relationship between relational dissatisfaction and any one relational problem. However, individuals rated their satisfaction lower when their partner was believed to have caused a *number* of communicative problems; for example, dissatisfaction stemmed from three or four of the problems' occurring over a few weeks' time or one problem recurring over the course of months. The greater the number of problems a partner causes, the greater the dissatisfaction. Vangelisti also found that attribution theory was important: of the serious problems listed by her interviewees, 44 percent of the problems were judged to be internally caused, and 63 percent were judged to be stable.

In sum, why do relationships fail? In part, relational partners decide to withdraw from relationships when relationships are inequitable and when there are serious, multiple problems that are judged to be stable, internally caused, and intentionally caused. Partners are likely to withdraw from the relationship if they perceive that the problems are not easy to solve.

Methods of Relational Disengagement

TACTICS USED IN RELATIONAL DISENGAGEMENT
Once the decision has been made to disengage, some message is usually used to communicate the initiator's intent. Table 10-6 presents a list of some of the tactics people report using when disengaging. The first type involves **positive-tone messages,** which have two important characteristics. First, positive-tone messages are

Table 10-6

MESSAGES USED IN RELATIONAL DISENGAGEMENT

Type	Example
Positive Tone	
Fairness	"I would say: 'It is unfair on my part and would be unfair to you to continue our relationship if one of us had to fake it. I care a great deal about you, but I don't feel as strongly toward you as you do toward me. It would be cheating you if I were to pretend I felt this way and would cause more heartache if I continue to do so. I think it would be wise if we stopped seeing so much of each other.'"
Compromise	"I would be very scared, I think. First, I would explain why I was dissatisfied with the relationship. Then I would say: 'I care about you and I want to be friends and there is no reason not to see each other.' We'd then talk and I would try to work out a compromise."
Fatalism	"In the kindest way possible I would say: 'My feelings have changed and I have really spent a lot of time praying about it and seeking God's guidance in this situation. I feel that it's not God's will for us to continue at this time.'"
De-escalation	
Promised friendship	"I would say: 'I think we need to stop seeing quite so much of each other. I am not ready to settle down yet. We can still see each other and remain great friends.'"
Implied possible reconciliation	"I would say: 'I'm sorry, but for a close relationship to work there must be mutual love, understanding, and close feelings, and at the moment I don't feel as close as I should. I think that it would be best to lay off for awhile. If this relationship was meant to work, it will. If not, then it was never meant to be.'"

Relationship fault	"I would say: 'I think we are becoming too dependent upon each other, so we have nothing individual to bring to the relationship at this point. If we take a period of time to do things on our own and make discoveries about ourselves and others, then we will be capable of continuing or beginning a new relationship.'"
Appeal to independence	"I would say: 'Now is not the time for us to be tied down. Maybe in the future we could pick it up again.'"
Test of relationship	"I would say: 'I think that maybe we have been seeing too much of each other. I think we should see other people, meet other people, to see if we really want to be together.'"

Withdrawal or Avoidance Tactics

"I wouldn't say anything. I would just avoid the person as much as possible.
Without explaining my intentions to break it off, I would avoid scheduling future meetings with the person.
I wouldn't bring up the topic of breaking up, I would just never call the person again and never return any of the phone calls."

Justification

Positive consequences of disengaging/target responsibility	"I would say: 'A good relationship meets the needs of both people and ours isn't meeting my needs. I don't want to change you and I would have to if you are going to meet my needs. So, I don't think we should see each other anymore.'"
Positive consequences of disengaging/disengager responsibility	"I would say: 'I'm really changing inside and I don't feel good about our relationship anymore. I think we'd better stop seeing each other.'"
Negative consequences of non-disengaging	"I would say: 'Continuing to see each other wouldn't work because we'd begin to hate each other and the relationship would really start to deteriorate.'"

(continued)

(table continued from previous page)

*Negative identity management
or manipulation*

Enjoyment of life	"I would say: 'Life is too short and we should enjoy other people and I myself would like to date other people, to see if we really want to be together.'"
Thought manipulation	"I'd beat around the bush for awhile, then ask: 'You're not very happy are you? What's wrong (hoping to create anger)? Well, I think we need to talk about us, like, why don't we date other people for awhile? If you don't want to, at least let me so I can figure out if I still feel the same way about us as I need to.'"
Nonnegotiation	"I would say: 'I think we should date around' (and then just date other people)."
Implicit expertise	"I would say: 'It would be better for the both of us, that we need more time to date others and be sure to find the right person to marry.'"

Source: Adapted from Cody 1982.

very emotional; they try to make the rejected partner not feel rejected and hurt and also release tension that the disengager experiences during disengagement. Second, the messages state or imply a desire to *de-escalate* (see less of each other) but not *terminate* the relationship. Some variations on this general tactic are labeled "fairness," "compromise," and "fatalism."

A second popular tactic used **de-escalation messages,** which also have two characteristics. First, as with positive-tone messages, the initiator explicitly proposes that the two "see less of each other"; however, de-escalation messages are not quite as emotional as positive-tone ones. Second, a reason is given for why the two should see less of each other. Reasons can involve spending too much time together, being too young, and needing to experience other people before getting serious.

A very different approach uses **withdrawal or avoidance tactics.** Sometimes disengagers say nothing to their partners concerning intentions to change. Sometimes disengagers avoid the partner, refuse to answer phone messages, decline to return calls, and keep encounters brief.

Some messages used to communicate disengagement are, in fact, "classic."

A fourth disengagement tactic uses **justification messages,** which have three important features. First, they communicate that the partners should terminate the relationship and "stop seeing each other." Second, a reason is given to support the decision, usually that there is a cause for dissatisfaction, that the relationship is not a good one, or that the relationship isn't meeting the needs of the disengager. Justification tactics may state or imply that the disengager believes that the problem cannot be solved or remedied, even claiming (in the variation called "negative consequences of not disengaging") that things will become worse if the two don't stop seeing each other.

Finally, the tactics of **negative identity management (or manipulation)** are in contrast to the positive-tone tactics. Instead of making an effort to help keep the disengager from feeling rejected, the very nature of negative identity management tactics is to arouse emotions in such a way as to quicken disengagement, with low regard for the partner's feelings of rejection. Several of the variations are insulting to the dating partner. For example, in the "enjoyment of life" version, the disengager says that he or she does not enjoy life with the partner, which is insulting to a person one has been dating for weeks or months. In the "implicit expertise" version, the disengager first claims to know what is "better for both of us" and then claims that one should find the "right person to marry" (which apparently is not the person he or she is currently dating). The "nonnegotiation" version flatly informs the partner what will happen ("we should date around") and implies that there is no room for discussion or compromise. The "thought manipulation" version is one of the cruelest: make the partner angry, and then propose that since things aren't working out, the two should end the relationship.

The negative identity management tactics sound very coldhearted, and the messages create the impression of a person who is unlikable. However, remember that some partners are highly resistant to the idea of a breakup. Some people do not take no for an answer, some people are possessive, and some people believe that they can win back the disengager's love. If a person doesn't first agree with positive-tone or other tactics, what would you do, especially if you were certain that you wanted out of a relationship? You would probably use a stronger message. Negative identity tactics are usually not the first messages disengagers employ when breaking up (unless they desperately need to get away from a very undesirable person). Although, in this section of the chapter, we have emphasized a typology of messages from the Cody (1982) study, similar messages have been uncovered in studies by Baxter (1982) and by Wilmot, Carbaugh, and Baxter (1985).

FACTORS AFFECTING DISENGAGEMENT TACTICS

Two simple propositions explain a good deal of the use of tactics. First, the more intimate the relationship, the more likely it is that the disengager will use some form of verbal message to communicate an intention to alter the relationship. Obviously, a disengager is obligated to say something to an intimate, and it is hardly effective or normative simply to disappear after becoming involved in an intimate long-term relationship. By contrast, withdrawal or avoidance tactics are used more often when the relationship is less intimate (after one or a few dates). Baxter (1982) also studied the impact of external versus internal causes and found that disengagers simply let a relationship die (they used more withdrawal tactics) when the cause was external (partner moved to a new city), compared to when the cause was internal (the two disagreed about life goals). In the latter case, friends and intimates are more likely to feel some obligation to explain the loss in intimacy or decline in relational closeness.

Second, when we want to stay friends with our ex-partners, we will use either positive-tone or de-escalation tactics, and when we want out of the relationship completely, we will use justification, withdrawal, or negative identity management tactics. A disengager would use positive-tone tactics to maximize the chance that the two partners would stay friends after the breakup.

Cody (1982) in fact found that positive-tone tactics were used more often when the relationship was intimate and the partner constrained the disengager but the partner was not guilty of serious faults or of failing to compromise. That is to say, when a disengager was relationally close and the significant problem was that the partner wanted a more serious relationship than the disengager, the disengager would be motivated to try to make sure that the partner would not have hurt feelings and the two stayed friends afterward. Banks and colleagues (1987) also found that positive-tone tactics were used when intimacy and constraint were high but were less likely to be used when the partner had faults. They also found that positive-tone tactics were used when there was network overlap—that is, when the couple shared many friends; therefore, they would want to maintain cordial, if not friendly, relationships.

De-escalation tactics were used in similar situations. The tactics were used when intimacy was high, the partner constrained the disengager, and the partner was not guilty of faults (Cody 1982). Banks and associates (1987) also found that de-escalation tactics were likely to be used when social networks overlapped and when the disengager claimed that the two formed a well-adjusted couple. The cause of the slowdown in the relationship, then, was due largely to the fact that the constraining partner wanted to move too quickly toward intimacy or wanted more than the disengager was willing to give.

Justification tactics were used when disengagers were in relationships that were intimate, the partner had faults, and the partner constrained the disengager (Banks et al. 1987; Cody 1982). Few people want to be in a serious, intimate relationship with a person with faults, so in situations like these, disengagers employ justification tactics to sever the relationship.

Banks and co-workers (1987) found that negative identity management tactics were used when a person was perceived as constraining the partner. However, Cody (1982) found that these tactics were likely to be used mostly by underbenefited partners when constraint and intimacy were high. Oddly, Cody thought that people who were angry about being underbenefited would use the cruel-sounding negative identity tactics; he actually found the opposite: people who were less angry were more likely to use the tactics. Why? It is probably the case that these tactics are used after the disengager has already decided that the relationship is over, perhaps as a third- or fourth-attempt message after the disengager has first used de-escalation and justification tactics. By the time negative tactics are used, the disengager may no longer feel angry so much as disappointed that the undesirable person hasn't complied with the request to go away. In fact, the feeling of being already free correlates highly with the use of negative identity management tactics (Banks et al. 1987).

The Consequences of Relational Disengagement

EMOTIONAL CONSEQUENCES

We have already noted that equity theory makes specific predictions about perceived inequity and emotional reactions. First, both underbenefited and overbenefited partners will experience distress, unhappiness, and discontentment. Second, underbenefited partners experience anger and depression, while overbenefited partners experience guilt.

Banks and associates (1987) also assessed emotional consequences. Disengagers felt a greater sense of freedom from their partners when the partners constrained them and the partners were rated low on desirability (a general index of beauty and popularity). To free themselves from their partners, disengagers employed negative identity management tactics and avoided the use of positive-tone tactics. Disengagers indicated that they were depressed when they were involved in intimate relationships with nonconstraining partners who failed to compromise; that is, disengagers reported being depressed if they wanted more out of the relationship than their partners did and the partners took them for granted. Depressed individuals also indicated that they had used more positive-tone and de-escalation tactics but had avoided justification tactics. The results suggest that the people who were most likely to become depressed were the ones who had been at a disadvantage in the relationship, who were more committed to it, and who had struggled to keep it going.

Hindy, Schwarz, and Brodsky (1989) and Mearns (1991) also argue that post-breakup depression is caused by how much the individual wanted to end the relationship, the duration of the relationship, how much the partner wanted to end it, the intensity of love and other feelings for the partner, and the partner's physical attractiveness. Mearns, however, found that physical attractiveness was unrelated to depression, but that gender was: women indicated greater depression than did men. Mearns also argued that people have learned different beliefs and expectations concerning how to cope with negative emotions. Some individuals have not learned to regulate negative moods and instead wallow in self-pity and depression and take few actions to cope with the traumatic event and to move on with their social lives. Alternatively, people who make plans to deal with traumatic events and to achieve closure (full adjustment) and who engage in activities they like with people they like experience less depression over time than do others.

Disengagers experienced anger when they were in intimate relationships in which the partner refused to compromise and was rated as untrustworthy. When the disengager was underbenefited (the partner failed to compromise), the disengager would become angry, even more so if the partner promised to do more and then didn't (was untrustworthy).

STAYING FRIENDS

Banks and colleagues (1987) found that people claimed to stay friends if the disengager had used de-escalation tactics and perceived the partner to be desirable (attractive, likeable, competent, etc.). The use of justification tactics and withdrawal or avoidance was related to terminating relationships in such a way that the two did not stay friends afterwards. In this study, however, the use of positive-tone or negative identity management tactics was unrelated to staying friends—sometimes people stayed friends, and sometimes they didn't.

Metts, Cupach, and Bejlovec (1989), however, examined the responses of both disengagers and disengagees. Disengagees claimed that they stayed friends if the two had been friends prior to becoming romantically involved and were likely to stay friends if the disengager had used positive tone and had avoided using any negative identity (or other manipulative) tactic during the breakup. Disengagers also claimed that the two stayed friends if they had been friends prior to becoming romantically involved. However, the disengagers claimed that different tactics affected the choice of staying friends: disengagers were less likely to stay friends after the breakup if they had been the underbenefited partner and if they had used withdrawal or avoidance tactics.

Very few studies have examined the question of staying friends after a relational disengagement. It would seem wise to recommend, if you want to stay friends, to use positive-tone or de-escalation tactics; to avoid the use of justification, manipulation, or withdrawal tactics; to treat the partner equitably; and to date a partner who is desirable and was a friend prior to the romantic involvement. Also, people may stay friends if the agreement to break up is mutual.

GRAVE DRESSING AND ADJUSTMENT

Breaking off a serious relationship can be traumatic and stressful. Several important works have addressed issues dealing with the process whereby individuals try to cope, resolve, and account for what occurred prior to and during the relational decay phases (Baxter 1984; Conville 1991; Lee 1984; Vaughan 1987; Weiss 1975). One recent program of research focusing on this matter has been conducted by Harvey, Orbuch, and Weber (Harvey, Agostinelli, and Weber 1989; Harvey, Orbuch, and Weber 1990; Harvey et al. 1992; Harvey et al. 1986; Harvey, Weber, and Orbuch 1990; Orbuch 1992). Their model is critically important because it focuses on psychological needs, communication, and mental health.

In Chapter 6 we talked about accounts as short-term tactics that we communicate to others when we defend ourselves from the accusation that we have been bad or that we are responsible for questionable actions. Harvey and colleagues argue that after a traumatic experience, such as the disruption of a loving relationship, we naturally experience a need to explain fully what happened to us. The accounting process in this particular context may require months or even years to develop fully because so much information, so many details, so much potential for second guessing (Did I try hard enough to repair it? What if I had given my partner one more chance? Did I make the right decision? What if I had changed?), so much intimate knowledge, and often so many other people in the couple's social networks are involved. The accounting process involves the construction of a detailed, coherent story or narrative about the relationship, what happened, when, why, and with what consequences.

Figure 10-2 presents a model of account making (Harvey et al. 1992). The sequence is initiated with the **traumatic event** (the breakup itself, or certain knowledge of the partner that prompted an immediate need to terminate the relationship); shock, numbness, and the feeling of being overwhelmed occurs naturally at this point in time. The second phase is **outcry,** in which the individual may experience a number of negative emotions—panic, despair, hopelessness, and exhaustion. This stage deals largely with the release of emotional tensions that inevitably follow a traumatic experience.

The third stage is **denial,** in which case the individual cuts off from others to be alone—staying at home, avoiding people at church or work, and so on. It is at this stage where the individual begins to think about the many reasons why the loving relationship soured. The interruption of daily routines facilitates thinking about

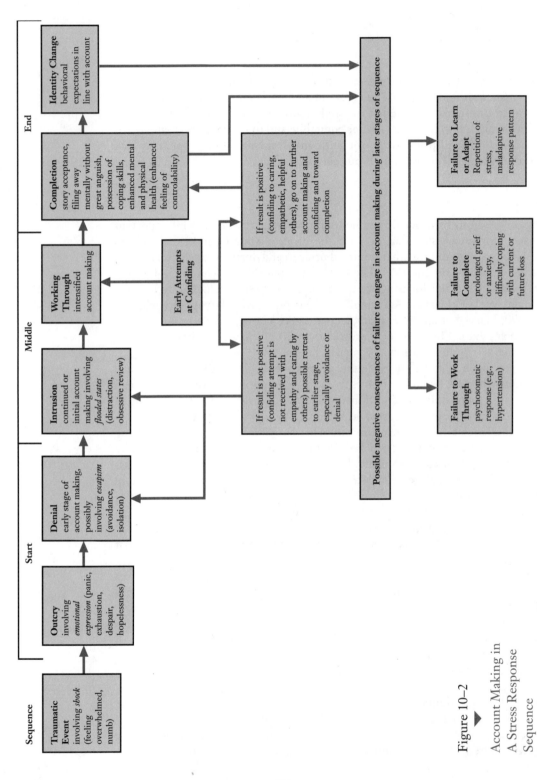

Figure 10–2

▶ Account Making in
A Stress Response
Sequence

Source: From Harvey et al. 1992. Used with permission of the authors.

In working through disengagement from a romantic relationship, it is important to discuss feelings with friends, for two reasons: to gain social support, comfort, and assistance and to check the accuracy of accounts used to explain the relationship's demise.

(W. Hill, Jr./The Image Works)

why the relationship failed; also, the depression the individual experiences at this stage facilitates a drive to come to closure or completion in providing an explanation so that the individual can close the door on the past and move on to new experiences and relationships. Alternatively, the maintenance of escapism and avoidance, without expressing grief openly or without talking with others about why events happened, may result in a number of psychological problems—as portrayed in the movie *The Prince of Tides* (dealing not with relational disengagement but with denial and escapism nonetheless).

In the middle stages, the individual will first experience **intrusion,** including occasional *flooded states* in which he or she cannot think about anything but the relational disengagement. For example, although back at work and back to "normal," the person might wake up one night trying to reconcile the breakup with the wonderful, romantic vacation the couple took only months before the breakup; or an old song or movie is unexpectedly overwhelming and the person has to reconcile certain feelings.

In the **working-through** stage, the individual provides explanations that are complete stories for various aspects on the relationship—the good and positive aspects, what went wrong, when things went wrong, when the realization dawned that

THE ACCOUNTING PROCESS: *WHEN HARRY MET SALLY . . .*

The movie *When Harry Met Sally . . .* provides excellent examples of how individuals proceed through an account-making sequence in response to stressful life situations. When they first meet, Sally and Harry seem incompatible, and after driving from Chicago to New York, they fall out of touch. Sally becomes romantically involved with Joe, and Harry marries Helen. After these two relationships decay, Sally and Harry rediscover each other and help each other cope with the emotional and social aftermath both are enduring.

Coping with Relational Decay: Early Phases

After breaking up with Joe, Sally enters a state of denial. She tells friends over lunch that the breakup was imminent, that she can find someone better than Joe, that the breakup wasn't very important, and that she needs no help. This accounting, it turns out, is incomplete and misleading. Sally represses her emotions and isn't ready to deal with the end of her relationship with Joe. She tries to appear strong, treating the rift as unimportant. Why? At this early stage of the accounting process, Sally is motivated by her self-presentation concerns (see Chapter 5), and she wants her friends to see that she is in control, competent, confident, mature. Some time later, Sally gives a fuller account to Harry. Sally admits that while playing a game with a child, she realized that she wanted to get married and have a family, but Joe wasn't committed to her and didn't share her interests in marriage or family life.

Harry first offers an account of his own relational decay to his friend Jess. From Harry's story, it is easy to infer that Harry experienced turbulent emotions during the traumatic stage. He undoubtedly felt shock, disbelief, uncertainty, devastation, and numbness: How could someone I loved and married manipulate me like this and treat me so poorly (the movers knew of his breakup before he did; Helen said that she wanted a trial separation but was actually moving in with someone else)? These emotional responses at the traumatic phase evolved into feelings of despair and hopelessness at the outcry phase.

In her accounting process, Sally remains for a long time at the denial phase. She claims that nothing is wrong, but she goes to sleep at 7:30 P.M. and, despite wanting a family, is reluctant to date. We can infer that during the traumatic phase, she felt betrayed by Joe's lack of commitment: How could someone I love so much and seem to have so much in common with turn out to be so different from me, not to love me enough to get married, not want to share the important things in life, like a family? These reactions later evolve, as mentioned, into exhaustion at the outcry phase and escapism, isolationism, and avoidance at the denial phase.

Coping with Relational Decay: Middle and Late Stages

Moving into the middle phases, both Harry and Sally experience intrusion, in which they are flooded with emotions. Harry experiences panic when he dates a woman who reminds him of Helen. When Harry and Sally run into Helen and her new love, Harry is at first speechless and becomes emotional afterward.

Harry and Sally become best friends because they respect each other and make few demands on each other; they talk, support, and advise, and their communication is not affected by any self-presentation goals other than to be themselves. They are busy working through their beliefs about men, women, and relationships.

Eventually, Harry confronts Sally about her denial, accusing her of not fully coming to grips with her feelings of loss, not getting on with her life. Sally defends herself, saying that it is her life and she can adjust just fine. Harry offers a full-blown apology (see Chapter 6) for accusing Sally of not facing (his perception of) reality, and Sally accepts his apology. In truth, as a good friend, Harry is right in acting as a "reality check" on Sally's denial.

Sally experiences intrusion when she hears that Joe is marrying someone else. Harry hurries to her side, and she finally passes through the denial phase, crying and asking the obvious, hurtful question: "Why didn't Joe want to marry me?" After Harry and Sally escalate their relationship to higher levels of intimacy, the movie, like the characters, relinquishes the focus on prior relationships. Both Harry and Sally have passed through the most troubling phases of the accounting process.

things had gone wrong, denials and acceptances for blame and responsibility, and so on. It is critically important for the disengager to confide these stories to others at this time, for several reasons. First, telling the stories to others and getting feedback from them provides a reality check on the account process; alternatively, an individual can create any number of scenarios that might be false, portraying the individual as too much of a hopeless victim or as too innocent, and so forth. In reality, no one is totally charming or perfect. Another critical role played by communicating these accounts is hearing one's friends verify and agree with the explanations concerning various aspects of the former relationship. Self-esteem is bolstered and tension is released as a person communicates accounts and gets beyond persistent and bewildering thoughts and doubts.

During this process, the individual puts together a fairly coherent, complete, detailed story concerning the dissolution and nearly all aspects of former relational life that has been reality-tested, verified, and accepted by friends and family members.

During the **completion** and **identity change** stages, the individual not only possesses stories and explanations about the breakup but has also developed coping skills and has perhaps altered his or her behavior in view of having learned from the account-making process. Coping skills may deal with certain behaviors revealed to be ineffective or even harmful in the previous relationship (placing work above family, drinking too much, being too quick to judge others, being too quick to anger, etc.) and changing personal habits, routines, and skills. Behavioral changes relate to how the individual pursues relational goals. For example, if a person has concluded that the last relationship ended because he or she moved too fast toward intimacy or had expectations that were too high, the individual might escalate the next relationship more slowly or adopt more realistic expectations.

As indicated in Figure 10-2, there are three possible negative consequences of failing to engage in account making: persistence of negative emotions (the flooded states characteristic of intrusion persist as hypertension, insomnia, etc.), prolonged grief and anxiety, and failure to learn and adopt more realistic standards of relational life, romance, and dating. Regarding this last consequence, if individuals place all the blame on the relational partner, fail to proceed through the account-making phase, and quickly return to dating, there is a good chance that they have not learned anything about themselves or about dating. Such individuals will tend to date people who are quite similar to the partners they just left and may end up in the same type of relationship from which they just exited.

Chapter Summary

This chapter began with a discussion of why some partners stay together and why others disengage from their relationships. A few of the factors contributing to relational longevity were: being in love, maintaining equitable relationships, dating someone similar to oneself, and being equally involved and committed to the relationship. A few of the factors contributing to disengagement were: boredom, differences in interests and backgrounds, conflicting ideas about marriage and sex, and the need to be independent.

We also discussed a number of disengagement tactics. Harsher tactics are more likely to be used when a disengager strongly desires to quickly terminate a relationship. Partners are more likely to stay friends after the breakup if the disengager uses a positive tone or de-escalation tactic; avoids the use of justification, manipulation, or withdrawal tactics; and when the relationship is marked by equity, the partner was considered desirable, the decision to break up was mutual, and the partners were friends prior to the disengagement.

Disengagement is a process that progresses through four stages: intrapsychic, dyadic, social, and grave dressing. We have emphasized grave dressing and other matters of adjustment in the last half of this chapter. Progressing through these stages can result in a "working through" of the process, bringing the individual not only a resolution of grieving, but also a new awareness of self.

KEY TERMS

▼

de-escalation	withdrawal or avoidance tactics
termination	justification messages
intrapsychic phase	negative identity management
dyadic phase	(or manipulation)
social phase	traumatic event
grave-dressing phase	outcry
psychological equity	denial
actual equity	intrusion
attribution theory	working-through stage
positive-tone messages	completion stage
de-escalation messages	identity change stage

EXERCISES FOR FURTHER DISCUSSION

▼

1. Write a short paragraph in which you discuss a romantic relationship that decayed or resulted in disengagement. Then write a short paragraph in which you discuss a friendship that deteriorated.
   a. What caused the relationship to decay?
   b. What were the consequences of the decay or disengagement?
   c. Was the intensity of emotional consequences greater in one type of relationship?
   d. Was staying in touch afterward equally important in both situations?
   e. What were the verbal messages used in each type of relationship to disengage? How were they similar or different?
   f. In what ways do you think the disengagement process is different for romantic relationships and friendships?
2. Equity can be used as a means of repairing a relationship if the partners succeed in balancing inputs and outcomes. Think of two characters, either from a book you have read recently or from a television series that you watch regularly, who

are in a long-term relationship that involves inequities. Now think about some of the ways in which these two characters use equity-restoring tactics.

   a. In what ways was the relationship initially inequitable?

   b. What sorts of tactics did the characters use to try to restore equity?

   c. Were the tactics effective? If so, which ones were the most effective?

3. Think of some situations you have either been in or observed, in which one partner tried to use jealousy to increase relational involvement.

   a. Was the tactic effective in increasing relational involvement?

   b. Were there any negative consequences to this tactic?

   c. In your experience, are men or women more likely to use this tactic? If there is a difference, why do you think it exists?

4. Think of a situation you have either been in or observed in which a relationship broke up but the partners remained friends. Now think of a situation in which a relationship broke up but the partners did not remain friends.

   a. Was there a difference in the tactics used to break up?

   b. In your experience, are men or women more likely to want to remain friends after disengaging?

   c. If one of the partners experiences depression or despair after a breakup, do you think it is better or worse for them to continue to be friends? What would some advantages be? What would some disadvantages be?

5. Think of a film you have seen recently in which relational decay and disengagement was an important theme.

   a. What was the source of the relational decay?

   b. Were the causes of the relational decay stable, controllable, intentional, and internal?

   c. Were the problems the couple experienced highly valenced (negatively charged)? In what ways?

   d. What repairs were attempted?

   e. What relational breakup communication tactics were used?

   f. What was the process of postdisengagement adjustment?

SUGGESTED READING

RELATIONAL DISENGAGEMENT

Duck, S. W., ed. 1982. *Personal relationships 4: Dissolving personal relationships.* New York: Academic Press. Duck has edited and written a number of books dealing with interpersonal relationships, their repair, and their decay. This book contains a number of chapters on making effective repairs of decaying relationships.

———. 1984. *Personal relationships 5: Repairing interpersonal relationships.* New York: Academic Press. This book contains a number of useful chapters on repairing relationships and on the topic of grave dressing and adjustment.

Duck, S. W., and Gilmour, R., eds. 1981. *Personal relationships 3: Personal relationships in disorder.* New York: Academic Press. This volume contains a number of useful chapters on the causes of relational decay, how to cope with relational decay, and messages used during disengagement.

Orbuch, T. L., ed. 1992. *Close relationship loss.* New York: Springer-Verlag. This volume contains a number of excellent chapters that focus on how the accounting process is involved in coping with relational decay.

ACCOUNTING FOR RELATIONSHIP DECAY

Harvey, J. H.; Orbuch, T. L.; and Weber, A. L. eds. 1991. *Attributions, accounts, and close relationships.* New York: Springer-Verlag.

Harvey, J. H.; Weber, A. L.; and Orbuch, T. L. 1990. *Interpersonal accounts: A social psychological perspective.* Cambridge, MA: Basil Blackwell.

Both of these volumes provide excellent examples of the accounts, or narratives, individuals employ when creating and communicating explanations for why relationships decayed. The 1990 volume is an excellent starting point for understanding accounts as stories or narratives we develop after a traumatic event. A number of examples from literature, biographies, and life stories are examined.

POST-DISENGAGEMENT ADJUSTMENT

Harvey, J. H.; Orbuch, T. L.; and Weber, A. L. 1990. A social psychological model of account-making in response to severe stress. *Journal of Language and Social Psychology* 9:191–207. The above article is a good place to read, in more detail, about the model we presented in this chapter on stages of the accounting process.

Hindy, C. G.; Schwarz, J. C.; and Brodsky, A. 1989. *If this is love, why do I feel so insecure?* New York: Atlantic Monthly Press. This book presents a more "pop psychological" view of the emotions people have during and after relational decay. This very readable book contains a number of case studies and stories concerning decay and adjustment.

REFERENCE LIST

▼

Banks, S. P.; Altendorf, S. M.; Greene, J. O.; and Cody, M. J. 1987. An examination of relationship disengagements: Perceptions, breakup strategies, and outcomes. *Western Journal of Speech Communication* 51:19–41.

Baxter, L. A. 1982. Strategies for ending relationships: Two studies. *Western Journal of Speech Communication* 46:233–242.

———. 1983. Relationship disengagement: An examination of the reversal hypothesis. *Western Journal of Speech Communication* 47:85–89.

———. 1984. Trajectories of relationship disengagement. *Journal of Social and Personal Relationships* 1:29–48.

Cody, M. J. 1982. A typology of disengagement strategies and an examination of the roles intimacy, reactions to inequity, and relational problems play in strategy selection. *Communication Monographs* 49:148–170.

Cody, M. J.; Kersten, L.; Braaten, D. O.; and Dickson, R. 1992. Coping with relational dissolutions: Attributions, account credibility, and plans for resolving conflicts. In *Attributions, accounts, and close relationships*, ed. J. H. Harvey, T. L. Orbuch, and A. L. Weber, 93–115. New York: Springer-Verlag.

Conville, R. L. 1991. *Relational transitions: The evolution of personal relationships.* New York: Praeger.

Duck, S. W. 1982. A typography of relationship disengagement and dissolution. In *Personal relationships 4: Dissolving personal relationships*, ed. S. W. Duck, 1–30. New York: Academic Press.

———. 1984. A perspective on the repair of personal relationships: Repair of what, when? In *Personal relationships 5: Repairing interpersonal relationships*, ed. S. W. Duck, 163–184. New York: Academic Press.

Harvey, J. H.; Agostinelli, G.; and Weber, A. L. 1989. Account making and the formation of expectations about close relationships. In *Close relationships*, ed. C. Hendrick, 39–62. Newbury Park, Calif.: Sage.

Harvey, J. H.; Orbuch, T. L.; and Weber, A. L. 1990. A social psychological model of account making in response to severe stress. *Journal of Language and Social Psychology* 9:191–207.

Harvey, J. H.; Orbuch, T. L.; Weber, A. L.; Merbach, N.; and Alt, R. 1992. House of pain and hope: Accounts of loss. *Death Studies* 16:99–124.

Harvey, J. H.; Weber, A. L.; Galvin, K. S.; Huszti, H. C.; and Garnick, N. N. 1986. Attribution in the termination of close relationships: A special focus on the account. In *The emerging field of personal relationships*, ed. R. Gilmour and S. W. Duck, 189–201. Hillsdale, N.J.: Erlbaum.

Harvey, J. H.; Weber, A. L.; and Orbuch, T. L. 1990. *Interpersonal accounts: A social psychological perspective.* Cambridge, Mass.: Blackwell.

Hill, C.; Rubin, Z.; and Peplau, L. A. 1976. Breakups before marriage: The end of 103 affairs. *Journal of Social Issues* 32:147–168.

Hindy, C. G.; Schwarz, J. C.; and Brodsky, A. 1989. *If this is love, why do I feel so insecure?* Boston: Atlantic Monthly Press.

Knapp, M. L., and Vangelisti, A. L. 1992. *Interpersonal communication and human relationships*, 2d ed. Newton, Mass.: Allyn & Bacon.

Leathers, D. G. 1992. *Successful nonverbal communication: Principles and applications*, 2d ed. New York: Macmillan.

Lee, L. 1984. Sequences in separation: A framework for investigating endings of the personal (romantic) relationship. *Journal of Social and Personal Relationships* 1:49–73.

Mearns, J. 1991. Coping with breakup: Negative mood regulation expectancies and depression following the end of a romantic relationship. *Journal of Personality and Social Psychology* 60:327–334.

Metts, S., and Cupach, W. R. 1986. *Disengagement themes in same-sex and opposite-sex friendships.* Paper presented to the Interpersonal Communication Interest Group, Western Speech Communication Association, Tucson, Ariz.

Metts, S.; Cupach, W. R.; and Bejlovec, R. A. 1989. "I love you too much to ever start liking you": Redefining romantic relationships. *Journal of Social and Personal Relationships* 6: 259–274.

Safran, C. 1979. Troubles that pull couples apart: A *Redbook* report. *Redbook*, January, pp. 138–141.

Vangelisti, A. L. 1992. Communication problems in committed relationships: An attributional analysis. In *Attributions, accounts, and close relationships*, ed J. H. Harvey, T. L. Orbuch, and A. L. Weber, 144–164. New York: Springer-Verlag.

Vaughn, D. 1987. *Uncoupling: How relationships come apart.* New York: Vintage Books.

Weiss, R. S. 1975. *Marital separation.* New York: Basic Books.

White, G. L. 1980. Inducing jealousy: A power perspective. *Personality and Social Psychology Bulletin* 6:222–227.

Wilmot, W. W.; Carbaugh, D. A.; and Baxter, L. A. 1985. Communicative strategies used to terminate romantic relationships. *Western Journal of Speech Communication* 49:204–216.

P A R T   I V

ACHIEVING

INSTRUMENTAL

GOALS

In Part IV, we focus on instrumental goals, looking at two general types: gaining compliance and managing interpersonal conflict. In Chapter 11, we look at some of the extensive research that has been done on compliance-gaining. This research focuses on the reasons why people comply (or do not comply) with requests. We then discuss some of the basic principles underlying compliance-gaining. Chapter 12 looks more closely at interpersonal conflict and the communication behaviors people use to manage conflicts. We present a definition of interpersonal conflict, look at some of the different styles and strategies of managing conflict, and then discuss some of the consequences of various types of conflict behaviors.

C H A P T E R   1 1

GAINING

COMPLIANCE

Laura got home from work and rushed to get ready for her jog. She was about to shoot out the front door when the doorbell rang. A nicely dressed thirty-five-year-old woman was at the door. "Hello," she said. "My name is _____, and I am with the Heart Fund. We are having our annual fund drive this month, and I am going door to door to obtain contributions. Will you contribute to the Heart Fund?" Laura grabbed some coins from the kitchen counter and gave them to the lady. The lady said, "You are a generous person. I wish more of the people I met were as charitable as you. Please take a leaflet that describes how the money you contributed is spent. Thank you." As the lady walked away, Laura looked at the leaflet. A card was stapled to the top. It said: "Charitable people give generously to help a good cause and those less fortunate than themselves. Are you one?" Laura put the leaflet on the table and went out for her jog.

Ten days later Laura was preparing for a barbecue when the doorbell rang. A twenty-five-year-old bearded man was on the doorstep. "Hello," he said. "My name is _____, and I am going door to door asking for contributions to help the handicapped. I've been working with handicapped people for a couple of years now, and today I volunteered to collect for multiple sclerosis. Would you like to contribute any money to multiple sclerosis?" Laura gave the man two dollars.

Laura didn't know it at the time, but she participated in a study conducted by Robert Kraut (1973). Kraut organized two requests—one for the Heart Fund and a second for multiple sclerosis. If people gave money to the Heart Fund, they were considered "donors," and the solicitor either called the donor a "charitable" person or merely thanked the donor and left a leaflet without the charitable label. Anyone who didn't donate to this fund was considered a "nondonor," and when this happened the solicitor either merely thanked the nondonor or actually called the nondonor "uncharitable."

Later, the man asked for donations to multiple sclerosis. Half of the time he presented himself as deeply involved by stating that he had worked for a "couple of years" with the handicapped. In half of the cases the man was *uninvolved:* "Everyone in my office had to go out today and spend some time collecting for charity, and I got assigned multiple sclerosis. . . . I think they do something with the handicapped. I'm supposed to be asking if you'd like to contribute any money to multiple sclerosis."

Salespersons use compliance-gaining tactics to make sales. Attentiveness is an obvious one; some tactics, however, can be very subtle.

(Dan Chidester/The Image Works)

How much money did people give to multiple sclerosis? Table 11-1 presents the results. In the donor half of the study, labeling a person as charitable when giving money to the Heart Fund prompted the person to give more money to a second charity—70 cents, versus 41 cents on the average. There was also a tendency for people to give more money to multiple sclerosis when the man was deeply involved with the cause (78 and 46 cents, versus 61 and 37 cents). Nondonors also gave more money to the highly involved man, compared to the uninvolved man (38 and 50 cents per person, versus 11 and 22 cents per person). Finally, people who were labeled as uncharitable gave slightly less (23 cents) than those who were not labeled (33 cents).

Why Do People Comply with Requests?

This chapter deals with the question of why people comply with requests, and we begin with a discussion of the Kraut study because it highlights two important reasons why people comply with requests. First, the nature of the request itself is im-

	Table 11-1 MEAN MULTIPLE SCLEROSIS CONTRIBUTIONS (IN CENTS)			
	Heart Fund Donor		Heart Fund Nondonor	
Involvement	*Charitable Label*	*No Label*	*Uncharitable Label*	*No Label*
High	78	46	38	50
Low	61	37	11	22
Average	70	41	23	33

Source: Adapted from Kraut 1973. Used with permission of the author and Academic Press, Inc.

portant. The man who worked with the handicapped and was personally involved has more credibility than the uninvolved solicitor and is deemed more worthy of our generosity.

Second, this study illustrates the importance of what we call **self-perception.** Self-perception means that when people take an action, they ask themselves questions like "Why am I behaving this way?" "Why am I acting like this?" "What causes my action?" Most people would want to keep their own money and not give money away unless they believed that there was a good reason for doing so. However, look carefully at Table 11-1. Not surprisingly, people who gave to one charity ("donors") were likely to donate money to the second charity (multiple sclerosis—people gave 37 to 78 cents). However, *why* did the group of donors who were labeled "charitable" give more (70 cents per person) than the group who were not labeled "charitable" (who gave only 41 cents per person)?

The answer rests in the types of self-perceptions the donors engage in when they comply with requests. When we give money, we think of some reason why we are giving away our cash, for example:

"I'll just give the solicitor 50 cents to get rid of her."

"I feel sorry for this solicitor, who has to walk around in this heat wave (or bitter cold), so I'll give some money."

"My nosy neighbor is probably watching, and I don't want her to think I'm a cheapskate."

"I can impress my date (who is in the next room) by looking like I was generous."

"I think the solicitor is cute, and I want him to like me, so I will give to the cause."

"Today is payday, so I can give a little."

Stop and think about the consequences. If any of these reasons was the reason why you gave money to the Heart Fund, would you give money to the second charity? Some of you would, but some of you wouldn't. Consider this: If you gave money because you felt sorry for the lady walking around in a heat wave, would you give money later to a man when the heat wave was over? If you gave because you thought the first solicitor was cute, would you give money later to a different person, for a different cause? Probably not.

Of course, there are other reasons why people comply with requests. Some of these reasons reflect the belief that the cause of the generosity is internal to the giver (this is the same notion of internality we discussed earlier in the context of attribution theory). Internal reasons reflect personal commitment to worthwhile causes:

"I am charitable, and charitable people help those who are less fortunate."

"I believe people should give to worthwhile causes. How else can we solve social and health problems?"

"Many people, some I know, suffer from heart-related health problems, and I believe it is important to help these people."

When we make self-perceptions like these, we are likely to comply and give money a second time (even to a different person) because we believe we are personally committed to helping good causes.

For example, when the solicitor for the Heart Fund identified the donors as "generous" people who help "the less fortunate," the solicitor was encouraging them to make the internal self-perception that they were indeed charitable and committed to helping the needy. If this labeling tactic were successful, more of the donors in the charitable-labeled group would make the internal self-perception and would consequently donate the second time, perhaps even more generously. In fact, Kraut (1973) found that 62 percent of the people labeled charitable donated the second time, compared to only 47 percent of the nonlabeled group. The people labeled charitable gave more; they were in fact more charitable.

Self-perception deals with the causes that people perceive for their own behavior. People make the "correct" or "desirable" self-perception when they judge their own internal attributions of generosity as the reason why they comply with requests. This process of self-perception is one of the important ways in which our behavior is altered. A critical feature of increasing compliance is to make sure that people make the "correct" self-perceptions of their behavior.

In Chapter 3 we introduced the idea of compliance-gaining messages, how we verbally go about asking other people for assistance, permission, advice, and so forth. These messages ranged from merely asking to threatening and forcing others to do what we want. This chapter deals with how we go about achieving instrumental goals that are far more subtle than most of these compliance-gaining messages. We will focus on how we employ psychological principles to get others to comply with our requests. Some of the verbal requests we discuss here involve asking for help from others. However, the reason why people comply with a simple request has to do with how the request is made and the context in which it is made. For example, the Kraut (1973) study structured the second request in two ways: labeling the donor influences the kinds of self-perceptions donors make, and the level of involvement of the solicitor influences the credibility of the request. Manipulating how people feel and what they believe *before* a request is made is how communication scholars alter one of the fundamental psychological principles of compliance. We manipulate the setting, some aspect of the environment, or the timing of a request when trying to tap into one of these psychological principles.

Cialdini (1993) argued that we need only a few fundamental psychological principles to explain compliance: anchoring and contrast effect, reciprocity, commitment, liking, social proof, authority, and scarcity.

Basic Principles of Compliance

ANCHORS AND CONTRAST EFFECTS

When people adapt to a standard amount of beauty, prices, generosity, violence, etc., and come to expect a certain amount as typical or normative, we say that they have "adapted" to that level. Psychologists have examined this phenomenon as part of **adaption level theory** (see Petty and Cacioppo 1981). An expectation can become an **anchor** for how someone perceives what is normative or typical. For example, people who see thin, beautiful women on television shows, commercials, and in movies may become anchored at a relatively high level of beauty that they then expect to see in others. Such people may develop an inflated view of how many beautiful people there are in the world.

After an anchor is established, a **contrast effect** is said to occur when some new object, person, or event is judged against the standard and is displaced away from the adapted level or anchor. For example, a $200 dress may appear to be a good buy relative to a set of $600 to $800 dresses that a shopper has seen all afternoon. Contrast effects are common. Brickman, Coates, and Janoff-Bulman (1978), for example, found that people who had experienced extremely high levels of happiness by winning the lottery actually rated everyday events like visiting friends, watching television, buying clothes, getting a compliment, hearing a joke, and reading a magazine as less pleasant than people who had never won the lottery. Both winners and nonwinners rated overall life satisfaction and happiness as equal, but winners of the lottery considered everyday events to be mundane in comparison to the thrill of winning the lottery. In several studies, Kenrick and Gutierres (1980) found that students rated a potential date, a photo of an average student, as less attractive if the students had just watched or evaluated a beautiful person but more attractive if the students had just watched an unattractive person.

Contrast effects are important in compliance settings in several ways. First, the generosity of others can be manipulated by making it appear that others are contributing a certain amount of money to a cause. Second, sales clerks can affect the sales process by showing customers the most expensive items first, so that other items do not seem quite as expensive. Consider a simple situation: A secretary is quitting, and the staff votes to take up a collection to buy a gift. A sign-up sheet is made, and people are asked to give money. When a study was done on this topic by Blake, Rosenbaum, and Duryea (1955) one-half of the people who were asked to make a contribution gave 50 cents, while the other half gave a dollar. The average contribution was 75 cents. We can imagine that 75 cents was the amount that people believed to be typical of what the average person would give. However, Blake and colleagues also constructed several bogus lists of contributions. On one list it appeared that people were giving an average of 25 cents each, while on another list it appeared that contributors were giving 75 cents each. What happened? When people thought that others were giving only 25 cents, they contributed only 32 cents on the average. When people thought that others were giving 75 cents each, they gave 63 cents on the average. People adapted to the standard of what they believed others were contributing.

This study is a good example of contrast effects and compliance because it demonstrates the two necessary conditions of the contrast effect. First, a standard is created—people thought that others were giving either 25 cents or 75 cents. Second, the amount that a person actually would give (75 cents) is viewed as "large" when compared (or contrasted) with the standard of what others are donating. People decline to give the large contribution, and they tend to give what others are contributing.

Although this study used the contrast effect to get people to give less money, it can be and often is used as a method for increasing contributions and tips by making it appear that the typical tip (in a bartender's tip container) is a dollar (or a larger bill), so that giving coins would be considered too little. Cialdini (1993) notes a project involving pool tables. During one week, customers were shown the least expensive pool tables first, and the next week they were shown the most expensive ones first. Customers purchased more expensive pool tables when they were shown the most expensive ones first—when their adaptation level or standard was anchored at the high end. When they saw the least expensive ones first, they settled for tables that were less expensive because they adapted to a lower standard.

Sometimes a contrast effect is used in a far more subtle way among friends. One partner might say, "Honey, could you do me a big favor?" "What?" (the other replies, expecting a big favor to be asked). "Could you get me a Coke from the re-frigerator?" The other might comply in part because the favor is "no big deal," at least relative to what was anticipated when first hearing the request.

RECIPROCITY

Reciprocity is fundamentally important in interpersonal relationships. As children, adults attempted to instill in us a basic belief in sharing, cooperating, and "doing unto others as they do unto us." If a friend invited us for a sleepover, to camp in the backyard, to play, and so forth, our parents would tell us, "It's your turn to have them over next time." When a friend does us a favor, we feel obligated to do a favor in return. When friends invite us to their homes, we reciprocate in kind. If we fail to reciprocate, we experience guilt, and we may be labeled a "moocher." We will lose friends.

The **reciprocity** principle is used to gain compliance from others in several ways. First, and most obviously, reciprocity is used to gain compliance through cre-ating a feeling of obligation on the part of others by doing them favors or giving them objects or services. Cult members go to airports and malls and give out "free" bookmarks, key chains, car stickers, and other objects. After having accepted these "free" gifts and spent a few moments in conversation, people are asked to make a donation. These cult members are trying to trigger a reciprocity-based obligation.

Businesses also use the reciprocity rule. Amway, for example, has its sales repre-sentatives leave a collection of product samples for potential customers to try "with-out obligation to buy." However, there is some felt obligation to buy something: the sales representative left a wide array of nice products for the customer's pleasure, and the least the customer can do is buy something. Other companies will offer sam-ples of food items in the stores to activate the reciprocity principle. Any parent who tries to teach a child to live by the reciprocity rule is put under a good deal of pres-sure when the child receives a free taste of juice by a nice lady at the store, who also happens to be distributing coupons for the product (see Cialdini [1993] for addi-tional examples).

Another way in which reciprocity is used in compliance has to do with the nature of **reciprocal concessions.** We feel obligated to comply with a request if the asker has made a concession to us. For example, when people bargain for a car or an item at a garage sale, they often make an offer lower than the asking price. The seller then lowers the price a certain amount; the seller has conceded a certain amount of the price. The potential buyer then increases the bid closer to what the seller wants; the buyer is also conceding. Buyer and seller determine the final price by each mak-ing concessions.

Using reciprocal concessions (bargaining) is common at garage sales and flea markets.

(Alan Reininger/Contact Press Images)

We don't have to look far to see many examples of reciprocal concessions. A political party may phone to ask if we would "buy" a table for eight at the governor's inaugural celebration for $10,000. When that is rejected, the phone solicitor will de-escalate the request to, say, dinner tickets for two or a cash gift of $100. Obviously, the solicitor is relying on the reciprocity principle because most people don't have a spare $10,000 or the time to go to the state capitol with seven friends for such an event. Virtually everyone will say no to this first request, but the well-trained phone solicitor has a prepared backup list of requests ready so that we'd agree to some smaller request. Many alumni associations conduct their fund raising in much the same way.

Cialdini and Ascani (1976) conducted a study to see if the reciprocal concession strategy can be used to get students to comply with requests. In this case, students were asked to donate blood. There were three different ways of asking for compliance. One group of students (the control group) was approached and simply asked to give blood:

We have our annual university blood drive tomorrow. We're asking students to come to our center here on campus to donate just one unit of blood sometime between 8:00 A.M. and 3:30 P.M. tomorrow. Would you be willing to donate just one unit of blood to our drive?

A second group, the "minimal-then-control-request group," was first asked to help in a small way, by advertising the blood drive. After these students agreed to place a sign on their door announcing the blood drive, they were then asked to give blood. No attempt was made to activate reciprocity obligations; however, the purpose of including this type of request was to see if an initial small request would make the students feel more committed to the cause and give blood. These students heard:

> We're asking students to help advertise our cause by taking one of these little cards [containing the local blood services organization logo] and displaying it somewhere, like on a window or on a door or even on a book, where people can see it. [After the student agreed, the solicitor continued:] Thanks. There's also another way you could help us, if you'd like. [The remainder was identical to the control group request.]

Finally, the third group, the "extreme-then-control-request group," heard a very large request first. When the students said no to the large request, the solicitor conceded to a smaller request, with the intention of getting more people to agree to give blood the next day. They heard:

> We're currently asking students to become involved in our long-term donor program. Long-term donors are those who pledge to give a unit of blood once every two months for a period of at least three years. This way we can be sure of a continuous supply of blood. Would you be willing to enroll in our long-term donor program? [After the student declined, the experimenter continued:] Oh. Well, maybe you'd be interested in another program we're asking students to participate in. [The remainder was identical to the control group request.]

There were three ways to examine how the students complied to the request: (1) verbal compliance—how many students verbally agreed to give blood the next day, (2) behavioral compliance—how many students actually gave blood the next day, and (3) future verbal compliance—of the students who gave blood the next day, how many agreed to give blood again in the future.

Table 11-2 presents the results. Look first at the rates of compliance for the students in the control group, who were only asked to give blood. Sixty-three students were asked to give blood, and twenty verbally agreed. Seven of the twenty students who verbally agreed to give blood actually gave blood (35 percent of the students who verbally complied). Only three of the seven who gave blood signed up to give blood again. Students in the minimal-then-control-request group behaved in a manner similar to those in the control group—31.7 percent verbally complied, 10 percent (two of the twenty) who verbally complied actually gave blood, and neither of the two who gave blood signed up to give blood again.

Table 11-2

VERBAL, BEHAVIORAL, AND FUTURE VERBAL COMPLIANCE WITH REQUESTS TO GIVE BLOOD

Group	Verbal Compliance		Behavioral Compliance		Future Verbal Compliance	
	%	N	%	N	%	N
Extreme-then-control-request	49.2	(31/63)	38.7	(12/31)	84.0	(10/12)
Minimal-then-control-request	31.7	(20/63)	10.0	(2/20)	0.0	(0/2)
Control	31.7	(20/63)	35.0	(7/20)	43.0	(3/7)

Source: Adapted from Cialdini and Ascani 1976. Copyright 1976 by the American Psychological Association. Adapted by permission.

Students in the extreme-then-control-request group gave more blood than students in the other groups: thirty-one of the sixty-three students verbally agreed to give blood the next day (49.2 percent), and twelve of the thirty-one who verbally agreed actually showed up and gave blood (38.7 percent of those who verbally complied), and ten of the twelve who gave blood signed up to give blood again (84 percent). This study clearly demonstrates the power of reciprocal concessions: students refused to join the long-term donor program, and when the solicitor conceded to a smaller request (from giving blood repeatedly over three years to giving blood once), the students felt obliged to concede from zero (no helping whatsoever) to giving blood at least once.

A special term is used for the reciprocal concessions procedure just described: the **door in the face.** Why? The procedure is used in situations in which people are supposed to say no to the first request; that is, the door is shut on the solicitor. After the rejection, the solicitor concedes, prompting the target (shopper, student, friend) into conceding. There are important guidelines in the effective use of the door-in-the-face tactic:

1. The initial request must be rejected by the target (the person we are asking to comply).

2. The second request must be clearly smaller than the first request—it must appear that the solicitor is conceding to a smaller request.

3. Recall our earlier discussion of self-perception in the charitable donations study. If people make a personal or internal judgment about why they are complying to a request, they are more likely to comply later to a second request. In the door-in-the-face procedure, however, people refuse to comply with the first request. In this type of situation, if people make a personal or internal judgment about why they are refusing to help, they probably won't help later. It is important, then, for anyone who uses this procedure to construct an initial large request in such a way that when people say no, they make one of the following types of judgments:

"I am in favor of the cause, but I can't promise to give for three years."

"I'd like to help, but I just don't have that much money right now."

"I'm sorry, but no reasonable person can do this. I wish I could help in some other way."

In sum, the first request must be large enough so that its rejection will be perceived by the target person as irrelevant for making internal self-perceptions.

4. The original request should not evoke resentment or be so large that the solicitor loses credibility. For example, a study on safe driving habits asked people to watch a busy intersection every Friday afternoon for two hours for two years. Not only did the targets refuse, but some laughed and reacted negatively to such an outlandish request.

5. The same solicitor must make the first and second requests—otherwise, there is no perception of concession making.

In short, an effective solicitor should make a first request that seems unreasonable or unreachable but not preposterous, then make a second, clearly smaller request that is seen as a concession.

COMMITMENT

Many people wear pins, publicly announcing their commitment to a sorority, fraternity, church, political party, or social or environmental cause. Pin wearing is but one form of commitment. Some people are only privately committed to causes—they send in money and buy calendars. Others wear pins, attend all the dances and mixers, and run for elected office. Later they attend the national conference and run for national office.

The **commitment principle** in compliance simply means this: the more a person is committed to a group, organization, or cause, the more likely the person will comply with requests to aid or assist that group, organization, or cause. Research on the commitment principle has focused on two procedures: the foot-in-the-door tactic and the lowball procedure.

THE FOOT-IN-THE-DOOR TACTIC. The **foot in the door** is so commonly used that examples are practically limitless. A person, for example, belongs to a church and attends services on a fairly consistent basis. The minister or priest approaches the person after services and asks him or her to help out next Sunday because one of the Sunday school teachers had to visit an ailing relative out of town. The person agrees and helps in the Sunday school. Afterward, the person is thanked and praised for doing a wonderful job in Sunday school. Some weeks later, the person is asked to help in Sunday school for a month and agrees. Agreement to a small initial request can blossom into an agreement to a large second (or third) request. The term *foot in the door* is used because the solicitor makes a small request to crack the door open so as eventually to get it open all the way.

The foot-in-the-door procedure is not guaranteed to work every time it is employed. Think back to the blood donation study. The commitment principle was attempted on the students who were asked to display a sign advertising the blood drive. The idea was to get them committed to the cause publicly, but in a small way, and then to ask them to give blood. The procedure was no more effective than the control request—in fact, fewer units of blood were obtained and less future behavioral compliance was obtained than in the control group.

There are a number of reasons why the procedure didn't work in this study. First, simply agreeing, verbally, to take a sign and display it may not really have made the students feel committed to the cause. Second, the students could have thought of external reasons for taking the sign ("Let me get this solicitor out of my face and throw this sign in the trash") instead of making the "correct" self-perception of commitment. In fact, we can think of better requests that might activate a commitment principle: First, ask the person to wear a pin advertising the blood drive. Second, have the person convince a friend to wear a pin as well. Third, have the person distribute blood drive pamphlets on one floor of the dorm. Then ask the person (now feeling committed) to give blood.

So much research has been conducted on the foot in the door that we can be fairly confident about these six guidelines concerning its effective use:

1. The first request must be clearly smaller than the second request, it must induce compliance, and it must be of sufficient magnitude to commit the individual to future compliance. If the first request is too small or trivial, the target will not feel committed to the cause, group, or organization.

2. The second request cannot be so large that few people would comply. Further, the second request cannot be so trivial that all people would comply (otherwise, why bother to use the foot-in-the-door procedure?).

3. If people believed that there were external pressures that led to their compliance on the first request, they will not perceive their own personal involvement to be the cause of the compliance, and there will be no foot-in-the-door effect.

4. Extending point three, compliance can be increased by employing tactics that act to ensure that people will make the appropriate self-perception of personal commitment to a cause. We demonstrated this earlier when we talked about the role of labeling in the charitable donation study.

5. Different solicitors can be used successfully to elicit the foot-in-the-door effect. The idea is that a person becomes committed to a cause, group, or organization, not to a particular person making a request.

6. The foot in the door works over time—the effects of committing oneself to the first request diminish slowly over time. More important than time is memory—does the target of the compliance remember, when receiving the second request, his or her commitment from the first request?

THE LOWBALL TACTIC.   Cialdini and associates (1978) note that a common sales tactic, especially prevalent among new-car dealers, is "throwing a lowball," or "lowballing." There are two ingredients to a **lowball** procedure. First, someone makes an offer or a request that is low or small, and you actively and freely agree to it. Second, after you are committed to the deal or to helping the solicitor, you find out that the deal was not as good as you first thought. In new-car sales situations, a dealer might agree with you on a price, and yet once you sit in the dealer's office, you find out that the price you agreed on earlier didn't include the special wheels and tinted glass you want; these will cost you extra. You were lowballed; this is a commitment-then-cost procedure. Many people are reluctant to retreat from an earlier agreement, so they don't walk out of the office and go shop elsewhere.

The lowball procedure is used outside of sales situations, of course. In one simple experiment, Cialdini and colleagues (1978) called students to participate in an experiment (for which they'd get credit in their introductory psychology classes). Half of the people were simply asked: "Can you participate in a project on Wednesday or Friday morning at 7 A.M.?" The other half of the students were lowballed— they were first asked to participate in a study on Wednesday or Friday, but were not told beforehand that the experiment required them to be present by 7 A.M. Only 31 percent of the students in the control group verbally agreed to show up at 7 A.M. However, 56 percent of the students verbally agreed to come to the study when the 7 A.M. time was not revealed to them. However, only 24 percent of the students in the control group actually showed up at 7 A.M. for the appointment, whereas 53 percent of the lowballed students showed up on time. Why? According to the researchers, people who are lowballed and who choose freely to agree with the

WHERE THERE'S SMOKE THERE'S . . . REACTANCE?

In this chapter we emphasized basic ways in which people try to get others to comply with a request. Don't think, however, that receivers of your tactics are going to stand by passively and merely comply with your requests. Many times, others will fight back and keep you from achieving your instrumental goals. People have a strong reaction to being influenced by others, especially when that influence takes the form of persistent and heavy-handed tactics.

When people believe that someone is forcing them to act contrary to their preferences and is restricting their freedom to behave, they experience "psychological reactance." This state of reactance generally occurs when people believe that their freedom to engage in an important behavior is being unjustly restricted by someone else. As shown in the article below, smokers react defensively and experience an increase in the desire to smoke when their freedom to smoke is threatened. Similarly, people who are in love become more and more in love if their parents try to keep them apart. Cialdini (1993) contains many other examples of the principle of psychological reactance.

Where there's smoke, there's ire.

A smokers' uprising, orchestrated by Phillip Morris Cos., is backfiring on Capitol Hill. A phone bank run by the cigarette maker asked thousands of smokers to call their congressional representatives to protest President Clinton's proposal for a "monster tax"—perhaps $2 a pack—to help finance health care reform. Members of the tax-writing House Ways and Means Committee were swamped—and angered—by the calls. "The intensity of this campaign blew away anything else we've had people call in on . . ." one aide said. . . . After a while, the messages sounded suspiciously similar, and aides determined that most calls had been transferred directly to their offices by Phillip Morris operators. The aides said some callers claimed they were offered free cigarettes for their surrogate lobbying, but Phillip Morris spokesman John Boltz denied it. He explained the call-in effort this way: "We've been deluged with calls from consumers asking for information about the tax and asking what they could do. We've provided an opportunity for them to make a call." "What made us so angry," fumed an aide to a prominent House Republican, "was that the constituents weren't calling on their own. Phillip Morris was paying for it." Rep. Bill Archer (R-Tex.), the ranking Republican on the Ways and Means Committee, got so smoked up that he called Phillip Morris and threatened to denounce the firm at a press conference. The calls ceased—but not before Hill staffers exacted revenge. They tied up Phillip Morris's Washington fax number with unwanted documents.

initial request feel a greater amount of commitment and responsibility to their obligation.

Students tell of being lowballed frequently. One group of students, in Texas, told a story in which a sorority sister asked for volunteers for a baton-twirling contest on Saturday. A group of volunteers quickly signed up. Later they were told that they had to be in a town an hour away at 8 A.M. on Saturday. They were lowballed, but they all went to the event because they felt committed and responsible. Another student related being asked to have lunch at the fraternity house with a transfer prospect from another university. Once there, he was asked to give a tour first of the house and then of the campus. He spent four hours with the transfer student and the student's family.

LIKING

We have already talked about the importance of being liked in this book—ingratiation tactics like rendering favors, praising others, and conforming opinions to others are used to increase liking (Chapter 5). We also like people who are physically attractive. The **liking principle** is simply this: we are more likely to comply to requests from likable, good-looking people than from people who are unlikable and unattractive.

This principle is so obvious that we will devote but little space to it. One classic study conducted by Shelly Chaiken (1979) will quickly show the power of beauty and liking. Chaiken had 110 students in a class act as solicitors and approach other students on campus, asking them to complete a questionnaire and to sign a petition demanding that the university "stop serving meat at breakfast and lunch at all dining commons."

Did students sign the petition simply because the solicitor was good looking? Some did (see Table 11-3). There are two important conclusions. First, attractive people generally got more people to sign the petition. This was especially true when females were approached by an attractive male (53 percent signed the petition) or by an attractive female (47 percent signed the petition) and when attractive females approached males (35 percent signed the petition). Second, Chaiken found that women were more likely to sign the petition than men—possibly because men may be more committed to a meat diet than women.

Nonetheless, when a good-looking person asked others to sign a petition, 29 to 53 percent of the students signed the petition. When the solicitor was judged as less attractive, only 24 to 38 percent of the students signed it. Being likable or attractive results in increases in compliance (also recall Chapter 4).

SOCIAL PROOF

Sometimes we just don't know how to behave—what the appropriate action should be or what etiquette requires. Some of us don't really know whether the band playing on stage is average, good, great, or fabulous. Some of us don't know the appro-

Table 11-3

PERCENTAGE OF STUDENTS WHO AGREED TO SIGN A PETITION DEMANDING THAT THE UNIVERSITY STOP SERVING MEAT AT BREAKFAST AND LUNCH

	Attractive Solicitor				Unattractive Solicitor			
	Male		*Female*		*Male*		*Female*	
Sex of target	Male	Female	Male	Female	Male	Female	Male	Female
Percentage signing petition	29	53	35	47	35	38	24	29

Source: Adapted from Chaiken 1979. Copyright 1979 by the American Psychological Association. Adapted by permission.

priate dress to wear to a particular social function, and some of us don't know the latest fashion trends. When we do not know what to do or have no guidelines, prior experience, evidence, or research, we are uncertain as to how we should behave, and we can be influenced by what is called **social proof:** we act the way others around us behave. Our proof of how to behave is based not on evidence, statistics, facts, logic, insight, individual preference, experience, or research but on the people in our immediate surroundings.

Social proof can influence us both directly and indirectly. The direct, explicit way is when people tell us, "This is what is currently popular," "This is what everybody is buying this year," "Four out of five people aged eighteen to twenty-four are voting in favor of Proposition A," and so on. The claim is that what is popular is good. In one study, certain shoppers in major clothing stores were told that a product (pants, shorts, etc.) was popular. The claim of popularity influenced the women shoppers—those who heard the claim spent more money ($110.53 each, compared to $56.98 spent by women who did not receive the appeal; see Cody, Seiter, and Montage-Miller 1994).

But social proof can influence us in subtle, more indirect ways. We can be influenced by both the verbal and nonverbal reactions of people who sit and stand around us. The fact that others are laughing at a stand-up comic tells us that there is some merit to the comedian's routine, and we may even think the comedian is funnier the more other people are laughing. Similarly, when we listen to a band play at a local establishment and see that some people in the audience scream and idolize the band, we conclude that the band must be good.

Research by communication scholars confirms that social proof can be used to influence our behavior and attitudes. We will mention two examples. First, most people say that they do not like "canned laughter," the laugh track we hear on TV situation comedies. However, chances are that we hate the laugh track only when we are aware of its presence. We can all be influenced by canned laughter when we are unaware of it, and some people believe that humorous material is funnier if they hear others laughing at it.

In a series of studies, Cupchik and Leventhal (Cupchik and Leventhal 1974; Leventhal and Cupchik 1975, 1976; Leventhal and Mace 1970) found evidence for three conclusions concerning canned laughter. First, the perceptions of the funniness of high-quality jokes may not be influenced by canned laughter; we would laugh at them anyway. However, low- and medium-quality jokes may be perceived as funnier if heard along with canned laughter. Second, people who score high on measures of expressiveness and laughter-proneness are not influenced by canned laughter, whereas those who score low on such measures rate jokes funnier if accompanied by canned laughter. Why? People who already do a great deal of laughing know how to evaluate jokes and are less influenced by the fact that other people are laughing, but individuals who are less knowledgeable or less informed about humor can be influenced by other people's laughter. Third, when people become aware of their behavior (e.g., a mirror is placed in the room), canned laughter ceases to have its impact. Knowledge and awareness can reduce the effectiveness of social proof.

Social proof can also influence the extent to which we evaluate live performances. One down-to-earth and excellent example was a project completed by Hocking, Margreiter, and Hylton (1976). Hocking had thirty students infiltrate a local campus bar featuring live entertainment on Thursday nights. On certain evenings the students provided positive feedback to the band. They screamed and yelled enthusiastically. On certain other evenings the students provided negative feedback—they sat quietly or acted bored. Members of the band had given permission for the study and played the same songs on the nights the experiment was being conducted.

While the one group of students went to the bar to either give positive or negative feedback, another group of students worked on an assignment to observe the nonverbal behavior of couples in public places. The instructor of this course required the students to attend the bar on certain Thursday nights (some went on positive-feedback nights, others on negative-feedback nights). This second group of students made their observations at the bar, and when they turned in their code sheets the next day, they were asked several questions, including how long they stayed at the bar, whether the band was good, and whether they would like to see the band again.

When other audience members yelled and screamed, providing the positive feedback, observers stayed longer (over 2½ hours), rated the band as better, and were also slightly more likely to see the band again (see Table 11-4).

Social proof is a common reason why we comply with requests. When we are uncertain of how to behave, we are likely to depend on how others behave, even if we are unaware of doing so.

Table 11-4

EVALUATION OF A LIVE BAND AS A
FUNCTION OF AUDIENCE FEEDBACK

	Negative Feedback	Positive Feedback	Significant Difference?
Number of minutes stayed	127.73	156.25	Yes
Overall quality of band[a]	6.73	7.90	Yes
See this band again?[a]	5.96	7.42	Weak

aRange 0 (low) to 10 (high).
Source: Adapted from Hocking et al. 1976. Used by permission of the authors.

AUTHORITY

The **authority principle** is quite common. We are taught to be obedient to people in positions of authority. Three types of authority derive from *titles, clothes,* and *trappings.* Titles are obviously important in seeking a position of authority over others. People labeled "doctor," "judge," "professor," "officer," or "commissioner" are more likely to gain compliance from others than people labeled "student," "worker," and so on. We are so strongly influenced by titles that pedestrians routinely follow the directions of any person in a uniform who holds a title, and nurses in a hospital comply quickly to requests made by "doctors," even ones who call in prescriptions and are never actually seen (Cialdini 1993).

"Clothes make the man," an old saying goes—even if the man is a criminal. Clothing is one of the most easily fakable signs of authority. Well-dressed people are helped more quickly and more readily when they shop, obtain better service, are seated at more desirable tables in restaurants, and are helped more quickly in emergencies. We frequently comply or follow the well-dressed person—for example, if we see a well-dressed businessperson jaywalk, we might be more inclined to do the same.

The trappings of status include jewelry, cars, briefcases, expensive pens, and all other objects that can be used to mark status, prestige, or social class. We are less likely to honk at the drivers of Jaguars or BMWs than we are at the drivers of Fords, and we are more likely to stop and give assistance to a driver of a disabled luxury car than to a driver of an average car or a car of low status. We are also more likely to comply with the requests of drivers who possess high-status trappings.

Another way to tap into the authority principle is through the use of expertise. Some of us go to speciality shops that feature gourmet coffees, imported chocolates, imported shoes, designer clothes, and so on. In such settings, an "expert" tells us information about how the products are made, materials that were used, the history of the company or family that makes the Scottish knits, and so forth. We often buy products on the basis of information supplied by purported experts.

SCARCITY

We love our freedom. We want to be able to go out and stay out as late as we want. We want to date whomever we please, without interference. We want to go to a store and buy an item we want without being told that the store ran out or that the store no longer stocks the item in the color or size or style we want. We want to chew gum without our teachers' trying to restrict our freedom.

The **scarcity principle** is tightly interwoven with this sense of freedom. The scarcity principle is simply this: opportunities to engage in some activity or to own some object seem more valuable when the opportunity is limited or restricted in some way. Our daily behavior is shaped by the scarcity principle in three ways: in the desirability of scarce objects, planned scarcity, and restricted freedom. First of all, people are willing to spend more money on "one-of-a-kind" objects that they will own and no one else will own. Collectors will spend considerable amounts of money to purchase such items as baseball cards, first-edition books, and coins or stamps printed with errors. Second, given that scarce objects will fetch higher prices, marketers actually plan shortages of certain desirable products so that shoppers will pay more. Many gift items advertised heavily at Christmastime are deliberately held in short supply to keep prices high.

Another example related to these two aspects of scarcity occurs when an individual sells a used car by placing an ad in the newspaper. When you arrive at 12:30 to look over the car, the seller may tell you that someone else is coming to see it at 1:00. Sure enough, someone does come to look at the car and engages in a lot of talking with the seller. If you liked the car when you first saw it, you would probably find it even more desirable when there appears to be competition for it. So you buy the car after only a little bargaining. Note that this could have been a stratagem—the guy selling the car could have had his cousin show up and act like an interested buyer just to motivate you to make a quick decision to buy it. You may have been manipulated without ever realizing it.

The third application of the scarcity principle involves restricted freedom. We have very strong reactions when a freedom we have enjoyed for a long time is restricted. Smoking cigarettes becomes more desirable when a smoker's freedom to smoke is restricted. Using lighter fluid to start a barbecue becomes more important to an outdoor cook if the city council plans to ban lighter fluid out of environmental concerns. People who have been free to buy and sell guns freely fight vigorously to maintain that freedom. The potential loss of freedom can also affect our feelings of being "in love." A study of dating students (Driscoll, Davies, and Lipetz 1972) found that the frequency with which parents attempted to interfere with their children's romantic partners caused the students to become more "in love" over a year's time. The researchers dubbed this the "Romeo and Juliet" effect.

A song by Mickey Gilley tells us that "all the girls get prettier at closing time—they all get to look like movie stars." Why? Earlier in the evening, we have the freedom to meet and get to know many people at a bar, spa, club, or other establishment, and when many people are available, we may perceive the typical person as fairly average. However, as closing time approaches, our options become more limited, and as our freedom to meet someone diminishes, the available people look more attractive.

Pennebaker and colleagues (1979) went to three drinking establishments and asked people to rate others on beauty. Posing as a dating pair, two people approached others in the bars and asked them to participate in an experiment. All agreed to help. They were then asked, "On a scale from 1 to 10, where 1 indicates 'not attractive,' 5 indicates 'average,' and 10 indicates 'extremely attractive,' how would you rate the opposite-sex individuals here tonight?" Next, they were asked: "If you were a member of the opposite sex, how would you rate members of your own sex here tonight, using the same scale as before?" Note that the participants were asked to make a global judgment about the people who were available. Pennebaker and colleagues asked people the judgments at 9:00 P.M., 10:30 P.M., and midnight. Considering that the bars in this location closed at 12:30, the scarcity effect should be strong by midnight.

Figure 11-1 presents the results. Look first at the line indicating the evaluation of same-sex people at the bar. There is little change in this judgment over the course of the evening, and people rated members of their own sex as fairly average (between 4.5 and 5.5). However, people judged members of the opposite sex as average (about

Figure 11–1

▼

Perceived Attractiveness of Others in a Bar As Closing Time Approaches

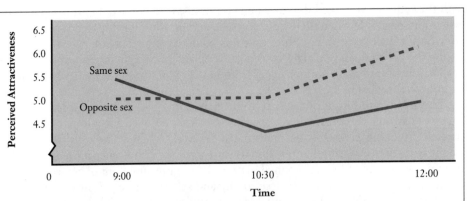

Source: From Pennebaker et al. 1979, fig. 1. Reprinted by permission of Sage Publications, Inc. and the author.

5.0) at both 9:00 and 10:30 but significantly and substantially more attractive at midnight (about 6.0). A more complex and involving study by Gladue and Delaney (1990) also investigated attractiveness in bar settings. They too found that men and women rated opposite-gender bar patrons as better looking as the evening wore on. They found that men even rated photographs of women to be even more attractive as midnight approached. The conclusion: scarcity increases desirability.

Chapter Summary

This chapter outlined a number of ways in which people get others to comply with requests. A contrast effect is commonly employed. In some settings, an individual can make a second request appear to be small if the first request is very large, and people will tend to grant the second request. In a selling context, a contrast effect is used to "anchor" a buyer at the expensive end of the sales spectrum, which encourages the shopper to buy a more expensive item.

Six other common ways of achieving instrumental goals were reviewed. The reciprocity principle is activated when we help someone who has helped us. The door-in-the-face tactic relies on the reciprocity principle in that the solicitor first makes a large request and then concedes to a small request; because we first say no to the large request, we feel obliged to concede to the smaller one—we make the concession from zero help to a small amount. The commitment principle is activated when we agree to a request for a cause and then start to think that we actually believe in or are committed to the cause. Two such tactics are the foot in the door (we agree to a small request to become committed in a small way and then agree to help in a larger way later) and the lowball (we agree to help before we know all of the costs that are involved—but by then we are committed and responsible for fulfilling our promise to help).

We are also more likely to comply if we like the people making the request, if we believe that something is popular, or if people in positions of authority (officials, experts, others of high status) make the request. Finally, we find that desirable things become even more desirable when they become scarce or may no longer be available to us.

KEY TERMS

adaptation level theory   commitment principle
self-perception   foot in the door
anchor   lowball
contrast effect   liking principle

reciprocity   social proof
reciprocal concessions   authority principle
door in the face   scarcity principle

EXERCISES FOR FURTHER DISCUSSION

1. Review the discussion of reciprocity, thinking about whether or not you were trained to reciprocate by people in authority.
   a. Do you agree that reciprocity is an important social norm and that people who violate it will eventually become friendless?
   b. Have you ever terminated or de-escalated a friendship with someone who failed to live up to your expectations of reciprocity?
   c. Have you ever been in a relationship in which you think you did not live up to someone else's expectations of reciprocity?
2. Review the section on lowballing.
   a. Have you ever been in a situation where you think you were lowballed? If yes, how did you handle the situation?
   b. If this type of situation occurred again, how would you handle it, based on the information presented in this chapter?
3. Watch a home shopping program or go to a store where the salespeople work on commission and sell aggressively. After watching the show or browsing in the store, write a few paragraphs in which you try to identify the compliance principles used by the salespeople.
   a. What compliance principles were used most frequently?
   b. Did you find any compliance principles that could be added to those listed in this chapter?
   c. Which compliance principles were the most effective, and why?
4. List the compliance principles that you think you use in your relationships.
   a. Which principle do you use most often with family members?
   b. Which principle do you use most often with friends?
   c. Which principle do you use most often in romantic relationships?
   d. If you use different principles in different relationships, why do you do so?
   e. Which compliance principles are most effective for you?
5. Which compliance principles would you use to pursue each of the following goals?
   a. To convince a professor to write a recommendation for you
   b. To convince a friend to take you to the airport
   c. To convince a stranger to buy raffle tickets from your school or church group
   d. To sell a used car to a stranger

e.   To convince someone in your family to loan you some money

f.   To convince an acquaintance to loan you notes for a class you missed

g.   To borrow some CDs or tapes from your roommate for a trip you are going on

h.   To convince your partner to go to a party that you want to go to rather than one that he or she wants to go to

i.   To convince your neighbor to start recycling

Discuss your answers with other class members, justifying the tactics you chose.

6.   Write a short paragraph in which you describe how the men you know shop and what sorts of sales tactics seem to be most effective in getting them to buy. Now write the same type of paragraph on how the women you know shop.

a.   Who shops more frequently, the men or the women?

b.   Who spends more money when they shop?

c.   Do you think men and women shop for the same reasons? What are their reasons?

d.   What sorts of sales tactics are most effective for the men?

e.   What sorts of sales tactics are most effective for the women?

f.   What sorts of sales tactics would be most effective for a couple shopping together?

7.   Most people feel that it is ethically wrong to manipulate other people. We feel that we have a right to know when we are being influenced and a right to defend ourselves against influence.

a.   Do any tactics described in this chapter violate this ethical principle?

b.   Are there any tactics that you would not use because they appear to be unethical?

c.   Can you think of some guidelines that you would use in deciding when and how to use the tactics discussed in this chapter?

SUGGESTED READING

▼

GENERAL COMPLIANCE PRINCIPLES

Cialdini, R. B. 1993. *Influence: Science and Practice,* 3d ed. New York: HarperCollins. This popular book first appeared in the early 1980s and is already in its third edition. Cialdini provides a plethora of examples of the use and misuse of the principles of compliance.

RECIPROCITY

Cialdini, R. B., and Ascani, K. 1976. Test of a concession procedure for inducing verbal, behavioral, and further compliance with a request to give blood. *Journal of Applied Psychology,* 61:295–300. The Cialdini and Ascani study was the first important study published on the topic of the door-in-the-face tactic or "matched concessions." Because it was a large-scale study involving several hundred participants, and because the topic of giving blood is an important area of study, this experiment is one of the most frequently cited studies on compliance principles.

LOWBALLING

Cialdini, R. B.; Cacioppo, J. T.; Bassett, R.; and Miller, J. A. 1978. Lowball procedure for producing compliance: Commitment then cost. *Journal of Personality and Social Psychology*, 36:463–476. This study was the first study demonstrating the importance of the lowball procedure in gaining compliance from others. Prior to this publication, the term "lowball" was used only in reference to sales tactics. Cialdini and others demonstrated that the principle of lowballing helps to gain compliance in non-sales encounters as well.

FOOT IN THE DOOR AND DOOR IN THE FACE

DeJong, W. 1979. An examination of self-perception mediation of the foot-in-the-door effect. *Journal of Personality and Social Psychology* 37:2221–2239. DeJong reviewed several hundred studies on compliance principles and offers a number of conclusions concerning the effectiveness of the foot-in-the-door or door-in-the-face tactics. The DeJong review is an excellent source for citations, since virtually every study is included (from every discipline and from every country).

Dillard, J. P.; Hunter, J. E.; and Burgoon, M. J. 1984. Sequential-request persuasive strategies: Meta-analysis of foot-in-the-door and door-in-the-face. *Human Communication Research* 10:461–488. Dillard, Hunter, and Burgoon offer a different review of the effectiveness of compliance principles, relying on a statistical procedure called a "meta-analysis." This review is far more recent than the DeJong review, but Dillard et al. excluded some studies from review which were difficult to find or which failed to publish the statistical evidence they needed in order to conduct the meta-analysis.

SCARCITY

Brehm, S. S., and Brehm, J. W. 1981. *Psychological Reactance: A Theory of Freedom and Control.* Orlando, Fla.: Academic Press. The Brehm and Brehm research team spent two decades conducting research on psychological reactance. Chapters detail male and female differences in psychological reactance, and detail the importance of this compliance principle in legal settings, interpersonal settings, and consumer settings.

Gladue, B. A., and Delaney, H. J. 1990. Gender differences in perception of attractiveness of men and women in bars. *Personality and Social Psychology Bulletin*, 16:378–391. A clever study by Gladue and Delaney demonstrated that the effect of looking prettier at closing time was not related to the amount of alcohol consumed, among other factors.

REFERENCE LIST

▼

Blake, R.; Rosenbaum, M.; and Duryea, R. 1955. Gift-buying as a function of group standards. *Human Relations* 8:61–73.

Brickman, P.; Coates, D.; and Janoff-Bulman, R. 1978. Lottery winners and accident victims: Is happiness relative? *Journal of Personality and Social Psychology* 36:917–927.

Chaiken, S. 1979. Communicator physical attractiveness and persuasion. *Journal of Personality and Social Psychology* 37:1387–1397.

Cialdini, R. B. 1993. *Influence: Science and practice*, 3d ed. New York: HarperCollins.

Cialdini, R. B., and Ascani, K. 1976. Test of a concession procedure for inducing verbal, behavioral, and further compliance with a request to give blood. *Journal of Applied Psychology* 61:295–300.

Cialdini, R. B.; Cacioppo, J. T.; Bassett, R.; and Miller, J. A. 1978. Low-ball procedure for producing compliance: Commitment then cost. *Journal of Personality and Social Psychology* 36:463–476.

Cody, M. J.; Seiter, J.; and Montagne-Miller, Y. 1994. Women and men in the marketplace. In *Gender, power, and communication in human relationships*, ed. P. Kalbfleisch and M. J. Cody. Hillsdale, N.J.: Erlbaum.

Cupchik, G. C., and Leventhal, H. 1974. Consistency between expressive behavior and the evaluation of humorous stimuli: The role of sex and self-observation. *Journal of Personality and Social Psychology* 30:429–442.

Driscoll, R.; Davies, K. E.; and Lipetz, M. E. 1972. Parental interference and romantic love: The Romeo and Juliet effect. *Journal of Personality and Social Psychology* 24:1–10.

Gladue, B. A., and Delaney, H. J. 1990. Gender differences in perception of attractiveness of men and women in bars. *Personality and Social Psychology Bulletin* 16:378–391.

Hocking, J. E.; Margreiter, D. G.; and Hylton, C. 1977. Intra-audience effects: A field test. *Human Communication Research* 3:243–249.

Kenrick, D. T., and Gutierres, S. E. 1980. Contrast effects and judgments of physical attractiveness: When beauty becomes a social problem. *Journal of Personality and Social Psychology* 38:131–140.

Kraut, R. E. 1973. Effects of social labeling on giving to charity. *Journal of Experimental Social Psychology* 9:551–562.

Leventhal, H., and Cupchik, G. C. 1975. The informational and facilitative effects of an audience upon expression and evaluation of humorous stimuli. *Journal of Experimental Social Psychology* 11:363–380.

————. 1976. A process model of humor judgment. *Journal of Communication* 26:190–204.

Leventhal, H., and Mace, W. 1970. The effect of laughter on evaluation of a slapstick movie. *Journal of Personality* 38:16–30.

Pennebaker, J. W.; Dyer, M. A.; Caulkins, R. S.; Litowitz, D. L.; Ackreman, P. L.; Anderson, D. B.; and McGraw, K. M. 1979. Don't the girls get prettier at closing time: A country and western application to psychology. *Personality and Social Psychology Bulletin* 5:122–125.

Petty, R. E., and Cacioppo, J. T. 1981. *Attitudes and persuasion: Classic and contemporary approaches.* Dubuque, Iowa: Brown.

C H A P T E R   1 2

MANAGING

INTERPERSONAL

CONFLICT

Jason and Scott thought it would be easy to share an apartment. They both played on the same softball team, they liked the same kinds of music, and they seemed to have the same values. Besides, they could cut down on rent if they shared an apartment.

After a few weeks it became clear that things wouldn't be as easy as they first thought. Jason often studied in the evening, typically in the living room. Scott didn't go to school, so he spent his evenings working out at the gym or going out on dates. Occasionally he would bring a woman back to the apartment, wanting to use the living room to listen to the stereo. But Jason was always there, either studying or watching TV.

Jason wasn't very tidy either. One thing that really bothered Scott was that Jason would never take out the trash. Two or three bags of trash would pile up at the kitchen entry, and Jason didn't even seem to notice. It was bad enough that Scott couldn't have any privacy when he wanted it, but the trash was embarrassing when he brought a guest home. At first Scott said nothing. Then after a few weeks, Scott asked Jason to take his trash out every day. Jason agreed, but he often forgot, which only made Scott more unhappy about the situation.

One night Scott almost fell over the bags of trash set in the hall. This time, and in less than a flash, Scott decided to confront Jason. Scott said, "Look, you may enjoy living like a pig, but I can't. So if you don't throw this trash out now, I'm gonna toss it in your room."

Jason wasn't about to be pushed around: "If you touch my room, I'll knock you flat."

Scott jumped up, grabbed the trash bags, and smashed them above Jason's bed.

Jason was shaking, "That does it—I'll get you back for this, believe me."

Scott mocked him. "Your threats are nothing but idle chatter."

On those words, the two began fighting, although not very well. The only thing they managed to do was put a hole in one wall, tear some curtains, and break a large window.

The next morning, Jason and Scott left the apartment. They forfeited that month's rent and their security deposit, due to the damage caused by the fight. Jason and Scott never saw each other after that morning.

This story illustrates a few aspects of interpersonal conflict. First, it shows that a particular conflict episode is probably not an isolated event. The issues at conflict between Jason and Scott occurred over several months. Second, this example shows that conflicts may never be "resolved." Instead, it is probably healthier to think of *managing* conflict over time. Obviously, Jason and Scott didn't manage their conflict very well. Finally, the example illustrates that people choose the way they respond to one another and that these responses often depend on what the other person has done.

Why Study Conflict?

There are several good reasons for studying conflict. Perhaps the best reason is to avoid the type of escalation to violence that Jason and Scott experienced. As we all know, people sometimes resort to physical violence or verbal abuse in conflict situations. Margolin (1990), for example, reports that about 20 percent of his sample of married couples had resorted to physical violence within the previous year. As this chapter reveals, there are more productive ways to manage interpersonal conflicts.

A second reason for studying conflict is to help you achieve your personal goals. Note that Jason and Scott failed to achieve what they wanted (friendship and saving money), in part because they cut off communication with each other. We are not saying that applying particular communication skills will solve all your interpersonal problems (see also Sillars and Weisberg 1987). We do contend that learning more about communication in conflict should better enable you to achieve your goals, even in emotionally charged situations. You can increase your ability to use the most appropriate and most effective communication strategies for managing conflict situations.

According to Deutsch (1973), conflict can be productive if managed properly. Conflict between family members, friends, lovers, and others can help the parties clarify their personal and relational goals. Conflict can also lead to the generation of new ideas and creative alternatives. Encouraging disagreement can promote effective decision making, but disallowing conflict can lead to poor decisions. In addition, interpersonal conflict can help people manage their lives better. You may very well be faced with a friend who wants to leave a party after having too much to drink; it is very possible that the only way your friend will live to see tomorrow is through confrontation with you.

A third and final reason to study conflict is that it is a natural and inevitable event, as Hocker and Wilmot (1991) indicate. Benoit and Benoit (1990) report that on the average, a person has *seven* conflicts a week, mostly among relatives, friends, and lovers with whom they've argued before (86 percent of conflicts are of this type). Conflict is natural and inevitable simply because people are not mere clones of one another. We each have our unique combination of beliefs, behaviors, and goals, which will inevitably conflict with others' beliefs, behaviors, and goals.

Defining Conflict

Conflict is defined as the disagreement between interdependent parties who perceive that they have incompatible goals (see also Cahn 1992; Hocker and Wilmot 1991; Putnam and Poole 1987). The key terms in this definition are *disagreement, interdependent,* and *perceived incompatible goals.* Interpersonal conflict occurs when there is some expression of disagreement, either verbal or nonverbal, between two people. When a person experiences internal conflict without expressing disagreement with others, this is known as **intrapsychic conflict,** not interpersonal conflict (Hocker and Wilmot 1991). Later in this chapter we describe various strategies and tactics that people use to express disagreement.

Interdependence means that the people in conflict depend on one another to accomplish their goals. You must coordinate behaviors in order to achieve your goals, but during conflict, the person with whom you must coordinate actions appears to block your goals. Probably the most important aspect of the definition concerns how goals might be perceived as incompatible. Note that goals may not in fact be incompatible; what really matters is that the parties in conflict *perceive* them as incompatible.

Other features of goals in conflict should be mentioned. As Sillars and Weisberg (1987) note, "In many conflicts, goals are quite complex and ephemeral" (p. 141). One reason is that goals change as the conflict progresses. Hocker and Wilmot (1991) identify three types of goals: *prospective goals* are the goals you initially have when entering the conflict episode, *transactive goals* are those that emerge during the interaction, and *retrospective goals* refer to how you look back at the interaction to make sense of it. For example, you might have the prospective goal of getting your roommate to give up the apartment on certain nights so that you have more privacy. Your roommate disagrees, and during the conflict you discover that your roommate doesn't go out due to shyness. Your goal might then change to persuading your roommate to go to a party with you. After the conversation, you might retrospectively decide that your goal was to help your roommate be less of a homebody. The point is that when you engage in conflict, your objectives may change. People who recognize the changing nature of goals can adapt their messages to achieve these goals.

Another factor that complicates conflict is that people have several goals at once. It is likely that no one single issue is relevant at a given moment of the conflict episode. For example, imagine that you need to type a report for a class, but your significant other wants to go out and makes a point of it. Your instrumental goal of completing your assignment conflicts with your partner's goal of going out. Yet at the same time you want to maintain the relationship (a second important goal), and you would prefer to get away from your homework as well.

Conflict Styles

Are people consistent in their use of conflict behaviors? That is the issue addressed by researchers who examine conflict styles. Investigations on the topic, by such researchers as Berryman-Fink and Brunner (1987), Kilmann and Thomas (1977), and Rahim (1986), have revealed five styles that people may use.

Perhaps the best way to explain the five styles of conflict is to place them on a graph that reflects the degrees to which an individual is concerned for others and for himself or herself. In addition, these styles are said to vary according to their degree of cooperation and assertiveness. Figure 12-1 shows the placement of the five styles according to these concerns.

As the graph indicates, a person who has a low concern for others and a high concern for self will likely have a **competing style.** This style is assertive, without real consideration for others' outcomes. By contrast, a person can have a high concern for others but a low concern for self. This person would be cooperative and unassertive, characteristic of an **accommodating style.** An individual could have a

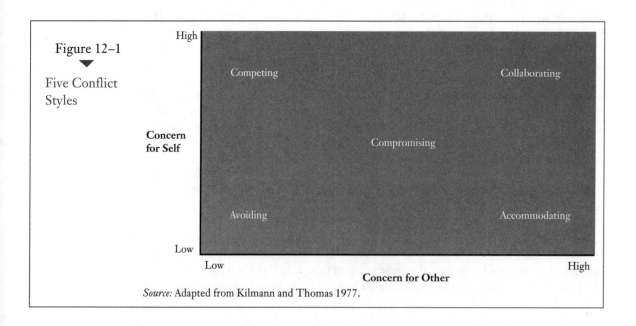

Figure 12–1

▼

Five Conflict Styles

High

Competing

Collaborating

Concern for Self

Compromising

Avoiding

Accommodating

Low

Low   High

Concern for Other

Source: Adapted from Kilmann and Thomas 1977.

high concern for both self and others, reflected in being assertive and cooperative. This is the **collaborating style.** Some people have little concern for themselves or others in conflicts. This lack of concern is seen in little assertiveness and little co-operation. Because such persons prefer to withdraw from the situation, this is referred to as the **withdrawing style.** Finally, there are people who have a moderate amount of concern for self and others. Accordingly, they show moderate amounts of assertiveness and cooperation. They are described as having a **compromising style.**

Which style is best? According to Hocker and Wilmot (1985), there is no simple answer. Rather, there are advantages and disadvantages to using each of these styles. Table 12-1 lists some of them.

Our view on conflict styles is that they describe how people tend to behave in general. Styles are useful because they let us see how we tend to behave in response to conflict. Moreover, the advantages and disadvantages of these styles are clear.

Although styles describe how people tend to behave, the research on what people actually do in conflict indicates that we make critical choices regarding when and how to manage conflict. These choices also lead to the use of particular strategies for managing conflict.

Choices in Managing Conflict

CONFRONT OR AVOID?

According to several researchers (e.g., Sillars, Wilmot, and Hocker 1993), one choice people make during conflict is to confront or avoid the other person. Imagine that you are waiting in your car at an intersection and the driver in front of you hasn't noticed that the traffic light has turned green. Should you confront the other driver (honk your horn), or should you withdraw from the conflict and wait quietly?

Several factors determine whether or not you confront or avoid the person. One of them is whether you have a "right to persuade" (Cody, McLaughlin, and Schneider 1981). If you believe that you have a right to pursue your goal, you will be more likely to confront the individual than if you are unsure about having the right to persuade. For example, if you noticed that the person in the car in front of you was reading a newspaper, putting on lipstick, or talking to a passenger, you would probably feel within your rights to honk your horn. But if you see that an elderly person is crossing in front of the other car, you wouldn't feel within your rights to honk your horn.

Another factor that determines whether you confront or avoid the other is how important the goal is to you. If you were late for an important meeting or a job interview, you would probably be less patient than if you were on your way to a party.

Status also affects the decision to confront or avoid. People tend not to confront those who have higher status but do tend to confront those with the same or lower status (see, for example, Putnam and Wilson 1982). Accordingly, you may not dis-

Table 12-1

ADVANTAGES AND DISADVANTAGES
OF THE FIVE CONFLICT STYLES

Style	Advantages	Disadvantages
Competing	Useful if instrumental goal is more important than relational or self-presentational goal; helpful if quick decisions are needed	Can hurt relational and self-presentational goals; can lead to escalation of conflict or avoidance by the other person
Accommodating	Can show reasonableness; can improve relationships, especially with superiors; can keep another from harming you	May communicate lack of power; ignores relational issues; requires sacrifice of instrumental goals
Collaborating	Can satisfy both parties; promotes creative solutions and commitment to them; enhances relational and instrumental goals; works well in long-term associations	Requires much energy, perhaps too much for a given goal; can be frustrating if not reciprocal; can be faked
Withdrawing	Acknowledges that some goals are not worth fighting for; protects against possible harm; appropriate if relationship is short-term	May be perceived as weak or uncaring; abandons goal; reinforces idea that conflict is unnatural and should be avoided at all costs
Compromising	Can let both parties accomplish some goals in an efficient manner; maintains most relational goals; seems reasonable to most people	Easy but may be counterproductive; requires sacrifice of both parties' goals to some degree; hampers use of creative alternatives

Source: Adapted from Hocker and Wilmot 1985.

Several factors determine whether you confront or avoid conflict with someone. Do you believe you are right to pursue your goal? How important is the goal to you? What is your status relative to the person you would be confronting? What public image do you want to present? What is the nature of the relationship between you?

(Michael Weisbrot/Stock, Boston)

agree with your supervisor about critical comments about your work, but you would be less willing to take the same criticism from a co-worker.

As Chapter 5 showed, self-presentation concerns how we groom our public image. Accordingly, the decision to confront or avoid the other person is affected by which public image we want to present. Recall that some people want to appear likable, so they ingratiate, while others want to appear dangerous, so they intimidate. Your various self-presentation goals likely affect your decision to confront or avoid conflict with others.

Finally, relational history affects your decision to confront or avoid. Sillars and colleagues (1983) found that for some couples (independents—see Chapter 9), satisfaction increases as their level of confrontation increases; but for other couples (separates—see Chapter 9), satisfaction decreases as their level of confrontation increases. In addition, friends probably feel more comfortable confronting each other than acquaintances do (Fitzpatrick and Winke 1979). Also, as you get to know someone, your confidence in making attributions about that person's behavior increases. A particular kind of silent response, a shrug of the shoulder, or a lukewarm "yes" is more readily interpreted by people who know one another well than by acquaintances. As you learn to interpret the other's nonverbal messages, you may become more likely to confront the other on the basis of those nonverbals.

COOPERATE OR COMPETE?

A second choice that you face when a conflict arises is whether to be cooperative or competitive. Again, several factors are decisive. They include perceived threat, reciprocity, and responses to inappropriate behavior. Research indicates that people who believe that their personal rights are being violated are more likely to lash out than those who do not see their rights as jeopardized. For example, Canary, Cunningham, and Cody (1988) found that people are more likely to use such competitive behaviors as shouting and sarcasm if they perceive that they are personally attacked.

Reciprocity affects your decision to cooperate or compete. As you may recall from earlier chapters, reciprocity refers to the way that dyadic partners mirror each other's behavior. As in self-disclosure, where one person tends to disclose at the same level of intimacy as the partner, reciprocity has a strong effect on selection of conflict behavior. Sillars (1980b), for example, found strong associations between one person's conflict behavior and the partner's conflict interaction. In addition, Burggraf and Sillars (1987) found that reciprocity had more effect on conflict behavior than relationship type or gender did. Simply stated, people treat others as they are treated themselves, especially during conflict. So when someone threatens you, the urge is to challenge back; when someone is patient and discloses feelings, the tendency is to offer disclosure in return (see Burggraf and Sillars 1987; Sillars 1980b).

Finally, certain kinds of inappropriate communication prompt negative reactions. Benoit and Benoit (1990) indicate that people are often drawn into a competitive mode when they are faced with insults, accusations, commands, or refusals of requests. Such messages prompt conflict; they are illustrated in Table 12-2.

Table 12-2
MESSAGES THAT PROMPT CONFLICT

Message	Type
"I don't like your singing."	Insult
"You acted silly at the party."	Insult
"You never clean up like you used to."	Accusation
"We're broke because you spend too much."	Accusation
"Stop talking with your mouth full."	Command
"Tell me when you won't be busy."	Command
"I can't see you because I'm too busy."	Refusal
"You'll just have to type this yourself."	Refusal

Source: Adapted from Benoit and Benoit 1990.

Decisions to confront or avoid and to cooperate or compete have important implications for managing interpersonal conflict. First, these decisions are under the control of the communicators. Everyone has the choice of whether or not to engage in conflict, and everyone has the choice of cooperating or competing. These choices happen almost instantly and are often made in a state of emotional upset. Nevertheless, these choices are ours to make, and we must accept responsibility for our conflict behaviors.

In addition, these choices are important because they lead to the use of strategies that reflect these decisions. If you decide to avoid the issue, you will probably engage in behaviors designed to minimize the conflict. If you decide to confront the person, you can do so in degrees of cooperation or competition. Several researchers (e.g., Cupach 1982; Putnam and Wilson 1982; Sillars et al. 1982) cite three basic conflict strategies that reflect decisions to avoid, to cooperate, and to compete. As these conflict strategies unfold, several kinds of patterns can be observed.

Conflict Strategies and Patterns

CONFLICT STRATEGIES

If you decide to avoid the conflict issue, you will likely use the **avoidance strategy.** Avoidance is intended to distract attention from the conflict. Table 12-3 offers examples of avoidance tactics.

Calvin and Hobbes reciprocate each other's conflict behaviors. Fortunately for Calvin, only his stuffed tiger heard his accusations and insults.

Table 12-3
AVOIDANCE TACTICS

Tactic	Description	Example
Direct denial	The communicator flatly denies that there is a problem.	"No, dear, nothing is wrong."
Evasion	The communicator tries to imply that the problem lies elsewhere.	"I can see how other couples have that problem."
Topic shift	The communicator simply changes the subject.	"That's interesting. Now as I was saying yesterday . . ."
Stalling	The communicator tries to delay or postpone discussion.	"It's too late to talk about that now."
Abstract remark	The communicator shifts the focus to a level that is removed from the issue.	"You say I'm impatient. Well, patience is a virtue that everyone needs to work at."
Procedural remark	The communicator focuses on manner rather than the conflict issue.	"I can't talk to you when you're like this."
Irrelevant remark	The communicator makes a statement that has little or no bearing on the conflict issue.	"There's a fly on the wall."

Source: Adapted from Cupach 1982; Hocker and Wilmot 1991; Sillars et al. 1982.

If you want to engage the other person in a cooperative manner, you would likely rely on an **integrative strategy.** Integrative behaviors are those that manage the conflict by taking into account both party's needs and wants—they attempt to integrate both person's resources and goals. Table 12-4 provides examples of integrative behaviors.

If you want to engage the other person in a competitive manner, you would probably use a **distributive strategy.** From a competitive posture, you distribute the resources and goals in a win-lose attitude, and you try to win as much as possible

Table 12-4

INTEGRATIVE TACTICS

Tactic	Description	Example
Descriptive statement	The communicator offers a factual explanation.	"There are three bags of trash in the hallway."
Disclosure	The communicator discloses personal feelings about the topic.	"I get very anxious when you speed like this."
Soliciting disclosures	The communicator asks the other person to disclose personal feelings.	"Please tell me what you're thinking."
Understanding and concern	The communicator demonstrates understanding and caring.	"I realize that this must be a tough decision for you."
Supportive remark	The communicator backs up the other person's point of view.	"I can see now what you meant."
Concession	The communicator conveys willingness to give in a little.	"OK, I'll try to drive more carefully from now on."
Acceptance of responsibility	The communicator accepts responsibility for part of the conflict.	"You're right—I can't manage money very well."
Common ground	Both communicators try to find a mutually satisfying solution.	"Can we agree on our major goals?"

Source: Adapted from Cupach 1982; Hocker and Wilmot 1991; Sillars et al. 1982.

regardless of the other's expense. Table 12-5 offers examples of behaviors that are distributive.

These tactics seldom occur in isolation. An individual rarely walks up to his or her partner, blurts out a disclosure or a prescription, and then leaves. Instead, an individual perceives that a valued goal is blocked and then decides whether to engage the partner in a conversation. Then these tactics unfold in various ways. Discussion of the various ways conflicts unfold reveals additional insights about communicative aspects of conflict.

Table 12-5

DISTRIBUTIVE TACTICS

Tactic	Description	Example
Personal criticism	The communicator faults the other person's character.	"You idiot! You don't think before you open your mouth."
Rejection	The communicator dismisses the other person's ideas.	"No way—that's out of the question."
Threat	The communicator warns of punishment if argument fails.	"If you don't throw out that trash, I'll toss it in your room."
Blame	The communicator attributes the entire conflict to the other person.	"It's your fault we're having this problem."
Hostile remark	The communicator tries to intimidate.	"Who the hell do you think you are?"
Shouting	The communicator tries to overcome the other person through sheer volume.	"DON'T YOU SHOUT AT ME!"
Sarcasm	The communicator uses intonation to convey that a statement is to be interpreted as its opposite.	"You sure looked macho on that mechanical bull."
Prescription	The communicator tells the other person what to do.	"You should stop thinking only of yourself—people might start liking you more."

Source: Adapted from Cupach 1982; Hocker and Wilmot 1991; Sillars et al. 1982.

CONFLICT PATTERNS

Sillars, Wilmot, and Hocker (1993) note that conflict tactics unfold along several organizational patterns or dimensions. These dimensions each reflect how specific instances of avoidance, integrative, and distributive tactics occur during interaction.

The five dimensions that these analysts discuss are *variety, continuity, symmetry, stationarity,* and *spontaneity.*

Variety refers to how flexible people are during conflict. As Sillars and colleagues (1993) note, lack of flexibility tends to occur among couples who are dissatisfied. Ting-Toomey (1983), for example, found that dissatisfied couples lapse into the same rigid patterns of defensive communication. Unhappy couples consistently responded to confrontational remarks and complaints with similar defensive statements. Gottman (1979) reports similar findings, indicating that negative, distributive behavioral cycles are hard to break for people in dissatisfying relationships. It appears that using a variety of conflict behaviors, particularly integrative responses, breaks the rigidity of the conflict interaction and increases the likelihood of productive conflict management.

Continuity refers to the range of topics covered during conflict. According to Sillars and co-workers (1993), intense conflicts about the same important relational issues (such as not trusting the partner or not showing affection) are unhealthy. At the same time, a conflict episode that entails many different topics (ranging from talking too much and eating habits to lack of trust and affection) reflects a dysfunctional relationship. For example, you may have been involved in a conversation where the parties couldn't focus on a single issue long enough to reach agreement or even understand each other. Or you may have felt the frustration of dealing with the same issue over and over again. People in satisfying relationships tend to develop their ideas before moving on to new issues. And satisfied couples avoid raising the same tired issues.

Symmetry refers to reciprocity of behavior, or mirroring the other's conflict. Symmetry references a quid pro quo (treat others as they treat you). Sillars and associates (1993) note that satisfied couples tend to reciprocate integrative behaviors but not distributive behaviors. Ting-Toomey (1983) also reported that satisfied couples engaged in symmetrical sequences of verbal teasing, confirmation, and description. Dissatisfied couples reciprocated defensive statements (Son: "There's no way I could have been out all last night." Father: "I doubt that." Son: "Well, I'm sure of it!" Father: "Don't lie to me!"). Recall from Chapter 9 that regressive spirals result from partners reciprocating negative messages. Severe regressive spirals can be quite damaging (Wilmot 1987).

Gottman (1982) reported that some of the most damaging symmetrical patterns were proposal–counterproposal, complaint–complaint, and metacommunication–metacommunication. The following is a proposal–counterproposal sequence:

Brad:	Let's order some Chinese food and rent a video.
Tracy:	No, let's do Italian and go dancing.
Brad:	Let's invite Ted and Lisa to join us.
Tracy:	No, let's go alone.

Or consider the following more explosive exchange:

Brad: You can leave me alone anytime you want.
Tracy: It's my house, so you check out.
Brad: Then you can go to hell.
Tracy: After you.

Cross-complaining can be common but destructive; for example:

Tracy: You didn't clean the kitchen like I asked.
Brad: So? You didn't wash the clothes.

or

Brad: I don't like your hair like that.
Tracy: You're no movie star either.

Metacommunication exchanges refer to reciprocating talk about talk. (You can find numerous examples of this kind of exchange on soap operas.) Consider the following symmetrical exchange:

Tracy: What do you mean by "be good"?
Brad: Why do you ask?
Tracy: I wouldn't ask if I didn't have a reason.
Brad: That's not a valid argument.
Tracy: Why not? It seems logical to me!
Brad: Logic and validity aren't the same thing.
Tracy: I should give you a few lessons in logic.

Of course, by now Tracy and Brad have forgotten the real issue they were discussing.

Although these examples reflect dysfunctional patterns, you can also use reciprocation to "guide the process in a potentially productive . . . direction" (Krueger and Smith 1982, 131). As Burggraf and Sillars (1987) note, it is difficult to engage in competitive, distributive confrontations with someone who offers cooperative, integrative behaviors. Accordingly, one method for breaking a destructive symmetrical pattern is simply to refrain from reciprocating distributive tactics.

Sillars and colleagues (1993) note that particular conflict behaviors do not occur at random. Instead, couples go through phases of conflict, a topic referred to as **stationarity.** Gottman (1979) discovered that couples typically follow a three-step process: first they offer observations or solutions to problems; next they agree or disagree; finally, they exchange information. During this exchange of information, people experience phases of conflict escalation and de-escalation. For example, some dyads begin with integrative messages, then move to more distributive tactics, then return to cooperative behaviors, perhaps because the conflict becomes too emotionally intense. Other dyads might begin and end their discussions with avoidant messages—talking about other people, denying that a problem exists, or shifting from topic to topic, not experiencing any phases of conflict escalation or de-escalation. Gottman and Krokoff (1989) noted that another common pattern begins with hostility and concludes with the partners avoiding each other.

According to Sillars and co-workers (1993), stationarity can also be observed across conflict episodes. In other words, although particular couples can engage in various phases within a given encounter, their tactical patterns are similar in different conflict encounters. So, for example, two people might begin every conflict with calm disclosures about their desired goals, which then gradually escalate into reciprocations of blaming and ridicule. Next one person realizes that the conflict is destructive and offers a conciliation tactic ("I'm sorry—I'll try to be more considerate"). The couple then goes out to dinner, during which they disclose their true feelings. Clearly, there are changes in the phases of conflict within one episode. But if this couple engages in the same tactical pattern of disclosure-blaming-conciliation-disclosure in every conflict episode, these people enact predictable conflict phases across episodes.

Sillars and associates (1993) use the term **spontaneity** to refer to the degree that the parties in conflict are not being overly strategic and guarded in what they say. You may have been involved in a conflict where you measured the effect of each and every word before it was spoken. The reason for this could be that the issue was very important or you didn't feel comfortable expressing your true feelings, or perhaps you felt intimidated by your partner.

Conversely, you may have observed a conflict where the other person plainly vented hostile feelings without thinking about the devastating effects of such "open and honest" communication. Clearly, being either overly cautious or careless about managing conflict may be unproductive. According to Sillars and colleagues, "Ideally, one would be spontaneous enough to be responsive enough to be collaborative, but strategic enough to modify destructive patterns when they arise" (p. 24).

In sum, Sillars, Wilmot, and Hocker have offered five organizational properties of conflict messages: variety, continuity, symmetry, stationarity, and spontaneity. Each property helps us observe how conflict tactics are exchanged and even how they may be modified.

Managing Relational Problems

Relational problems are inevitable. Some of these problems are resolved quickly; others take months or even years to manage. Responses to relational problems are important because such problems constitute an important conflict domain.

330

Discussing the problem (voice) is one of several options people have when they encounter problems in their relationships. The other options include separating (exit), staying with the partner and hoping things will work out (loyalty), or making the present situation more difficult for the partner (neglect).

(Gatewood/The Image Works)

Rusbult (1987) has identified four general responses that people use in dealing with problems in relationships. The first response type is **exit:** the couple separates formally, or the individuals think or talk about leaving (see also Chapter 10). The second approach is **voice.** Voice includes such actions as "discussing problems" and "suggesting solutions." The third approach is **loyalty:** the person decides to wait and hope that things will work out. Or loyalty could be shown in supporting the partner in the face of personal criticism." Finally, a person can use **neglect**—avoid the partner, refuse to discuss the relational problems, and perhaps show hostility.

Sheila has been married for about twenty years to Doug. She is moderately satisfied with her marriage and her family, but Doug is very controlling: he monitors her communication with other people; he reads her mail, listens on the extension when she receives phone calls (even from her daughter), and never allows Sheila to go out alone. Nor does he let her drive the family car. Sheila sacrificed her career in teaching to be with Doug, and she continues to be primarily responsible for raising their four children (three of whom still live at home). Doug, however, enjoys a different life. He goes out whenever and with whomever he pleases, and he refuses to answer to Sheila. Because of his carousing, the family budget is always tight. Often, Sheila

---

CONFLICT IS DEADLY IN *THE WAR OF THE ROSES*

In the film *The War of the Roses*, we see the serious damage that can result from an unremittingly competitive approach to managing conflict. Oliver Rose is a professional, and his wife, Barbara, is a homemaker who later begins a business of her own. With his income, they purchase a large house, which she makes elegant through years of hard work. Though initially happy, the Roses ultimately grow apart.

Barbara wants a divorce and the house, but Oliver refuses to relinquish it. The house becomes a trophy to be won. To manage the impasse, the Roses decide to divide the house into three zones—an area for each of them, plus a neutral zone. When his lawyer suggests that Oliver give Barbara the house, Oliver insists that he must win. His lawyer advises, "Oliver, there is no winning in this, only degrees of losing." But Oliver misses the point—that using a distributive strategy is counterproductive—and responds, "I got more square footage." For Oliver the house is a battleground, and the outcome of the conflict is measured by the territory occupied.

The Roses then escalate their negative behaviors to the point of violence. Oliver ruins a party Barbara throws for her clients; she reciprocates by destroying his sports car with her truck. He dismantles her oven; she in turn demolishes their prized porcelain collection, which she also loves but values more as a means of hurting Oliver. Despite attempts to manage the conflict in a cooperative fashion, these people cannot resist the urge to reciprocate negative behaviors, and that mishandling of interpersonal conflict ultimately costs them their lives.

Throughout *The War of the Roses*, both parties consciously decide to escalate the conflict. Neither one is willing to back down, so both end up losing. A great many people decide to manage conflict in the same destructive manner, partly due to the shortsighted belief that winning is a major goal in itself.

---

must ask Doug for money to purchase groceries for the household. But the cash is low, even for groceries. Every month or so they have the same conflict: she must buy the groceries, but there is not enough money to purchase what the family would like to eat. Doug gets very upset, criticizes Sheila, and demands that she "find some way" to make ends meet. In a word, Doug responds to this ongoing problem by using neglect. What is Sheila's response to Doug? She displays loyalty.

Rusbult (1987) has demonstrated that the use of the four responses to relational problems is tied to a person's commitment to the relationship. For Rusbult, commitment is born of a combination of satisfaction with the relationship, the amount of investment already made in the relationship (such as money and emotional energy), and the quality of alternatives (another potential partner, a support group).

In the scenario presented, why does Sheila respond to her relational problems with loyalty? Part of the reason is that she has invested so much in this relationship—her career, her time raising the children, her friendships. Another reason is that she has no alternatives. She has no income, no job prospects, no conceivable way to meet others, and no transportation. Her options are very limited. And as Sheila gets older, her costs become more reason to stay in the relationship (see Rusbult, Johnson, and Morrow 1986b).

If Sheila's options were not limited—if she had maintained her career and friends who could offer her support—what might her approach be to this situation? Sheila would probably use voice. Table 12-6 indicates when people theoretically use exit, voice, loyalty, and neglect, depending on the combination of commitment factors. It predicts that Sheila would threaten to leave or actually leave the relationship (that is, use exit) if she were dissatisfied with her partner, did not have much invested in the relationship, and had other friends, activities, or even lovers. Sheila might use neglect if she were dissatisfied, had little invested, but felt that she had nowhere else to turn.

Rusbult, Johnson, and Morrow (1986a) found that the use of voice in mild relational problems helped stabilize the relationship. Moreover, voice and loyalty have been positively related to commitment (Rusbult 1987). However, as might be expected, the use of exit and neglect were negatively associated with commitment and satisfaction. Rusbult and colleagues (1986a) also found that women reported using voice for mild problems and loyalty for all kinds of problems more than men did. These authors also found that men reported using neglect more often than women did.

Table 12-6
TYPICAL RESPONSES TO RELATIONAL PROBLEMS

Likely Response	Properties of Commitment		
	Satisfaction	*Investment*	*Alternatives*
Exit	Low	Low	High
Voice	High	High	High
Loyalty	High	High	Low
Neglect	Low	Low	Low

Source: Adapted from Rusbult 1987. Reprinted by permission of Sage Publications, Inc.

In an extension of this research, Metts and Cupach (1990) found that the exit-voice-loyalty-neglect typology is associated with certain irrational beliefs that college students have about their romantic relationships: (1) that disagreement is destructive (it's not OK to disagree); (2) that partners are expected to be mindreaders (your partner should be able to know your thoughts and feelings without your voicing them); (3) that partners cannot and do not change; (4) that the relationship must achieve sexual perfectionism (your sex life with your partner must be the best there is); and (5) that men and women are different (hence they cannot agree on anything).

Metts and Cupach (1990) found that each of these irrational beliefs correlated *positively* with a participant's use of exit and neglect and *negatively* with use of voice. For example, if you believed that your partner could not change an aspect of his or her behavior, you would see no reason to express your concern over the issue. Metts and Cupach also found that exit and neglect correlated negatively with relational satisfaction, whereas voice correlated positively. Clearly, the use of the various methods for dealing with relational problems reflects as well as affects the nature of a relationship.

Consequences of Conflict Behaviors

The premises of attribution theory were presented in Chapter 6. In Chapter 10 we discussed the fact that attributions are related to the causes of relational breakups. Now we will discuss the consequences of conflict in terms of attributions and relational outcomes.

ATTRIBUTIONS

You may recall that people attribute the causes of events to external (situational) versus internal (dispositional) factors. So, for example, you might believe that the cause of a conflict is external (e.g., he is under a lot of stress right now; she didn't make the swimming team; his wife just left him), or you might attribute the cause for the conflict to be an internal factor (he is impatient and short-tempered; she is a witch). In general, negative (distributive) behaviors tend to be attributed to the internal properties of the other person, whereas positive (integrative) behaviors tend to be attributed to oneself (see Bradbury and Fincham 1990).

In a study of college roommates, Sillars (1980a) found that the use of both distributive and avoidance behaviors was positively related to believing that the other person (in this case a roommate) was the cause of the conflict, whereas integrative behaviors were positively associated with believing that oneself was the cause of the conflict. Of course, the irony is that when distributive behaviors are used, *both* partners see the other as the cause of a conflict. In the example at the beginning of the chapter, Jason saw Scott's attitude as the cause of the conflict, while Scott saw Jason's lack of cleanliness as the cause.

Other causal factors that affect how we perceive conflict are *stability* and *globality* (Bradbury and Fincham 1990). **Stability** refers to the consistency of a conflict over time, and **globality** refers to the number of issues that are in conflict. Research concerning these causal dimensions reveals that perceptions of stability and globality of a conflict's causes are positively related to negative behaviors. Sillars (1980a) also found that stability was positively associated with the use of avoidance tactics ("If he's a slob, why try to change him?").

Karen was the copyeditor of a small magazine. According to Karen, the editor, Mark had goals that conflicted with most of the staff—especially the women. Mark consistently made rude, sexual remarks to many of the women on staff. In addition, he would ask for their ideas about articles, but he would never use them. Because he was disorganized, the magazine copy would be rushed at the last possible minute to Karen, who would have to work all night to meet the deadline. Karen concluded that Mark's "professional and sexual immaturity" was the cause of all the magazine's problems. Karen also concluded that the magazine was a success due to her diligence and her editing skills. Mark attributed the success of the magazine to his creativity and hard work. He realized that he had a few conflicts with the staff, but problems with his staff were seen as part of the pressure to meet deadlines, and they were isolated issues that changed from staff member to staff member.

Fincham, Bradbury, and Scott's (1990) review of the literature reveals that compared to satisfied couples, dissatisfied couples perceive the causes of negative events as internal to the partner, stable, and global; but dissatisfied couples perceive the cause of *positive* events as external to the partner, unstable, and less global. In the story just presented, Karen attributed the causes of her conflict to Mark, and these attributions were internal, stable, and global. But Mark perceived the causes of conflict with his staff as external (deadlines) and isolated (varying from person to person).

Why do people tend to blame others for their negative encounters? There are several plausible explanations. Thomas and Pondy (1975) argue that people cannot know their partners' motives. In this light, we cannot see the external stressors that others are experiencing. Storms (1973) found that people are focused more on the partner than on themselves during interaction, and this external focus leads to over-attributing responsibility to the partner. That is, the cause for the partner's behavior is seen as internal, but the causes for our own behavior are seen as more external (a phenomenon also known as the actor-observer bias). A final reason we attribute the causes of negative conflicts to others is the "self-serving" bias—we do not want to believe that we are capable of negative actions, so we attribute the causes to others

("I don't mean to call you all those nasty names, but you force me to every time you get me so upset"). Again, the irony is that both parties to the conflict are making similar attributions (it's the other guy's fault).

RELATIONAL CONSEQUENCES

Besides affecting causal attributions, conflict messages affect fundamental relational features. One very important relational feature is satisfaction. The research findings reveal that in general, integrative tactics are positively associated with relational satisfaction, but distributive and avoidant tactics are negatively associated with relational satisfaction (e.g., Sillars 1980a). Researchers have also found that the use of integrative behaviors appears to be linked to increases in trust, commitment to the relationship, and cooperation (e.g., Canary and Cupach 1988; Canary and Spitzberg 1989; Sillars et al. 1983).

Gottman and Krokoff (1989) obtained an interesting result. These authors found that expressions of conflict, including showing anger, were negatively associated with relational satisfaction when conflict and satisfaction were measured at the same time. But reports of satisfaction taken three years later were positively associated with the previous confrontational conflicts and were negatively associated with whining and withdrawal (especially when the husband whines or withdraws). Gottman and Krokoff suggest that husbands should express their feelings openly and that wives should encourage such expressions and discourage avoidance to keep a relationship satisfactory in the long run.

There are two reasons why the expression of emotions during conflict is associated with later but not current relational satisfaction. First, family members, friends, and lovers learn from these conflicts what is important to each person. Second, over time these dyads reach consensus on important relational issues, such as showing consideration, trust, and household chores. According to Sillars and colleagues (1993), consensus on such issues probably leads to increased relational functioning.

It appears that conflict behaviors are first interpreted during the conflict episode, and these interpretations then affect the character of the relationship. More specifically, people determine how satisfied they are with the conversation and how competently their partners managed the conflict. These episode-specific judgments then affect the character of the relationships, as several studies have found (Canary and Cupach 1988; Canary and Spitzberg 1987, 1989, 1990; Cupach 1982).

That evaluations of the partner's conflict behavior affect relational outcomes has two implications. First, in most of these studies, appropriateness and effectiveness are used as criteria to judge the acceptability of the partner's conflict behavior (see also Chapter 14). It is not enough that the partner is appropriate; he or she should also be effective. Likewise, even though the partner may be effective, the person could still violate relational rules (perhaps through the use of distributive tactics) and thus be seen as inappropriate. Both appropriateness and effectiveness are criteria we use to judge others' conflict messages. Second, behaviors that comprise these competence criteria may change from relationship to relationship. What is appropriate and effective in one conflict may not be in another.

Chapter Summary

Conflict may lead to productive or destructive outcomes, depending on the communication behaviors we use. Individuals have conflict styles, or tendencies to respond to conflict. Each style has its advantages and disadvantages. In specific conflicts, however, communicators must decide how they want to deal with the conflicts at hand. Their decisions to confront or avoid and to cooperate or compete lead to their initiating particular strategies—integrative, distributive, and avoidance strategies. These strategies are reflected in specific conflict tactics and patterns of interaction. The literature suggests that people in functional relationships do not reciprocate negative, distributive tactics; they are moderately spontaneous; and they do not fix on a single issue or discuss many different issues in a given conflict.

The causes of negative conflicts are generally attributed to the partner, and dissatisfied couples see these conflicts as internal to the partner, stable, and global. In general, integrative tactics are associated positively with relational satisfaction, and distributive and avoidance tactics are associated negatively with relational satisfaction. In addition, people assess their partners' conflict behaviors according to standards of appropriateness and effectiveness, and these evaluations also affect the relationship. Although the relationship is affected by conflict messages and attributions about the conflict, the nature of the relationship (satisfying versus dissatisfying, high or low in trust, etc.) probably then leads to the choices of communication behavior in future conflicts.

KEY TERMS

conflict

intrapsychic conflict

competing style

accommodating style

collaborating style

withdrawing style

compromising style

continuity

symmetry

metacommunication

stationarity

spontaneity

exit

voice

avoidance strategy	loyalty
integrative strategy	neglect
distributive strategy	stability
variety	globality

EXERCISES FOR FURTHER DISCUSSION

1. Examine the advantages and disadvantages of the various conflict styles described in Table 12-1.
   a. Can you think of any advantages and disadvantages that you would add to this table?
   b. What style do you use most frequently in your personal relationships?
   c. What are the advantages and disadvantages of the style you use?
2. Working with another person in your class, role-play how you would respond to each of the messages presented in Table 12-2. Now switch roles and allow the other class member to respond to you. After completing the role playing, revise each of the messages to be less threatening; then repeat the role playing and see if you were effective.
3. Review the discussion of the strategies of avoidance, integrative, and distributive tactics.
   a. What are the advantages and disadvantages of each?
   b. Do you think that people decide to use these strategies during conflict, or do they just occur?
   c. If you were to choose one of these strategies as a way of handling all conflicts, which one would you choose? Try to justify your choice by providing examples of how it would be effective in a range of situations.
4. Note the various ways that conflict unfolds according to patterns of variety, continuity, symmetry, stationarity, and spontaneity.
   a. Does one of your relationships involve the use of any of these patterns?
   b. Do you think you can recognize such patterns of conflict as they unfold?
5. Using Rusbult's typology of exit-voice-loyalty-neglect, examine the communication behavior of a television character's way of handling relational troubles (a soap opera character would work well for this exercise).
   a. Do this character's behaviors fit within Rusbult's typology?
   b. Do the character's responses to relational problems seem realistic to you?
   c. In what ways do the character's behaviors differ from the ones used by you and the people you know? Why do you think you might use different behaviors?

6. Write a short paragraph describing a recent conflict you have been involved in.
    a. Were the causes of the conflict internal or external? Stable or unstable? Global or isolated?
    b. Do you think the other person would make similar attributions about the conflict?
    c. Does the way in which the conflict was resolved affect the way you make attributions about the conflict's causes? How?
7. Try to identify five rules that you have for managing conflict. These might not be rules that you have consciously articulated before but just ideas that govern your sense of fair play. Working with a group of class members, discuss the rules you came up with, and see if you can agree on five rules that all of you would use to govern conflict.

SUGGESTED READING

▼

CONFLICT THEORY

Cahn, D. 1992. *Conflict in intimate relationships.* New York: Guilford Press. Cahn reviews research findings and methods used from different theoretical perspectives. Cahn emphasizes marital conflict and mediation.

STRATEGIES AND TACTICS

Hocker, J. L., and Wilmot, W. W. 1991. *Interpersonal conflict,* 3d ed. Dubuque, Iowa: Brown. This text discusses fundamental aspects of conflict. Definitions, goals, power, strategies, and tactics are reviewed.

Sillars, A. L.; Wilmot, W. W.; and Hocker, J. L. 1993. Communication strategies in conflict and mediation. In *Communicating strategically: Strategies in interpersonal communication,* ed. J. Wiemann and J. Daly. Hillsdale, N.J.: Erlbaum. As the title indicates, various approaches for managing conflict are reviewed. An important section of this chapter examines various structural features of conflict patterns. The chapter also includes a major section on mediation.

ATTRIBUTIONS IN CONFLICT

Bradbury, T. N., and Finchman, F. D. 1990. Attributions in marriage: Review and critique. *Psychological Bulletin* 107:3–33. This article extensively reviews how people make attributions in marriage. Emphasis is placed on how people make different kinds of attributions about conflicts depending on whether they are in a satisfying or unsatisfying marriage.

Sillars, A. L. 1980a. Attributions and communication in roommate conflicts. *Communication Monographs* 47:180–200. An interesting study is conducted on how roommate attributions are linked to their communication behavior. Cooperative and competitive behaviors were found to differ according to the types of attributions made about the conflict.

REFERENCE LIST

▼

Benoit, P. J., and Benoit, W. E. 1990. To argue or not to argue. In *Perspectives on argumentation: Essays in honor of Wayne Brockriede*, ed. R. Trapp and J. Schuetz, 55–72. Prospect Heights, Ill.: Waveland Press.

Berryman-Fink, C., and Brunner, C. C. 1987. The effects of sex of source and target on interpersonal conflict management styles. *Southern Speech Communication Journal* 33:38–48.

Bradbury, T. N., and Fincham, F. D. 1990. Attributions in marriage: Review and critique. *Psychological Bulletin* 107:3–33.

Burggraf, C. S., and Sillars, A. L. 1987. A critical examination of sex differences in marriage. *Communication Monographs* 54:276–294.

Cahn, D. 1992. *Conflict in intimate relationships*. New York: Guilford Press.

Canary, D. J.; Cunningham, E. M.; and Cody, M. J. 1988. Goal types, gender, and locus of control in managing interpersonal conflicts. *Communication Research* 15:426–446.

Canary, D. J., and Cupach, W. R. 1988. Relational and episodic characteristics associated with conflict tactics. *Journal of Social and Personal Relationships* 5:305–322.

Canary, D. J., and Spitzberg, B. H. 1987. Appropriateness and effectiveness perceptions of conflict strategies. *Human Communication Research* 14:93–118.

———. 1989. A model of the perceived competence of conflict tactics. *Human Communication Research* 15:630–649.

———. 1990. Attribution biases and associations between conflict strategies and competence outcomes. *Communication Monographs* 57:139–151.

Cody, M. J.; McLaughlin, M. L.; and Schneider, M. J. 1981. The impact of intimacy and relational consequences on the selection of interpersonal persuasion strategies: A reanalysis. *Communication Quarterly* 29:91–106.

Cupach, W. R. 1982. *Communication satisfaction and interpersonal solidarity as outcomes of conflict message strategy use*. Paper presented at the International Communication Association conference, Boston.

Deutsch, M. 1973. *The resolution of conflict: Constructive and destructive processes*. New Haven, Conn.: Yale University Press.

Fincham, F. D.; Bradbury, T. N.; and Scott, C. K. 1990. Cognition in marriage: Retrospect and prospect. In *Cognition in marriage: Basic issues and applications*, ed. F. D. Fincham and T. N. Bradbury, 118–119. New York: Guilford Press.

Fitzpatrick, M. A., and Winke, J. 1979. You always hurt the one you love: Strategies and tactics in interpersonal conflict. *Communication Quarterly* 27:3–11.

Gottman, J. M. 1979. *Marital interaction: Experimental investigations.* Orlando, Fla.: Academic Press.

———. 1982. Emotional responsiveness in marital conversations. *Journal of Communication* 32:108–120.

Gottman, J. M., and Krokoff, L. J. 1989. Marital interaction and satisfaction: A longitudinal view. *Journal of Consulting and Clinical Psychology* 57:47–52.

Hocker, J. L., and Wilmot, W. W. 1985. *Interpersonal conflict*, 2d ed. Dubuque, Iowa: Brown.

———. 1991. *Interpersonal conflict*, 3d ed. Dubuque, Iowa: Brown.

Kilmann, R. H., and Thomas, K. W. 1977. Developing a forced-choice measure of conflict-handling behavior: The MODE instrument. *Educational and Psychological Measurement* 37:309–325.

Krueger, D. L., and Smith, R. 1982. Decision-making patterns of couples: A sequential analysis. *Journal of Communication* 32:121–134.

Margolin, G. 1990. Marital conflict. In *Methods of family research: Biographies of research projects, vol. 2: Clinical populations*, ed. G. H. Brody and I. E. Siegel, 191–225. Hillsdale, N.J.: Erlbaum.

Metts, S., and Cupach, W. R. 1990. The influence of relationship beliefs and problem-solving responses on satisfaction in romantic relationships. *Human Communication Research* 17: 170–185.

Putnam, L. L., and Poole, M. S. 1987. Conflict and negotiation. In *Handbook of organizational communication: An interdisciplinary perspective*, ed. F. M. Jablin, L. L. Putnam, K. H. Roberts, and L. W. Porter, 549–599. Newbury Park, Calif.: Sage.

Putnam, L. L., and Wilson, C. E. 1982. Communication strategies in organizational conflicts: Reliability and validity of a measurement scale. In *Communication yearbook 6*, ed. M. Burgoon, 629–652. Newbury Park, Calif.: Sage.

Rahim, M. A. 1986. *Managing conflict in organizations.* New York: Praeger.

Rusbult, C. E. 1987. Responses to dissatisfaction in close relationships: The exit-voice-loyalty-neglect model. In *Intimate relationships: Development, dynamics, and deterioration*, ed. D. Perlman and S. W. Duck, 209–237. Newbury Park, Calif.: Sage.

Rusbult, C. E.; Johnson, D. J.; and Morrow, G. D. 1986a. Impact of couple patterns of problem solving on distress and nondistress in dating relationships. *Journal of Social and Personal Relationships* 50:744–753.

———. 1986b. Predicting satisfaction and commitment in adult romantic involvements: An assessment of the generalizability of the investment model. *Social Psychological Quarterly* 49: 81–89.

Sillars, A. L. 1980a. Attributions and communication in roommate conflicts. *Communication Monographs* 47:180–200.

———. 1980b. The sequential and distributional structure of conflict interactions as a function of attributions concerning the locus of responsibility and stability of conflicts. In *Communication yearbook 4*, ed. D. Nimmo, 217–235. New Brunswick, N.J.: Transaction Books.

Sillars, A. L.; Coletti, S. F.; Parry, D.; and Rogers, M. A. 1982. Coding verbal conflict tactics: Nonverbal and perceptual correlates of the "avoidance-distributive-integrative" distinction. *Human Communication Research* 9:83–95.

Sillars, A. L.; Pike, G. R.; Jones, T. S.; and Redmon, K. 1983. Communication and conflict in marriage. In *Communication yearbook* 7, ed. R. N. Bostrom, 414–429. Newbury Park, Calif.: Sage.

Sillars, A. L., and Weisberg, J. 1987. Conflict as a social skill. In *Interpersonal processes: New directions in communication research*, ed. M. E. Roloff and G. R. Miller, 140–171. Newbury Park, Calif.: Sage.

Sillars, A. L.; Wilmot, W. W.; and Hocker, J. L. 1993. Communication strategies in conflict and mediation. In *Communicating strategically: Strategies in interpersonal communication*, ed. J. Wiemann and J. Daly. Hillsdale, N.J.: Erlbaum.

Storms, M. D. 1973. Videotape and the attribution process: Reversing actor's and observers' points of view. *Journal of Personality and Social Psychology* 27:165–175.

Thomas, K. W., and Pondy, L. R. 1977. Toward an "intent" model of conflict management among principal parties. *Human Relations* 30:1089–1103.

Ting-Toomey, S. 1983. An analysis of verbal communication patterns in high and low marital adjustment groups. *Human Communication Research* 9:306–319.

Wilmot, W. W. 1987. *Dyadic communication*, 3d ed. New York: Random House.

P A R T   V

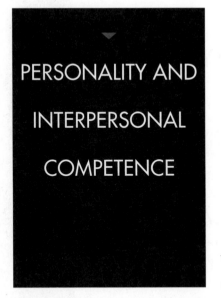

PERSONALITY AND INTERPERSONAL COMPETENCE

In our final section, we look at the important issue of interpersonal communication competence. Chapter 13, on personality and interpersonal communication, presents a model for understanding how personality affects communication behavior and then discusses seven general types of personality constructs that can be identified. Chapter 14, our final chapter, presents some of the criteria scholars use for assessing competence and includes a self-test, so that you can practice assessing your own level of interpersonal communication competence. The chapter concludes with a review of the book, looking at all of the issues—fundamentals, self-presentation, relational development, instrumental objectives, and personality—in terms of their implications for interpersonal communication competence.

C H A P T E R 1 3

PERSONALITY AND

INTERPERSONAL

COMMUNICATION

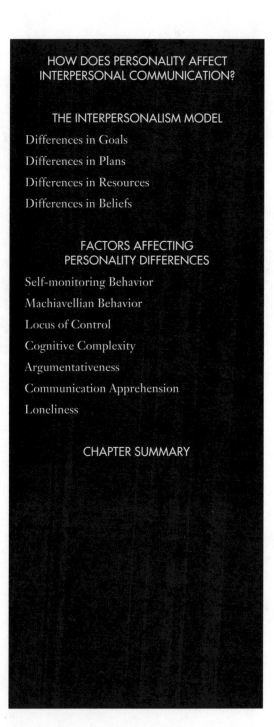

After a vigorous game of racquetball, Gordon Gekko and Bud Fox were in the locker room when Gekko shared some of his philosophy of life and business:

"I don't throw darts at a board. I bet on sure things. Read Sun Tzu, *The Art of War.* Every battle is won before it's ever fought. Think about it. [Pause.] You're not as smart as I thought you were, buddy-boy. Have you ever wondered why the fund managers can't beat the S and P 500? Because they're sheep, and sheep get slaughtered. I've been in this business since '69. Most of these Harvard MBAs—they don't amount to [beans]. Give me a guy who is poor, smart, and hungry—and no feelings! You win a few, you lose a few, but you keep on fighting. And if you need a friend, get a dog. It's trench warfare out there, pal."

Later, Gekko also parts with advice to the stockholders at Teldar:

"Greed, for lack of a better word, is good. Greed is right. Greed works. Greed clarifies and cuts through and captures the essence of the evolutionary spirit. Greed in all its forms—greed for life, for money, for love, for knowledge—has marked the upward surge for mankind, and greed—you mark my words—will save not only Teldar Paper but that other malfunctioning corporation called the USA."

Communicators differ greatly in their goals, plans, resources, and beliefs. For example, our scenario, adapted from the movie *Wall Street*, dramatizes how one type of person, Gekko, is driven by the need to compete and win, even if he has to lie, cheat, and violate laws to do so. We call this type of person a *Machiavellian*, a term synonymous with *manipulator*.

The movie illustrates how Gekko used communication to manipulate others so that he could achieve his goals. Gekko seduced the young Bud Fox to join the world of ethics-free affluence. Gekko rewarded Fox with riches and beautiful women, showed him the "good life" at the finest restaurants, and confided in him as if Bud Fox were a "good friend." However, Gekko also challenged and berated Bud Fox ("You're not as smart as I thought you were, buddy-boy"), manipulating Fox into wanting to do more and more to appease Gekko. Eventually, Bud Fox engaged in more frequent, and more blatant, unethical actions. Greed conquered. Communicators who place so much emphasis on being competitive and on winning use communication much differently than other types of communicators.

How Does Personality Affect Interpersonal Communication?

Anyone who wants to understand human behavior needs to appreciate the impact of individual differences in goals, plans, skills, and communication behaviors. Some people enter into relationships (and break them off) very easily and very quickly; others demonstrate considerable devotion to one person for a long period of time; still others are lonely and seem to have great difficulty making friends. Personality differences account for the radical differences in interpersonal relationships.

Personality is the totality of an individual's behavioral and emotional tendencies, the organization of the individual's distinguishing character traits, abilities, and habits. This definition has been criticized as vague and simplistic. For example, what precisely is a "trait"? And two communicators may display the same "habit" or "behavioral pattern" (being friendly to others), but for vastly different reasons. One person may be genuinely friendly out of a desire to give and win affection. The second person may act friendly primarily for the purpose of exploiting others. (Recall authentic and illicit ingratiation from Chapter 5.)

The Interpersonalism Model

Miller and Read (1987; Read and Miller 1989) argue that any personality construct should be viewed as involving four components: (1) goals, (2) the plans for attaining those goals, (3) the resources required for pursuing those goals, and (4) beliefs about the world that affect how plans are put in motion and executed. They call this the **interpersonalism model** of personality. Table 13-1 presents an example of the four components for one extreme of each of three individual difference variables: gender (women versus men), loneliness (high versus low), and self-monitoring (high versus low).

DIFFERENCES IN GOALS

Goals are the states or achievements to which we aspire. We overviewed goals in Chapter 1, noting that goals vary along a supraordinate, basic, and subordinate dimension. We are interested here in goals at the supraordinate level—the overarching goals that motivate people to act in many ways to pursue an important end state. When communicators possess different supraordinate goals, it follows that they will pursue different basic goals and, of course, enter into different types of specific situations. For example, a communicator socialized to emphasize friendliness should pursue goals by frequently acting in ways complementary to the friendliness motive: frequently sharing activities with others, giving assistance to others, giving advice and support to others, and eliciting support for others. Conversely, a

Table 13-1

A COMPARISON OF THREE PERSONALITY VARIABLES IN TERMS OF THE FOUR COMPONENTS OF THE INTERPERSONALISM MODEL

Component	Personality Variable		
	Gender: Female	*Loneliness: High*	*Self-monitoring: High*
Goals	• Wanting to make friends	• Wanting to make friends	• Wanting to make a good impression
	• Wanting a sense of community	• Wanting to be with people	• Wanting others to have a high opinion of self
	• Wanting egalitarian, high-quality interpersonal relationships	• Wanting to please and win affection	• Being able to get things out of others
	• Wanting to please and win affection		
Plans	• Doing things with groups	• Doing things with groups	• Focusing on others, imitating others
	• Showing interest in others	• Not taking risks	• Adapting to the situation at hand
	• Disclosing appropriately	• Focusing on self	• Showing interest in others
	• Treating others as equals	• Making inappropriate disclosures (nonreciprocal, too intimate or not intimate enough)	• Doing and saying what is appropriate to the situation
Resources	• Good social skills	• Lack of social skills	• Good social skills
	• Access to people—ability to seek out and be with people	• Lack of access to people	• Access to people
	• Skill at sending and receiving nonverbal messages	• Inaccuracy in receiving nonverbal messages	• Competence in sending and receiving nonverbal messages and monitoring the nonverbal behavior of others
Beliefs	• People are fun.	• People are fun—maybe.	• People are fun.
	• People are rewarding.	• People are rewarding—usually.	• People are rewarding.

(continued)

(continued from previous page)		
Beliefs	• Interpersonal relationships are worth the effort needed to keep them growing.	• People generally don't like me.	• People generally like me.
	• Most people can be trusted.	• I'm not sure I can trust others.	• People are easily impressed by public performances.

Source: Adapted from Miller and Read 1987. Used with permission of Plenum Publishing Corp.

person who was raised and socialized to be a winner, like Gekko, would spend little time on friendliness but a good deal of time planning how to achieve his own personal goals and grooming an image of competence, strength, and intimidation (recall Chapter 5).

In fact, the term *social participation* is used to denote the quality and quantity of activities that individuals actively construct for themselves (Reis et al. 1982; Smith et al. 1990; Wheeler and Nezlek 1977). Some individuals have a restricted level of social participation. They date less, seek out others less, and communicate less than others. Other individuals find it difficult to stay home; they seek out others, initiate relationships frequently and with apparent ease, and go on dates more often and with more people.

Women differ considerably from men in terms of the goals pursued (see Table 13-1). Women are more expressive, affiliative, cooperative, status-neutralizing, and communally oriented (see Deaux 1977; Deaux and Major 1987; Smith et al. 1990). Cody, Canary, and Smith (1993) studied the social participation of men and women and found that women more frequently pursued goals of sharing activities with others, gaining assistance from others, giving advice to others, engaging in volunteer work, proposing relational changes (planning relational escalations, devising tests of relational trust, and devising ways to initiate relationships), and protecting rights and enforcing obligations with others.

What do these differences in social participation mean? Nearly all of them can be explained in terms of the fact that women pursue more communal goals in which they engage in more status-neutralizing activities (also see Deaux 1977; Reis et al. 1982), whereas men pursue more competitive, individualistic goals in which they engage in more status-assertive activities. Communal goals are reflected by the fact that females give more advice to each other, share more activities with one another, are more preoccupied with the quality of their interpersonal relationships, and are more concerned with ensuring that people adhere to rights and obligations (friends and roommates should reciprocate favors and fulfill obligations in rent, cleaning, bills, and so on; people should treat one another fairly). The status-assertive versus status-neutralizing aspect of these relationships can be seen at any party: many men want to talk and mingle with women, especially beautiful ones, or talk to high-status and powerful people. Women, however, are more likely to circulate, mingle, and mix with *all* guests (thereby attempting to neutralize status differences).

DIFFERENCES IN PLANS

Plans (also discussed in Chapter 1) deal with the sequences of communicative actions a person will employ to attain a goal. To pursue the goal of quality relationships and communal goals, women are more likely to ask friends to do things together (shop, eat, spend time together visiting), whereas males typically have to have some focal activity when they get together with other males (watch a game, work on some task). Plans for pursuing relational goals also include showing interest in others, avoiding bragging, disclosing appropriately, and being open to others and equal.

DIFFERENCES IN RESOURCES

The implementation of any plan requires that the individual possess certain resources that make it possible to pursue the goal. There are three basic types of resources in the interpersonalism model: personal, situational, and relational. Personal resources include all the knowledge, physical characteristics, and communicative skills of the individual; possessions; power; and the ability to cope with anxiety, stress, or emotion. Clearly, some individuals possess greater knowledge, more insight into human nature, and greater understanding of how others will react; some may have special talents and abilities that might be used to pursue a goal; others are taller, more beautiful, or more expressive; and still others may have power, money, or status that make achieving goals easier.

Situational resources include access to people who may help in achieving goals (knowing others who have power, status, money, etc.), provide access to objects (e.g., having a computer and a high-quality printer that make it easier to print nice-looking résumés for a job search), or access to experiences (e.g., having a hospital nearby in which to do volunteer work in high school, paving the way for the offer of a paying job later). Relational resources include the emotional support stemming from being in a relationship and any other resources a couple can generate together.

Throughout this book we have commented on the fact that women and men possess different resources. Women communicate most emotions accurately, smile more, use higher levels of eye contact, adopt a more direct position to other speakers, display increased levels of involvement, and are more expressive (Chapter 4). Men use more space, are louder, are more likely to interrupt others, make more speech errors, and employ more "filled pauses." Women and men also have a different orientation toward self-disclosure (Chapter 7): women are more concerned with making sure that the person they disclose to is discreet, trustworthy, sincere, liked, respected, good at listening, warm, and open. They employ more detailed and more elaborate apologies when communicating accounts (Chapter 6).

DIFFERENCES IN BELIEFS

Finally, our beliefs about the world and about interpersonal relationships will affect whether we will devote our resources to a plan in the interest of achieving a goal. Beliefs such as "people are rewarding" or "people are fun" support the use of resources to pursue the goal of wanting to make friends. However, any two individuals may share the same goals (to make friends), the same resources and skills, and the same plans (knowledge of how to gain friends) yet communicate and behave in vastly different ways because of the beliefs they currently hold. For example, one person might believe that "people are rewarding, fun, and trustworthy," while another believes (possibly after a failed relationship) that "people can be rewarding, are often fun, and are trustworthy about half of the time." Obviously, the first person would seek out people, spend more time with them, disclose information, and so on far more than the second. The point is that all four components in the interpersonalism model are necessary in order to fully account for why people differ from one another.

We see from Table 13-1 that lonely individuals of both sexes share some of the same goals as women: wanting to make friends, wanting to be with people, wanting to please and win affection. However, the plans, skills, and beliefs are quite different. Lonely individuals do not like to take risks, they focus on themselves and not on others, and they fail to disclose appropriately. Unfortunately, lonely individuals lack many of the resources necessary to pursue their interpersonal goals—they lack access to skills and are unable to develop such skills because they lack access to people, and quality contact with people is necessary to build social skills and competence in nonverbal communication. Finally, because of their previous experiences, they only hold tentative beliefs about the rewards provided by people.

As a third example of the model, we have included the high-self-monitoring individual. This type of person subscribes to the beliefs that "people are fun" and "people are rewarding"; however, the supraordinate goals pursued by high self-monitors deal with making a good impression and wanting others to think highly of them. To pursue such goals, high self-monitors develop a number of personal resources that can be used to make a good impression: good social skills, access to people, and monitoring others' nonverbal behaviors. This type of person's plans to change include focusing attention on others, learning to imitate others, adapting to the situation at hand, showing interest in others, and doing and saying what is situationally appropriate. This type of communicator differs fundamentally from others in regards to a wide range of goals and skills.

We raised the question earlier of what we mean by a "personality construct" or an "individual difference variable." The answer is that any individual difference among communicators may reside in any one feature of goals, plans, resources, and beliefs. Any pair of individuals may be exactly the same in three of these but behave very differently with regard to the fourth. Of course, others may differ on most of the components—as in the case of the lonely individual and the high self-monitor. Now let's focus on the goals, plans, skills, and beliefs of seven types of communicators.

Factors Affecting Personality Differences

SELF-MONITORING BEHAVIOR
Table 13-2 presents items that are used in a self-monitoring questionnaire. Read each statement and state whether it is basically true or false with respect to you. The more often you answer yes, the more likely it is that you are a high self-monitor.

Self-monitoring is a personality construct that is intimately linked to a person's view of the self. High self-monitors pay close attention to their own behavior and to the behavior of others in a social situation, and they behave in ways that are appropriate for a given situation. When looking for information concerning how they should behave, high self-monitors look at others around them. They are social chameleons who routinely blend in with their current environment. Snyder (1987) refers to the high self-monitor as a person who presents a *pragmatic* conception of the self that defines his or her identity in terms of specific social situations and roles.

Table 13-2

SAMPLE ITEMS FROM A SELF-MONITORING SCALE

1. I would probably make a good actor.
2. I have considered being an entertainer.
3. I can look anyone in the eye and tell a lie with a straight face (if for the right end).
4. In different situations and with different people, I often act like very different people.
5. I can make impromptu speeches even on topics about which I have almost no information.
6. I guess I put on a show to impress or entertain others.
7. I'm not always the person I appear to be.
8. I may deceive people by being friendly when I really dislike them.

Source: Adapted from Snyder and Gangestad 1986. Copyrighted by the American Psychological Association Adapted by permission.

High self-monitors have acting ability, like being at the center of attention, and can deceive by acting friendly even with people they dislike.

Whereas the high self-monitor presents a pragmatic view of the self, the low self-monitor presents a view of the self that is *principled*, defining his or her identity in terms of personal characteristics and attributes. The self is a coherent identity of attributes, values, and attitudes that are held as enduring "for all time and for all places," unchanging as the communicator moves from situation to situation. A low self-monitor might say, "I am friendly, I am even-tempered, I am reliable," and so on, as if immutable. Low self-monitors have a rich and accessible knowledge of themselves, and they "choose words and deeds that accurately reflect their under-lying beliefs, attitudes, and dispositions" (Snyder 1987, 50).

Principled individuals are likely to maintain strong ethical standards, rejecting goals and situations in which they cannot "be themselves" and the use of tactics that they consider manipulative. In fact, Smith and colleagues (1990) found that low self-monitors, especially low-self-monitoring males, rejected the use of emotional ma-nipulations (putting on a happy face, pouting, sulking, etc.) and the use of pressure or force, relying instead on direct requests and logic.

Let us review the relevant features of self-monitoring (see Snyder 1987):

1. In social situations, high self-monitors focus efforts on reading and inter-preting what is occurring around them, to aid them in choosing their own self-presentations. High self-monitors are also likely to attend to information useful for making inferences and predictions about other people's intentions. Low self-monitors behave in ways compatible with their notion of their "true self" and accept people at face value.

2. High self-monitors are skilled "impression managers," displaying high levels of acting ability, flexibility, and adaptability. High self-monitors have groomed these skills over the years to provide presentations of the self that are appropriate for the situations in which they find themselves. However, high self-monitors may commu-nicate little about their private beliefs, feelings, or intentions. Low self-monitors present themselves in ways that reflect their true, authentic attitudes, values, and beliefs.

3. During conversations, high self-monitors are more highly motivated to work on ensuring that the conversation is smooth-flowing, prompting others to talk about themselves, conveying an immediate sense of closeness or intimacy, using humor, reciprocating self-disclosures, and employing other skills to keep the conversation going.

4. High and low self-monitors differ in social participation. High self-monitors typically select specific friends for particular activities, and usually only for those se-lected activities. So high self-monitors have certain friends they go to football games

with and different friends with whom they play golf, who are different from their tennis partners and the people with whom they go dancing. Further, these different friends may be separated by large geographic distances and may rarely (if ever) interact. In short, high self-monitors "segment" their social life. Low self-monitors share a wide range of activities with the same friend or group of friends. When asked to list whom they select for leisure activities and why, high self-monitors indicate that they prefer to play tennis with "good" tennis players and dance with "good" dancers. High self-monitors prefer to engage in activities with experts, thereby comparing their own abilities with experts and improving on these skills. Low self-monitors prefer to engage in activities with the people they like.

5. Although most high self-monitors have low self-monitors as casual friends, they prefer other high self-monitors as close friends; high self-monitors feel more comfortable with other people who understand and prefer the life of diversity. Low self-monitors prefer other low self-monitors as both casual and close friends. However, because friendships are intimately linked to specific activities, it is far easier (and more likely) for high self-monitors to replace friends to play tennis with, dance with, and so on. As high self-monitors' skills improve, they "trade up" to better experts in tennis, dancing, and so forth.

6. Low and high self-monitors differ radically in the quality of their friendships. Low self-monitors view friendship "in terms of an *affect-based* orientation, a definite sense of depth of friendship, considerable conception of compatibility and endurance beyond the present context, and much evidence of a conception of nurturance and sympathy within friendship" (Snyder 1987, 68). High self-monitors view friendship as an *activity-based* orientation, with a "somewhat shallow sense of friendship, little conception of compatibility beyond [the here and how], and little conception of nurturance" (p. 68).

7. When selecting dates, high-self-monitoring males spend more time studying a potential date's physical characteristics; in fact, when given the choice, the high-self-monitoring male would select a date with a beautiful woman even after she was described as "moody, withdrawn, and self-centered." Low-self-monitoring men focused more on the potential date's psychological characteristics. High self-monitors date exclusively for briefer periods of time (relative to low self-monitors), date more different people in a year, have sex with more people in a year, and have more one-night stands than low self-monitors (especially low self-monitoring females) do. The relatively low level of commitment on the part of high-self-monitoring individuals means that it is easier for them to de-escalate or terminate one relationship while starting new ones at their leisure. Low self-monitors adopt a committed orientation in dating relationships. They prefer to spend time with their current dating partner, are more likely to date others exclusively and for longer periods of time, and date fewer people over the years.

MACHIAVELLIAN BEHAVIOR

Niccolò Machiavelli in 1513 wrote *The Prince*, which detailed how to achieve and retain power through deception, exploitation, and cruelty. Christie and Geis (1970) developed a test of **Machiavellianism** that measures a person's general tendency to be manipulative. However, over the years, people have raised questions about the accuracy of such a test. Hunter, Gerbing, and Boster (1982) argue that the tendency to be manipulative is not measured with a single set of questions. Rather, at least four different beliefs are involved in a Machiavellian orientation. Further, at the core of this personality type is the very high need to compete. In fact, manipulative characters are more likely to come from families in which there has been intense sibling rivalry between brothers and sisters, causing intense feelings of "beating out" the rival.

Table 13-3 presents items that measure four aspects of the Machiavellian orientation: attitude toward deceit, attitude toward flattery, beliefs concerning immorality, and cynicism. A Machiavellian is highly cynical, has a positive attitude toward deceit and flattery, and believes that people are basically immoral. Machiavellians

---

Table 13-3
SAMPLE ITEMS FROM A MACHIAVELLIANISM SCALE

Topic	Sample Items
Deceit	• There is no excuse for lying to someone else. • Honesty is the best policy in all cases.
Flattery	• It is wise to flatter important people. • The best way to handle people is to tell them what they want to hear.
Immorality	• Most people who get ahead in the world lead clean, moral lives. • Most people are basically good and kind.
Cynicism	• Anyone who trusts anyone else completely is asking for trouble. • It is safest to assume that all people have a vicious streak that will come out if given the chance.

Source: Adapted from Hunter et al. 1982. Copyright by the American Psychological Association. Adapted by permission.

(called "high Machs") are more interested in pursuing (and achieving) their own personal goals, whereas low Machs focus on both personal and relational goals. High Machs prefer to win, sometimes at any cost; low Machs place more emphasis on maintaining interpersonal relations, perhaps giving less importance to winning if doing so embarrasses a friend or lessens a friendship.

Here is a brief outline of relevant research findings (see Steinfatt 1987):

1. High Machs place emphasis on winning over the maintenance of interpersonal relations.

2. High Machs manipulate others and change manipulative tactics quickly as a situation unfolds. For example, high Machs can switch easily during games and during bargaining contexts so fast and so easily that they sometimes adamantly advocate a position that they had rejected only a few minutes earlier. Also, emotions are easily manipulated as well—a high Mach may be friendly one minute, make you feel guilty the next minute, and then use a threat to get you to do something.

3. During encounters, low Machs focus on how people in the situation differ from each other, whereas high Machs focus on how people in the situation differ from themselves, looking for weaknesses to exploit.

4. High Machs are more resistant to social influence than low Machs; high Machs are less likely to change their beliefs just to please someone else or due to social pressures.

5. High Machs are effective in bargaining because they look for ways to bargain effectively as the session progresses, show great flexibility in their behaviors, use emotional appeals, and enjoy the experience of bargaining.

6. High Machs are more effective when the situation is unstructured (no time constraint, no limits placed on behaviors or roles, etc.), communication is face to face, and interpersonal manipulation is allowed; if high Machs had to send messages and memos through a formalized chain of command, they would be no more effective than low Machs.

7. High Machs tend to have fewer close friends than low Machs; further, high Machs tend to prefer friends who are substantially lower than themselves in Machiavellian beliefs—possibly because low-Mach friends may be more easily influenced and may be naive and fail to understand the full range of a high Mach's manipulative behavior. However, even though high Machs may not have other high Machs as friends, they have a good deal of respect for other high Machs (who are other "winners").

8. When money and rewards are at stake, high Machs are more likely to lie, and may lie more effectively, than their low-Mach counterparts (Geis and Moon 1981). One study had students first identify people they liked, didn't like, or were ambivalent about and then describe these people honestly or dishonestly ("Describe a person you like as if you liked him or her," "Describe a person you dislike as if you liked him or her"). This study revealed that Machiavellians engaged in "hamming" (using more expressive facial and hand movements when lying than when telling the truth), and their deception was more difficult to detect accurately (De Paulo and Rosenthal 1979). However, when motivation is low (no money or rewards are at stake), high and low Machiavellians do not differ in their nonverbal behaviors (O'Hair, Cody, and McLaughlin 1981).

LOCUS OF CONTROL

The concept of **locus of control** stems from work initiated by Rotter (1966), who argued that behavior is a function of expected reinforcement, the value of that reinforcement, and the situation, as defined by the person (Steinfatt 1987). As people mature, they learn that they receive **reinforcements** for behaviors. If people behave in a certain way, receive reinforcement, and believe that their behavior *caused* the reinforcement, they have developed an internal locus-of-control orientation. People who have developed an internal orientation believe that their achievements will be rewarded, that they can have an impact on the world and help shape their own destinies. Internals believe that control of their behaviors stems from their own motivations, abilities, and achievements and that their behaviors are the cause of the reinforcements. By contrast, people who have developed an external locus-of-control orientation have little hope of controlling outcomes, feel that effort is not necessarily rewarded (one has to be in the right place at the right time to get rewards), and believe that their behavior is not motivated internally but rather that they are responding to external pressures.

Table 13-4 presents some of the items that are used to measure the locus-of-control orientation for an important domain in interpersonal communication, affiliation. If you have an internal locus of control, you would strongly agree with the items listed for ability and effort (internality = ability + effort; recall our discussion of ability and effort in Chapter 5). Internals believe that they earn rewards because they have the ability to earn them and made the effort to do so. Externality, however, is derived from the belief that rewards are obtained either because of luck or something else external to the individual (externality = context + luck).

Research indicates that locus of control has a very strong impact on goals, plans, skills, and beliefs (Canary, Cody, and Marston 1986; Canary, Cunningham, and Cody 1988; Lefcourt 1982; Lefcourt et al. 1979, 1985; Steinfatt 1987).

Table 13-4
SAMPLE ITEMS FROM A LOCUS-OF-CONTROL SCALE FOR AFFILIATION

Component	Sample Items
Ability	• It seems to me that getting along with people is a skill. • Having good friends is simply a matter of one's social skill. • I feel that people who are often lonely are lacking in social competence.
Effort	• Maintaining friendships requires real effort to make them work. • In my case, success at making friends depends on how hard I work at it. • If I didn't get along with others, it would tell me that I hadn't put much effort into the pursuit of social goals.
Context	• My enjoyment of a social occasion is almost entirely dependent on the personalities of the other people who are there. • Some people can make me have a good time even when I don't feel sociable. • No matter what I do, some people just don't like me.
Luck	• Making friends is a funny business; sometimes I have to chalk up my successes to luck. • In my experience, making friends is largely a matter of having the right breaks. • Often chance events can play a large part in causing rifts between friends.

Source: Adapted from Lefcourt et al. 1979. Used with permission of the authors.

1. Compared to externals, internal locus-of-control communicators are more willing to enter into a wider range of influence goals, rated goals as easier to imagine, claimed greater confidence, and indicated that they would be more persistent when attempting to influence others.

2. Internals are more resistant to influence and pressure than externals.

3. Internals employ personal powers of persuasion when attempting to influence others. Internals employ rationality (reasons, evidence), dyad-oriented tactics, and the manipulation of positive (but not negative) emotions when persuading others (Canary et al. 1986). In an organizational simulation, Goodstadt and Hjelle (1973) found that internals used more personal powers of persuasion, meaning that they worked with the employee on improving performance, set goals and schedules, and praised the employee to encourage performance. Externals employed more threats to convince others to work. What explains this? Internals and externals employ tactics that are compatible with their own view of why people are rewarded. Externals believe that behaviors, and rewards for those behaviors, are caused externally by the context or by luck. To prompt workers to work more, externals try to apply external pressure on them (threats). Internals believe that the individuals' own behaviors cause the rewards to be given; the philosophy is to communicate to workers that hard work will be noticed and rewarded. Hence externals apply external pressure on workers, whereas internals use a set of tactics designed to create a reward system (Goodstadt and Hjelle 1973).

COGNITIVE COMPLEXITY

Communicators differ substantially in the extent to which they have developed detailed ways of viewing and describing objects and people around them. This is known as **cognitive complexity.** Eskimos have many ways to describe snow, and Americans have many ways to describe automobiles. People also differ in the ability for characterizing people and for differentiating among different types of people. When asked to write out descriptions of one's friends, some can provide very detailed, thorough, and complex descriptions, noting friends' habits, beliefs, mannerisms, ways of treating others, traits, and personality characteristics. People who provide such detailed descriptions are considered to be cognitively complex because they have developed, and use, a "relatively differentiated, abstract, and organized system of interpersonal constructs" (Burleson 1987, 308). Some other people can provide only minimal descriptions of a person's characteristics ("He is big, tall. He runs fast. He's a good dancer").

Descriptions people make of others vary along three criteria: the number of constructs or terms used to describe people (called "interpersonal construct differentiation"), the abstractness of these constructs (concrete, physical, descriptions are low in abstractness; describing values and ethical principles would be highly abstract), and the degree of organization of the constructs (merely listing features reflects a low level of organization). Most research in the area of cognitive complexity has relied on construct differentiation (Applegate 1982; Burleson 1984, 1987; Sypher and Applegate 1984).

People with well-defined systems for characterizing others display a number of social perception skills (Burleson 1987): (1) the ability to infer multiple causes for and consequences of the actions of others; (2) the ability to recognize and understand other people's emotional states; (3) the ability to reconcile and integrate potentially inconsistent information about others; (4) the ability to avoid making simplistic, global evaluations of others; and (5) the ability to convey and understand the cognitive, emotional, and motivational aspects of other people's perspectives.

Because of their cognitive development and skills, cognitively complex people are more likely to employ "person-centered" messages when communicating with others. In person-centered speech, the communicator is able to construct and communicate a message that takes into consideration the perspective of the target; the target's values, beliefs, and emotional needs are incorporated into the communicator's message, thus making the communicator more effective at persuasion, in conflict episodes, and when comforting others.

Table 13-5 presents an example of what we mean by different levels of perspective taking (Delia, Kline, and Burleson 1979). There are nine levels that span from inability or lack of taking the receiver's perspective (levels 0, 1, and 3) to full accommodation of the receiver's perspective (levels 6, 7, and 8; also see Chapter 8 for a discussion of comforting messages). Cognitively complex communicators employ higher levels of other-perspective-taking, person-centered messages and comforting messages when pursuing their relational and instrumental goals. This personality variable has been shown, in research with children, parents, and college students, to be important in achieving goals and in maintaining interpersonal relationships.

ARGUMENTATIVENESS

Infante (1987; Infante, Chandler, and Rudd 1989; Infante and Rancer 1982; Infante et al. 1984; Infante and Wigley 1986) proposes that people vary in the degree to which they are argumentative. **Argumentativeness** is seen as the motivation to defend one's own view and attack the position of others. It also reflects a lack of motivation to avoid arguments. Accordingly, Infante and Rancer (1982) offer a measure of argumentativeness that is composed of two factors, approaching arguments and avoiding arguments. Table 13-6 (see p. 362) presents examples.

Argumentativeness indicates who likes to confront others' ideas. For example, Rancer and Infante (1985) found that for highly argumentative people, motivation to argue was increased when the conversational partner was also thought to be highly argumentative. But those who were low in argumentativeness were not motivated to argue regardless of the conversational partner's score. Thus argumentative people enjoy debating other argumentative people. Theoretically, engaging in debate is enjoyed most by highly argumentative couples.

It is important to distinguish argumentativeness from verbal aggressiveness. **Verbal aggressiveness** refers to the tendency to attack the self-concept of the part-

---

Table 13-5

LEVELS OF PERSPECTIVE TAKING

I. No Discernible Recognition of and Adaptation to the Target Perspective

   0. No statement of desire or request; no response given.

   1. Unelaborated request

      a. "Mommy, can I have someone over to sleep on my bed?" "Could I have a party please?"

      b. "Could you please take care of this puppy?" "Could you keep this dog?"

   2. Unelaborated statement of personal desire or need. This level also includes pleas, begging, or a repeated statement of the request or personal need.

      a. Simple statement of desire: "I want a party. Can I have one?" "I would enjoy a party."

      b. Please: "Please, pretty please and sugar on top?" "I'd tell her. Please, Mommy, it really means a lot. Please." "Oh, please don't say no."

II. Implicit Recognition of and Adaptation to the Target's Perspective

   3. Elaboration of the necessity, desirability, or usefulness of the persuasive request.

      a. Elaboration of persuader's need: "I've never had this before or anything so why don't you let me really have a party cause I've been wanting to do this for a long time." "Well, I'm going away pretty soon and I think it's really important to me to have a slumber party because I won't be here that much longer."

      b. Elaboration of need from the perspective of an involved party other than the persuader or target: "Would you keep this dog safe so he won't run out in the street and would you keep it in your house so it won't be scared and fight with the other dogs?" "My friends like me a lot. They would like to have a party and want you to let them come over. They'll be really disappointed if they can't cause they've been wanting to come over for a long time." "This dog is really skinny and he doesn't have any place to go."

   4. Elaboration of persuader's or persuasive object's need plus minimal dealing with anticipated counterarguments.

      a. Request refutes anticipated counterargument. "This is a lost puppy. Could you maybe keep it for a day or two, cause I can't keep it at my house?" "Will you please keep this dog for me cause my Mom won't let me keep it."

     b. Request is limited or altered to become more acceptable: "This poor puppy, he's been lost and he's hungry. Will you keep this dog while I try to find its owner?" "Mom, could I have a slumber party for my birthday and *just* invite about five girls?"

     c. Appealing to general principles: "I think that you should give me more responsibility by letting me have the party." "It's part of humanity you know. You have to take something."

5. Elaborated acknowledgment of and dealing with multiple anticipated counterarguments.

     a. Refuting anticipated counterarguments: "Hi, I just found this puppy on the street and he didn't have a collar. If I took it home I know my father and mother wouldn't let me keep him because we already have a big dog. My father would have to get it shots, and we really don't have any place to keep him. Our dog would probably hurt the puppy. So could you keep him?"

     b. Alleviating effects of anticipated counterarguments: "It's big enough to stay outside and you only have to feed him and water him and that doesn't take all day." "And I'd make sure everything's cleaned up and I'd pay for all the food. And there wouldn't be any beer." "Mother, can I have six kids over? We'll make up our sleeping bags and we'll fix our own popcorn." "There wouldn't be a lot of running around and there would only be about five people. I'd tell her what kind of entertainment we were going to have to show that we'd stay out of trouble."

III. Explicit Recognition of and Adaptation to the Target's Perspective

  6. Truncated efforts to demonstrate relevant consequences to the target of accepting (or rejecting) the persuasive request.

     a. General advantage to anyone granting this request: "You know, a dog's a good playmate for kids." "It would be good for you to have a dog around as protection or a friend."

     b. Bribes: "If you let me have a party, I'll make something that my father likes to eat." "If you keep the puppy I'll wash your car every day."

  7. Elaboration of specific consequences of accepting (or rejecting) the persuasive request to one with characteristics of the target.

     a. "You look kind of lonely. This dog would be a good companion, somebody to talk to and everything." "You need a watchdog around here because like there have been some break-ins around here. This dog might be able to help you."

     b. "You've been saying you wanted to get to know my friends better. If you let me have a party, you can get to know them."

(continued)

(continued from previous page)

8. Demonstrable attempts by the persuader to take the target's perspective in articulating an advantage or attempts to lead the target to assume the perspective of the persuader, another person, or the persuasive object.

   a. Demonstrable attempts to take the target's perspective in articulating an advantage: "If I were you and I lived alone, I'd like a good watch-dog like this one."

   b. Leading the target to take the perspective of an involved party: "I'd tell her how he might have an owner and if she was in the same situation, if she had lost her puppy, she would want somebody to take care of it for her." "If you were out in the cold and everything, wouldn't you want somebody to come and pick you up and give you a home. That's what this puppy wants."

Source: From Delia, Kline, and Burleson 1979, fig. 1. Copyrighted by the Speech Communication Association. Reprinted by permission of the publisher.

ner verbally with the intention of causing hurt (Infante and Wigley 1986). Argumentativeness and verbal aggression are different in the *locus of attack*. That is, an argumentative person attacks the partner's ideas, but a verbally aggressive person attacks the partner. Infante and colleagues (1990) identified ten types of verbally aggressive behavior: character attacks (saying unfavorable things about the partner's

Table 13-6
SAMPLE ITEMS FROM AN ARGUMENTATIVENESS SCALE

1. Arguing over controversial issues improves my intelligence.
2. I enjoy avoiding arguments.
3. I am energetic and enthusiastic when I argue.
4. Once I finish an argument, I promise that I will not get into another.
5. I have a pleasant, good feeling when I win a point in an argument.
6. When I've finished arguing with someone, I feel nervous and upset.
7. I enjoy a good argument over a controversial issue.
8. I enjoy defending my point of view on an issue.
9. I feel refreshed to do well in an argument.
10. I have the ability to do well in an argument.

Source: Adapted from Infante and Rancer 1982. Used with permission of the authors.

It is important to distinguish between argumentativeness and verbal aggressiveness. An argumentative person attacks another person's ideas, whereas a verbally aggressive person attacks the other person.

(Ulrike Welsch/Photo Researchers)

character), competence attacks (attacking the person's ability to be a good partner), background attacks (attacking the person's upbringing), criticism of physical appearance, maledictions (wishing evil for a person), teasing, ridicule, threats, swearing, and nonverbal emblems (using facial expressions, gestures, and eye behaviors to attack another).

Studies indicate that argumentativeness is either unrelated to verbal aggressiveness or that being argumentative can actually decrease the tendency to be aggressive. Infante and Wigley (1986) found that argumentativeness was unrelated to verbal aggressiveness. Similarly Infante and co-workers (1984) found that highly argumentative people were unlikely to revert to aggressive communication when confronted with a stubborn roommate. Infante, Chandler, and Rudd (1989), in fact, found support for a "skill deficiency model" of interpersonal violence. This means that interpersonal violence is partly due to an *inability* to present one's ideas. These researchers found that violent marriages were characterized by lower self-reported argumentativeness and higher reports of spousal verbal aggressiveness. Argumentativeness appears to be related to constructive outcomes, and aggressiveness is linked to negative outcomes (such as abuse).

Why do people engage in aggressive communicative behaviors? According to Infante and associates (1992), the reasons can be that they use aggressive behavior to reciprocate hurt or disdain for the partner or to vent anger; that they resort to aggression when they are unable to think of an effective argument or when a rational conversation degenerates into a fight; that they are taught to handle conflict with aggression; that something in the present situation triggers an aggressive reaction to a previous unresolved hurt; that they are imitating action seen on TV; that they want to appear tough; or that they want to be mean to the partner. These authors found that four of these motivations distinguished the most aggressive persons from the least aggressive ones: wanting to appear tough, degenerating from rationality to aggression, wanting to be mean, and disdain for the partner.

COMMUNICATION APPREHENSION

Many individuals suffer from high levels of anxiety over how they might be evaluated in a given situation or how they might behave. This is referred to as **communication apprehension.** There are substantial differences between anxious and nonanxious individuals in both social relations and in communicative behaviors (see Daly and Stafford 1984; McCroskey 1982).

1. Anxious individuals date less often and possess fewer social skills than nonanxious individuals. Anxious individuals also rate themselves lower in physical attractiveness. Anxious individuals are more likely to date one person exclusively for a relatively long time and are not likely to accept blind dates. Anxious individuals also have fewer friends, are shy and conformist, and are less likely to accept a position of leadership in a group. Anxious individuals are not as capable as nonanxious ones to construct strategies or plans for how to make friends.

2. Anxious individuals are much more likely to display their anxiety via nonverbal behaviors: greater body tension, greater disinterest, less eye contact, more fidgeting, less nodding, more leaning away from others, less facial pleasantness, and greater space needs.

3. Anxious individuals differ from nonanxious ones considerably in a number of variables relevant to maintaining conversations and controlling interactions. Anxious individuals speak less frequently and speak for briefer durations than nonanxious communicators. They are less likely to interrupt others effectively and are relatively ineffective in initiating or controlling a conversation. Anxious communicators are more likely to speak with disfluencies and make speech errors and to exhibit more nervous smiling, more frequent silences, more verbal repetitions, and longer latencies when speaking. Anxious individuals recall fewer previous interactions and make more mistakes in what they recall than nonanxious speakers.

Very high levels of anxiety or apprehension are detrimental to the communicator's personal life, limiting the ability to achieve a number of instrumental goals. Some campuses or schools have developed programs for anxiety *desensitization* that enable students to cope more effectively with high levels of anxiety that interfere with daily life. At a minimum, communicators who suffer from high levels of communication apprehension should concentrate on developing the social skills necessary to meet people, make friends, and achieve interpersonal goals.

LONELINESS

Loneliness refers to the pain experienced due to the discrepancy between desired and actual social contacts (Bell 1985; Spitzberg and Canary 1985; Zakahi and Duran 1985). Loneliness is very common, especially among students. It is related to a lack of social skills and is negatively related to goal achievement.

For example, Bell and Roloff (1991) found that loneliness was negatively correlated with choosing situations where a person might find potential partners. They also found that it was negatively associated with disclosures about one's personality and about one's activities and interests—lonely individuals do not disclose or reveal information that is highly personal, preferring revelations of a nonintimate nature, such as demographics (age, place of birth, etc.). Hawken, Duran, and Kelly (1991) found that lonely individuals failed to develop rapport with their roommates, failed to maintain composure in social settings, made self-disclosures that were judged as inappropriate, and experienced a limited range of social contacts (they had fewer kinds of friends and acquaintances). Similarly, Solano, Batten, and Parrish (1982) found that lonely people disclosed less intimate topics to a member of the opposite sex than nonlonely people did.

Margulis, Derlega, and Winstead (1984) suggested four conditions that underly the experience of loneliness (though others are also important): (1) the unavailability of a person or group of people to help the individual achieve valued goals; (2) the belief that this unavailability will continue for some time; (3) the unavailability of a companion, friend, or acquaintance at times when it is extremely important or when publicly expected to have one (holidays, weddings, formal dinners, etc.); and (4) a steady desire, unsatisfied over an extended period of time, to have such a social partner.

It is important to realize that there are two kinds of loneliness, *situational* and *chronic*. Situational loneliness is the temporary loneliness that people experience now and then. Chronic loneliness tends to be severe and lasts months and perhaps even years. Chronic loneliness, much more than situational loneliness, has been associated with dysfunctional social behaviors. For example, Spitzberg and Canary (1985) found that chronically lonely people are seen as less communicatively competent than situationally lonely and nonlonely people.

Why do some people become chronically lonely while others experience only transient situational loneliness? Spitzberg and Canary (1985) feel that chronic loneliness is explainable in terms of attribution theory (recall Chapters 6 and 10):

> Persons who attribute loneliness to unstable, external, and controllable causes are more likely to take steps to remedy their loneliness than those who attribute loneliness to stable, internal, and uncontrollable causes. Furthermore, chronically lonely people are much more likely than situationally lonely people to attribute their loneliness to stable, uncontrollable causes. (p. 389)

Imagine that you move to a new city because of a change in job or a transfer to a new university. This may well involve losing touch with valued friends and family and even a breakup with a romantic partner. You feel the loss of these relationships, but you attribute that feeling to factors that are external, unstable, and controllable. That is, the move, not your specific actions, caused the loss of friendships; this type of change is unusual, rather than a stable, recurring process; and you believe that your ability to meet and gain new friends is something that you can control. Given this scenario, you probably experience situational loneliness and will probably make new friends in time. Chronically lonely people, by contrast, see their loneliness as

Both communication apprehension and loneliness reflect a limited social environment. To be emotionally healthy, people in such circumstances must work at developing skills that will let them communicate and connect with others.

(Joel Gordon)

HOW HIGHLY APPREHENSIVE WORRIERS DIFFER
FROM "NORMAL" NONWORRIERS

Our text says a good deal about highly apprehensive individuals and lonely individuals. As the following newspaper article suggests, people who are chronic worriers are also probably highly apprehensive and probably more lonely than nonworriers. Chronic worriers apparently think much differently from nonworriers.

How to help the chronic worrier? Besides seeking counseling, the article recommends two ways. First, it is unproductive to worry all the time, so one recommendation is to set aside a certain time to worry. The second recommendation involves interpersonal communication—being assisted by friends who communicate social support and who help the worrier understand what is and isn't worth worrying about.

We all know them: the walking worried. The worry warts of the world. The woe-is-me, hand-wringing . . . well, you get the idea.

Generally, chronic worriers have been considered somewhat annoying people who could stop worrying if they wanted but who instead get a perverse pleasure from it.

That view may be unsympathetic. In recent years, chronic worriers have attracted greater interest among psychologists, who now believe that extreme worrying is an addictive thought pattern that can lead to serious mental and physical consequences. But they also say it is something that can be successfully "treated" with hard work.

"In therapy it has always been considered as not very serious and that there was not much you could do about it," says Dr. Gary Emery, a worry expert and director of the Los Angeles Center for Cognitive Therapy. "Surprisingly, for how prevalent it is and how much suffering it causes, it hasn't been studied much."

Experts' efforts over the last decade have been devoted to defining chronic or obsessive worrying. After all, everyone worries. But what is the difference between worrying a little and worrying a lot?

A chronic worrier, Emery says, is "someone who has a morbid preoccupation with what can go wrong. Chronic worrying is unrealistic in the sense that it's unhelpful and it's counterproductive. It's realistic in the sense that what you're worried about could actually happen. It's not paranoia like, "The CIA is after me." . . .

In a recent study, [Michael Vasey at Ohio State University] looked at 48 college students, half of whom were found to be chronic worriers. When asked what worried them, both groups gave similar responses: academic success, relationships and health.

(continued)

(continued from previous page)

The students were then asked, "What is it about getting good grades that worries you?" And this is where the difference stood out. Worriers produced much longer lists of possible consequences.

For example, chronic worriers saw a stronger likelihood that not getting good grades would eventually result in pain, physical deterioration and death. To a non-worrier, the result might be unhappiness and strain, but nothing beyond that. . . .

[Vasey] was stunned to see how large a role worrying seemed to play in some people's lives. The worriers in his group said they spent at least half of their waking hours worrying. In contrast, the others said they worry less than 10% of each day. . . .

But worriers can learn to break the habit, experts point out. . . .

"The problem is that people worry any place and every place, but . . . never get past that initial stage of thinking about what may go wrong," Vasey says. "But if you devote enough time to it [in one sitting], then maybe you can begin to come up with solutions." . . .

The key to giving up the worry habit is realizing that worrying doesn't help, Emery says.

"It comes from the insight that it's a waste of time. . . . It doesn't solve things. It's a substitute for action. When people realize this, they can let go of it." . . .

Some people find it helps to ask themselves, "What is the worst thing that can happen?" he says—and to realize that almost none of those "worst things" happen.

According to Vasey, people who cope well with worries often do so because they ask other people, "Do you think I should be worried about this?"

"When someone says, 'I think you're overreacting,' most people can use this information to stop worrying," he says. "But serious worriers are probably going to need more help than that."

From Shari Roan, "Oh, No! *Now* What Could Go Wrong?" Copyright 1993, *Los Angeles Times*. Reprinted by permission.

something that will not end, due in part to their character, previous experiences, and lack of social skills.

Over time, as the experience of loneliness progresses, the chronically lonely's social skills worsen, even "atrophy," and the lonely person may give up on interpersonal goals. In particular, lonely people become less involved in various social circles and display less involved behavior. Bell (1985), for example, reported that lonely people communicated less involvement in conversations, paying less attention to what was said, recalling less of the conversation, and talking less than nonlonely people.

The most popular measure of loneliness is the Revised UCLA Loneliness Scale (Russell, Peplau, and Cutrona 1980). Table 13-7 presents sample items from this

Table 13-7

SAMPLE ITEMS FROM THE REVISED
UCLA LONELINESS SCALE

1. I lack companionship.
2. There is no one I can turn to.
3. I am no longer close to anyone.
4. My interests and ideas are not shared by the people around me.
5. I feel left out.
6. My social relationships are superficial.
7. No one really knows me well.
8. I feel isolated from others.
9. I am unhappy being so withdrawn.
10. People are around me but not with me.

Source: Adapted from Russell et al. 1980. Used with permission of the author.

measure. As you examine these items, you may also want to determine if they apply to you over the past two weeks. If so, it would indicate situational loneliness. If the items apply to you over the past two years, this would indicate chronic loneliness. Regardless, you should understand that the remedy for loneliness is communicating with others. Not to communicate perpetuates loneliness.

Chapter Summary

In this chapter, we first discussed the fact that women are more expressive, communal, status-neutralizing, and affiliative than men. We saw evidence that self-monitoring individuals varied fundamentally in the presentation of self in everyday life. High self-monitors adapt to groom public images so that they fit in appropriately to the situation, and they seek out new people to date and experts in various areas of play, leisure, and work.

Machiavellians are well equipped to manipulate others and occasionally lie and manipulate emotions so as to compete better and win. Internal locus-of-control individuals have higher confidence in influencing others than externals, and internals employ more tactics, including rationality and persistence, to influence others. Cognitive complexity, the ability of individuals to describe the people they know, is strongly related to the ability of the communicator to employ messages that adopt the receiver's perspective, thus helping achieve a number of relational and instrumental goals. Argumentative individuals seek and obtain satisfaction from oral argument and from the mental work involved in researching evidence, using logic, and applying their minds. People suffering from communication apprehension and loneliness have constructed for themselves a limited social environment. Interpersonal communication can help them overcome these barriers.

KEY TERMS

▼

personality	cognitive complexity
interpersonalism model	argumentativeness
self-monitoring	verbal aggressiveness
Machiavellianism	communication apprehension
locus of control	loneliness
reinforcement	

EXERCISES FOR FURTHER DISCUSSION

▼

1. List your three supraordinate goals—the three goals that you consider the most important to achieve. Then outline a plan for achieving each of those goals.
   a. What resources that you possess will help you achieve these goals?
   b. What resources do you need to achieve your goals that you don't already have? How might you go about obtaining those resources?
   c. Discuss your plan with someone who knows you well, and see if that person thinks your plans sound workable.
2. Review the material in Chapter 5 on self-presentation styles (ingratiators, intimidators, exemplifiers, supplicators, self-promoters). Now make a list of the personality constructs (or individual differences) discussed in this chapter, and write next to each the self-presentation style (or styles) that you believe the personality type would most likely use. Compare your answers with those of other class members.
3. Think about your own reactions to the personality constructs discussed in this chapter.
   a. Do you personally know individuals that you would identify as cognitively complex? Lonely? Apprehensive? Argumentative?
   b. Which of the personal styles discussed do you find most appealing?

    c.   How would you describe yourself in terms of the personality constructs presented?

4.   Write a short paragraph in which you describe one of your favorite television or movie characters in terms of the personality constructs presented in this chapter.

5.   Speculate on the relationship between personality construct and relational decay, disengagement, and adjustment.

    a.   What personality construct do you think would stay in a relationship the longest? Why?

    b.   What personality construct would work the hardest to keep a relationship going? Why?

    c.   What personality construct would be most likely to initiate a breakup? Why?

    d.   What type of disengagement tactic (manipulation of negative feelings, positive tone, de-escalation, etc.) would each personality construct use?

6.   Consider the relationship you have with your family in terms of the personality constructs that you identified in yourself.

    a.   Are you similar to or different from your brothers and sisters?

    b.   Was there a lot of sibling rivalry in your family? If so, what effect do you think it had on your personality?

    c.   Do you think your personality is similar to that of one of your parents? If so, in what ways do you try to adjust your personality to either be more or less like that parent?

SUGGESTED READING

▼

GENDER

Deaux, K., and Major, B. 1987. Putting gender into context: An interactive model of gender-related behavior. *Psychological Review* 94:369–389. Deaux and Major review literature on gender displays and male/female differences, and propose a model of the contexts within which females may be expected to display certain types of behaviors.

SELF-MONITORING

Snyder, M. 1987. *Public appearances, private realities: The psychology of self-monitoring.* New York: Freeman. Snyder reviews fifteen years of research he has done on self-monitoring. Chapters include discussions of measuring the high and low self-monitoring individual, dating preferences, preferences for being in (or avoiding) situations, and behaviors that are displayed by high and low self-monitors during interactions.

MACHIAVELLIANISM

Christie, R., and Geis, F. L., eds. 1970. *Studies in Machiavellianism.* Orlando, Fla.: Academic Press. Christie and Geis present the classic works on the Machiavellian construct in this volume. An excellent reference for anyone interested in knowing more about Machiavellianism.

Steinfatt, T. M. 1987. Personality and communication: Classical approaches. In *Personality and interpersonal communication*, ed. J. C. McCroskey and J. Daly, 42–128. Newbury Park, CA: Sage. Steinfatt's extensive review of "classic" personality constructs includes material more contemporary than the Christie and Geis volume, and includes more material on Machiavellianism and tactics of manipulation.

LOCUS OF CONTROL

Lefcourt, H. M. 1982. *Locus of control: Current Trends in Theory and Research* (2d ed). Hillsdale, N.J.: Erlbaum. Lefcourt and his students review two decades of research on locus of control, with attention given to its measurement, and its importance in interpersonal and marital contexts.

COGNITIVE COMPLEXITY

Applegate, J. L. 1982. The impact of construct system development on communication and impression formation in persuasive contexts. *Communication Monographs* 49:277–289. Applegate's well-written paper on impression formation is recommended for two reasons: the review of literature on cognitive complexity and the clearly written description of a coding system demonstrating the complexity of impressions people make on others.

ARGUMENTATIVENESS

Infante, D. A., and Rancer, A. S. 1982. A conceptualization and measure of argumentativeness. *Journal of Personality Assessment* 46:72–80. Infante and his students have devoted two decades of research to the issues of argumentativeness versus other constructs (e.g., assertiveness). This 1982 study provides a well-written rationale for this line of research and an examination of how to measure the construct.

COMMUNICATION APPREHENSION

McCroskey, J. C. 1982. Oral communication apprehension: A reconceptualization. In *Communication yearbook 6*, ed. M. Burgoon, 136–170. Newbury Park, Calif.:

Sage. McCroskey and his students have devoted almost three decades to the measurement of communication apprehension and the consequences of possessing high levels of communication apprehension. This 1982 article provides an extensive review of the research in this area, along with comments on the measurement of communication apprehension.

LONELINESS

Spitzberg, B. H., and Canary, D. J. 1985. Loneliness and relationally competent communication. *Journal of Social and Personal Relationships* 2:387–402. Spitzberg and Canary not only provide an extensive review of the literature on loneliness, but also provide a model of loneliness and competence in maintaining relationships.

REFERENCE LIST

Applegate, J. L. 1982. The impact of construct system development on communication and impression formation in persuasive contexts. *Communication Monographs* 49:277–289.

Bell, R. A. 1985. Conversational involvement and loneliness. *Communication Monographs* 52: 218–235.

Bell, R. A., and Roloff, M. E. 1991. Making a love connection: Loneliness and communication competence in the dating marketplace. *Communication Quarterly* 39:58–74.

Burleson, B. R. 1984. Comforting communication. In *Communication by children and adults*, ed. H. E. Sypher and J. L. Applegate, 63–104. Newbury Park, Calif.: Sage.

———. 1987. Cognitive complexity. In *Personality and interpersonal communication*, ed. J. C. McCroskey and J. A. Daly, 305–349. Newbury Park, Calif.: Sage.

Canary, D. J.; Cody, M. J.; and Marston, P. J. 1986. Goal types, compliance-gaining, and locus of control. *Journal of Language and Social Psychology* 5:249–303.

Canary, D. J.; Cunningham, E. M.; and Cody, M. J. 1988. Goal types, gender, and locus of control in managing interpersonal conflict. *Communication Research* 15:426–446.

Christie, R., and Geis, F. L., eds. 1970. *Studies in Machiavellianism.* Orlando, Fla.: Academic Press.

Cody, M. J.; Canary, D. J.; and Smith, S. W. 1993. Compliance-gaining goals: An inductive analysis of actor's goal types, strategies, and successes. In *Communicating strategically*, ed. J. M. Wiemann, Hillsdale, N.J.: Erlbaum.

Daly, J. A., and Stafford, L. 1984. Correlates and consequences of social-communicative anxiety. In *Avoiding communication: Shyness, reticence, and communication apprehension*, ed. J. A. Daly and J. C. McCroskey, 125–144. Newbury Park, Calif.: Sage.

Deaux, K. 1977. Sex differences in social behavior. In *Personality variables in social behavior*, ed. T. Blass, 357–378. Hillsdale, N.J.: Erlbaum.

374

Deaux, K., and Major, B. 1987. Putting gender into context: An interactive model of gender-related behavior. *Psychological Review* 94:369–389.

De Paulo, B. M., and Rosenthal, R. 1979. Telling lies. *Journal of Personality and Social Psychology* 37:1713–1722.

Delia, J. G.; Kline, S. L.; and Burleson, B. R. 1979. The development of persuasive communication strategies in kindergartners through twelfth-graders. *Communication Monographs* 46:241–256.

Geis, F. L., and Moon, T. H. 1981. Machiavellianism and deception. *Journal of Personality and Social Psychology* 41:766–775.

Goodstadt, B. E., and Hjelle, L. A. 1973. Power to the powerless: Locus of control and the use of power. *Journal of Personality and Social Psychology* 27:190–196.

Hawken, L.; Duran, R. L.; and Kelly, L. 1991. The relationship of interpersonal communication variables to academic success and persistence in college. *Communication Quarterly* 39:297–308.

Hunter, J. E.; Gerbing, D. W.; and Boster, F. J. 1982. Machiavellian beliefs and personality: Construct invalidity of the Machiavellianism dimension. *Journal of Personality and Social Psychology* 43:1293–1305.

Infante, D. A. 1987. Aggressiveness. In *Personality and interpersonal communication*, ed. J. C. McCroskey and J. A. Daly, 157–192. Newbury Park, Calif.: Sage.

Infante, D. A.; Chandler, T. A.; and Rudd, J. E. 1989. Test of an argumentative skill deficiency model of interspousal violence. *Communication Monographs* 56:163–177.

Infante, D. A., and Rancer, A. S. 1982. A conceptualization and measure of argumentativeness. *Journal of Personality Assessment* 46:72–80.

Infante, D. A.; Riddle, B. L.; Horvath, C. L.; and Tumlin, S. A. 1992. Verbal aggressiveness: Messages and reasons. *Communication Quarterly* 40:116–126.

Infante, D. A.; Sabourin, T. C.; Rudd, J. E.; and Shannon, E. A. 1990. Verbal aggression in violent and nonviolent marital disputes. *Communication Quarterly* 38:361–371.

Infante, D. A.; Trebling, J. D.; Shepard, P. E.; and Seeds, D. E. 1984. The relation of argumentativeness to verbal aggression. *Southern Speech Communication Journal* 50:67–77.

Infante, D. A., and Wigley, C. J. 1986. Verbal aggressiveness: An interpersonal model and measure. *Communication Monographs* 53:61–69.

Lefcourt, H. M. 1982. *Locus of control: Current trends in theory and research*, 2d ed. Hillsdale, N.J.: Erlbaum.

Lefcourt, H. M.; Martin, R. A.; Fick, C. M.; and Saleh, W. E. 1985. Locus of control for affiliation and behavior in social interactions. *Journal of Personality and Social Psychology* 48:755–769.

Lefcourt, H. M.; Von Bayer, C. L.; Ware, E. E.; and Cox, D. J. 1979. The Multidimensional-Multiattributional Scale: The development of a goal-specific locus of control scale. *Canadian Journal of Behavioral Science* 11:286–304.

Margulis, S. T.; Derlega, V. J.; and Winstead, B. A. 1984. Implications of social psychological concepts for a theory of loneliness. In *Communication, intimacy, and close relationships*, ed. V. J. Derlega, 133–160. Orlando, Fla.: Academic Press.

McCroskey, J. C. 1982. Oral communication apprehension: A reconceptualization. In *Communication yearbook 6*, ed. M. Burgoon, 136–170. Newbury Park, Calif.: Sage.

Miller, L. C., and Read, S. J. 1987. Why am I telling you this? Self-disclosure in a goal-based model of personality. In *Self-disclosure: theory, research, and therapy*, ed. V. J. Derlega and J. H. Berg, 35–58. New York: Plenum.

Miller, P. C.; Lefcourt, H. M.; Holmes, J. G.; Ware, E. E.; and Saleh, W. E. 1986. Marital locus of control and marital problem solving. *Journal of Personality and Social Psychology* 51: 161–169.

O'Hair, H. D., and Cody, M. J. 1987. Machiavellian beliefs and the social influence process. *Western Journal of Speech Communication* 51:279–303.

O'Hair, H. D.; Cody, M. J.; and McLaughlin, M. L. 1981. Prepared lies, spontaneous lies, Machiavellianism, and nonverbal communication. *Human Communication Research* 7:325–339.

Rancer, A. S., and Infante, D. A. 1985. Relations between motivation to argue and the argumentativeness of adversaries. *Communication Quarterly* 33:209–218.

Read, S. J., and Miller, J. C. 1989. Inter-personalism: Toward a goal-based theory of persons in relationships. In *Goal concepts in personality and social psychology*, ed. L. A. Pervin, 413–472. Hillsdale, N.J.: Erlbaum.

Reis, H. T.; Nezlek, J.; and Wheeler, L. 1980. Physical attractiveness in social interaction. *Journal of Personality and Social Psychology* 38:604–617.

Reis, H. T.; Wheeler, L.; Spiegel, N.; Kernis, M. H.; Nezlek, J.; and Perri, M. 1982. Physical attractiveness in social interaction: II. Why does appearance affect social experience? *Journal of Personality and Social Psychology* 43:979–996.

Rotter, J. B. 1966. Generalized expectancies for internal vs. external locus of control of reinforcement. *Psychological Monographs* 80 (Whole No. 609).

Russell, D.; Peplau, L. A.; and Cutrona, C. E. 1980. The Revised UCLA Loneliness Scale: Concurrent and discriminant validity evidence. *Journal of Personality and Social Psychology* 39:472–480.

Smith, S. W.; Cody, M. J.; Lo Vette, S.; and Canary, D. J. 1990. Self-monitoring, gender, and compliance-gaining goals. In *The psychology of tactical communication*, ed. M. J. Cody and M. L. McLaughlin, 91–135. Clevedon, England: Multilingual Matters.

Snyder, M. 1987. *Public appearances, private realities: The psychology of self-monitoring.* New York: Freeman.

Snyder, M., and Gangestad, S. 1986. On the nature of self-monitoring: Matters of assessment, matters of validity. *Journal of Personality and Social Psychology* 51:125–139.

Solano, C. H.; Batten, P. G.; and Parrish, E. A. 1982. Loneliness and patterns of self-disclosure. *Journal of Personality and Social Psychology* 43:524–531.

Spitzberg, B. H., and Canary, D. J. 1985. Loneliness and relationally competent communication. *Journal of Social and Personal Relationships* 2:387–402.

Steinfatt, T. M. 1987. Personality and communication: Classical approaches. In *Personality and interpersonal communication*, ed. J. C. McCroskey and J. A. Daly, 42–128. Newbury Park, Calif.: Sage.

Sypher, H. E., and Applegate, J. L., eds. 1984. *Communication by children and adults.* Newbury Park, Calif.: Sage.

Wheeler, L., and Nezlek, J. 1977. Sex differences in social participation. *Journal of Personality and Social Psychology* 35:742–754.

Zakahi, W. R., and Duran, R. L. 1985. Loneliness, communicative competence, and communication apprehension: Extension and replication. *Communication Quarterly* 33:50–60.

CHAPTER 14

IMPLICATIONS FOR

INTERPERSONAL

COMMUNICATION

COMPETENCE

It was my first job interview after completing my Ph.D. I had trouble falling asleep because I was excited about the possibility of working at a major university. After four hours of counting backward, sleep came.

The hotel operator forgot to deliver the wake-up call. So when the phone finally rang in the morning, it was the department chair's loud voice wondering, "Hello, are you ready yet? I am waiting for you in the lobby." Ten minutes later, unshaved and without umbrella, I greeted the chair. I felt good about getting ready in ten minutes, but the chair didn't seem to have enjoyed his wait.

Having no time for breakfast, I was glad for the coffee in the faculty lounge. "Sugar?" the chair asked. I nodded yes. "That is a very special sugar container," said the chair. "Our wonderful secretary for over thirty years gave us this splendid present just last month." That was the first time the chair smiled, recollecting his lifelong co-worker. I noticed the other dozen or so faculty members were smiling too. I attempted to return their sugar container.

Without apparent cause, the container flew from my hands to the center of the faculty lounge, where it crashed into a thousand pieces of glass intermingled with white sugar. Broken were thirty years of memories. And next to those, no one really cared about my future. After several gasps and an awkward silence, the chair announced, "The presentation begins in five minutes. Be sure to take your umbrellas because it's starting to rain."

The presentation began well, then slowly fell apart. I had difficulty articulating some of my ideas because the topic I had chosen was rather esoteric. At one point during the presentation, it was clear that the entire audience was bored. Still, I was determined to present all my ideas. The question-and-answer session also went very poorly. My attempts to evade questions I couldn't answer only generated direct and vicious follow-up questions. Afterward, only one person complimented me: "That was interesting," was all he said.

Interpersonal competence seems easy for some people. Some people appear at ease no matter where they are. They know how to act and what to say. They seem genuinely involved in the conversation, change the topic at will without offending others, and listen well. Other people are less competent at times. They don't know how to act or what to say. Instead of showing interest in the conversation, they either talk about themselves or withdraw.

Communication scholars have spent considerable energy researching interpersonal **communication competence** (e.g., Bostrom 1984; Cegala 1991; Duran 1983; McCroskey 1982; Parks 1985; Pearce and Cronen 1980; Rubin 1985; Spitzberg and Cupach 1984; Wiemann and Backlund 1980). This research suggests that communication competence is determined by both conversational partners, involves knowing how to communicate, references actual communication behavior, and reflects the communicator's success at achieving his or her goals.

The energies spent to investigate communication competence are justified. Spitzberg and Cupach (1989) show that a lack of communication competence is linked to mental illness, depression, anxiety, shyness, loneliness, developmental disorders, academic problems, sexual offenses, and drug abuse. Communication competence, by contrast, is positively associated with having friends and the ability to function personally.

A Component Model of Competence

Perhaps the most comprehensive theory of communication competence is Spitzberg and Cupach's (1984). Part of their theory is a "component model." According to these scholars, evaluation of competence occurs in three components: *motivation, knowledge,* and *skill.*

MOTIVATION

Spitzberg and Cupach (1984, 1989) conceive of motivation as an individual's approach or avoidance orientation in various social situations. For a variety of reasons, individuals are drawn to particular social episodes (approach) and are discouraged from engaging in other social episodes (avoidance).

As indicated in Chapter 1, goals motivate individuals to act. Also as noted in Chapter 1, interpersonal goals refer most generally to self-presentation, relational, and instrumental objectives. At the less abstract (basic) level, goals are more specific regarding what the communicator wants and with whom. Self-efficacy (see also Bandura 1989) alters whether a person approaches or avoids a particular kind of interaction goal. In other words, an individual's confidence in being successful in a particular type of interaction will increase the likelihood that the person will approach that particular type of interaction. Conversely, if the person lacks confidence regarding success or believes that he or she will fail, the person will likely avoid those goals.

You may ask yourself about your motivation for various self-presentation, relational, and instrumental goals. Knowing your own motivation for personal goals is vital if you are to understand your behavior. Of course, this does not imply that you take stock of your wants and impulses before every conversation. It does mean, however, that you have a set of values that indicate what is important in life. Knowing what you want and how much you are willing to sacrifice to get it will guide your interpersonal contacts and communication.

KNOWLEDGE

In addition to motivation, the communicator must know how to act. Spitzberg and Cupach (1984) observe that once an individual decides to pursue a conversational goal, the usual kinds of interaction for that situation are imagined, and applicable schemas or plans are analyzed and adopted. As mentioned in Chapter 1, goals lead to plans for action. Once you are motivated toward a goal, you begin constructing plans to obtain it. Previous experience informs your knowledge of what constitutes a workable plan, and you tend to adopt plans that have worked in similar situations instead of re-creating new plans for each situation (Berger and Jordan 1992). In this vein, competence would entail having a repertoire of plans that can be used to achieve valued goals.

Greene (1984) calls knowing how to act **procedural knowledge.** Procedural knowledge refers to the ways people read social situations and decide on a course of action that yields desired outcomes. According to Greene, people recall procedural knowledge obtained from previous experience and watching others and within moments make a decision as to how to behave. Of course, people know how to behave in many situations, so the process of assembling the best action procedure requires almost no time. People may have learned procedural knowledge from many sources, including a *prototype* of interpersonal competence (Pavitt and Haight 1985). A prototype is a model representative. Accordingly, you may observe different prototypes that indicate to you what action should be performed in social situations. In novel situations, you must work harder to construct an appropriate plan of action (Greene 1984).

SKILL

The third component in Spitzberg and Cupach's model is skill. In this model, skills refer to behaviors actually performed. Spitzberg and Cupach (1984) review several studies showing that a person may be motivated to act and know how to act but may not actually behave as desired. How many times have you been motivated to perform well and knew how but failed to enact the behavior as you wished?

Recall the story at the beginning of this chapter. The candidate for the university position was quite motivated and knowledgeable about how to communicate in an interview setting. But the candidate lacked some basic social skills that day. First, although he made his prospective chair wait for ten minutes, he did not apologize for his failure to be prompt (see Chapter 6). Second, he dropped the valued sugar container, obviously because he was not careful to hold it firmly. He had forgotten his umbrella, so you can imagine that the day was filled with awkward requests to borrow or share someone's umbrella. Finally, he had several problems delivering his speech and did not adjust to the audience even though he realized they were bored.

Is there a list that informs us what most people consider to be competent? The literature on interpersonal communication competence provides several standards, or criteria for assessing what constitutes competent performance. Meeting these criteria means performing at competent levels. Let us discuss these standards.

Criteria for Assessing Competence

Many criteria are presented in various studies. Here we will briefly review six, selected because they have received much theoretic and empirical attention for several years. All six criteria apply to interpersonal contexts; furthermore, they are representative of the competence literature—they are rough synonyms for factors not reviewed. Finally, each of these criteria is relevant to the goals-based view offered in this book. The six criteria are *adaptability, conversational involvement, conversational management, empathy, effectiveness,* and *appropriateness.*

ADAPTABILITY

According to Spitzberg and Cupach (1989), **adaptability** (or flexibility) is the most commonly cited standard for judging competence. Communicative adaptability refers to the ability to change behaviors and goals to meet the needs of the inter-action (see Duran 1983). As several studies have shown, being adaptable is important to interpersonal competence.

According to Duran (1991), adaptability is comprised of six factors: *social experience, social composure, social confirmation, appropriate disclosure, articulation,* and *wit.* Social experience refers to having participated in various social interactions. Having various interactions allows for "the development and refinement of a social communication repertoire" (p. 6). Having developed a range of communication behaviors permits people to select the most optimal communication behaviors. Social composure refers to keeping calm. The ability to keep calm is related to the ability to perceive situations accurately (Duran 1991). Social confirmation refers to acknowledgment of the partner's self-presentation efforts. Understanding the partner's self-presentation goals helps the communicator adapt. Appropriate disclosure refers to being sensitive to the amount and type of information presented to the partner (see also Chapter 7). Articulation refers to the ability to express ideas through language. Developing a range of verbal skills allows people to express their ideas to various conversational partners. Finally, Duran (1991) states that the ability to use humor assists in adapting to the social situation. A person's humor can make dull interactions brighter. Wit can also ease tensions between people and alleviate embarrassment.

CONVERSATIONAL INVOLVEMENT

A second standard for assessing communication competence is **conversational involvement.** Cegala (1991) reports that being involved in the conversation is critical to communication competence. Conversational involvement represents a behavioral as well as a cognitive activity. In other words, communicators must be cognitively involved in the conversation and demonstrate their involvement through their interaction behaviors (head nods, vocal cues, etc.).

According to Cegala (1984), conversational involvement is assessed according to the factors of *responsiveness, perceptiveness,* and *attentiveness.* Responsiveness references such behaviors as knowing what to say, what your role is, and feeling part of the interaction. Perceptiveness concerns being aware of how others perceive you, how others respond to you, and how observant you are of others. Attentiveness refers to listening carefully to others, focusing on the conversation, and not being preoccupied with your own thoughts. The conceptual opposite of involvement is being overly concerned with yourself in interaction—what Vangelisti, Knapp, and Daly (1990) call **conversational narcissism.** In sum, you are said to be conversationally involved to the degree that you are cognitively and behaviorally responsive, perceptive, and attentive to your conversational partner.

CONVERSATIONAL MANAGEMENT

Conversational management concerns how communicators regulate their interactions (Wiemann and Backlund 1980). Skilled interactants understand their role in managing interaction. Managing conversations also implies that people do not adapt to social situations only; they also control them. Accordingly, competence is assessed in terms of who controls the interaction ebb and flow and how smoothly the interaction proceeds.

The conversational ebb and flow is witnessed in such activities as turn taking and yielding, topic shifts and extensions, asking questions, intonation, nodding, interrupting, and the like (Spitzberg and Cupach, 1984, 138). Conversational turn taking and yielding simply refer to how communicators alternate at speaking (only one communicator tends to talk at one time). How topics proceed and change is a matter of conversational management. In addition, people indicate where attention should be directed by asking questions, varying the intonation in their voice, nodding their heads, and even interrupting one another.

EMPATHY

For many years now, researchers have known that **empathy** is an important skill in interpersonal communication (e.g., Keefe 1976). Empathy refers to the ability to show your conversational partner that you understand his or her situation and that you share his or her emotional reactions to the situation (Gladstein 1986). Empathy should not be confused with sympathy; sympathy is feeling sorry for another person to the extent that you want to help the person (see Wispe 1986). Empathy need not necessarily lead to helping the other person (Gladstein 1986; Miller, Stiff, and Ellis 1988).

According to Gladstein (1986), empathy entails both cognitive understanding (also called role taking or perspective taking) and feeling parallel emotions (also called emotional contagion). Empathy involves a process of suspending your own attitudes and values about a particular event and allowing the conversational partner's experience to guide your thoughts and feelings. Thus empathy involves putting aside your attitudes, adopting the perspective of your conversational partner, and feeling the emotions that he or she feels (see Gladstein 1986; Keefe 1976). Of course, empathy may involve positive or negative emotional responses and may even lead to "occupational burnout" in environments where people work with others' stressful situations (Miller et al. 1988).

EFFECTIVENESS

Effectiveness refers to achieving the objectives you have for your conversations. According to Parks (1985), communication competence refers to the degree to which you achieve your personal goals in a given situation without jeopardizing other important secondary goals. For example, your conversational goal may be to obtain a particular two-week vacation so that you can visit some high school friends. Accordingly, you would judge the quality of the exchange with the supervisor by your degree of success at obtaining the vacation time you wanted. But you would not want to risk other important goals (salary increases, being perceived as a loyal worker, etc.).

If communication is assessed according to the standard of effectiveness, certain communication behaviors would appear to be more competent than others. For example, asserting your desires in conflict, being persistent in compliance-gaining situations, and directly or indirectly obtaining the information you want are communication behaviors that function primarily to achieve personal goals.

APPROPRIATENESS

Spitzberg and Cupach (1984) define communication competence as the degree to which the communicator's goals are achieved through appropriate interaction (p. 100). **Appropriateness** refers to upholding the expectations for a given situation. According to Spitzberg and Cupach, appropriateness is one of two fundamental criteria for determining competence. Effectiveness, already discussed, is the other criterion.

You may readily think of situations where a person is appropriate but not effective or where the communicator is effective but inappropriate. For example, in a conflict situation, it is possible to agree with the other person to the extent that you never argue for your own position. In this instance, you could meet the criterion of appropriateness but in doing so sacrifice your primary goal. By contrast, you could

Appropriateness and effectiveness are two fundamental criteria for assessing communication competence. If you can achieve your goals (effectiveness) without violating what other people expect of you (appropriateness), you fulfill these criteria for competence and are seen as competent.

(Barbara Ries/Photo Researchers)

be overly competitive in your use of conflict strategies. In this instance, you may achieve your primary goal, but at the expense of violating the expectations others have of you. According to Spitzberg and Cupach (1984), *both* appropriateness and effectiveness contribute to competence in communicating.

Assessing Your Own Interpersonal Communication Competence

Using Spitzberg and Cupach's components, we can more precisely assess communicator competence according to each of the six competence criteria. For the purposes of this book, we will limit the evaluation of interpersonal competence to you. Answer each of the items in Table 14-1 to assess how well you believe you fare on

Table 14-1

A SELF-EVALUATION OF INTERPERSONAL COMMUNICATION COMPETENCE

Instructions: Answer each item honestly as it currently applies to you in typical conversations with others. Use a 5-point scale for your responses. Write 5 if you *strongly agree*, 4 if you *slightly agree*, 3 if you are *unsure*, 2 if you *slightly disagree*, and 1 if you *strongly disagree*.

_____ 1. I want to adapt my communication behavior to meet others' expectations.

_____ 2. I have enough knowledge and experiences to adapt to other people's expectations.

_____ 3. I use a wide range of behavior, including self-disclosure and wit, to adapt to others.

_____ 4. I want to be involved in the conversations I have with other people.

_____ 5. I know how to respond to others because I am perceptive of social situations and attentive to others' behaviors.

_____ 6. I show my involvement in conversation both nonverbally and verbally.

_____ 7. I want to make my conversations with others go smoothly.

_____ 8. I know how to change topics and control the basic tenor of the conversations I have with others.

_____ 9. It is easy for me to manage conversations the way I want them to proceed.

_____ 10. I want to understand other people's viewpoints and emotions.

_____ 11. Truly understanding another person means both taking the role of that person and feeling the feelings that the person feels.

_____ 12. I demonstrate my understanding of others by reflecting their thoughts and feelings to them.

_____ 13. I am motivated to obtain the conversational goals I set for myself.

_____ 14. Once I set a goal for myself that involves another person, I know the steps to take to achieve it.

_____ 15. I achieve my interpersonal goals.

_____ 16. I want to communicate with others in an appropriate manner.

_____ 17. I am aware of the rules that guide social behavior.

18. I act in ways that meet situational demands for appropriateness.

Scoring: To assess *motivation*, add items 1, 4, 7, 10, 13, and 16. To assess *knowledge*, add items 2, 5, 8, 11, 14, and 17. To assess *skill*, add items 3, 6, 9, 12, 15, and 18. *Adaptability* subscale = 1, 2, 3; *involvement* subscale = 4, 5, 6; *conversation management* subscale = 7, 8, 9; *empathy* subscale = 10, 11, 12; *effectiveness* subscale = 13, 14, 15; *appropriateness* subscale = 16, 17, 18. *Overall self-evaluation = 1–18 (possible range = 90 to 18 points).*

each of the six criteria according to your motivation, knowledge, and skill. There are many other measures of competence that have established reliability and validity (for a review, see Spitzberg and Cupach 1989). However, the items in Table 14-1 operationalize the concepts we have presented in this chapter. So use Table 14-1 as a tool for learning and discussion rather than as a measure for scientific research purposes.

Using Table 14-1, you can determine how well you meet the competence criteria. You can assess your own competence in terms of motivation, knowledge, and skill. Also, each subscale score profiles your competence according to the criteria of adaptability, involvement, conversational management, empathy, effectiveness, and appropriateness. Finally, you can obtain a very general measure of your competence by simply summing all the items.

Implications for Competence: A Review

Throughout this book we have presented many communication strategies, tactics, and other behaviors that are functionally related to people's goals. Research has shown which behaviors are more or less related to successful outcomes. We are aware that many of these communication behaviors seem new or even strange to you. You may have responded, "I could never do this" or "I can't imagine saying that." Nevertheless, by presenting these various communication strategies, tactics, and behaviors, we hope to increase your range of communication options.

Moreover, throughout this book we have framed the material within the context of the communicator's goals. Although this focus coincides with our view of communication, it may give the impression that once you establish your goals, know how to enact the plans to achieve your goals, and engage in certain communication strategies, you should be effective in getting what you want. We want to dismiss such a simple conceptualization of the communication process. Instead we stress that in interpersonal interaction, two people are constructing goals and plans, two people have various motivations for their desires, two people are presenting a public image of who they are, two people are attempting to define their relational desires, and two people have instrumental objectives that may correspond to or conflict with each other's instrumental objectives. In addition, as Chapter 13 suggests, these two people may have various individual differences that complicate the goals-plus-communication model. In other words, we assume that two people have the right to set each of their goals and to pursue them interdependently with others.

Finally, throughout this book we have attempted to present theory and research that show how we can be more competent interpersonal communicators. Each discussion has implications for interpersonal communication competence. The remainder of this chapter reviews some of what was said, emphasizing particular implications. (Each of the eighteen implications has been noted by a boldfaced number in parentheses.)

LESSONS FROM *THE JERK*

Many critics hold that the primary function of comedy is to ridicule ourselves so that we can learn from our shortcomings. And many of the best comedians are fine instructors in human error. If we pay attention to what comedians tell us, we might gain insights about our foolish behaviors, to remedy them.

In *The Jerk*, Steve Martin portrays a simpleminded person who doesn't seem to have a clue about how to present himself, how to develop a relationship, or how to succeed in business. Martin plays Navan Johnson, a rhythmless white man raised by a black family. Late one night, Navan hears some elevator music that inspires him to seek his own identity. So he hitchhikes to the big city and takes a job at a gas station.

One day Navan is talking with the owner of the station, Mr. Artunian, when a van arrives delivering phone books.

Navan: The new phone book is here! The new phone book is here!
Artunian: (*sarcastically*) I wish I could get that excited about nothing.
Navan: Nothing! Are you kidding? (*he reads*) Page 73: "Johnson, Navan R." I'M SOME-
            BODY NOW. Millions of people look at this book every day! This is the kind of
            spontaneous publicity—your name in print—that MAKES people. Things are going
            to start happening to me now!

Indeed they do start happening. He meets Marie (played by Bernadette Peters) and attempts to ask her on a date, but all he can do is mumble the words. She tells him to stomp his feet "once for no, twice for yes." He stomps twice and they meet the next day.

Navan: Are you a model?
Marie: No, I'm a cosmetologist.
Navan: Really? That's unbelievable. That's impressive. It must be tough to handle weight-
            lessness. Do you have a boyfriend?
Marie: Sort of.
Navan: Do you think, the next time you make love to your boyfriend you could think of me?
Marie: I haven't made love to him yet.
Navan: That's too bad. Do you think it's possible that someday you could make love to me
            and think of him?
Marie: Who knows—maybe you and he could make love and you could think of me.
Navan: I'd just be happy to be in there somewhere.

Marie and Navan continue seeing each other, and Navan decides to propose marriage. Navan is in a bathtub and calls out to Marie as she is gathering her things to leave him:

Navan: Honey, guess what! I wrote a song for you this morning:

Oh, I'm picking out a thermos for you.
   Not an ordinary thermos for you.
But the extra best thermos you can buy,
   with vinyl and stripes and a cup built right in.
I'm picking out a thermos for you
   and maybe a barometer too.
And what else can I buy so on me you'll rely?
   A rear end thermometer too!

Honey, there's a question I've been wanting to pop, but I've been afraid you'd say no. But this seems like the right time and place, so here goes: Honey, will you marry me?

The dog then barks twice, and Navan mistakes that for a yes. He shouts "Yahoo!" But during the proposal, Marie had slipped out the front door.

In the remainder of the film, Navan earns millions of dollars through luck and loses it because of ineptitude. But because he remembered to send a few dollars home each week, he salvages some of his wealth. The film concludes as it began, with Navan back on the farm, not quite keeping time to a favorite family hymn.

We can see from the excerpts of dialogue how Navan presented himself—as a jerk. His first date and proposal to Marie are examples of how not to present yourself and develop a relationship. The fact that he didn't save any substantial amounts of money and lost a fortune overnight also indicate his incompetence.

The Jerk exaggerates people's incompetent behaviors—or does it? Can you think of other comedians who offer insights about people by making fun of their incompetence? What would they have us laugh at? What can we learn from their insights?

Excerpts from *The Jerk* by Steve Martin, Carl Gottlieb, and Michael Elias. Copyright © by Universal City Studios, Inc. Courtesy of MCA Publishing Rights, a division of MCA Inc.

FUNDAMENTALS OF COMMUNICATION COMPETENCE

Part I of this book presented concepts fundamental to communication. Chapter 1 discussed how important interpersonal communication is used to achieve your self-presentation, relational, and instrumental goals. One clear implication (1) is that competent communicators are aware of their self-presentation, relational, and instrumental goals they attempt to achieve interpersonally. In addition (2), optimal competence refers to achieving your main goals without sacrificing your less important goals (see also Parks 1985).

Two people make up a relational system; in other words, two individuals' goals are involved in interaction. Accordingly, assessments of competence must account for both parties, not just one person's behavior (see also Spitzberg and Cupach 1984, 1989). Given that each person is assessing the conversational partner's communication, both parties need to satisfy the situational and relational expectations for behavior held by the partner. The more interdependent the parties are, the more interwoven are their goals. Kelley (1979) postulated that people become interdependent in terms of their "fate" and behaviors. That is, interdependence means changing someone's future outcomes as well as his or her behavioral patterns. One implication (3) of this is that the more interdependent the behavioral patterns, the more the assessments of self and partner competence are linked.

Chapter 2 presented four different perspectives on communication. The implication (4) is that there is not one accurate way to examine communication behavior. Your understanding of the communication process can vary dramatically from the next person's, and what you stress about communication may be quite different from what your partner stresses. For example, you may feel that ambiguous messages are poor symbols, whereas your partner may feel that ambiguous messages are powerful symbols. What is important is that (5) you have an *informed understanding* of communication processes.

Chapters 3 and 4 presented many concepts concerning exchanging messages verbally and nonverbally. One clear implication (6) from these chapters is that messages are communicated through multiple channels. For example, liking another person is communicated both verbally and nonverbally. A second implication (7) of these chapters is that messages may be interpreted variously. More to the point, *your* messages may be interpreted in many ways that diverge from your intention. The competent communicator is not surprised when a message is interpreted in an unintended manner.

COMPETENCE IN SELF-PRESENTATION

Chapter 5 noted that self-presentation is so common that you seldom think about it. But you do think about your desired public image when it is called into question. Chapter 5 highlighted the direct self-presentation strategies of ingratiation, intimidation, self-promotion, supplication, and exemplification. You probably learned these concepts for the first time and applied them to yourself. One implication (8) for competence answers this question: What communication behaviors do you choose to develop your public image? Answering this question may reveal to you why you use certain messages rather than others.

Chapter 6 discussed communication behaviors used to defend a threatened public image—accounts. You will recall that accounts are messages offered in response to a perceived social failure. *Excuses* attempt to show that the communicator is not to blame for the event. *Justifications* seek to lessen the impact of the failure event by claiming that the consequences are not important. *Concessions* involve admitting responsibility for the failure. *Apologies* admit to the failure and promise remediation of the problem. Finally, *refusals* involve a claim that the event did not occur, denial of the right of the partner to question you about the event, or evasion. In addition, Chapter 6 indicated which of these accounts are seen as effective. Using accounts has several implications for interpersonal competence, including **(9)** the issue of whether we should become adept at using them. After all, why should socially competent people learn various ways to recover from social failures? The answer lies in the fact that we all fail occasionally.

Chapter 7 concerned self-disclosure. We implied that self-disclosure is best conceptualized as the decision to reveal something about yourself or to remain private. Factors affecting your decision to disclose or to remain private were emphasized. Chapter 7 also presented research on the consequences of self-disclosure, indicating that you should not disclose a lot of intimate information early in a conversation. In addition, the norm of reciprocity is met by disclosing information about the topic at hand or by reciprocating information at the same level of intimacy. Finally, research suggests that you should avoid disclosing negative aspects of yourself in most encounters. Given all these research findings, it appears that **(10)** self-disclosure should be reserved for few situations and a select person. We agree with this conclusion and Duran's (1991) observation that we should be sensitive to the amount and kind of information we disclose to others.

COMPETENCE IN RELATIONAL DEVELOPMENT

Relational development is seen as the outcome of people's goals to escalate (Chapter 8), maintain (Chapter 9), and de-escalate or terminate (Chapter 10) their relationships. These chapters imply that there is no one correct way to pursue your relational goals. Relationships develop in many different ways, and they are maintained successfully according to the relational definitions the partners choose to adopt. In addition, there are many factors and communication approaches people consider when de-escalating a relationship.

Chapter 8 focused on relational escalation. You will recall that people are attracted to others for a variety of reasons. Chapter 8 also showed that research suggests that the escalation of relationships progresses with increases *and* decreases of intimate messages. Finally, Chapter 8 reviewed turning points. The literature shows that some couples escalate their relationships quickly through a few relational turning points, while other couples experience more turning points and take longer to commit to each other. One implication **(11)** for competence is that you should anticipate variation in the progression of intimacy. Some relationships escalate to intimacy more quickly than others; some relationships involve different types of love; and there are periods when the relationship does not escalate but shelters ordinary conversations and conflict.

Chapter 9 presented several strategies people use to maintain their personal relationships: *positivity, openness, assurances, social networks,* and *sharing tasks.* Each of these strategies has been shown to be effective in preserving both romantic and nonromantic relationships. In addition, Chapter 9 featured relational spirals and dialectics. The implication (**12**) from this material is to recognize that change is a fundamental feature of maintaining a relationship (Montgomery 1993). Hence when we think of relational maintenance processes, we should think of fluctuations in relational properties (such as intimacy and trust, or in terms of dialectics) and recognize that we use communication strategies to keep our relationships within a desired range of fluctuation.

Chapter 10 focused on various issues and communication behaviors associated with relational de-escalation and termination. The process of de-escalation was depicted according to Duck's (1982) four-phase model (intrapsychic phase, dyadic, social, and grave-dressing phase). Various attributions for de-escalation were reviewed. Chapter 10 also presented five strategies people use in de-escalating or terminating their relationships: positive tone (emotional attempts to not hurt the rejected partner), de-escalation tactics (reasons for de-escalation without alleviating the partner's hurt feelings), withdrawal or avoidance (avoiding the partner), justification tactics (citing positive consequences of disengaging or negative consequences for not disengaging), and negative identity or manipulation tactics (which show little regard for the partner, as they arouse feelings that lead to a quick end). Discussing the ways in which people can competently de-escalate or terminate a relationship sounds cold and ruthless. Still, we need to recognize that (**13**) most of our relationships require some kind of communication to bring about separation, and Chapter 10 indicated when people use these various de-escalation strategies.

COMPETENCE IN INSTRUMENTAL OBJECTIVES

We all have personal goals regarding self-advancement, or instrumental objectives. You may need a favor from someone or some material assistance (e.g., a car loan or a ride to the airport). Chapters 11 and 12 discussed principles related to gaining such compliance from others and how to manage situations where you perceive your goals are blocked.

Chapter 11 reviewed rules that associate the success of interpersonal influence attempts with underlying principles. These rules involved *anchoring and contrast effects, reciprocity, commitment, liking, social proof, authority,* and *scarcity.* The implication (**14**) of these rules at the strategic level is that competent communicators can use these principles to persuade others. In addition, (**15**) competent communicators recognize these rules when others use them. Do people really use these principles to influence others? Of course they do.

Chapter 12 discussed the manner in which conflict is managed. At least two implications arise from this chapter. First (**16**), people choose to use various conflict strategies. *Integrative* behaviors are cooperative and seek areas of mutual agreement. *Distributive* tactics are competitive and seek self-advancement, even at the partner's expense. *Avoidance* tactics minimize the conflict. There are advantages and disadvantages to each strategy, and the communicator must choose the most effective strategy in a given conflict episode. Second (**17**) Chapter 12 shows that these strategies unfold in different patterns. These patterns can be characterized according to their *variety, continuity, symmetry, stationarity,* and *spontaneity.* The competent communicator is sensitive to the manner in which his or her communication progresses during conflict and alters his or her behavior to make the conflict episode more productive.

PERSONALITY AND COMPETENCE

Chapter 13 indicated that people have various reactions to different social situations and reviewed seven personality factors: *self-monitoring,* Machiavellianism, *locus of control, cognitive complexity, argumentativeness, communication apprehension,* and *loneliness.* This material shows that people vary in their preferred social situations. For example, highly argumentative people enjoy participating in social debates and seek to initiate conversations with others who are also argumentative. In a similar vein, low self-monitors seek relationships with people whose beliefs correspond to their own. In addition, Chapter 13 demonstrated that people communicate differently according to these personality factors. The implication (**18**) is that we should realize people vary in their preferred social situations and communication behaviors. Knowing these differences may enable us to communicate with a wider range of people more competently.

Final Comments

This book has been about using interpersonal communication to achieve your personal goals. As with all books and studies, you should adapt the principles that are presented to your own interpersonal situations and life experiences. Sometimes the principles we present are based on many studies and personal experiences. At other times, the concepts we present are based on very recent research that has not yet been replicated. Throughout, however, we have presented the best information on the topic we knew. Nevertheless, you must use judgment regarding the practical application of all the material presented in this text.

Finally, we hope that this book has increased your interest in studying more about interpersonal communication. Many universities offer advanced courses on the topic of interpersonal communication. These courses will no doubt extend your knowledge and make you aware of other approaches to the topic. Our hope is that this text has provided you with the basic tools you need to understand the field of interpersonal communication and that it has whetted your appetite for further inquiry about interpersonal communication processes.

My second and third job interviews gave me other opportunities to improve my "personal marketing skills." I couldn't tell if the first presentation topic was too abstract or if I just could not impart the ideas. So I switched the presentation topic to something less abstract. I also prepared handouts and a relevant cartoon (to lighten the presentation).

My chief concern was running into the unexpected. I learned that when seeking a job, surprise is inevitable. I also learned from my past mistakes. I read a lot before going to bed, not allowing the next day's worries to bother me. I also made sure that the hotel alarm clock was set. And as luck would have it, the hotel operator was 15 minutes late with the wake-up call for my third (and most important) interview. Regardless, I was ready when the chair walked into the lobby.

I also made sure there was plenty of time for breakfast and coffee. So I felt energetic and awake when I met my future colleagues. I tried to be sensitive to their issues and direct in answering their questions. I believed—correctly—that honesty was essential for our continued working relationship. I must admit to lying to one of the faculty members, however. When asked if I cared for any sugar in my coffee, I smiled and replied, "No, thank you."

KEY TERMS

▼

communication competence	conversational management
procedural knowledge	empathy
adaptability	effectiveness
conversational involvement	appropriateness
conversational narcissism	

EXERCISES FOR FURTHER DISCUSSION

▼

1. One of main ideas in this book has been that knowing our own motivation for personal goals is vital if we are to understand our behavior. Do you agree or disagree with this premise? Discuss why or why not.

2. Make a list of five people whom you think of as competent communicators, people who could serve as models for your own interpersonal communication competence.
   a. What behaviors do these people use that make them competent?
   b. What behaviors do they use that you would like to begin to use as well?
3. Complete the self-evaluation of interpersonal communication competence in Table 14-1.
   a. How did you score yourself in terms of motivation? Knowledge? Skill?
   b. In what ways do you think you are already a competent communicator? What is your greatest strength?
   c. In what ways do you think you could improve as a communicator?
4. Review the eighteen implications presented in the final section of this chapter.
   a. Which three of these implications are the most relevant to your life?
   b. Which three of these implications constitute principles that you can adopt for your own interaction behaviors?
5. Look again at the communication competence story presented at the beginning and end of this chapter. Now write a story of your own that shows differences in competent and incompetent communication behaviors.

SUGGESTED READING

COMMUNICATION COMPETENCE THEORY AND RESEARCH

Spitzberg, B. H., and Cupach, W. R. 1984. *Interpersonal communication competence.* Newbury Park, Calif.: Sage. These authors review different conceptualizations of competence. They emphasize various components of competent interaction, stressing that competence is a relational accomplishment.

Spitzberg, B. H., and Cupach, W. R. 1989. *Handbook of interpersonal competence research.* New York: Springer-Verlag. Various measures of competence are reviewed. This is an excellent sourcebook for anyone doing research on the topic.

ADAPTABILITY

Duran, R. L. 1991. *Communicative adaptability: A review of conceptualization and measurement.* Paper presented at the Speech Communication Association convention, Atlanta. Major aspects of adaptability are presented. Duran also shows how his research has been linked to other research on competence.

CONVERSATIONAL INVOLVEMENT

Cegala, D. J. 1991. *Conversational involvement: Ten years later*. Paper presented at the Speech Communication Association convention, Atlanta. Cegala reviews how the research on conversational involvement has evolved over ten years. Both survey and observational studies are highlighted.

CONVERSATIONAL MANAGEMENT

Wiemann, J. M., and Backlund, P. 1980. Current theory and research in communicative competence. *Review of Educational Research* 50:185–199. Although one of the first reviews of communication competence, the issues discussed are still current. Conversational management is discussed as one of several important features of competence.

EMPATHY

Gladstein, G. A. 1986. Understanding empathy: Integrating counseling, development, and social psychology perspectives. *Journal of Counseling Psychology* 30:467–482. This is an excellent review and synthesis of definitions and theoretical perspectives on empathy.

APPROPRIATENESS AND EFFECTIVENESS

Spitzberg, B. H., and Cupach, W. R. 1984. *Interpersonal communication competence*. Newbury Park, Calif.: Sage. Two key features of communication competence (appropriateness and effectiveness) are presented. Other criteria of competence are also discussed.

REFERENCE LIST

Bandura, A. 1989. Self-regulation of motivation and action through internal standards and goal systems. In *Goal concepts in personality and social psychology*, ed. L. A. Pervin, 19–85. Hillsdale, N.J.: Erlbaum.

Berger, C. R., and Jordan, J. M. 1992. Planning sources, planning difficulty, and verbal fluency. *Communication Monographs* 59:130–149.

Bostrom, R. N. 1984. *Communication in competence: A multidisciplinary approach*. Newbury Park, Calif.: Sage.

Cegala, D. J. 1984. Affective and cognitive manifestations of interaction involvement during unstructured and competitive interactions. *Communication Monographs* 51:320–338.

————. 1991. *Conversational involvement: Ten years later.* Paper presented at the Speech Communication Association convention, Atlanta.

Duck, S. W. 1982. A typography of relationship disengagement and dissolution. In *Personal relationships 4: Dissolving personal relationships,* ed. S. W. Duck, 1–30. Orlando, Fla.: Academic Press.

Duran, R. L. 1983. Communicative adaptability: A measure of social communicative competence. *Communication Quarterly* 31:320–326.

————. 1991. *Communicative adaptability: A review of conceptualization and measurement.* Paper presented at the Speech Communication Association convention, Atlanta.

Gladstein, G. A. 1986. Understanding empathy: Integrating counseling, developmental, and social psychology perspectives. *Journal of Counseling Psychology* 30:467–482.

Greene, J. O. 1984. A cognitive approach to human communication: An action assembly theory. *Communication Monographs* 51:289–306.

Keefe, T. 1976. Empathy: The critical skill. *Social Work* 21:10–14.

Kelley, H. 1979. *Personal relationships: Their structure and process.* Hillsdale, N.J.: Erlbaum.

McCroskey, J. C. 1982. Communication competence and performance: A research and pedagogical perspective. *Communication Education* 31:1–8.

Miller, K. I.; Stiff, J. B.; and Ellis, B. H. 1988. Communication and empathy as precursors to burnout among human service workers. *Communication Monographs* 55:250–265.

Montgomery, B. M. 1993. Relationship maintenance versus relationship change: A dialectical dilemma. *Journal of Social and Personal Relationships.*

Parks, M. R. 1985. Interpersonal competence and the quest for personal competence. In *Handbook of interpersonal communication,* ed. M. L. Knapp and G. R. Miller, 171–201. Newbury Park, Calif.: Sage.

Pavitt, C., and Haight, L. 1985. The "competent" communicator as a cognitive prototype. *Human Communication Research* 12:225–241.

Pearce, W. B., and Cronen, V. E. 1980. *Communication, action, and meaning.* New York: Praeger.

Rubin, R. B. 1985. The validity of the communication competence assessment instrument. *Communication Monographs* 52:173–185.

Spitzberg, B. H., and Cupach, W. R. 1984. *Interpersonal communication competence.* Newbury Park, Calif.: Sage.

————. 1989. *Handbook of interpersonal competence research.* New York: Springer-Verlag.

Vangelisti, A. L.; Knapp, M. L.; and Daly, J. A. 1990. Conversational narcissism. *Communication Monographs* 57:251–274.

Wiemann, J. M., and Backlund, P. 1980. Current theory and research in communicative competence. *Review of Educational Research* 50:185–199.

Wispe, L. 1986. The distinction between sympathy and empathy: To call forth a concept, a word is needed. *Journal of Personality and Social Psychology* 50:314–321.

INDEX

Instructor's Manual
to Accompany

Prepared by
Bonnie Farley-Lucas, Susan J. Messman,
Lisa A. Wallace, and Daniel J. Canary

Instructor's Manual to Accompany

INTERPERSONAL COMMUNICATION: A GOALS-BASED APPROACH

Daniel J. Canary
Ohio University

and

Michael J. Cody
University of Southern California

Prepared by:
Bonnie Farley-Lucas
Susan J. Messman
Lisa A. Wallace
and
Daniel J. Canary

all at
Ohio University

Manufactured in the United States of America.
8 7 6 5 4
f e d c b a

For information, write:
St. Martin's Press, Inc.
175 Fifth Avenue
New York, NY 10010

ISBN: 0-312-03695-7

CONTENTS

INTRODUCTION

This instructor's manual accompanies <u>Interpersonal Communication: A Goals-Based Approach</u>. The purpose of this manual is to assist instructors in planning class sessions and to provide a variety of test items focusing on key concepts.

Planning the Course

<u>Interpersonal Communication: A Goals-Based Approach</u> focuses on how communication is used to achieve self-presentation, relational, and instrumental goals. Accordingly, the text provides a rich topic area where the instructor can blend conceptual issues with everyday examples. Students should readily relate to the concepts discussed in the text and be able to offer examples. (Students using early drafts of the book have shown much enthusiasm for discussing its content.) Moreover, the book is designed so that instructors of beginning as well as advanced interpersonal courses can present relevant theory and research on the topic.

If you are teaching an introductory-level interpersonal communication course, we suggest that you begin with Part I. The links between goals and interpersonal communication are explored in Chapter 1, and interpersonal communication is defined in Chapter 2. Fundamentals involving verbal and nonverbal communication are discussed in Chapters 3 and 4.

If you are teaching an upper division interpersonal communication course, you may want to skip Chapters 2-4. Or to obtain alternative perspectives or review in advanced courses, you can include them. Be aware that most of the material presented in Chapters 2-4 will be new to both beginning and advanced students of interpersonal communication.

Parts II through IV present material that reflects the thesis presented in Chapter 1, that important personal goals are achieved primarily through interpersonal communication. Part II explains how the various goals of presenting, defending, and disclosing the self are achieved; Part III discusses the goals of escalating, maintaining, and de-escalating relationships; and Part IV describes how instrumental goals are pursued by gaining compliance and managing interpersonal conflict. The instructor will find that many traditional as well as contemporary research areas can be discussed within the framework self-presentation, relational, and instrumental goals. But we encourage the presentation of other ways to cast the literature, as students often appreciate a counterbalance of approaches (a point also stressed in Chapter 2).

Part V offers a discussion of how personality affects interpersonal communication (Chapter 13). Several personality factors that have been shown to affect interpersonal behavior are reviewed. Finally, the book concludes by analyzing the implications for interpersonal communication competence (Chapter 14). This last chapter also offers a sense of completion to the course.

Your use of the book may simply depend on the number of weeks you have available. If so, the following schedules are suggested for semester (16-week) and quarter (10-week) terms.

<u>Semester System (16 weeks)</u> <u>Quarter System (10 weeks)</u>

<u>Week</u>

	Semester System (16 weeks)	Quarter System (10 weeks)
1	Introduction to course; in-class exercise	Introduction to course; Chapter 1
2	Chapter 1	Chapter 2
3	Chapter 2	Chapter 5
4	Chapter 3	Chapter 6
5	Chapter 4	Chapter 7; midterm exam
6	Chapter 5	Chapter 8
7	Chapter 6	Chapter 9
8	Chapter 7; midterm exam	Chapter 10
9	Chapter 8	Chapter 11
10	Chapter 9	Chapter 12; final exam
11	Chapter 10	
12	Chapter 11	
13	Chapter 12	
14	Chapter 13	
15	Chapter 14	
16	Final exam	

In the schedules, you will notice several assumptions at work. First, these schedules assume that instructors may not assign reading the first week. If you do assign reading the first week, you can certainly get right into the text. Second, the schedules assume that the typical class will cover one chapter a week. Of course, you may want to adjust the amount of material covered per week to your own course objectives. Finally, we assume that midterms and final exams are used. You may want to use a different examination schedule, including one that is organized around the major parts of the text.

About the Instructor's Manual

We have included a variety of discussion questions, class activities, and multiple-choice, true-or-false, and short-answer test items for each chapter. The discussion questions and class activities supplement exercises in the back of each chapter. Our goal is to offer the instructor many options for stimulating and informative class discussions and activities. The discussion questions and activities in the instructor's manual encourage students to develop and practice critical thinking skills. The discussion questions and class activities will help you do the following:

-- Explore theoretical issues regarding the study of interpersonal communication
-- Guide students through a sample of ethical dilemmas they are likely to confront in their quest for achieving personal goals
-- Reflect on the implications of the research results featured in the text.

Test items highlight main points covered in the text. There are an average of twenty-five items per chapter. We suggest the combined use of multiple-choice, true-or-false, and short-essay items. The short essays are most useful when you want students to extend the material, offering personal thoughts. Of course, you will probably want to supplement the test items with others on material not discussed in the text but covered in lecture. Correct answers to manual questions are indicated either in parentheses or by an asterisk (*).

You will also likely tailor this material to meet the specific needs and interests of your students. We have attempted to include scenarios and test material that nontraditional or returning students may find relevant to their life experiences. We have also included some items that demonstrate sensitivity to gender and cultural issues.

We hope that you will find this manual helpful in achieving your teaching objectives and that you find it promotes a pleasurable, fruitful learning environment for your students.

Bonnie Farley-Lucas
Susan J. Messman
Lisa A. Wallace
Daniel J. Canary

CHAPTER 1: THE IMPORTANCE OF INTERPERSONAL COMMUNICATION IN ACHIEVING PERSONAL GOALS

Chapter Objectives

1.   To present the conceptual framework that guides this book

2.   To discuss how communication can be studied from a goals-based perspective that focuses on three major types: self-presentation, relational, and instrumental goals

3.   To preview the remainder of the book

Discussion Questions

1.   Ask students to provide two separate examples: one in which an individual has attempted to maintain a public image of a competent, friendly person and one in which the same individual has attempted to portray a public image of a weak, indecisive person. Ask students to think about the communication behaviors behind each attempt. How do they differ? How would your students react in similar situations?

2.   Discuss the concept of "facework." Do students think that self-presentation is something we do continuously or just in certain situations?

3.   Have students consider the goal of relational escalation, perhaps even recalling a recent relationship they wanted to escalate. Have them discuss how this goal might vary according to the seven properties of goals: abstractness, clarity, degree of challenge, number of goals, time, communication influence, and planning. By linking relational escalation to goals, are we making it seem overly strategic? In other words, do relationships evolve over time without a clear intention of this evolution? What about the other goals presented in the chapter--for the most part, are they obtained strategically or mindlessly?

Class Activities

1.   Discuss the self-presentation goal of interpersonal communication. Then choose a few participants (a new employee, his or her romantic partner, and a boss) to role-play a "real-life" scenario in front of the class. The situation is as follows:

You are new at your job, and so far, you are doing quite well. However, you have been spending very little time with your partner. You decide to cook a special dinner and have a romantic evening at home. As you and your partner are shopping for your special meal, you come face to face with your new boss, who stops to chat and invites you to be a member of a special departmental committee that is meeting that evening.

You are stuck in the predicament of maintaining an image as a caring lover, while still looking competent and eager to please your boss. What do you say? What types of communication behaviors do you display? Which public image do you wish to convey, or do you compromise both?

Following the role-playing, have students discuss these questions with the classroom audience. Include a discussion about the self-presentation image of the boss and mate as well as that of the new employee. Have students consider the types of communication behaviors they employed.

2. Divide the class into groups of three or four students each. Have each member take turns being the "communicator." Attempting to be as persuasive as possible, each student should communicate one of the following personal goals to the rest of the group:

a. Your two friends have obtained four tickets to a concert that you have been dying to go to. You want them to take you and another mutual friend rather than the dates they had planned to take. Persuade them to take you.
b. You owe two months' rent on your apartment, and your landlord is getting very hostile. You've applied for a student loan, but it hasn't come in yet. You hope that it will come through soon. Persuade a friend to let you borrow more money to tide you over.
c. You've had a terrible fight with a very good friend, and you were in the wrong. To make up for your behavior, your friend, who is not very attractive, has begged you for a fix-up with an old high school friend of yours. You realize that the high school friend is not interested, but it means a lot to you right now to please the friend you fought with. Persuade the high school friend to go on the date.
d. You are switching careers, and you are applying for a job for which you have little direct experience. You find out that a professor whose course you've taken previously has strong connections in this company. You received an average grade in this professor's class, but a reference from this teacher will almost secure the job for you. Persuade the professor to write a strong letter of recommendation for you.

During the role-playing, have students observe and list the types of communication behaviors used by the communicators. Ask students to focus on the behaviors they thought were effective in achieving the goals. Then ask if any students have had similar experiences in reality and, if so, what they did and how they fared. Finally, you may want to have students compare role-playing with real-life situations to determine when role-playing can be informative. (Role-playing is often informative when the situation is plausible and the students act as if they are engaged in that situation. If the situation is not plausible or if the students are not engaged in it, role-playing may not bring about realistic behaviors.)

Multiple-Choice Questions

1.   Which type of goal involves "facework"?
    * a.   self-presentation
      b.   relational
      c.   instrumental
      d.   none of the above

2.   Which of the following is not one of the three levels of abstractness of a communication goal?
      a.   basic
    * b.   identifiable
      c.   supraordinate
      d.   subordinate

3.   Joan has the goal of getting Tom to support her in her attempt to persuade their parents to give her $50. Which of Tom's following responses demonstrates an example of Joan's "transactive goal"?
      a.   "Sure, Joan, I'll help you win them over."
      b.   "I really would like to help you, Joan, but I can't."
    * c.   "Do you need $50? I could lend it to you."
      d.   "Why do you want me to help you?"

For questions 4 through 8, classify the following goals in terms of level of abstractness. Use the following levels:

      a.   basic   c.   supraordinate
      b.   identifiable   d.   subordinate

4.   My goal is to become very successful in my career. (c)

5.   My goal is to get my spouse to drive the children to piano lessons on Tuesday night when it is my turn. (d)

6.   My goal is to get Chris to go out with me on a date. (a)

7.   My goal is to persuade my professor to let me turn in my final paper next Friday rather than this Friday. (d)

6

8. My goal is to be seen as a friendly, cheerful, honest, and intelligent person. (c)

9. Which of the following is <u>not</u> an instrumental goal?
    * a. wanting your friend to go shopping with you
    b. wanting your friend to lend you money so you can go shopping
    c. wanting your sister to give you a ride to work
    d. wanting your friend to help you construct a graph for your paper

10. Which of the following is true of our communication and our personal relationships?
    a. Our personal relationships have very little to do with communication.
    * b. Communication both affects and reflects our personal relationships.
    c. Personal relationships are affected by our communication, but communication does not reflect our relationships.
    d. Our communication is <u>not</u> affected by personal relationships.

11. Which of the following is <u>not</u> one of the six properties of goals?
    a. Goals vary in time.
    b. Goals vary in terms of clarity.
    c. There can be multiple goals.
    * d. Goals vary in terms of assessment.

<u>True-or-False Questions</u>

1. According to Bandura, a person with high self-efficacy tends to go after a goal full force until presented with a failure. Failures are seen as damaging to the person's self-image, so the person finds a new goal to achieve. (F)

2. Goals that are in the distant future are called proximal goals. (F)

3. Secondary goals can change your communication behavior toward your primary goals. (T)

4. Wanting your friend to change an annoying habit is a routine relational goal. (F)

5. People who rely on each other to accomplish their goals are said to be interdependent. (T)

6. Giving advice to a family member is considered a routine relational goal. (T)

7. Protecting a threatened personal right is considered a routine relational goal. (F)

8. Prolonging an obligation (such as waiting to pay back your sister until your student loan check arrives) is a routine self-presentation goal. (T)

9. Attempting to change your partner's beliefs and opinions is a routine instrumental goal. (T)

10. Goals are important because they enable us to make sense of the world around us. (T)

Short-Answer Questions

(Ask for a rationale for each answer.)

1. Are the three general goals outlined in this chapter comprehensive? That is, can you think of other general goals people seek through interpersonal communication?

2. Which of the six properties of goals do you find most important to communication?

3. Is self-efficacy important for seeking goals?

4. Is "facework" a routine activity people engage in?

5. Distinguish between supraordinate and subordinate goals. Give an example of each. If you were to study interpersonal communication, which level would be more informative?

CHAPTER 2: DEFINING INTERPERSONAL COMMUNICATION

Chapter Objectives

1. To show that there is more than one perspective on interpersonal communication

2. To present the authors' definition of interpersonal communication

3. To offer the assumptions underlying the authors' definition of interpersonal communication

4. To generate discussion about the various views on interpersonal communication and their underlying assumptions

Discussion Questions

1. Have students recall the text's definition of interpersonal communication. The text also gives five assumptions of the definition. Ask, "Are these assumptions compatible with yours? What assumptions might you have regarding interpersonal communication?"

2. Discuss the models of the various perspectives for the study of communication. Ask which model of the four looks most like how they envision communication. You might probe their reasons for their answers as well.

3. Interpersonal communication serves many functions. Ask your students to offer some examples of these functions. Are some of these functions performed simultaneously? Which can be? Which cannot?

4. Present the following material (written by one of book's authors) on dancing as a metaphor for the perspectives on communication. Ask students to discuss how the dancing analogy may inform us on the nature of the perspectives.

> Dancing is very much like communication. Dancing is highly symbolic, it usually requires interaction (in a general sense), and when done right, it is highly enjoyable.
> We extend the analogy to perspectives on communication to illustrate what you would emphasize about dancing if you looked at dancing from each of the perspectives.
> The mechanistic view. According to the mechanistic view, dancing is understood as actions you take with your partner in coordination to music. There are steps for each dance that indicate how the dance is to be performed. The waltz, the jitterbug, and the mambo each require certain basic steps. Once these steps are learned, they can be used to dance with anyone else who also knows the steps. All you have to do is begin using the steps for a dance that fits the music and see if the other person responds in the same way. Once the basic steps have been learned, you can change the steps and see how the dance partner responds.
> But if either person does not know the steps to a dance, the dancers will be unable to understand what to do. This most likely occurs at the beginning of the dance, when one partner first discovers that the other does not know the steps. In similar fashion, one might begin a new variation of the dance that the partner might not understand. A breakdown of the dance could also occur if the band isn't very good or if one of the dancers has had too much to drink.

A psychological view. From a psychological perspective, dancing doesn't focus so much on the steps involved as it does the perceptions and feelings within each person. Of course, there are some learned behaviors, and you would respond to the music with behaviors that have been repeated and reinforced over time.

On another psychological level, there are also interpretations of the situation and your partner's behavior. You might identify the situation as highly intimate and having significant relational consequences. In this instance you feel warm and begin dancing closer to your partner. If you perceived the dance as low in intimacy and low in its relational consequences, you would probably not try to dance too close.

Remember, "dancing is in the mind, not in the steps." So any problems you have understanding how to dance should focus on the degree to which you share perceptual congruence. And one other thing: partners are more likely to blame each other if the dance wasn't good.

An interactionist view. From an interactionist perspective, dancing is a combination of impulse and watching what other people, especially your partner, are doing. Although you have an urge to swing your arms without reservation, you notice that other people dancing have particular movements that signify to one another what they are doing. So you begin dancing, comparing your partner's movements to your own. You also compare the two of you to others on the dance floor, and you notice that others are watching you as well.

You learn to create a dance and then re-create it. You understand your partner's responses to you because of your ability to shift your role as a dancer. There are times when you can't imagine what some movements indicate because you can't always imagine you are acting as if you are the other person.

A pragmatic view. From the pragmatic perspective, dancing focuses on how both persons move together, not as two separate dancers. This view does not focus on the steps for each dance unless looking at such steps helps in the predictability of understanding the couple's moves. We might see if the partners are coordinating their actions, with one taking the lead and the other following. If both people try to lead (or if both follow), dancing will soon cease.

We also would focus on the phases of dancing. For example, we could see that dancing involves the partners orienting themselves to the dance floor and one another, that there might be some initial awkwardness (like both people trying to lead), but that after this awkwardness the couple establishes a predictable pattern of moves. But if the pattern becomes too predictable, the dancers will probably stop dancing.

Class Activities

1. Divide the class into four groups. Have each group prepare to argue that one of the perspectives is ideal for the study of interpersonal communication. You may want to have a fifth group of students remain neutral in order to vote on which perspective was presented best.

The discussion following the debate should focus on how perspectives interact with the subject matter of interpersonal communication. Differences between perspectives should be highlighted. The discussion should also illustrate how different the nature of interpersonal communication is in each case.

2. Present a clip of a video that portrays an interpersonal relationship--for example, clips of the movie Dad with Ted Danson and Jack Lemmon. Have students identify how the different functions of communication are present in the interactions.

Multiple-Choice Questions

1. Why are different perspectives on the study of communication valuable?
   * a. Perspectives focus our attention on particular elements of communication.
   b. Perspectives limit insights into the nature and process of communication.
   c. Perspectives reduce the tendency of scholars to maintain conflicting definitions of communication.
   d. All of the above

2. From the mechanistic perspective, communication is effective when
   * a. the decoded message matches the encoded message.
   b. the encoded and decoded messages occur simultaneously.
   c. both participants encode and decode messages.
   d. all of the above

3. Which perspective on the study of communication is particularly useful for identifying the components of the communication process?
   * a. mechanistic   c. interactionist
   b. psychological   d. pragmatic

4. Which perspective has spawned the most interpersonal communication research?
   a. mechanistic   c. interactionist
   * b. psychological   d. pragmatic

5. Which perspective holds that people use what others think to define their self-concept?
    a. mechanistic   c. interactionist
* b. psychological   d. pragmatic

6. The pragmatic perspective does all of the following except
* a. focus on the behaviors of individuals' communication rather than on the relationship as a whole.
    b. focus on how both parties communicate with each other over time.
    c. examine patterns of interaction in order to assess change.
    d. none of the above

7. When communication is studied as a transaction, all of the following are studied except
* a. two persons' behavior combined.
    b. both persons' recall.
    c. immediate feedback.
    d. meaning as a product of both persons' communication experience.

8. Which of the following is true regarding the process of being?
    a. People change very little over the life cycle, as evidenced in their interpersonal communication style.
    b. People develop strategies for adapting to their social world.
    c. Communication exchanges are fleeting and therefore may be replicated.
* d. none of the above

9. Which of the following is not a function of interpersonal communication?
    a. to achieve self-presentation, relational, and instrumental goals
    b. to help us define who we are
* c. to make sure that other people or events do not change our personality
    d. to provide structure to our social world

10. Critical components of the pragmatic perspective include all of the following except
    a. the whole is greater than the sum of its parts.
    b. systems are influenced by those outside the system.
    c. systems are organized.
* d. systems deal with events and material objects.

True-or-False Questions

1. Social symbols are both nonverbal and verbal, and they represent ideas, emotions, objects, or events. (F)

2. Strategic communication means that a decision is made on how to communicate with another person to achieve a goal. (T)

3. Mindless communication occurs when a person is unclear how to achieve a certain goal in an interaction. (F)

4. One can be competent at achieving instrumental goals while also achieving self-presentation and relational goals. (T)

5. Links to social systems outside the relationship vary in their extensiveness, that is the extent to which partners engage in talk about the external world. (F)

6. Schutz's postulate of compatibility indicates that interpersonal needs are met whenever individuals complement each other's giving and receiving of these particular needs. (F)

7. The principle of nonsummativity holds that systems have spatial and functional relationships to one another that evolve over time. (F)

8. Noise is best defined as internal or external feedback that distracts from the sender's message. (F)

9. According to the interactionist perspective, society refers to the cooperative behaviors of individuals. (T)

10. According to the mechanistic perspective, humans have choices and attempt to reduce uncertainty. (F)

Short-Answer Questions

1. Identify and define the four perspectives on communication presented in this chapter. What are the key differences among them?

2. Do you agree with the definition of interpersonal communication in the text? Do you agree or disagree with the authors' assumptions accompanying this definition?

3. Describe the three ways to study messages as acts, interacts, and transacts.

4.   Describe the fundamental properties of competent communication. How do these operate in interpersonal communication?

5.   Discuss the concept of the process of being. How is this related to interpersonal communication?

CHAPTER 3: FUNDAMENTALS OF VERBAL COMMUNICATION

Chapter Objectives

1. To discuss the nature of language as it pertains to seeking goals

2. To use the three levels of messages--valence, strategy, and argument--as a way of understanding verbal messages

3. To show that people's interpretation of messages occurs at several levels, using Pearce and Conklin's model of hierarchical meaning

4. To differentiate deliberative from empathic listening and suggest that the two are sometimes merged in practice

Discussion Questions

1. Have students discuss "arbitrary metaphors" and the semantic triangle. Ask them how the semantic triangle can illustrate the following statement: "The first time I met Paul, he reminded me of my favorite brother, Jack. I thought Paul was very friendly and had a great sense of humor, just like Jack."

2. Have students offer examples of how they know what someone wants and how they use that to interpret what the person says to them.

3. Discuss the three types of message design logics. Ask students to provide examples of expressive, conventional, and rhetorical design logics. What are the differences between content and control aspects of communication? How can we illustrate control in communication content?

4. Ask students, what are some of the common misconceptions regarding verbal communication? What is at the root of these misconceptions? Where might they originate? How are they perpetuated? Why might we incorrectly assume that

more communication is better communication? Why might we incorrectly assume that communication leads to happiness?

Class Activities

1. This class activity compares dictionary meanings with social meanings. Its objective is to show that many of our meanings are socially constructed. First, write the following words on the board: COLLEGE, PIG, SUCCESS, MARRIAGE. Next, ask students to write down on paper the first word that comes to their minds for each of the words on the board.

Ask students to share these "first impressions." As each is stated, write it on the board. If it is already on the board, place a check next to it and move on to the next student. When all students have finished giving their impressions for each of the words, read the dictionary definition for each of the words, and then read the list of students' first impressions.

Class discussion should focus on the following points: Why are there so many different interpretations for each word? What kinds of words are we most likely to misinterpret or place many meanings on? How often do you think we assume that the other person knows exactly what we mean? How can we help reduce ambiguity in communication? Other topics might include connotative versus denotative language, forces shaping our definition of words, and the importance of context in assigning meaning.

Note: It is important to write down responses without commenting on them or editing them. The neutral manner will not inhibit or encourage any other particular responses.

2. Have the class practice coding the following conversation according to the argument coding scheme presented in Table 3-2. Do not worry if students appear frustrated; in fact, that could lead to a discussion about how difficult it is to conduct research and about how there can be many interpretations for the same behavior.

    Todd: See that guy over there?
    Mary: The old guy sitting on the bench?
    Todd: No, no. The one wearing the skirt.
    Mary: Oh! He really is wearing a skirt? What is a man doing wearing a skirt?
    Todd: Actually, he has great, muscular legs. It is hot out today. Maybe he's just comfortable in it.
    Mary: What do you mean? Only women can wear skirts!
    Todd: Well, Scottish men wear kilts, and those are skirts.
    Mary: Yeah, but that guy is wearing a silky pleated skirt, and it looks really feminine.
    Todd: Hey, if women can wear pants and T-shirts, men should be allowed to wear anything they want!

Mary: I don't suppose you're going to start wearing skirts now. Are you? Because unless it's Halloween, I wouldn't want to be seen in public with you!

Todd: You are so closed-minded! I feel like just running into a store, buying a flowery dress, prancing around town in it, and screaming, "Mary Smith is my friend!"

Mary: I am not closed-minded. You're just saying that to make me angry.

Todd: You deserve it!

3. Using the conversation in Activity 2, ask two pairs of students to role-play the scenario in front of the class while the other students identify confirming and disconfirming behaviors. The first pair should be instructed to act angry, and the second pair should be instructed to act as if they are joking (or even flirting) with each other. Discussion could then focus on how verbal messages can mean different things, depending on one's relational goal.

4. In small groups, have students brainstorm examples of both disconfirming and confirming messages they have received in the past week and their reactions to each type of message. Next, have groups identify confirming and disconfirming messages they have intentionally or unintentionally communicated to others in the past week. Discussion should focus on similarities of the messages and how these messages affected them as both sender and receiver. What are the implications of confirming and disconfirming communication in achieving personal goals?

<u>Multiple-Choice Questions</u>

1.   The semantic triangle illustrates all of the following <u>except</u> which statement?
    a.   The meanings of words depend on shared symbols.
    b.   References are composed of one's previous experience.
    c.   There is a relationship between words and the reality words represent.
*   d.   People have the same references for symbols.

2.   Words make sense to the extent that they are relevant to actors' goals. This is called
    a. message design logics.   *   c. pragmatic coherence.
    b. effectiveness via quantity.   d. arbitrary metaphors.

3.   The expressive message design logic refers to
*   a.   presenting ideas and feelings as they are experienced.
    b.   creating one's social world.
    c.   the rules of the game.
    d.   none of the above

4. The rhetorical message design logic refers to
   a. presenting ideas and feelings as they are experienced.
 * b. creating one's social world.
   c. the rules of the game.
   d. none of the above

5. Verbal messages can be examined according to
   a. valence.   c. argument.
   b. strategy.   * d. all of the above

6. Valence refers to
 * a. the positivity or negativity of a statement.
   b. how ideas are used to support other ideas.
   c. a chemical reaction to a social situation.
   d. none of the above

7. Confirming messages are <u>not</u> characterized by
   a. recognizing your partner's existence.
   b. accepting your partner's way of experiencing life.
 * c. communicating imperviousness.
   d. expressing a willingness to become involved with your partner.

8. Juan asked Ronald to join him for lunch, but Ronald ignored Juan's invitation and walked right by him. Ronald was communicating
 * a. indifference.   c. a tangential response.
   b. imperviousness.   d. a monologue.

9. According to Wheeless, messages intended to make promises or threaten others would most likely belong to the power base of
 * a. consequences.   c. altruism.
   b. relationship identification.   d. values.

10. Pearce and Conklin's hierarchical meaning model illustrates that
    a. messages can be perceived both negatively and positively.
    b. people consciously choose which messages they attend to.
  * c. people interpret messages in various ways.
    d. all of the above

True-or-False Questions

1. Verbal messages as strategy refers to convergence seeking on the part of the communicator. (F)

2. Verbal messages as argument refers to seeking convergence on ideas. (T)

3.   A conventional message implies appropriateness norms and links one's goal to the fulfillment of these norms. (T)

4.   A rhetorical message not only follows the rules, but it also breaks the rules. (F)

5.   A speech act is a communicator's behavior immediately following the interpretation of a verbal message. (F)

6.   Communicators understand connections among words because of their inferred links to communicator goals. (T)

7.   Disconfirming messages are false, or untrue verbal statements that cannot be verified. (F)

8.   Message strategies can be divided into power bases such as consequence, relationship identification, and values. (T)

9.   When a message is analyzed at the level of valence, the focus is on how ideas are developed and shared. (F)

10. Episodes are coherent sequences of interaction that have an identifiable beginning and end. (T)

Short-Answer Questions

1.   The text holds that words are arbitrary metaphors. Do you see anything wrong with this claim?

2.   What is the difference between strategies and tactics? Give an example of each as it relates to asking a friend for a favor.

3.   It is often said that people are not rational. Do you agree with this? What implication does this have for studying messages as argument?

4.   Distinguish between empathic and deliberative listening. Which do you think people engage in more?

CHAPTER 4: FUNDAMENTALS OF NONVERBAL COMMUNICATION

<u>Chapter Objectives</u>

1. To introduce some topics of research in nonverbal communication

2. To introduce theories of interaction, including Patterson's arousal theory and the speech accommodation theory or communication accommodation theory

3. To examine the role of nonverbal messages as they convey liking, intimacy, and deception

<u>Discussion Questions</u>

1. Discuss channel discrepancy. Have students describe situations in which they misread a nonverbal or verbal act. Describe situations in which someone misread your nonverbal or verbal act. What were the consequences? Offer some possible theoretical explanations of why it was misread.

2. Ask students, what are some of the well-known adapters, illustrators, emblems, and regulators in our culture? Discuss some of the cultural variations that they have undergone. How does the use of these differ in bars, classrooms, and other environments?

3. Discuss why nonverbals are so difficult to interpret. What are some of the gender differences (supported by research) in nonverbal communication? Why are emotions so difficult to interpret?

4. Discuss arousal theory. How does Burgoon's model differ from Patterson's model? Ask students to critique the models and offer their experiences to back up their claims.

<u>Class Activities</u>

1. Have two students of the same sex stand in front of the class about ten feet apart. Then have them begin walking closer toward each other until one of them says "stop." Ask the students to keep their arms at their sides and to face each other. Have them take one-step increments until they almost touch. At this point, ask them what they are experiencing. Then tell them to stand at a comfortable distance, noting how far apart they stand. Repeat this exercise with other pairs of students, varying the combination of genders.
    After several such encounters, have the participants discuss their own feelings and observations they may have regarding others whom they watched. Students should be able to offer theoretical explanations of their comments from the text.

Class discussion could be extended to include off-campus issues regarding personal space in differing environments and situations, such as home, work, restaurants, or bars.

2. This activity could be used as an alternative to Exercise 5 at the end of Chapter 4. Ask students to write two short stories about themselves, one true and the other untrue. Ask for volunteers to tell their two stories in front of the class, presenting both as if they were true. (Or the instructor or a confederate can do this.)

Other students should observe verbal and nonverbal behaviors during the stories to determine which is true and which is not. After both stories have been told, have students vote on the true and untrue versions. Then ask students to list the characteristics or behaviors that led them to vote as they did. Write these on the board to serve as data for discussion. Only at this point should you reveal which story was true. Ask volunteers to describe their experiences as the "deceiver."

Discussion should focus on the following issues: What are characteristics of deception? How accurate can we be in detecting deception from nonverbal behavior alone? What are some of the factors that may affect our ability to detect deception (knowledge of the communicator, knowledge of the subject, ability to observe channels, etc.)?

3. Write each of the following on an index card:

I'm thirsty.	I'm bored.
I'm tired.	A nice-looking female
OK	Time out.
It is over there.	It is up there.
I have a headache.	I have a stomachache.
I am very happy.	I am very sad.
I am very nervous.	Painting a picture
This is important.	Listen to this.
I am confused.	I don't care.
It's your fault.	I'm cold.
I'm hot.	You have said enough.

A big circle	A rabbit
Driving a car	Dancing
Money	Typing a paper
Reading a book	Flirting
A drunk	An infant

Hand one card to each student, and have students use nonverbals <u>only</u> to convey the words or phrases on the cards to their classmates. After students have guessed the correct word or phrase, have them identify whether the message was an adapter, a regulator, an emblem, or an illustrator.

<u>Multiple-Choice Questions</u>

1. Physically attractive people
   a. are often seen as trustworthy and sociable.
   b. are assumed to share our attitudes.
   c. report a higher frequency of dates.
   * d. all of the above

2. Which of the following is <u>not</u> a basic emotion?
   a. fear   c. sadness
   * b. contempt   d. disgust

3. John was at a friend's party and was not having a good time. However, when his friend asked him if he was having fun, John smiled and said, "Hey, this is great! What a party!" John was engaging in
   * a. masking.   c. internalizing.
   b. inhibiting.   d. externalizing.

4. The body type most associated with attractiveness and sociability is that of the
   * a. mesomorph.   c. physomorph.
   b. endomorph.   d. ectomorph.

5. Which person rarely shows how he or she feels?
   * a. withholder   c. ever-ready expresser
   b. blanked expresser   d. frozen-affect expresser

6. Which person shows the trace of an emotion, even when not actually feeling that emotion?
   a. withholder
   b. blanked expresser
   c. ever-ready expresser
 * d. frozen-affect expresser

7. Nonverbals used to maintain turn taking between two or more interactants are
   a. adapters.
   b. illustrators.
   c. emblems.
 * d. regulators.

8. Hand movements that are used to satisfy a person's physical or psychological needs are called
 * a. adapters.
   b. illustrators.
   c. emblems.
   d. regulators.

9. According to Patterson's arousal theory, if Person A perceives Person B's increase in intimacy as positive, A will most likely
   a. compensate.
   b. implicate.
 * c. reciprocate.
   d. all of the above

10. The five stages to courtship are
   a. attention, positioning, invitations and sexual arousal, resolution, recognition.
   b. attention, recognition, invitations and sexual arousal, positioning, resolution.
 * c. attention, recognition, positioning, invitations and sexual arousal, resolution.
   d. attention, positioning, recognition, invitations and sexual arousal, resolution.

True-or-False Questions

1. Interpreting emotions is very difficult because there are over twenty basic human emotions. (F)

2. Eye contact is fundamental to how people attempt to manage impressions. (T)

3. Externalizers tend to bottle up emotions and display neutral or muted facial expressions. (F)

4. Compared to women, men generally stand closer to other speakers. (F)

5. Immediacy refers to the degree of psychological closeness we feel with another person. (T)

6. The orotund vocal quality is often negatively stereotyped because it implies weakness and lack of enthusiasm. (F)

7. Communicators will attempt to converge toward the speech and nonverbal patterns of others when they desire to communicate a contrasting self-image. (F)

8. Communicators exhibit mutual accommodation when they both switch their speech styles to move toward both parties' speech rate, volume, etc. (T)

9. Arousal theory holds that individuals are in a constant state of arousal. The goal of the communicator is to provide opportunities for positive arousal. (F)

10. According to Burgoon (1989), the nonverbal expression of intimacy involves communicating several different yet related themes that jointly characterize the overall degree of intimacy and liking. (T)

Short-Answer Questions

1. What is the functional approach to the study of nonverbal communication? Do you agree with this approach?

2. What is meant by channel discrepancy? How could this be useful in the study of deception detection?

3. What are self-fulfilling prophecies? How do they relate to our attribution of physical beauty to others?

4. List four possible reasons why it is difficult to interpret a person's nonverbal communication. What implication do these have for your own efforts to interpret other people's nonverbal messages?

PART II ACHIEVING SELF-PRESENTATION GOALS

CHAPTER 5: PRESENTING THE SELF

Chapter Objectives

1. To discuss how communication is used in the service of the major interaction goal of self-presentation

2. To survey the reasons why people hold on to particular self-presentations

3. To discuss five direct methods or strategies of self-presentation, emphasizing how people ingratiate and self-promote

4. To discuss indirect strategies of self-presentation

Discussion Questions

1. Solicit students' opinions regarding these questions: Do you think that it is really possible to raise your self-esteem simply by changing your self-presentation strategies? Why or why not? Can you think of any examples to illustrate your points?

2. Have students discuss a situation in which they may wish to keep a negative identity. (Would it simply be too much work to maintain the positive identity?) You could follow up with this question: Would you go from a positive identity to a negative identity in any situation?

3. Ask students if they believe that we are continuously able to monitor our self-presentation and that we can go from latent mindfulness to expressed mindfulness so quickly. Ask students to provide reasons for their answers and examples to back their positions.

4. Have the class discuss the three indirect strategies of self-presentation: basking in reflected glory, blasting the opposition, and boosting. Inquire whether these strategies are more common, less common, or just as common as Jones and Pittman's direct strategies. Have students provide examples of each indirect strategy.

5. Present students with this question: Are there any ethical issues involved in meeting self-presentation goals? For example, is it ethical for us to study self-presentation in order to learn better how to ingratiate? To self-promote? Another ethical question is whether people should change their modes of self-presentation or simply remain true to themselves.

Class Activities

1. Divide the class into groups of four or five. Give students a few minutes to familiarize themselves with Jones and Pittman's taxonomy. Then have them write one personal example of each strategy (ingratiation, intimidation, self-promotion, exemplification, supplication) that they have experienced. Next, take a few minutes to have each group discuss where the strategies were used and whether or not they were successful. Finally, have all group members combine their answers and present them to the class as a whole. Were there any similarities? Differences?

2. Divide the class into groups of four or five. Have students share examples of either their own or a friend's faux pas. Wait until each group has at least ten examples. Have them categorize these examples into self-presentation strategies. What type of image were they trying to create? What happened to tarnish that image? (Note: This activity could also be used when discussing Chapter 6, or as a transitional exercise to Chapter 6, which also discusses types of embarrassment, including faux pas, and strategies for reducing embarrassment.)

Multiple-Choice Questions

1.　The ability to monitor the success of our self-presentation goals at a nonconscious level is called
　　a.　preattentive skills.　　c.　self-monitoring.
　*　b.　latent mindfulness.　　d.　social watchfulness.

2.　We strive for self-identities that are
　*　a.　believable and beneficial to us.
　　b.　believable and obvious to ourselves
　　c.　beneficial and inobvious to ourselves.
　　d.　inobvious and beneficial to others.

3.　One factor that determines whether we will enact ingratiating behavior is the subjective probability of success. Which of the following is not considered under this factor?
　　a.　determining whether the target will be receptive or resistant to our attempt
　　b.　sizing up the situation to determine success of the attempt
　　c.　assessing own skills and resources relating to the attempt
　*　d.　comparing our skills with the target's skills to determine who would be more successful in the attempt

4.　Which of the following strategies attempts to portray the self as dedicated and worthy?
　　a.　ingratiation　　　　c.　self-promotion
　*　b.　exemplification　　d.　supplication

5.　Which of the following strategies attempts to arouse affection from others?
　*　a.　ingratiation　　　　c.　self-promotion
　　b.　exemplification　　d.　supplication

6. Jill tries to present herself as being dangerous and ruthless; however, on this particular occasion, Jill was perceived as being "all talk" or wishy-washy. What might have happened that changed her intended image?
   a. She let others know that she was willing to cause them embarrassment to get what she wanted.
   b. She let others know that she has a low tolerance for anger and could become revengeful.
   c. She let others know that she was not likely to give in to sentiment or compassion.
   * d. She let others know that she would never cause herself pain or embarrassment to get her way.

7. Which of the following strategies might backfire, making you look like a hypocrite?
   a. ingratiation   c. self-promotion
   * b. exemplification   d. intimidation

8. Which type of ingratiation occurs when someone acts nice or complementary to get something else, such as a favor?
   a. authentic ingratiation   c. motivational ingratiation
   b. situational ingratiation   * d. illicit ingratiation

9. Which type of ingratiation occurs when one's primary motivation in using such behaviors is to meet the demands of the situation?
   * a. authentic ingratiation   c. motivational ingratiation
   b. situational ingratiation   d. illicit ingratiation

10. Relative to others, braggers are seen as
    a. more competent and more likeable.
    * b. more competent and less likeable.
    c. less competent and less likeable
    d. none of the above

11. Which of the following is not an indirect self-presentation strategy?
    a. blasting the opposition with derogation
    * b. blinding the opposition with irrelevant stories
    c. basking in reflected glory
    d. boosting one's assessment of an association

12. Which of the following is not one of the qualities to be emphasized in the strategy of self-promotion?
    a. natural ability   c. help of others
    * b. motivation   d. effort

13. You appear to be a caring person by giving money to the needy and joining organizations that support social causes. You have engaged in a form of
    a. ingratiation.   c. self-promotion.
    * b. exemplification.   d. supplication.

True-or-False Questions

1. We are able to monitor our self-presentation skills continuously on a nonconscious level. (T)

2. If a positive identity requires us to fulfill new responsibilities, we may elect to keep a negative identity. (F)

3. Our self-presentation can help raise our self-esteem. (T)

4. Negative feedback can enhance our motivation to present ourselves in a positive way. (T)

5. Conscious monitoring of our self-presentation skills is known as latent mindfulness. (F)

6. The motivation to create a desired identity can be so strong as to make us engage in violent acts or acts that are damaging to ourselves. (T)

7. As the need to be liked increases, the probability of successful ingratiation decreases. (T)

8. One of the negative attributions that you risk when employing intimidation strategies is that you will appear conceited. (F)

9. The emotion that you are attempting to arouse when employing supplication is guilt. (T)

10. Self-promoters should outwardly declare accomplishments to ensure the successful outcome of respect. (F)

11. The desire to boost your associations may occur when your only audience is yourself. (T)

12. Your self-presentation strategies change depending on how you want the other person to see you. In three different conversations, you may use three different strategies. (T)

1. Identify and define three indirect strategies and three direct strategies of self-presentation. Which are most effective, in your opinion--direct or indirect?

2. What is the relationship between self-presentation and self-esteem?

3. What is the role of positive and negative feedback in self-presentation?

4. List three things you might consider when presenting yourself to a new acquaintance.

CHAPTER 6: DEFENDING THE SELF

Chapter Objectives

1. To present account giving as an important self-presentation goal

2. To present the different types of accounts, including excuses, justifications, apologies, and denials, and to show under what conditions these messages are considered effective

3. To discuss how we manage embarrassment predicaments

4. To discuss how we manage accounts when dealing with bureaucrats (as in traffic court)

5. To present attribution theory as a means of understanding the viability of accounts

Discussion Questions

1. Have students provide recent examples of controversies involving politicians, actors, and other public figures. Three issues could be considered: First, should public officials be required to account for their personal lives (drinking, extramarital affairs, marijuana use, etc.)? Second, do your students think that their own private lives are private, or must they give accounts for their own behaviors and relationships? Finally, what types of accounts that they have seen are viable? Have students offer specific examples.

2. Have students cite examples from their own experience of accounts that were received well and those that were not received well. Specifically, have students think of a personally embarrassing situation and how they responded. Ask them to identify which accounts were successful and which were not and to explore reasons for the differences.

3. Ask students to consider how people might act like "naive social scientists" when they are about to offer an account or when given accounts by others. Have them give examples from their experience when they have acted as "investigators," "jury members," or "news reporters" when trying to understand other people's behavior. How much time and effort do we spend finding out why, is it fair, or what are the facts?

4. You may want to discuss the ethical implications of teaching the literature on accounts. Should students use the information on account giving to achieve their communication goals? Are there any ethical problems in being a "good account giver"? Or should we not worry about teaching people to be effective in understanding and communicating accounts?

Class Activities

1. This activity is a fun way to show in concrete terms how people offer different kinds of accounts in different predicaments. (We heard of these predicaments from our students.) The activity involves having students make up accounts by combining the predicaments with the types of accounts. First, on note cards, write one of each of the following predicaments:

a. You are two hours late for Thanksgiving dinner, and your host is extremely upset because all of the other guests had to wait to eat while the food got cold. What do you say to the host?

b. You borrowed a friend's textbook and sold it back to the bookstore for cash. Your friend asks for the book back. What will you tell your friend?

c. Your parents are paying for your education. Although you tried to hide it from them, they discover that you failed three classes last year. What account do you offer your parents?

d. You didn't do the dishes again, and your roommates are really mad at you for not keeping up with your share of the housework. How do you respond to your roommates?

e. You threw some papers in the trash. Later you found out that these were important papers that your mate had to complete and return to a superior at work. How do you account for this?

f. You turn in a paper late to your professor, and you are afraid that your grade will suffer as a result. The professor asks you why your paper is late. What do you say?

g. You injure your back and need to ask for time off from work. Your boss doesn't think that anyone should miss work under any circumstances and suggests that you are not a good employee. How do you respond?

h. You have been driving in the passing lane for over twenty minutes. Your passenger turns to you and asks, "Why are you driving like this? You know bad driving is a sign of immaturity." What do you say in response?

i. You are caught leaving your work premises for lunch without signing out or gaining permission. This is against company policy. What do you say to your boss?

j. You are pulled over by a police officer for driving 80 miles per hour in a 55-mph zone. The officer asks for your driver's license, but you do not have it because it was taken away after your third speeding ticket. How do you account for this?

k. It is 4:58 P.M. and you are scheduled to begin work at 5:00. You rush toward the changing room to put on your uniform and discover that the room is already occupied. Changing in the break room is against company policy, but you strip down and start changing clothes anyway. Before you have your uniform on, your manager walks into the room, catching you red-handed and red-faced. What do you say?

l. Your romantic partner walks into your room and finds you kissing his or her best friend. Your partner is very jealous and angry. What do you say?

m. Your romantic partner comes home unexpectedly and finds you in the middle of reading some of his or her personal letters. What do you say to defend yourself?

n. Your fiancé or fiancée, who has been saving every possible penny for your wedding costs, happens to find your charge card statement and discovers that you have made a number of purchases for things that are not strictly necessary and confronts you for "spending money foolishly." What do you say in response?

o. You happened to be traveling through a town where an old friend lives, but you did not call or stop to visit. Somehow, your friend finds this out and is hurt and angry. What is your account for this?

Next, copy each of the following account types on separate note cards:

Concession (full-blown apology)
Concession (partial confession of guilt)
Concession (admission of guilt or responsibility)
Concession (full confession of guilt)
Excuse (appeal to own shortcomings)
Excuse (appeal to accidents)
Excuse (scapegoating)
Excuse (appeal to shortcomings of others as a frame of reference)
Excuse (reasons for the appeal to shortcomings)
Excuse (appeal to defeasibility)
Excuse (appeal to own effort and care during event)
Excuse (biological drives or fatalism)
Refusal (claim that event did not occur)
Refusal (unrestricted attribution of guilt to the accuser)
Refusal (reference to other sources of information)
Refusal (denial of the right of the reproach)
Refusal (refusal to confess guilt for the event)
Refusal (evasion)
Justification (condemnation of condemners)
Justification (self-fulfillment)
Justification (sad tale)
Justification (denial of injury or minimization of harm)
Justification (denial of victim)
Justification (appeal to loyalties)
Humor

Shuffle the two decks of cards separately so that each is in random order. Have students, one at a time, take a predicament card and read it to the rest of the class. Next, have them take an account card, read the account aloud, and role-play the account to fit the given predicament. Have students take turns, with each taking three tries. (After several turns, reshuffle the cards so that variations occur.) Time permitting, you may want students to experiment with two or three different types of accounts for each predicament. After the activity is over, ask students to discuss which of the accounts were believable.

2. Break the class into dyads or small groups. Using the predicaments in Activity 1, hand each dyad or group one of the cards. Ask groups to brainstorm the many possible ways to account for each predicament. After the accounts are offered, have them identify which type each is. Class discussion could then focus on contextual factors in account giving, which types of accounts are most effective in achieving goals, and so on.

Multiple-Choice Questions

1. Apologies and excuses
   * a. are more likely to be perceived as polite, preferable, and effective than justifications and refusals.
   b. are seen as most competent because the communicator presents himself or herself as in control of the situation.
   c. are less likely to be perceived as polite, preferable, and effective than justifications and refusals.
   d. interfere with a person's ability to defend the self.

2. Justifications
   a. are more likely to be perceived as polite, preferable, and effective than excuses and apologies.
   * b. are seen as most competent because the communicator presents himself or herself as in control of the situation.
   c. are less likely to be perceived as polite, preferable, and effective than excuses and apologies.
   d. interfere with a person's ability to defend the self.

3. Examples of concessions include all of the following except
   a. acknowledgment of one's own responsibility or guilt.
   * b. appeal to loyalties.
   c. expression of regret.
   d. appeal to restitutions already performed.

4. The appeal to accident excuse is
   a. used quite frequently.   c. less effective if it is overused.
   b. often honored by others.   * d. all of the above

5. Suzanne claimed that since she did not know how to use quotes or footnotes, she should not be charged with plagiarism. This is an example of which type of justification?
   a. scapegoating   c. self-fulfillment
   b. an appeal to loyalty   * d. an appeal to defeasibility

6. Pat said, "So what if I play my music loud? Our neighbors are so old that their hearing is probably bad anyway!" This is an example of which type of justification?
   a. scapegoating   * c. denial of victim
   b. sad tale   d. condemnation of the condemner

32

7. "I'm sorry I was speeding, officer. I'm twenty minutes late for work, and we are having an important meeting today." This is an example of which type of justification?
    a. scapegoating
    b. denial of victim
    * c. appeal to loyalty
    d. self-fulfillment

8. Dispositional causes of behavior are believed to originate in
    a. the environment.
    * b. the actor.
    c. the viewer or perceiver of the behavior.
    d. none of the above

9. Distinctiveness judgments deal with
    * a. whether or not a person's behavior is different from one situation to another.
    b. the extent to which a person's behavior is the same over time.
    c. the perception of similar others in similar situations.
    d. whether or not a person's behavior is acceptable in a certain situation.

10. Which attributions are most effective in offering an excuse?
    a. unintentional, stable, internal, uncontrollable causes
    * b. unintentional, unstable, external, uncontrollable causes
    c. intentional, stable, internal, controllable causes
    d. intentional, unstable, external, controllable causes

True-or-False Questions

1. Scott and Lyman defined an account as "a linguistic device employed whenever an action is subjected to evaluative inquiry." (T)

2. Since concessions are the denial of responsibility, they are the opposite of an apology. (F)

3. A justification attempts to exonerate the accounter, whereas an excuse makes an action seem less negative. (F)

4. Scapegoating excuses involve appeals to fate. (F)

5. People are most likely to accept accounts that combine justifications, refusals, and concessions. (F)

6. Attribution theory states that we study other people's behavior in order to judge why people act the way they do. (T)

7. Justifications are more likely to be seen as competent than excuses. (T)

8.   Conflict is likely to occur if a person justifies an unintentionally planned failure event. (T)

9.   Derogations of self-esteem are likely to be met with neutral questions. (F)

<u>Short-Answer Questions</u>

1.   What is involved in presenting a "full-blown" apology? Do all of these features sound realistic?

2.   You are twenty minutes late for class, and your professor asks for an account of your behavior. Give an example of an excuse that offers unintentional, unstable, external, and uncontrollable causes; then give an example of an excuse that is related to intentional, stable, internal, and controllable causes.

3.   What are the two main goals people pursue in the management of embarrassing situations?

4.   Explain how an ineffective account may lead to conflict between two people.

CHAPTER 7: DISCLOSING THE SELF

<u>Chapter Objectives</u>

1. To position self-disclosure as an important self-presentation activity within the goals-based approach

2. To define self-disclosure and to present its dimensions

3. To discuss self-disclosure in conjunction with privacy regulation

4. To present the factors that encourage and inhibit self-disclosure

5. To discuss the consequences of self-disclosure in terms of its dimensions

Discussion Questions

1. Raise the general issue of the use of self-disclosure in meeting interpersonal goals, especially self-presentation goals. The book claims that self-disclosure is a very direct method of presenting the self. Have your students consider if this is true or not. Then ask if meeting our own goals through self-disclosure interferes with the goals of others.

2. Have students discuss how the media present disclosure and disclosers. You may want to assign students to bring in an example of a novel, a television program, or a movie in order to discuss whether or not the media present disclosure accurately.

3. Have the class break into groups of three or four to address the following questions: How do couples, friends, and acquaintances manage their privacy boundaries? In other words, what kinds of behaviors do people engage in to maintain privacy? Do these behaviors vary across relationship type? Should people respect each other's needs for privacy? What about needs for disclosure?

4. Ask students to consider how self-disclosure is also used to achieve goals of relational escalation, maintenance, and de-escalation. That is, ask if disclosure is used to obtain relational goals as well as self-presentation goals. (The authors believe that disclosure does further all kinds of goals, especially self-presentation goals.)

5. Ask students to discuss the factors that affect disclosure, offering examples from their own experience. Can they think of factors not mentioned in the book that affect disclosure?

Class Activities

1. Divide the class into groups of five members each. Give each group a disclosure situation. Situations might include:

   a.   Two male best friends hanging out on a Tuesday afternoon
   b.   A male and female acquaintance meeting for lunch
   c.   Newlyweds spending their second weekend together after the honeymoon
   d.   A mother and her college-age daughter spending a Saturday shopping
   e.   Two good female friends having dinner together

   Have the groups generate lists of disclosure topics for their situation. They should be able to create a list of potential topics and one of taboo topics. Finally, have students put the topics in the appropriate intimacy category: valuative, topical, or descriptive.

2. Divide the class into groups of five members each. Using situations like those in Activity 1, have the groups create dialogues that might occur in these situations. You may want to assign a topic, such as dating or sex.

The groups should include in their dialogues disclosure that would be appropriate and disclosure that would not be appropriate. Have two members from each group interpret the dialogue in front of the class. Students from other groups will attempt to identify appropriate and inappropriate disclosure given the situation and to explain why statements are inappropriate. Students can also identify barriers to disclosure in each of the particular situations.

3. Show a clip of a movie (e.g., <u>Sweet Heart's Dance</u>) or a television program (e.g., <u>thirtysomething</u>) in which the characters are engaged in disclosure. Have the class discuss the nature of the disclosure in terms of its dimensions of breadth, depth, valence, and so on.

<u>Multiple-Choice Questions</u>

1. "I can't stand spiders--they are dirty, disgusting creatures." This is an example of
   * a. evaluative intimacy.
      b. topical intimacy.
      c. descriptive intimacy.
      d. none of the above

2. Kris knows all about Julie's family, but only her family. According to social penetration theory, Kris and Julie's disclosure has
      a. primarily breadth.
   * b. primarily depth.
      c. both breadth and depth.
      d. neither breadth nor depth.

3. Tina does not disclose often. However, once she gets started, she tends to tell everything about herself. According to Wheeless, Tina's disclosure lacks which dimension?
      a. valence
      b. honesty or accuracy
      c. amount or frequency
   * d. control of depth

4. According to Miller, the reasons why people disclose include all of the following <u>except</u>
      a. to be the center of attention.
      b. to avoid rejection.
      c. to achieve acceptance.
   * d. to develop distance from another person.

5. Jourard's dyadic effect indicates that if Bob tells Jerry that he is no longer attracted to his wife, Jerry's responding disclosure will most likely
      a. be less disclosive.
      b. be more disclosive.
   * c. be equally disclosive.
      d. change the subject.

6. Consider the following communication exchange:
   Sarah: I wish we could spend more time together.
   David: I'm just not ready to be in love or to live with someone.
   Petronio would identify this coordination of boundaries as
   a. satisfactory.   c. deficient.
 * b. overcompensating.   d. equivocal.

7. According to Ludwig et al., who are more likely to reciprocate depth of disclosure?
   a. extroverts   * c. high self-monitors
   b. introverts   d. low self-monitors

8. Which of the following is <u>not</u> true regarding married couples and disclosure?
   a. Married couples' amount of disclosure tends to decrease over time.
   b. The valence of married couples' disclosure tends to become more negative.
   c. Married couples tend to disclose to each other more than outsiders.
 * d. Married couples' disclosure tends to be more evaluative than descriptive.

9. Petronio, Martin, and Littlefield found that women place more importance on prerequisites for self-disclosure than men do. These prerequisites for characteristics of receivers include all of the following <u>except</u> that they be
   a. discreet.   c. liked.
 * b. same-sex.   d. open.

10. Which of the following statements about the association between self-disclosure and liking or satisfaction is true?
 * a. Negative disclosures usually lead to negative evaluations.
    b. Amount of self-disclosure is more important than how it is offered.
    c. People who reciprocate on the same level or topic of intimacy are perceived less favorably than those who do not reciprocate.
    d. Generally, disclosures offered early in conversations rather than late are viewed positively by listeners.

True-or-False Questions

1. If the relational rewards outweigh the costs, a decrease in intimacy is sought. (F)

2. According to Altman and Taylor, most self-disclosure occurs after people get to know each other, after the initial stages of the relationship. (F)

3. Wheeless and Grotz found that trust was more related to control of depth and intent to disclose dimensions of self than to the honesty dimension. (T)

4. The most common reason why college students do not disclose is that they want to maintain a positive self-presentation. (T)

5. Tolerance of vulnerability is a function of both the need to be open and the need to protect oneself. (F)

6. Women tend to use a status-assertive disclosure style more than men. (F)

7. In general, Japanese people value self-disclosure more than Americans. (F)

8. When people believe that a disclosure they are hearing is not targeted specifically for them, the discloser is seen as more open and therefore more likable. (F)

9. Often an intimate message without intense language is viewed favorably even when the message responded to is a low-intimacy, low-intensity message. (T)

10. Research indicates that communicators who offer negative disclosures are viewed as more honest and are therefore viewed more positively. (F)

Short-Answer Questions

1. This book places the discussion of self-disclosure in the chapters concerned with self-presentation. Would it not be better to discuss self-disclosure as a relational goal?

2. What does social penetration theory tell us about self-disclosure?

3. In privacy boundary management, what are the considerations of disclosers versus respondents? Compare and contrast two considerations of each.

4. Discuss the relationship between disclosure and liking or satisfaction. What factors influence this relationship, and how?

5. Is honesty always the best policy? Answer using material presented in the text.

CHAPTER 8: ESCALATING RELATIONSHIPS

Chapter Objectives

1. To show that relationships vary qualitatively in the way they develop

2. To discuss the different bases of attraction, emphasizing the importance of communication

3. To emphasize that escalation involves both increases and decreases in intimacy, with the more highly developed relationships maintaining a level of intimacy that can be sustained over the long haul

4. To discuss turning points as a method for tracing the escalation of relationships

Discussion Questions

1. Ask students to discuss the following questions: Do you share any personal idioms with a romantic partner? With a family member? With a friend? How did these idioms originate? Do you ever catch yourself using them in public, or do you consciously use them in public? Do idioms make you feel closer to your partner?

2. Have students discuss Andersen's six cognitive schemata. Ask if all of these schemata are relevant in every incident and if there are other important factors that have not been identified in Andersen's model.

3. Have students consider their romantic relationships or those of close friends or family members. Ask if they would characterize each relationship as "accelerated," "intermediate," or "prolonged." What reasons do they have for their answers? Ask if partners can change the rate of escalation, or is it predetermined by the way the relationship began?

4. Do your students think that too much emphasis is placed on escalating relationships? That is, do they feel pressured to begin and develop relationships when they prefer to be alone?

<u>Class Activities</u>

1. Divide the class into groups of four or five, with males and females in each group. Have the groups take a few minutes to study Andersen's cognitive valence theory. Using his model, have the groups consider the following situations in which they are always Person B:

   a. You are sitting in a secluded booth in a dark restaurant with your boss of the opposite sex. The boss moves closer to you and slides a hand over yours.

   b. You are on a first date with someone you do not find at all attractive or interesting. At this moment you are walking side by side down a public sidewalk; it is around 8:30 P.M., and you are wondering how you will get through the evening. Your date stops walking and suddenly kisses you on the cheek very close to your lips.

   c. You are eating dinner in your apartment with your best friend of the opposite sex. Your friend suddenly stops eating and tells you that he or she is in love with you and always has been.

   d. You are walking down Main Street at noon with your lover of three months, who all at once kisses you passionately.

   e. You are at a party, and you have been drinking. You go into a spare bedroom to "sleep it off." Someone of the opposite sex whom you do not know very well follows you into the room and lies down beside you.

In each of these situations, how would you react as Person B? Do the males react differently than females in any or all of the situations? Trace your reactions for each situation through Andersen's model.

2. Have class members discuss in pairs how different relationships can develop in different ways. Have them think of three different relationships and identify the ways they began and escalated. Then ask them to recall any differences in communication that typify these relationships. What might explain these differences?

Multiple-Choice Questions

1. According to Perlman and Fehr, which of the following is <u>not</u> one of the qualities of intimate relationships?
    a. Interaction increases in frequency, duration, and settings.
    b. Partners become skilled at predicting each other's behavior.
    * c. Partners decrease their investments in the relationship.
    d. Partners feel that their separate interests are linked to the well-being of the relationship.

2. Which are the fundamental interpersonal needs according to Schutz?
    a. inclusion, knowledge, control
    b. knowledge, control, affection
    * c. inclusion, control, affection
    d. none of the above

3. Which of the following is an advantage of pursuing closer relationships?
    a. You have reason to fear your own destructive impulses.
    b. You may be abandoned.
    c. You may lose control over the situation.
    * d. You reduce uncertainty about the other person.

4. Which of the following is <u>not</u> one of McCroskey and McCain's dimensions of attraction?
    a. social   * c. physical
    b. communication   d. task

5. Which of the following is <u>not</u> one of Berger et al.'s (1977) dimensions of attraction?
    a. supportiveness   * c. communication
    b. character   d. sociability

6. According to Wallace's study on attraction, which of the following is negatively related to liking?
    a. supportiveness   c. sensitivity
    * b. talkativeness   d. flirtatiousness

7. According to Andersen's cognitive valence theory, if Person A increases intimacy and Person B reacts positively on five of the six cognitive schemata, what would the predicted relational outcome be?
    a. Positive relational outcomes will occur.
    * b. Negative relational outcomes will occur.
    c. Neutral relational outcomes will occur.
    d. Person B will increase intimacy also.

41

8. Which of Knapp's stages of relational escalation is characterized by small talk?
    a. bonding
    b. integrating
    c. initiating
    * d. experimenting

9. Which of Knapp's stages includes using verbal shortcuts that both people understand?
    a. bonding
    * b. intensifying
    c. experimenting
    d. integrating

10. Which "love way" is communicated primarily through nonverbal messages?
    a. committed
    b. traditional
    c. collaborative
    * d. none of the above

True-or-False Questions

1. Interdependence in your relationship helps you achieve desired personal outcomes. (T)

2. Escalation of relationships means the successful negotiation of both intimacy and control. (T)

3. Clatterbuck's cognitive class of attraction deals with communication behaviors. (F)

4. Clatterbuck's anthropological class of attraction deals with physical beauty. (T)

5. Physical beauty is often defined more by individual preferences than by cultural standards. (F)

6. Couples in short-term romantic relationships have higher need complementarity than couples in long-term relationships. (F)

7. Altman and Taylor state that uniqueness of interaction increases as the relationship matures. (T)

8. Rings are probably exchanged in the intensifying stage of Knapp's model. (F)

9. Prolonged courtship types have more love and more conflict than accelerated types. (T)

10. Committed love is seen in messages of togetherness that reference the present as well as the future. (T)

1.   What are Clatterbuck's four approaches to the study of attraction?

2.   What is the "norm of reciprocity"? Why is this an important factor in interpersonal communication?

3.   Do you think that Knapp's five stages of relational escalation accurately describe the subject, in your experience?

4.   Do you think the study of relational turning points offers insights into the ways in which relationships escalate?

CHAPTER 9: MAINTAINING RELATIONSHIPS

Chapter Objectives

1.   To present equity theory as a way of understanding why some relationships are maintained and others are not. (Equity theory is again presented in Chapter 10, on relational de-escalation.)

2.   To discuss proactive and constructive strategies people report using for maintaining close personal relationships

3.   To discuss positive and regressive spirals of messages

4.   To introduce relational dialectics and responses to dialectics

5.   To discuss different marital types, as found in the research of Fitzpatrick

Discussion Questions

1.   Ask students to think about a current or recent romantic relationship. Ask them to offer examples of positivity, openness, assurances, social networks, and sharing tasks.

2.   Ask students to reflect on a failed relationship of any type. Would Stafford and Canary's maintenance strategies have helped maintain this relationship? How? Why? Were any used?

3. Ask students to identify maintenance strategies in their favorite television shows (soaps, sitcoms, dramas) and in movies. How might they learn to recognize these strategies and to determine their effectiveness?

4. Discuss the concept of spirals. Ask students if the upper and lower limits are fixed or clearly defined, especially as they are experiencing these spirals. In other words, when do you know that the progressive or regressive spiral is approaching the limit?

Class Activities

1. Have the class divide into pairs. Each member of each pair will be role-playing an involvement in several different situations.

   a. You are involved in what you had considered to be a happy, albeit predictable, marriage. You had noticed nothing wrong with your relationship until this evening. Tonight you discovered evidence that leads you to conclude that your spouse has been having an affair for the past year. You don't want a divorce; you want to continue this marriage, but you are justifiably angry and hurt. Convey all of this to your spouse.

   b. Your roommate of the opposite sex has been acting very oddly. You suspect that he or she is becoming romantically inclined toward you. You decide to approach your roommate with your suspicions because you don't feel the same way. However, you know that you could never find a better roommate. Communicate your feelings to your roommate while sustaining an environment in which you can remain friends as well as roommates.

   c. You have never gotten along with your father, yet you no longer actively disagree. Your relationship is simply a distant one. Recently, while visiting, you overheard a conversation between your parents in which your father expressed his regret at the lack of closeness in your relationship. You feel as if you should make some effort to promote a more fulfilling relationship. Go about doing this.

   d. Your best friend, a photography major, has spent weeks putting together the final portfolio for an important class and is apparently satisfied with the results. You think that some of the pictures are of low quality and that the overall effect is disappointing. When asked for your opinion, you decide to tell the truth. Do this in such a way as to maintain the relationship.

Discuss the various means of maintaining relationships through communication. How might you have communicated differently than your partner if the roles had been reversed?

2. Have students write accounts by creating or recalling a personal situation in which one member of a relationship is severely underbenefited and the other overbenefited. Have them exchange their accounts with another class member. Have the pairs of students answer the following questions:

    a. Which of you created a more extreme situation?
    b. Is there a difference in your perceptions of over- and underbenefited members?
    c. Why might this be so?

Have students trade again with two other class members. Then have the class discuss as a group if they saw any clear differences in the kinds of situations they wrote about.

3. Ask students to think about a relationship in which they want to maintain closeness but are unhappy about how things have been going although they aren't exactly sure what is wrong. Which of the following strategies would they be more likely to use?

    a. Positivity--I would act nice and cheerful so that my partner would reciprocate.
    b. Assurances--I would comfort the other person and see to it that his or her needs were met.
    c. Openness--I would discuss my unhappiness with my partner to try to change things.
    d. Social networks--I would talk to some mutual friends to see if they could offer support or advice.
    e. Sharing tasks--I would work harder to perform my share of our duties.
    f. Antisocial--I would act rude or manipulative if my partner did not change.
    g. Avoidance--I would detract attention from our problems in the hope that they would diminish.

Multiple-Choice Questions

1. What is achieved when the ratios of inputs to outputs is the same for both partners?
   * a. equity   c. reciprocity
     b. equality   d. none of the above

2. Which of the following is not one of Stafford and Canary's five types of communication strategies in maintenance?
     a. positivity   c. assurances
   * b. acknowledgments   d. social networks

3. Which particular strategy involves not criticizing the partner?
   * a. positivity
   b. active strategy
   c. assurances
   d. social networks

4. Using which strategy most implies commitment to the relationship and its future?
   a. positivity
   b. active strategy
   * c. assurances
   d. social networks

5. Accepting that dialectics are a natural part of relational life is known as
   a. selection.
   b. revitalization.
   c. neutralization.
   * d. reframing.

6. Compromising dialectics or handling the topics ambiguously is known as
   a. reframing.
   * b. neutralization.
   c. discussion.
   d. acquiescence.

7. According to Fitzpatrick's typology, which couples are autonomous and avoid conflict?
   a. traditionals
   b. independents
   * c. separates
   d. propers

8. According to Fitzpatrick's typology, which couples are interdependent and experience conflict?
   a. traditionals
   * b. independents
   c. separates
   d. propers

9. Which of the following would portray an "interdependence-autonomy" dialectic?
   * a. a son wanting to move out of his parents' home but being afraid that he couldn't make it on his own
   b. a wife wanting her husband to talk to her but not knowing how to get him to do so
   c. a teacher wanting to instill religious values in his students but the school system wanting to keep religion out of the schools
   d. a husband wanting to go bowling and his wife wanting to go golfing instead

10. Who would be most likely to seek an extramarital relationship first?
    * a. underbenefited partners
    b. overbenefited partners
    c. equitably treated partners
    d. Both partners are equally likely to seek an extramarital affair.

True-or-False Questions

1. Having discrepant goals usually leads to progressive spirals. (F)

2. Revitalization is an indirect way of dealing with dialectics. (T)

3. According to Fitzpatrick's marital typology, independents are "emotionally divorced." (F)

4. According to Fitzpatrick's typology, separates used "guerrilla-like" communication to persuade partners; they constrained the others' behavior but appealed to their values. (T)

5. People increase their use of protective and detective jealousy strategies according to their degree of suspicion and emotional distress. (T)

6. Doing household chores is nice, but it cannot help maintain a relationship. (F)

7. In explicit recognition responses, the communicator offers acknowledgment and explanation. (F)

8. Talking about the state of the relationship can be a taboo topic. (T)

9. If you answer someone with a response that is related but not directly relevant to the issue under discussion, it is known as a nonapplied disclosure. (T)

10. Partners must stop both positive and negative spirals before they hit a critical point, or the relationship will be jeopardized. (T)

Short-Answer Questions

1. Briefly explain the relevance of equity theory to relational maintenance.

2. Do you agree with the four actions you should take when dealing with regressive spirals?

3. Discuss relational dialectics. Do these provide us with a helpful way of considering what it is like to relate to another person over time?

4. Review Fitzpatrick's marital typology. Is one type more desirable than another? Also, is there another marital type that is not covered in this typology? If so, what would it be?

CHAPTER 10: DE-ESCALATING RELATIONSHIPS

Chapter Objectives

1. To discuss why people de-escalate and terminate relationships

2. To present Duck's model as an effective means to describe the process of de-escalation

3. To reintroduce equity theory as it applies to relational stability and satisfaction

4. To discuss how people use communication strategies to de-escalate relationships

5. To discuss how people cope with breakups

Discussion Questions

1. Have students discuss Duck's model of relational disengagement. Ask if, in their experience, the model provides an accurate portrayal of the process? What would they add to or delete from the model?

2. Ask students, why is understanding equity theory important in understanding relational disengagement?

3. Ask students, is the high divorce rate in the United States a sign of failure, or is the divorce rate a more realistic reflection of the nature of human relationships?

4. Ask your students if there is a kind way to end a relationship. Also, ask if it is kind to be cruel, as the text suggests, when the other person resists the breakup.

Class Activities

1. Have students discuss the following question in groups of three or four: What can you do in a relationship in which the person treats you badly? That is, what can you do if the person intimidates, is inconsiderate, and perhaps is verbally or physically aggressive? Once some suggestions have been offered, you may want to discuss the issue as a class.

2. Have students form dyads. Have them suggest instances when each of the communication tactics for relational termination would be effective and appropriate. Are some tactics always or never good tactics?

Multiple-Choice Questions

1. Hill, Rubin, and Peplau found that certain factors were related to relational de-escalation. Which of the following factors is <u>not</u> related?
   a. seasons
   * c. living together
   b. equity
   d. similarities in character and attitudes

2. Which of the following statements is true about involvement and relational maintenance and decay?
   a. Relationships are more likely maintained when men are more involved than women.
   b. Relationships are more likely maintained when women are more involved than men.
   c. Relationships decay when men are more involved than women.
   * d. Relationships are more likely maintained when the partners are equally involved.

3. In which of the following months is a breakup more likely to occur?
   * a. June
   c. January
   b. November
   d. October

4. Hill, Rubin, and Peplau found that women rated more relational problems as important than men did--with one exception. Which of the following problems did men rate as more important?
   a. differences in interests
   * b. living too far apart
   c. a desire to be independent
   d. interest in someone else

5. During which of Duck's phases of relational decline is a person likely to compare the partner to potential partners?
   a. social phase
   * c. intrapsychic phase
   b. grave-dressing phase
   d. dyadic phase

6. During which of Duck's phases is a person likely to confront the partner with the dissatisfaction?
   a. social phase
   c. intrapsychic phase
   b. grave-dressing phase
   * d. dyadic phase

7. According to Metts and Cupach, which of the following reasons for relational decay is more common for men than for women?
   a. drifting apart
   c. third-party involvement
   b. rule violation
   * d. relational definition

49

8. Which of the following communication tactics for disengagement involves suggesting that the two see less of each other and provides a reason why?
   a. positive tone
   * b. de-escalation
   c. justification
   d. negative identity management

9. An underbenefited partner can engage in a number of ways to perceive equity. Which of the following is <u>not</u> one of the ways?
   a. devaluing the self
   b. comparing this relationship to ones that were even less equitable
   c. distorting inputs and outcomes
   * d. seeking compensation

10. When a disengaging couple wants to remain friends, which strategies are most often used?
    a. positive tone and withdrawal
    b. negative identity management and justification
    * c. positive tone and de-escalation
    d. withdrawal and justification

11. In Harvey, Orbuch, and Weber's model of responses to termination, which phase involves the person's avoiding others and considering the reasons for the breakup?
    a. traumatic event
    b. outcry
    * c. denial
    d. none of the above

True-or-False Questions

1. Moving from one level of intimacy to a less intimate one while hoping to remain friends is referred to as de-escalation. (T)

2. The probability of being in a long-term relationship is increased when people are similar to each other. (T)

3. A partner's net gains for being in a relationship are the person's outcomes from the relationship plus the person's inputs into the relationship. (F)

4. The principle of least interest states that the person less interested in establishing and maintaining a relationship will have less power in the relationship. (F)

5. One strategy that is particularly useful in improving long-term relationships involves overbenefited partners' restoring psychological equity by minimizing the victim's suffering. (F)

6.	The more intimate the relationship, the less likely it is that the disengager will use some form of verbal message to communicate an intention to alter the relationship. (F)

7.	One reason that people intentionally cause jealousy in their partners is to bolster their self-esteem. (T)

8.	After a breakup, men tend to be more hurt emotionally than women. (F)

9.	Couples are more likely to remain friends after a breakup if the female initiates the disengagement. (F)

10.	In terms of emotional reactions to perceived inequity, underbenefited partners experience anger and depression, while overbenefited partners experience guilt. (T)

Short-Answer Questions

1.	Would you predict any changes in the 1976 Hill, Rubin, and Peplau study findings if you were to investigate why people break up today? Or do you feel that the reasons for breaking up remain the same today as they did two decades ago? Are any of the reasons different for adults older than 25?

2.	What is the filtering process, and how is it connected to relational termination?

3.	Review Cody's (1982) causes for relational disengagement. Can you add any others to this list?

4.	Differentiate between underbenefited and overbenefited partners. Which do you think is better off, and why? What options do people in both situations have for restoring psychological and actual equity?

PART IV ACHIEVING INSTRUMENTAL GOALS

CHAPTER 11: GAINING COMPLIANCE

Chapter Objectives

1. To extend the discussion of compliance gaining that was introduced in Chapter 3, focusing on instrumental goals (obtaining favors or resources)

2. To present Cialdini's six principles to summarize how people succeed in gaining compliance from others

3. To discuss the tactics of the foot in the door, the door in the face, and lowballing in interpersonal contexts

Discussion Questions

1. Corporations and nonprofit organizations often agonize over the yearly budgeting process. Every department is struggling to receive a substantial piece of the budget pie. Many managers exaggerate their initial budget requests. Ask students to discuss this process in light of reciprocal concessions procedures to describe how management-union negotiations tend to follow reciprocal concessions.

2. Ask students if they have experienced any situations in which someone used a compliance technique that made them feel taken advantage of or misled. Ask them to think about how prevalent such activities are. Also inquire if people who trust others are naive. (You may also want to ask this question after reading Chapter 13's discussion of Machiavellianism.)

3. Ask students if they can identify in their own experience any principle of compliance gaining besides those presented in the text. If they can, ask them to provide examples.

Class Activities

1. Have students form small groups. Ask them to focus on brainstorming the various rules of compliance that they encounter or that influence their lives. Ask them to differentiate rules they employ from rules that are used by others to influence them.

   Then debrief the class by having each group share the rules they identified as the most common compliance procedures experienced. Discuss similarities and differences among the groups. Also discuss some of the compliance procedures that were unique to certain individuals or that seemed to be encountered less often.

2. Hand out three index cards to each student. Each card will have one of the three types of authority (titles, clothes, and trappings) printed at the top. Have the students take one card at a time and do the following: Take five minutes to write down personal examples of compliance or behavior related to the authority type. For example, how many individuals with formal or informal titles influence their behavior? (Have the students be specific.) For clothes, the example could be the number of times students have recently been influenced by the way a person was

dressed; or have them identify the kinds of dress that seem to influence them (and situations in which this effect occurs). Develop a similar question for trappings.

Open a classwide discussion by asking students to share some of their stated behaviors. Then discuss the general level of compliance that these students seem to be experiencing based on these types of authority.

3. Videotape a ten-minute series of television commercials that represent a variety of products and services. After each commercial segment, pause and have students identify the compliance-gaining messages in each commercial.

After all commercials have been shown, discussion could focus on questions like these: . Which messages are most common? Which messages seem most effective? Which are least effective? Do certain products lend themselves to certain compliance-gaining procedures?

4. Collect a variety of items, such as a paper bag, a stapler, a book of matches, a candy bar, a mug, and a book, and place them in a box. Let students examine the contents of the box and choose one item to sell to their classmates. After they have chosen their item, ask for volunteers to practice selling the items to the class. After each student has given a sales pitch, ask the class to identify each compliance-gaining strategy used.

Multiple-Choice Questions

1. Kraut's (1973) study highlighted two reasons why people comply with requests. Which statement is most accurate regarding these two reasons?
    a. The nature of the request itself is important; a person's self-perception is irrelevant.
    b. The nature of the request itself is of little importance compared to a person's self-perception.
*   c. Both the nature of the request and a person's self-perception are important when discussing compliance.
    d. none of the above

2. The reciprocity rule is best described as
*   a. a culturally instilled belief in returning to others the things they do for us.
    b. a means of forcing others to do what we want.
    c. the physical act of taking what belongs to us.
    d. a belief that all things will come full circle.

3. The special term for reciprocal concessions, which means that people are supposed to say no to your first request, is
    a. pie in the sky   *   c. door in the face
    b. just say no   d. foot in the door

4. The commitment principle states that
   a. the less committed a person is to a group, the more likely the person is to comply with a request from that group.
   * b. the more committed a person is to a group, an organization, or a cause, the more likely the person is to comply with a request.
   c. a person's commitment has little or nothing to do with compliance.
   d. people who are committed to a course of action are highly principled individuals.

5. A friend tells you that he will sell you his stereo for $150. You agree, knowing that he had originally paid a lot more for the system. When you go to give your friend the money and pick up the stereo, he informs you that the speakers will cost an additional $100! According to the commitment principle, you have just been
   a. shot in the foot.   c. ripped off.
   * b. lowballed.   d. squeeze-played.

6. Social proof can influence you in which of the following ways?
   a. directly--people tell you what to do
   b. forcibly--people simply force you to do something
   c. indirectly--you are influenced by both verbal and nonverbal reactions of people around you
   * d. both directly and indirectly

7. "Well-dressed people are helped more quickly when they shop." Which basic rule of compliance is demonstrated in this statement?
   a. scarcity   c. social proof
   b. commitment   * d. authority

8. You have been shopping at expensive mall stores for two years. You know that a pair of hot-selling name-brand jeans is going to cost you around $80. According to contrast effects, you have come to accept a typical price for those jeans. This is known as
   * a. an adaptation level.   c. self-perception.
   b. a reciprocal concession.   d. none of the above

9. During one Christmas season, Cabbage Patch dolls (which retailed for $39) were being auctioned off by some stores for as high as $100. Not enough dolls were being made to meet the demand. Which basic rule of compliance best fits this situation?
   a. contrast effect   c. liking
   b. commitment   * d. scarcity

10. If we are using an example of selling and buying a car, which one of the following explanations best describes what reciprocal concessions means?
    a. The buyer simply pays the seller the price being asked.
    b. The seller concedes to the buyer.
    c. The buyer concedes to the seller.
 * d. The seller lowers the price by a certain amount, and the buyer increases the bid by a certain amount.

True-or-False Questions

1. Self-perception relates to the causes or reasons people perceive for their own behavior. (T)

2. To use reciprocal concession as an approach to get someone to donate money to your charity, you would first have to ask for an amount of money that the person would definitely say no to. (T)

3. When Jack first filled in for his boss at the hotel's front desk, it was only supposed to be every other Wednesday afternoon. Jack now finds himself working not only every Wednesday afternoon but also Thursday and Friday mornings. Jack has been subjected to one of the procedures regarding the commitment principle. (T)

4. When using the foot-in-the-door procedure, different solicitors can be used because the person is committed to a cause, group, or organization and not to just one person. (T)

5. The lowball procedure is also known as the commitment-then-cost procedure. (T)

6. More men will respond to a request to sign a petition when asked by an attractive female than when asked by an unattractive female; however, the attractiveness of the female solicitor has no effect on the responses of women. (F)

7. When first starting out, some stand-up comedians have friends sit in the audience to generate laughter. They are trying to use one of the authority principles. (F)

8. Manufacturers of clothing try very hard to get early adopters or trendsetters to buy their new designs. These manufacturers are actually using one of the procedures of the social proof principle. (T)

9. Contrast effects involve both an adaptation level (an established standard) and a contrast effect (evaluation against the standard). (T)

10. The reciprocity concept enables a person to gain compliance by creating a sense of obligation. (T)

<u>Short-Answer Questions</u>

1. Discuss the foot in the door and the door in the face. What are the procedures for each? When would it be advisable to use each?

2. Give three examples of behaviors that friends might engage in to use the commitment principle on you.

3. Give an example of how you have personally experienced the social proof principle. Analyze exactly what the proof consisted of.

4. Explain what the word <u>trappings</u> has to do with the authority principle. Are there other ways to communicate authority, in your opinion?

CHAPTER 12: MANAGING INTERPERSONAL CONFLICT

<u>Chapter Objectives</u>

1. To discuss why it is important to study interpersonal conflict

2. To discuss conflict as a natural event that arises because of perceptions of incompatible goals

3. To present conflict styles as tendencies to behave, conflict strategies as approaches that people decide to use, and conflict tactics as the behavioral unfolding of strategies

4. To discuss five dimensions of conflict

5. To present Rusbult's exit-voice-loyalty-neglect model of responding to relational problems

6. To discuss attributional and relational outcomes of conflict strategies

Discussion Questions

1. Ask your students for metaphors to describe conflict situations (see Hocker & Wilmot, 1991, for examples). Have them think about the origins of their metaphors and how their metaphors shape their response to conflicts.

2. Remind students of Rusbult's (1986a) findings that women report using voice for mild problems and loyalty for all kinds of problems more than men do. Why do students believe these differences in behavior exist?

3. Metts and Cupach found that the exit-voice-loyalty-neglect typology is associated with irrational beliefs that college students have about their romantic relationships. Have students discuss the degree to which they themselves adopt the stated irrational beliefs and how (or if) their personal behaviors correlate positively or negatively with their use of exit, neglect, and voice.

4. Ask students to discuss the authors' explanations of why people tend to blame others for their negative encounters. Then have the students discuss how people could actually attempt to change this behavior. Have them also consider what specific language people can use to prevent them from making the attribution that "It's the other guy's fault."

Class Activities

1. Have students form dyads or small groups. Have them brainstorm ways that instructors could initiate and encourage productive conflict in the classroom. Have groups share their most effective strategies for encouraging productive conflict, using theories and concepts from the chapter to back their claims. (If the class environment is not conducive, forgo this activity.)

2. In small groups, have students brainstorm various conflict situations in which they have been involved in the past week. Have them classify and group conflicts according to the type of goal that they and others were trying to accomplish and the strategies (integrative, distributive, avoidant) that they and others used. Class discussion might focus on the prevalence of conflict in our everyday lives, why we use certain strategies, and the role of goals in conflict escalation or de-escalation.

Multiple-Choice Questions

1. The authors cite three reasons for studying conflict. These are
    a. to avoid escalation to violence, to eliminate personal goals, and to recognize conflict as a natural and inevitable event.
    b. to avoid escalation to violence, to help achieve personal goals, and to avoid conflict.
  * c. to avoid escalation to violence, to help achieve personal goals, and to recognize conflict as a natural and inevitable event.
    d. to justify physical and verbal abuse, to help achieve personal goals, and to recognize conflict as a natural and inevitable event.

2. In relation to the definition of conflict, interdependence means that people in conflict
    a. do not depend on one another to accomplish their goals.
    b. have the same goals.
  * c. depend on one another and coordinate behaviors in order to accomplish their goals.
    d. none of the above

3. Hocker and Wilmot (1991) identify three types of goals. These are
    a. prospective, transactive, and metaperceptive goals.
    b. prospective, transactive, and validating goals.
    c. prospective, metaperceptive, and functional goals.
  * d. prospective, transactive, and retrospective goals.

4. What can be said about styles of conflict?
    a. There are basically five styles that people adopt.
    b. Style has to do with concern with self versus concern for others.
    c. Styles vary according to degree of cooperation and assertiveness.
  * d. all of the above

5. What are advantages of the avoiding conflict style?
    a. Some goals are not worth fighting for.
    b. It reinforces the idea that conflict is unnatural.
    c. It can keep you out of harm's way.
  * d. Both a and c are true.

6. In specific conflicts, communicators must decide how they want to deal with the conflicts at hand. They decide to
    a. confront or avoid the situation or person.
    b. cooperate or compete with the other person.
  * c. both confront or avoid and cooperate and compete.
    d. none of the above

7. Regarding conflict strategies, which of the following are avoidant tactics?
    a. direct denial
    b. evasion
    c. abstract, procedural, and irrelevant remarks
    * d. All of the above

8. Which of the following are distributive tactics?
    * a. shouting, blaming, and sarcasm
    b. descriptive statements and disclosures
    c. supportive remarks
    d. topic shifts and forestalling

9. Think of couples who have conflicts that never focus on a single issue long enough to reach an agreement or have arguments over the same issue time after time. Which conflict dimension would they be exhibiting?
    a. variety   c. symmetry
    * b. continuity   d. stationarity

10. Rusbult identified four responses that people have regarding problems in their relationships. If a person is comfortable enough within a relationship to discuss problems and suggest solutions, which approach or response would that person be exhibiting?
    a. exit   c. loyalty
    * b. voice   d. neglect

True-or-False Questions

1. Interpersonal conflict can lead to new ideas, creative solutions, and more effective decision making. (T)

2. People may perceive their goals as incompatible (in conflict) even if they are not incompatible. (T)

3. Individuals' goals very rarely change during a conflict process. (F)

4. The compromising conflict style can hamper the use of creative alternatives, resulting in the implementation of a less than optimum solution. (T)

5. As you get to know someone, your confidence in making attributions about that person's behavior increases. (T)

6. Perceived threat, reciprocity, and responses to inappropriate behavior determine your level of cooperation or competition during a conflict. (T)

7. If you want to engage a person in a competitive manner, you would probably use an integrative strategy. (F)

8. "That's the most ridiculous idea you ever had!" This is a rejection statement and an example of an integrative tactic. (F)

9. Dissatisfied couples often fall into routine, rigid patterns of defensive communication. (T)

10. Regarding responses and approaches to problems in a relationship, low satisfaction, low investment, and low alternatives would most likely lead to a neglect response. (T)

11. We tend to blame ourselves for a conflict if the other person uses distributive tactics. (F)

Short-Answer Questions

1. What are the advantages of studying both conflict styles and conflict strategies?

2. Explain how status affects a person's choice either to confront or to avoid another person during conflict.

3. Cite and briefly describe the three basic conflict strategies, reflecting decisions to avoid, to cooperate, and to compete.

4. How are distributive and integrative behaviors usually attributed to self or others?

PART V PERSONALITY AND INTERPERSONAL COMPETENCE

CHAPTER 13: PERSONALITY AND INTERPERSONAL COMMUNICATION

Chapter Objectives

1. To show how personality affects interpersonal interactions

2. To present Miller and Read's interpersonalism model as a framework for examining personality factors

3. To discuss the social activities of men and women

4. To summarize the research on seven personality factors

5. To have students inquire about their own personality factors by referring them to samples of the factors' measures

Discussion Questions

1. Show a film, such as <u>Wall Street</u> or <u>My Cousin Vinny</u>, that exemplifies the personalities of the characters. Solicit students' opinions on ways in which the personality attributes discussed in this chapter are identifiable in these characters. Which aspects of these characters would they want to change and not change? Based on the material summarized on gender differences in this chapter, must these characters necessarily be men?

2. Ask students to discuss how goals and personality are related, according to this chapter.

3. High self-monitors are able to influence people by being friendly even when they actually dislike others. Ask students if this is ethical behavior. High self-monitors also have the ability to adapt to many interaction settings. This is how they earned the name <u>social chameleons</u>. In your students' opinion, which is the more competent communicator, the high or low self-monitor?

4. Scoring either high or low on Machiavellian orientation is extreme. Most people fall somewhere in the middle, which indicates that most people have some of this trait. Ask students to discuss these questions: Does this mean that the high Machs are correct in assuming that by nature, people are essentially bad? When could manipulation be considered positive in our interactions with others?

5. Have students consider where control of behavior originates. Is control really external, meaning that people with an internal locus of control are really not as much in control as they think? Or is control of behavior genuinely internal, and those with an external locus actually relinquishing control?

Class Activities

1. Have students form groups of four. Ask them to generate examples of people from movies or television who fit each of the personality types discussed in the chapter. Discussion can focus on different levels of each personality type as well as how the different types combine within certain characters.

2. Have students fill out a form that has them check the personality types that they think fit them best (high Mach, low Mach, etc.). Then group students into dyads and have them complete the same form on the other person. Together students can then compare their self-concept with how they are perceived.

Multiple-Choice Questions

1. According to Miller and Read's interpersonalism model, personality involves which four components?
   * a. goals, plans, resources, beliefs
   b. thinking, feeling, intuiting, minding
   c. ethos, pathos, logos, philos
   d. none of the above

2. Which of the following is true regarding self-monitoring?
   a. High self-monitors accept people at face value and focus efforts on reading and interpreting what is occurring around them.
   b. High self-monitors tend to be highly disclosive, revealing much about their beliefs and feelings.
   c. Low self-monitors tend to prompt others to talk about themselves in an attempt to keep the conversation moving smoothly.
   * d. Low self-monitors conceptualize friendship with an affect-based orientation.

3. The beliefs involved in measuring a Machiavellian orientation revolve around all of the following except
   a. flattery.   c. cynicism.
   b. immorality.   * d. probability.

4. People who score low on Machiavellian orientation focus on
   a. personal goals.
   b. relational goals.
   * c. both personal and relational goals.
   d. no goals.

5. A high mach would prefer all of the following situations except
   a. face to face.   * c. impersonal.
   b. unstructured.   d. personal.

6. Which of the following is true regarding locus of control?
   * a. Internals claim greater confidence than externals.
   b. Externals rate goals as easier to imagine.
   c. Internals employ more threats in order to get others to work.
   d. All of the above

7. Which of the following personality types is most resistant to influence?
   a. cognitively complex   c. high self-monitor
   b. low Machiavellian   * d. internal locus of control

8. Which of the following is <u>not</u> an ability that is definitive of cognitively complex people as discussed in the text?
   a. the ability to infer multiple causes for and consequence of others' actions
   b. the ability to recognize and understand the emotional states of others
   * c. the ability to make global evaluations of others
   d. none of the above

9. Verbal aggressiveness includes all <u>except</u> which of the following behaviors?
   a. maledictions
   b. threats
   c. competence attacks
   * d. presenting evidence

10. Which of the following is <u>false</u> regarding communication apprehension?
   a. Anxious individuals date less often than nonanxious individuals.
   * b. Anxious individuals are less likely to conform to others in group settings than nonanxious individuals.
   c. When speaking, anxious people tend to use numerous verbal repetitions.
   d. More anxious people recall fewer previous interactions.

<u>True-or-False Questions</u>

1. Males are more successful than females at obtaining permission from parents. (T)

2. Males tend to be more status-neutralizing in their interactions than females. (F)

3. A low self-monitor presents a pragmatic conception of the self that defines personal identity in terms of specific social situations and roles. (F)

4. Most high self-monitors have low self-monitors for friends because low self-monitors present a view of self that is principled. (F)

5. Because low self-monitors value friendship so highly, they tend to have high expectations of friends and can be quite persistent in asking friends for favors. (F)

6. High Machs are better than low Machs at predicting the characteristics of other persons in situations. (F)

7. High Machs have fewer close friends than low Machs and prefer friends who are similar in their Machiavellian beliefs. (T)

8. If a person behaves in a certain way, receives reinforcements, and believes that his or her behavior caused the reinforcements, the person is said to have an external locus of control. (F)

9. Verbal aggressiveness and argumentativeness are similar in terms of locus of attack. (F)

10. Situational loneliness has been strongly associated with dysfunctional social behaviors. (F)

Short-Answer Questions

1. How do the social worlds of men and women differ in terms of the interpersonalism model?

2. Define self-monitoring. What are the key differences between a high and a low self-monitor?

3. Define the trait of Machiavellianism. Evaluate the nature of a person who is considered high Mach. Give an example of a high Mach, describing the person and his or her behavior.

4. List and describe the components of the locus-of-control scale.

5. To test for cognitive complexity, people are asked to describe various things. Define the three criteria that indicate variations in complexity.

CHAPTER 14: IMPLICATIONS FOR INTERPERSONAL COMMUNICATION COMPETENCE

Chapter Objectives

1. To present Spitzberg and Cupach's componental model of interpersonal competence

2. To review six criteria that determine competence

3. To have students think of their own interpersonal competence by completing the Self-evaluation of Interpersonal Communication Competence (Table 14-1)

4. To review the book's implications for the study of interpersonal competence

Discussion Questions

1. Have students discuss how communicators can be effective yet not appropriate and vice versa. Ask students to give examples of each type of communicator.

2. Ask students to reflect on the following questions: What is the nature of communication competence? Who are communicatively competent role models? How can you tell?

3. In most of the chapters, strategies were presented that operate to achieve particular goals (e.g., direct self-presentation strategies, relational maintenance strategies). Ask students if learning about these strategies makes a competent communicator. Probe what else is needed besides knowledge of how to behave.

Class Activities

1. Break the class into small groups. Based on the information in this chapter, have students build the ideal communicator. Obviously, not everything can be included, and students will have to make choices. Each group should then present its ideal communicator to the rest of the class. In so doing, students will have to defend their inclusion of certain aspects of interpersonal communication and their exclusion of others.

2. Break the class into dyads. Have them discuss how they feel their communication behavior might change after reading this text. Are there particular improvements that they want to focus on in the future? What aspects of their interpersonal communication are they most comfortable with or would they not like to change?

3. Discuss students' responses to the Self-evaluation of Interpersonal Communication Competence (Table 14-1). Ask why they responded the way they did. You also might inform them that in a pilot test of this measure, all the subscales had acceptable reliabilities (coefficient alpha ranged from .6 to .9, with most subscales above .8).

4. Have students form groups of three to five. Have them write a situation, like the one at the beginning of this chapter, in which they were communicatively incompetent, giving as many details as possible. Then have students talk about these stories in their groups. Next, have them rewrite the situation, portraying a competent communicator. Have them discuss the changes they made in their groups.

1. Which of the following statements about communication competence is false?
    a. Competence is determined by both conversational partners.
    * b. Competence is simply knowing how to communicate.
    c. Competence is determined in part by the ability of the communicator to achieve goals.
    d. All of the above are true.

2. Lack of communication competence is associated with all of the following except
    a. mental illness   c. drug abuse
    b. depression   * d. none of the above

3. Which of the following is one of the six factors of adaptability?
    a. articulation   c. social composure
    b. wit   * d. all of the above

4. What are the three factors that measure conversational involvement?
    a. responsiveness, listening skills, empathy
    * b. responsiveness, perceptiveness, attentiveness
    c. perceptiveness, empathy, attentiveness
    d. perceptiveness, empathy, responsiveness

5. Conversational ebb and flow is not witnessed in
    a. intonation.   c. interruptions.
    b. head nods.   * d. smiles.

6. The evaluation of communication competence involves which three components?
    a. knowledge, empathy, effectiveness
    b. effectiveness, appropriateness, empathy
    c. skill, motivation, appropriateness
    * d. none of the above

7. Which of the following is true regarding the component model of competence?
    a. A person's self-efficacy alters whether the person approaches or avoids a particular kind of interaction.
    b. Procedural knowledge refers to the ways people read social situations and decide on a course of action.
    c. People may know how to act in a given communication situation and still not behave as they desire.
    * d. All of the above are true.

8.   Which of the following is true regarding empathy?
      a.   Empathy leads to helping others.
  *   b.   Empathy is the cognitive understanding of another's views and feeling parallel with that person.
      c.   To be empathic, one must sympathize with the other person.
      d.   None of the above is true.

True-or-False Questions

1.   Communication effectiveness refers to the ability to change one's behaviors and goals to meet the needs of the interaction. (F)

2.   Social confirmation refers to having participated in various social interactions. (F)

3.   Conversational management means that communicators must be cognitively involved in the conversation and demonstrate their involvement through their interaction behaviors. (F)

4.   Managing conversations implies that people do not adapt to social situations only; they also respond to them. (F)

5.   Empathy refers to feeling parallel emotions with another person. (F)

6.   It is possible in some communication situations to be appropriate without being effective, as only one of those aspects is essential to competence. (T)

7.   The two underlying dimensions of the six criteria for competence are control and consideration. (F)

8.   Scripts are highly routinized sequences of behavior that require awareness and contemplation on the part of communicators. (F)

9.   To be competent, a person need only be motivated. (F)

10.   Without knowledge of how to behave, interpersonal competence is difficult to achieve. (T)

1. List and describe the criteria for assessing communication competence.

2. Describe conversational involvement. Can you think of other factors relevant to involvement? Can one be adaptable but not involved?

3. Completely describe the component model of communication competence.

4. Discuss how the Self-evaluation for Interpersonal Communication Competence (Table 14-1) was constructed. Does this seem a valid way to have you determine your interpersonal competence?

5. Analyze five implications for competence discussed in Chapter 14.

St. Martin's